# Anime and the
# Visual Novel

T0130857

# Anime and the Visual Novel

*Narrative Structure, Design and Play
at the Crossroads of Animation
and Computer Games*

DANI CAVALLARO

McFarland & Company, Inc., Publishers
*Jefferson, North Carolina, and London*

To Paddy,
with love and gratitude

LIBRARY OF CONGRESS CATALOGUING-IN-PUBLICATION DATA

Cavallaro, Dani.
    Anime and the visual novel : narrative structure, design and
play at the crossroads of animation and computer games /
Dani Cavallaro.
        p.    cm.
    Includes bibliographical references and index.
    ISBN 978-0-7864-4427-4
    softcover : 50# alkaline paper ∞

    1. Animated films — Japan — Themes, motives.
    2. Computer games — Japan.   I. Title.
    NC1766.J3C374    2010
    791.43'340952 — dc22                         2009039280

British Library cataloguing data are available

Cover art by Kasuga

Manufactured in the United States of America

*McFarland & Company, Inc., Publishers*
  *Box 611, Jefferson, North Carolina 28640*
   *www.mcfarlandpub.com*

# Contents

# Preface

*We live immersed in narrative, recounting and reassessing the meaning of our past actions, anticipating the outcome of our future projects, situating ourselves at the intersection of several stories not yet completed.*

— Peter Brooks

*Imagination is always the fabric of social life and the dynamic of history.*

— Simone Weil

This study is the fruit of a deep-rooted dedication to the animated medium at large and to the art of anime in particular, progressively consolidated over time by the exploration of diverse studios and of their multifarious productions within that sector of the contemporary culture industry. Its goal is to delineate the thematic, structural and aesthetic traits of a relatively new-sprung and increasingly popular development within the realm of anime: namely, animated series adapted from visual novels. In the realm of anime, the term "visual novel" connotes a gaming event of an eminently participatory nature, consistently harnessing the player's own productivity to the generation of the narrative fabric and thus circumventing many of the constraints entailed by more author-centered videogames. The visual novel characteristically dramatizes alternate and intersecting story arcs and its ending therefore varies depending on the choices made by the player at certain pivotal "decision points." For the player to experience all of the available — and always partial — solutions potentially entailed by a visual novel, it is necessary to replay the game several times, opting for different routes on each occasion. Relatedly, multiperspectivalism is accorded a cardinal status within the cumulative diegetic construct insofar as the game's take on the action alters according to the point of view from which it is tackled by different personae. Taken

1

in tandem, ramifying plot strands and plural viewpoints buttress at virtually every turn the medium's cultivation of fictionally elaborate situations and adventures. Narrative and ludic priorities are steadily regarded as interdependent and inseverable.

The visual novel's composite diegesis is articulated by recourse to lengthy textual passages that record either conversations or interior monologues. These are complemented both by frames with character sprites intended to designate the speaker and by visually enticing natural and architectural backgrounds. Such settings characteristically exude a unique sense of painterly opulence abetted by alternately exuberant and mellow palettes, as well as a painstaking attention to details. Finally, it is in the areas of character design and development that the visual novel most sonorously declares its distinctiveness by yielding richly nuanced galleries of psychologically complex actors and a panoply of varyingly intricate or even tortuous relationships. This book argues that anime productions based on visual novels represent an art-within-the-art characterized by particular modalities of perception and reception, on the one hand, and by an original take on philosophical and societal issues of cross-cultural relevance on the other. Their aesthetic and diegetic characteristics are deeply influenced by many of the formal conventions and graphic flourishes associated with the parent games. This makes them a form of animation *sui generis*: a unique microcosmic constellation within the macrocosm of anime.

In assessing the present cogency of a study of anime productions based on visual novels, it is important to stress that the existing works are already very popular, as demonstrated by numerous online databases, review panels and discussion groups. Several of these have already been released on DVD in the West, while others are slated for release in the near future. Even prior to their licensing for global distribution and marketing, all the works have thus far been widely available in the form of top-quality fansubs and are enjoyed in this format by extensive audiences the world over. The rapidly growing nature of the medium indicates that additional titles of wide appeal will go on materializing in years to come. The book's most plausible readership within academic establishments includes students in the areas of film studies generally and animation studies in particular, interested in exploring a burgeoning expression of the art of anime. Given its conceptual scope, however, it is also likely to appeal to wider audiences, especially in the field of cultural studies. Both established and developing courses currently offered by U.S. and U.K. colleges that use anime as a component of their syllabi (in areas as varied as popular culture, art history and Asian studies among others) are some of the book's most likely beneficiaries.

Chapter 1, *Anime and the Visual Novel: Theoretical Approaches,* opens with an assessment of anime's relationship with the realm of videogaming at large. It then evaluates the most salient characteristics of the visual novel as a ludic format within the broader context of role-playing games (RPGs), as well as the impact of the medium's stylistic formulae and thematic foci on the anime it has spawned. The chapter subsequently outlines the principal recurrent themes and motifs articulated by the narratives explored in the book. Special attention is paid to the articulation of creative quests and related inclusion of self-reflexive gestures; the deployment of dreams and visions; the relationship between individuals and collectivities; the collusion of mythical and mundane realities; the depiction of both the natural environment and architectural sceneries; the dramatization of mnemonic disorders connected with hidden traumas; and the synthesis within a single text of diverse generic codes and conventions. Finally, the chapter engages in an evaluation of some of the principles underpinning the visual novel's (and related anime's) execution of characters and settings with reference to pertinent aspects of indigenous aesthetics and architectural history.

Each of the ensuing chapters opens with an assessment of theoretical perspectives relevant to the visual novel, and hence to the shows deriving from it. These include: the debate surrounding the relationship between ludology and narratology (Chapter 2); the player's role as an active producer of the story (Chapter 3); the concept of immersion as a ludic and narrative phenomenon (Chapter 4); and the importance of character presentation and its intimate relationship with broader developments in the domain of indigenous graphic design (Chapter 5). In the course of the analysis, it will emerge that these issues are intimately interrelated. Indeed, the evaluation of a game's narrative import, which is at the heart of the narratology-versus-ludology debate, inevitably invites reflection on the player's part in the construction of stories. This, in turn, encourages an assessment of the specifically immersive component of the player's experiences. Finally, immersion itself could be addressed as a corollary of effective character and background portrayal. Cumulatively, Chapters 2 to 5 thereby trace the analytical trajectory mapped out below.

- Although the visual novel may not constitute a narrative *as such*, it contains the materials (characters, structures and events) of a *potential* or *virtual* story.
- It is up to the player to *narrativize* the game — i.e., to constellate those materials into an *actual* story.
- To ensure the player's creative involvement, the visual novel seeks to draw him or her into its textual skein through *immersive* strategies. In so doing, however, it challenges the mimetic imperatives of narrative absorption by self-consciously foregrounding its *artificiality*.

- *Design* principles hold a key role in encouraging the player to operate as a productive agent. Subtle character portrayals and effective depictions of both natural and architectural habitats supply the player with a wealth of visual and emotive stimuli.

While the book applies these ideas to visual novels, it also assesses their pertinence to the anime adapted therefrom, proposing that they are no less applicable to the animated medium than to the videogaming one.

Chapter 2, *Parallel Worlds*, examines a set of titles devoted to the portrayal and investigation of imaginary realities in which parallel existences coalesce and clash by turns. The chapter also proposes that the assiduous return to this topos in the anime here studied attests to the value accorded to the notion of recurrence in Japanese art and tradition. In this context, it specifically communicates an inveterate human concern with the coexistence of alternate and interpenetrating dimensions within a superficially singular reality across variable cultural milieux. The following productions are discussed:

- *Air*
- *Yami to Boushi to Hon no Tabibito*
- *Touka Gettan*
- *Shuffle!*
- *Soul Link*
- *Aria*

In Chapter 3, *Returns to the Past*, the focus is on shows that present their personae's decision to revisit locations and attendant memories buried in the past as vital to the unraveling of haunting fears and anxieties. Individual agents are typically posited as inseparable from their communities (encompassing familial, scholastic and professional networks). Concomitantly, the collusion of past and present is complemented by the integration of legendary and prosaic elements in the anime's narrative orchestrations. This chapter tackles the titles listed below:

- *Kanon*
- *Kanokon*
- *Myself; Yourself*
- *true tears*
- *ef—a tale of memories* and *ef—a tale of melodies*
- *H2O Footprints in the Sand*

Chapter 4, *Epic Exploits*, engages with productions concerned with simultaneously private and collective quests driven by a desire to decipher sinister enigmas enshrined in both recorded history and fiction-coated lore. While such ventures deserve their designation as "epic" due to their heroical proportions, they are often coursed by dark inchoate urges that threaten to cloud the laudability of their objectives, which adds a felicitously sobering note to what could otherwise have come across as an overidealistic scenario. The following anime are employed as case studies:

- *Tsukihime, Lunar Legend*
- *Utawarerumono*
- *Fate/stay Night*
- *The Familiar of Zero*
- *When Cicadas Cry* (a.k.a. *When They Cry: Higurashi*)

In Chapter 5, *Journeys of Self-Discovery*, the book addresses a set of anime concerned with the alternately auspicious and baleful facets of the Bildungsroman curves charted by their characters' life stories. The medium's tenacious aversion to bluntly adversarial ethical opposites proclaims itself most audibly in these interrelated pilgrimages. The shows here examined include:

- *To Heart*
- *D.C. ~ Da Capo ~*
- *Clannad*
- *Tsuyokiss*
- *Rumbling Hearts*
- *School Days*
- *White Album*
- *Kashimashi — Girl Meets Girl*

The discussion is supplemented by a filmography, notes and bibliographical references.

\* \* \*

Please note that the anime lists offered above only include the principal titles. Full details of all productions are supplied in the filmography.

*A life spooled out like thread, strength uncertain, length unknown; whether it will cease abruptly or run out endlessly, binding more lives together as it goes; in one instance no more than cotton, barely sufficient to gather a shirt together at its seams, in another a rope — triple-woven, turk's-head closures, each strand and fiber tarred and twisted to repel water, blood, sweat, tears; a rope to raise a barn, to fashion Portuguese bowlines and bring a near-drowned child from a flooded run-off, to hold a roan mare and break her will, to bind a man to a tree and beat him for his crimes, to hoist a sail, to hang a sinner.*

— R. J. Ellory

# 1

# *Anime and the Visual Novel: Theoretical Approaches*

*Children may just as well play as not. The ogre will come in any case.*
— James Joyce

*The creation of something new is not accomplished by the intellect but by the play instinct acting from inner necessity. The creative mind plays with the objects it loves.*
— Carl Jung

## *Anime and Videogaming*

Anime-based graphic styles have deeply influenced the Japanese videogame industry practically from inception. This is partly explained by the fact that in contrast with their early Western colleagues, many Japanese game developers benefit from training in art and design colleges rather than in computer programming and hence started out as manga illustrators and anime artists. Historically, the anime-videogame cross-pollination has been significantly affected by commercial imperatives. Although the earliest games in Japan often regarded anime as a superior source of inspiration, there came a point when their status changed from that of spin-offs to that of free-standing market forces. Indeed, as the budgets allocated to the production of anime shows began to decrease in the mid–1990s, several artists shifted from TV animation to gaming design. Anime's influence is now omnipresent and infiltrating the designs of Western gaming companies. Furthermore, Western spectators are becoming more responsive to videogames produced by Japanese companies due to their prior experience of anime and related familiarity with indigenous graphic conventions, while game players already accustomed to Japanese styles by games are becoming more responsive to anime itself. The market for games directly inspired by popular anime releases (and by the manga on which these are in turn often based) is rapidly expanding. At times, the game in question merely uses a group of characters from the original program and a set of contexts for them to act in. Increasingly, however, this approach is being revised, allowing games to express autonomous narrative and aesthetic values rather than blandly formulaic imitations of their antecedents. This is enabling the gradual ascent of games to the status of fine art.

While anime has been the source of inspiration behind a plethora of videogames for decades, a more recent development is the reverse trend, namely the adaptation of games as animations. Some of the most cherished, visually appealing and diegetically complex anime titles of recent years have been based upon a very specific type of computer game generally known as "visual novel." In the context of anime culture, the phrase "visual novel" ("*bijuaru noberu*") designates a multibranching and interactive ludic experience that enlists the player's creativity alongside the production studio's own artistry and thus transcends the boundaries of other types of more controlling videogaming. The visual novel typically articulates its narrative by means of extensive text conversations complemented by lovingly depicted (and mainly stationary) generic backgrounds and dialogue boxes with character sprites determining the speaker superimposed upon them. At certain pivotal moments in the story, more detailed images drawn especially for those scenes and enhanced by more cinematic camera angles and CGI are included. A visual novel's ending alters according to the player's choices at key turning points, which provides a motivation to replay the game and opt for alternative decisions each time. Pictorial sumptuousness, vibrant palettes, meticulous devotion to plot depth and character design and development are absolutely vital aspects of the medium.

An important formal point requires elucidation at this stage. Western audiences sometimes tend, erroneously, to regard visual novels as synonymous with "dating simulations" (or "dating sims"), a videogame subgenre of simulation games. In dating sims, the player typically controls a male avatar whose goal is to date, and converse with, various female characters in order to form a romantic relationship. While the high-school environment is the most common scenario, dating sims may also be set in fantasy worlds where the player's task consists of protecting girls from monsters. The gameplay is largely dependent on statistics. For example, the player's success in conversation with a girl may be measured according to his or her choice of apposite lines of dialogue, and the overall score improves or worsens accordingly. Although visual novels and dating sims often share analogous graphic formats, treating them as interchangeable is, quite simply, incorrect. For one thing, visual novels are not simulations but rather role-playing games. Additionally, and more crucially, the equation of visual novels to dating sims ignores the visual novel's generic diversity. The most prominent generic roles are played by romance and by drama in the classic sense of the term: namely, a situation involving an intense conflict of forces capable of eliciting powerful emotional reactions from the audience. However, the dramatic element is not uniformly or repetitively doled out since it is actually couched in a variety of scenarios, including domestic affairs, psychological crises and high-school dynamics. At the same time, the supernatural yarn, comedy, the mythological epic, mystery, adventure, fantasy and action also feature regularly among the form's favorite repertoires. Horror and science fiction also make sporadic yet memorable appearances.

In examining the synergetic dialogue between videogaming and anime with a specific focus on the relationship between visual novels and their animated offshoots, it is also worth noting that a growing number of anime titles are concurrently being adapted into visual novels. The choice of shows amenable to translation into visual novels is by no means accidental. In fact, the titles in question lend themselves to that process due to specific stylistic and narrative traits: most notably the articulation of multibranching and intertwining stories, the depiction of deftly nuanced character galleries and a consummate devotion to lavishly painted settings and backgrounds. This book includes examples of anime that have spawned visual novels in order to complement satisfactorily its pivotal area of investigation.

In evaluating the visual novel's distinctive features, it is important to grasp its status as a ludic product within the broader context of the videogaming industry at large. What deserves particular consideration is the visual novel's status as a distinctive typology within the Adventure/RPG (Role-Playing Game) category. This type of game is characterized by a style of gameplay that casts the player as the story's protagonist, requiring him or her to interact with various characters and their worlds and to solve assorted puzzles in the process. Such a game does not include action elements and is therefore able to unfold at a deliberate pace, allowing the player to linger on its dense and highly detailed graphics and thus enjoy the game's textual dimension and sheer artiness in ways not afforded by markedly kinetic packages predicated on rapid-fire action within strict time constraints. These features have made the Adventure/RPG configuration appealing even for people not customarily adept at videogaming. The relatively straightforward point-and-click interface they typically adopt has abetted this trend. An inceptive form of Adventure/RPG is the Text Adventure game: an exercise in interactive fiction (IF) revolving around puzzle-laden treasure hunts and eager to experiment with storytelling techniques capable of maximizing audience engagement. The Text Adventure game was at first heavily reliant on written language, but the development of increasingly sophisticated technologies for the production of CGI created scope for the evolution of a further type, the Graphical Adventure. Visuals thus began to complement and even replace written passages at a considerable rate as integral to the player's experience of the given game world and interaction with it by means of icons and buttons. A subsequent development is marked by the Dialogue game, where the interactor progresses through a narrative not by completing tasks but by virtue of verbal skills deployed in conversation with virtual characters. An even more recent upgrowth within the sector is marked by LAPR games: live-action role-playing games.

## Features of Visual Novels and Their Anime Spin-offs

As a form of interactive fiction, the visual novel overtly calls upon players to participate in the production of the text as integrated agents. In placing the interactor in a finely grained imaginary setting wherein he or she is required to deploy both text-analysis capabilities and puzzle-solving skills, the visual novel forges an innovative way of presenting and receiving the narrative experience. In exploring the visual novel's simulated environment to discover and apply its guiding rules while simultaneously figuring out how to influence its events, the player is encouraged to navigate the text in an attitude of sustained and conscious alertness. In this regard, the visual novel could be regarded as a paradigmatic instance of the narrative discourse designated by Espen J. Aarseth as "ergodic literature." The term derives from the Greek "*ergon*" ("work") + "*hodos*" ("path") and economically describes a type of literature in which "nontrivial effort is required to allow the reader to traverse the text" (Aarseth, p. 1).

Anime based on visual novels exhibit stylistic and narratological attributes that emanate directly from the characteristic mold, gameplay codes and graphic styles of the ludic format they follow. They thus evince a narrative and aesthetic constitution of unique allure. Hence, the decision to embark on a detailed assessment of recent anime productions based on visual novels is not merely an outcome of their popularity among both Eastern and Western audiences, although this is a factor to be taken into account to situate those works adequately in the contemporary cultural scene. No less importantly, it results from the realization that those shows constitute a form of animation *sui generis*: a distinctive galaxy within the anime universe. Just as the visual novel is an art form in its own right within the gaming world, as borne out by its contextualization vis-à-vis other game typologies, so anime inspired by visual novels could feasibly be regarded as an art-within-the-art.

Grasping the formal specificity of the games themselves is vital to an adequate appreciation of their animated offshoots. It is particularly crucial to bear in mind, in this regard, that when a show is based on a standard videogame replete with graphics, the animation team has plenty of source material at its disposal. However, when the parent text is a visual novel, this is not the case. Insofar as the original consists largely of text, it is up to the director and the animation team at large to ideate the elements that do not appear on the computer screen at all. The degree of explicitness with which the visual novel as a ludic template enlists the player's participation cannot be automatically expected of a piece designed for televisual or theatrical exhibition. Nevertheless, interactivity is metaphorically replicated by means of particular diegetic methods that tenaciously shun authorial mastery. These demonstrate that just as visual novels prioritize the player's engagement with text and static graphics over dynamic spectacle, so anime programs based on visual novels ask the spectator to focus on the narrative weave and its collusion with images rather than breakneck action. In both visual novels and the anime based upon them, reflection and speculation are the activities invoked by the experience over and above passive absorption. Relatedly, the viewer of anime inspired by visual novels is not presented with a casket housing a mindlessly consumable prize but rather placed in the position of a vigilant gambler enjoined to take chances at each corner of a textual maze composed of numerous forking paths. The viewer's ongoing engagement in the production of the story as an open-ended enterprise makes the anime highly rewatchable, in much the same way as the player's creative involvement in the parent games ensures their replay ability over time. Other features of the visual novel outlined earlier are concurrently echoed by the animated progeny. The games' reliance on often lengthy textual passages is paralleled by the shows' incorporation of elaborate conversations and interior monologues, so that even though written text is not overtly brought into play, the discursive dimension holds a prominent role, often in preference to kinetic spectacle. Moreover, textuality is frequently foregrounded through dialogues that address the nature of storytelling and dramatic performance, and on the very practices of writing, reading and watching. Thus, the anime provide metacommentaries on the narratological devices intrinsic in all manner of visual and graphic constructs.

The visual novel's devotion to studiously rendered backgrounds is replicated by the anime's consistent use of settings of autonomous artistic caliber. Dialogue boxes and sprites make occasional appearances in frames that allude self-referentially to the show's affiliation with the visual novel. Additional self-reflexive gestures consist of the inclusion of images that make explicit reference to the production process at the levels of both basic drawings and elaborate animation effects. Nimbly varied camera angles meant to enhance the mood of a scene and to influence its perception by the viewer with different degrees of intimacy or distance are assiduously deployed. At the same time, CGI prove especially versatile in the creation of visual effects intended to maximize the solidity and textural density of objects — e.g., clothes, accessories, mechanical equipment, furniture and food, alongside many other organic and inanimate entities. The visual novel's painterly richness, notably evinced by its luscious chromatic modulations, is likewise integral to the anime. It is key to the evocation of the environmental, atmospheric and seasonal properties of both single scenes and recurrent scenarios, and indeed contributes vitally to the articulation of a story's emotional drift. Last but not least, the dedication to plot complexity and character depth typically exhibited by the visual novel is no less salient a trait of the anime based on that format. The supple manipulation of interwoven arcs is vital to their narrative effectiveness, and bolstered by the psychologically acute portrayal of personae that evolve in credible ways even within seemingly formulaic boundaries. Hence, a cast of characters that may superficially appear to be composed of conventional types with predictable personality traits is capable of revealing levels of complexity on a par with stage drama or live-action cinema at their most proficient.

The strategies adopted by anime based on visual novels to promulgate their artistic approach make them distinct cultural products buttressed by salient theoretical preoccupations. The following narrative techniques play a notable role in advancing those concerns:

- narrative multiperspectivalism;
- branching and crisscrossing yarns;
- deliberately inconclusive resolutions;
- unconventional blend of the mundane and the supernatural;
- interweaving of domestic and mythological milieux.

The multiperspectival approach entails that while the story is perceived from different angles by diverse personae, the audience itself is continually engaged in the formulation of alternate and even conflicting readings. The injunction to engage with the characters' fluctuating emotions — including anxiety, fear, loneliness and vulnerability — heightens the mood of instability evoked by multiperspectivalism in the first place. Concomitantly, the ongoing genesis of plot ramifications, allied to a penchant for open-endedness, questions the notion of narrative coherence and the plausibility of organizing the text's intermeshed threads according to hierarchical criteria. This scenario mirrors the preference for adumbration and inconclusiveness over explicit statement traditionally evinced by Japanese art. If an analogy were to be surmised between the kind of animated drama here examined and the realm of literature, it could be argued that its affective import and aesthetic allusiveness draw it closer to lyrical poetry than to classic realist fiction.

Moreover, in harmonizing the prosaic and the extraordinary, the earthbound and the transcendental, the shows also bring together two linchpins of Japanese aesthetics: the bittersweet contemplation of the evanescence of worldly pleasures encapsulated by the concept of *mono no aware*, and the striving for the infinite and the eternal associated with the principle of *yugen*. The accordance of pivotal significance to accidental and indeterminable factors in the processing of the graphic narrative calls to mind two further categories central to Japanese aesthetics: *sabi*, a passion for imperfection, and the related notion of *wabi*, a predilection for the frayed and the lacunary. Given its openness to multiple and discordant interpretative trajectories, the anime under scrutiny place emphasis on notions of chance, contingency and randomness. The meanings they disclose for different viewers are not, of course, utterly fortuitous insofar as the audience's decoding choices, decisions and inferences are routed, albeit unobtrusively, by the shows themselves. Yet, the exact fashion in which individual spectators will string those elements together remains unpredictable. This scenario is redolent of chaos theory. In this context, dynamic systems that may appear to be governed solely by chance and hence to lack any deterministic drive can in fact be seen to contain a principle of order. This is based on the idea that slight variations in the initial conditions of those systems (commonly referred to as the "butterfly effect") may have momentous repercussions on their entire fabric. However, this controlling law does not provide any dependable guarantee of stability since it is impossible to predict exactly how a situation may develop as a result of the initial change, let alone be measured and calculated. With both the anime here examined and chaos theory, order and randomness are posited as ultimately inextricable from each other.

For the sake of documentary accuracy, it should be noted that within the relevant industrial sector, the axial player (so to speak) is the company Visual Art's/Key, the original creator of some of the most popular visual novels adapted into anime — e.g., *Kanon, Air* and *Clannad*. Other notable enterprises include Type-Moon (*Fate/stay Night* and *Tsukihime, Lunar Legend*), La'cryma (*true tears*), Yeti (*Myself; Yourself*), Circus (*Da Capo* and *Da Capo II*), Minori (*ef—a tale of memories* and *ef—a tale of melodies*), Makura (*H2O Footprints in the Sand*), Alchemist (*Rumbling Hearts, Aria*), Age (*Rumbling Hearts*), PrincessSoft (*Rumbling Hearts, Tsuyokiss*), Candy Soft (*Tsuyokiss*), Navel (*Shuffle!, Soul Link*), Aquaplus/Leaf (*To Heart, Utawarerumono, White Album*), Seventh Expansion (*When Cicadas Cry*), Root (*Touka Gettan, Yami to Boushi to Hon no Tabibito*), Overflow (*School Days*), Marvelous Interactive (*The Familiar of Zero*), Vridge (*Kashimashi*) and 5pb. (*Kanokon*).

## Recurrent Themes and Motifs

The paragraphs that follow outline some of the most assiduously recurrent themes and motifs articulated by the narratives under scrutiny. These include:

1. creative quests and self-referential reflections on artistic production;
2. oneiric and visionary experiences;
3. the relationship between the individual and the community;
4. the interpenetration of the legendary past and the contingent present;
5. the relationship between nature and the built environment;
6. amnesia associated with repressed traumas;
7. the interweaving of contrasting generic formulae.

Several of the key characters portrayed in the anime here explored endeavor to give their predicaments a metaphorical form through artistic self-expression. Thus, they engage in activities such as fiction writing, stage drama, filming, street theatre, music, drawing and painting (amongst others). This motif provides scope for self-reflexive speculations regarding the nature of textual construction and presentation. Thus, it could be regarded as a thematic correlative for the visual novel's structural emphasis on textuality. The notion of "art" also stretches beyond the realms of the fine and performing arts to embrace practical activities such as martial and culinary arts. In all instances, emphasis is placed on the corporeal qualities of the product rather than on abstract aesthetic values.

The anime's engagement with the materiality of art reflects an important aspect of Japanese culture: namely, the reverential attitude towards their materials characteristically exhibited by Japanese artists throughout the ages. This preference does not only manifest itself in the treatment of objects and practices that can explicitly be considered "artistic" in the Western sense of the term. In fact, it is also notable in pursuits enmeshed in everyday life, such as garden design, flower arrangement, interior design and fashion design, the tea ceremony and various gastronomic practices, as well as both artisanal and industrial packaging. According to Lenor Larsen, the value of the physical element is cardinal to the creation of all manner of artifacts within both traditional and contemporary Japanese society: "Craftmakers working within Japan's ancient traditions respond to the generations of passed-on knowledge. This collective memory includes a deep respect for material and process, and respect too for the intended user" (Larsen, p. 12). As Haruo Shirane emphasizes, the classical Japanese poem (*waka*) likewise attached paramount value to its corporeal dimension: "Japanese poetry" constitutes "a material object for which calligraphy, paper, and packaging were probably as important as the poem itself.... The type, color, and size of the paper were also important. The poet could also add a sketch, attach a flower or leaf, or add incense or perfume to the poetry sheet. The poem as material object was often a gift for the host, friend, or lover. Matching the poem or paper with the social occasion or season was a key factor in its effectiveness or performativity." *Waka*, the critic concludes, was "meant to be *seen* both as text and material object" (Shirane, pp. 223–224). Given the concurrent emphasis placed on textuality and materiality by both the visual novel and its animated brood, it is hard to imagine more apt an antecedent than the case examined by Shirane.

Dreams feature prominently as diegetic and symbolic motifs in several of the works assessed in this book. At times, the shows orchestrate their plots as though they were dreams undergone by their own characters. At others, they deploy oneiric elements as metaphors for a broader spectrum of affects and experiences. In so doing, they invite reflection on allegorical analogies between the phenomenon of dreaming and the processes of filmmaking and film viewing. The filmmaker is always involved in the construction of imaginary worlds by recourse to structural and rhetorical mechanisms akin to those of oneiric discourse — cutting, editing, condensation, displacement, symbolic allusion. Simultaneously, the viewer, like the dreamer, interacts with images that are capable of absorbing his or her entire sensorium, yet are not empirically palpable or indeed, strictly speaking, "real." This is most emphatically the case with animation, where images do not capture any physical referents other than the graphics they record on film, and the visionary dimension of filmmaking and film viewing is therefore exponentially highlighted. The animated tale, like the dream, consists of a translation of thoughts into visual events. Moreover, just as dreams can be regarded as dramatic constructs comprising various acts that are not always obviously linked and may even unfold in tandem, the anime here discussed tend to articulate parallel story arcs whose interconnections are often cryptic rather than instantly accessible. Deploying the characters themselves as dreamers in the ways several of the anime here studied do adds an extra dimension to the aforementioned correspondences. The work indeed becomes so imbricated with the language of dreaming that it may, as Bruce Kawin suggests, "appear to dream itself" (Kawin, p. 5). Additionally, a parallel is formed between the dreaming character and the audience witnessing the character's dream on the screen. Just as the character has no immediate access to the dream's message but may only reconstruct it through secondary revision, so the audience is enjoined to assess the dream's significance, often with hindsight, in the larger context of the film's overall diegesis rather than as a transparent statement.

In the specific context of Eastern philosophy, mythology and lore, dreams are often used as ways of portraying the coalescence of disparate dimensions, cathartic journeys into the unfathomed and radical suspensions of the boundary between fantasy and reality. Hayao Kawai has indeed proposed that the treatment of oneiric experience in Japanese folk literature and mythology features three main aspects: "the free interpenetration of this world and the dream world" (Kawai 1995, p. 15); the undertaking of a journey to "the land of death" (p. 17); the notion of "multiple realities" (p. 19), which posits reality as many-layered and therefore intensely mutable, depending on the nature of the stratum occupied at any one point in time. The erosion of the boundary between the empirical and the hypothetical enacted by many of the titles addressed in this study gains considerable momentum from the portrayal of mutually permeating realms in which the characters' hold on their spatial and temporal coordinates is so flimsy as to feel virtually non-existent. This scenario fully warrants the use of a multiperspectival approach to the narrative, insofar as no single perspective can be unproblematically trusted. The semi legendary father of Taoism himself, Lao Tzu, is reputed to have wondered, after dreaming that he was a butterfly, whether he might effectively be a butterfly's own dream (Lao Tzu). (Please note that the butterfly image concurrently echoes the principles of chaos theory outlined earlier.) The oneiric trope, moreover, could be said to echo a fundamental tenet of Hindu philosophy: namely, the proposition that the physical and mental reality human beings experience on a daily basis is an illusory veil (*Maya*) concealing the mysteries and complexities of the cosmos. In treating their stories as though they were dreams, and their worlds as no more tangible or empirically verifiable than dreamworlds, the chosen anime tangentially ask us to ponder the oneiric character of the very lives we lead beyond the screen.

In the anime pivotal to this discussion, the oneiric component is handled in the light of a specifically Eastern perspective, whereby animated dreams do not amount to innocently pleasing scenarios intended to keep their audiences warm and cozy. In fact, the dreamworlds charted by these productions are rarely, if ever, unequivocally benign, let alone reassuring. Even at their quietest, the dreams in question allude to sinister realities, traversed by the threats of violence and chaos. Evoking something of an unconscious as yet untouched by the policing agency of consciousness, the dreams hark back to a pointedly Shintoist tradition imbued with animistic values, and hence sensitive to every object's vitality and dynamism. This approach to the oneiric parallels the intrinsic character of Japanese animation as a challenging medium unafraid of exposing the painful and the terrifying, in contrast with the world view promoted in the West by Disney-driven animated spectacle.

Practically all of the titles under investigation posit the singular subject and the social web as inseparable, by alternately focusing on a person's interaction with, or alienation from, a group. This may take the microcosmic guise of a domestic setup (such as an actual or surrogate family, a gang of friends or a club) or else the macrocosmic form of a larger institution or organization (such as a school, a business outfit or a hospital). Large-scale ensembles may also feature in the shape of imaginary bodies governed by rules indigenous to the fictive worlds of the anime where they appear, especially in the cases of fantasy and sci-fi shows. This motif strikes its roots in the very core of Japanese culture, where vital importance has been traditionally accorded to the concept of group affiliation, and the related imperative to subordinate private interests to the priorities of a community, its network of relationships, its hierarchy, its practices and rituals, and its codes of conduct. On the one hand, this ethical tenet could be seen as a logical corollary of Japan's high demographic density, requiring people to live in close proximity with one another and hence harbor quite a different notion of "privacy" to the one generally fostered in the West. On the other, the principle of allegiance to a group can be historically related to samurai culture and the code of *bushido* ("the way of the warrior"), where loyalty, understood as duty to one's leaders, plays a key part. This is paralleled, at the familial level, by the principle of piety as duty to one's elders. Both loyalty and piety were firmly enthroned as twin moral precepts by Confucianism. The reciprocal entanglement of individuals and communities provides the anime with ample scope for the elaboration of multiple points of view and crisscrossing story arcs of the kind favored by the visual novel, since no one perspective or yarn related to a single character can be pursued in isolation to the exclusion of the social fabric in which it is situated.

Even as they engage in the portrayal of frankly mundane circumstances, documenting with loving attention their characters' everyday experiences in domestic and scholastic settings, the anime insistently draw attention to the incidence of otherworldly agencies and supernatural phenomena. This entails that contemporary and quotidian situations, however prosaic these might appear to be, hold the potential to hark back to time-honored traditions wherein those unearthly forces find inception. At times, myths and legends are explicitly summoned as either diegetic infrastructures or symbolic motifs. These encompass both actual tales enshrined in Japanese culture and new-fangled fables indigenous solely to the world of a specific anime. At others, the enduring legacy of legend is subtly alluded to — most notably in the dramatic use of plot twists that lend themselves to ambivalent interpretation as empirically measurable occurrences, on the one hand, and miraculous interventions on the other. The blend of prosaic and preternatural events favored by the visual novel itself is thus emphatically respected.

The anime's attention to the ubiquity of mystical elements finds a graphic correlative in their depiction of both natural and urban settings. These are primarily characterized by a vibrant sense of aliveness, whereby verdant meadows and ordinary streets, glittering waters and humble pylons, sublime mountain ranges and common dining-rooms alike come across as elementally animate presences even at their most inert. In this respect, the shows again invoke a native tradition steeped in the teachings of the Shinto creed. Whereas in the Judeo-Christian system God is thought of as external to both time and space, in Shinto the divine principle is regarded as a spiritual energy pervading the universe in its entirety — rocks and mountains, oceans and rivers, plants and both human and other animals. Relatedly, in Judeo-Christian cultures it is generally believed that a happier and more balanced world could only be engendered by God as a transcendental agent. In Shinto, the notion that the spiritual principle courses through the universe as a whole implies that the world might be changed by any living force. In highlighting the aliveness of both the natural realm and man-made settings in keeping with a quintessentially Shintoist lesson, the anime here studied loyally emulate their parent texts, honoring the visual novel's own devotion to pictorially opulent backgrounds of all sorts.

Several narratives take as their premise the proposition that their protagonists labor under the curse of buried, repressed or submerged pasts beset by juvenile traumas. Time and again, characters are enjoined to confront physical landscapes scarred with emotions: love, loss, loneliness and a now doleful, now corrosive anguish. Often this ordeal is unleashed by a person's return to a place not seen in years that feels uncomfortably familiar and uncanny at once. Memories thought to have been conclusively buried surge back — stark, insistent, piercing, and above all, no longer deniable. Recuperating and accepting the past is posited as an integral part of the maturation process. In dramatizing this Bildungsroman element, the shows enjoin both their personae and their spectators to address the meaning of "truth": what it might be, how it might be found, and what to do with it if and once it is found. The theme of mnemonic occlusion is most typically orchestrated by recourse to the flashback (analepsis), an interspliced scene that loops the story back in time from the stage it has reached. At times, the flashback takes us to an earlier point in the narrative presented in the actual anime (internal analepsis); at others, it switches back to a point prior to the start of the visual experience as such (external analepsis): These strategies give the shows precious opportunities to foreground the process of their production, and thus offer an implied self-referential commentary on their constructedness. In this respect, they echo directly the visual novel's accent on the textual dimension and its construction. By presenting many of their characters' memories as fragmented and lacunary, the anime find a perfect way of maximizing at least three of the parent form's most distinctive attributes: multiperspectivalism, open-endedness and interwoven narratives. Indeed, the emphasis placed on the unreliability of individual personae's mnemonic baggages requires that the truth of their circumstances can only be approximated by weighing discordant perceptions and evaluating diverse experiences against one another, in the knowledge that no truth thus reached is ever likely to be anything other than tentative.

Echoing the visual novel's generic suppleness, the anime here examined move fluidly and even irreverently across diverse genres. It is not uncommon, therefore, for a scene pregnant with a baleful sense of foreboding unexpectedly to give way to a moment of sheer comedy or for images saturated with carefree joy suddenly to be clouded by consternation or gloom. Moreover, the source games themselves have sometimes undergone generic metamorphosis through the refinement of the original releases as classier editions and through their adaptation as anime shows. For example, several visual novels contain graphic depictions of sexuality in their original form that have been removed from both later versions of the games and from their anime offspring. Thus, though some of the shows may periodically feature erotic overtones or saucy innuendoes, they do not indulge in explicit or gratuitous sexual scenes and are therefore enjoyable by wider audiences. Shaped by a number of sign systems — social, cultural, literary, cinematic, theatrical, pictorial — the discourse deployed by the visual novel as a unique form of RPG is itself a medium to negotiate multibranching, rambling and even conflicting interpretations of reality by embracing disparate generic formulae and conventions within a single fabulistic framework.

## *Characters and Settings: Design Philosophy*

As adumbrated in the preceding pages, two of the most remarkable features of visual novels and of anime based upon them are thoughtfully designed characters and backgrounds. Some theoretical observations concerning these two aspects of the titles under scrutiny deserve detailed consideration at this juncture, due to their profound relevance to this book's entire scope and subject matter. All of the productions here explored rely on depth of characterization in conjunction with meticulous background designs in order to achieve the various objectives pursued by their yarns, as outlined in the preceding segment of this discussion. Ultimately, proficient character design is integral to a game's or an anime's ability to lure us into its fictive domain. Nevertheless, as will be underscored in Chapter 4 apropos of the phenomenon of immersion, neither visual novels nor the shows adapted from them are intent on drawing their players and viewers so deeply into their realms as to make them oblivious to the works' constructedness, their artfulness. In fact, revealing once again their allegiance to traditional Japanese aesthetics, those artifacts never presume to be holding the mirror up to nature, so to speak, and hence delivering a world indistinguishable from reality itself (whatever this might be). Reminding their audiences of the process of production underlying their visuals and their stories while concomitantly inviting them to participate in that process are vital priorities for both visual novels and their televisual progeny.

While the pleasure gleaned from playing a visual novel or watching an anime based upon that ludic form owes much to immersive involvement in the experiences of various characters and their milieux, it depends no less crucially on the concurrent awareness that one is playing a game or watching a show. To ensure that we never quite lose sight of this artificially staged enactment, the works under investigation assiduously expose the strategies underpinning their construction — e.g., by drawing attention to specifically cinematographical techniques they deploy, such as particular camera angles or framing devices, or else to the sketches and paintings behind the fully realized personae and settings we actually see on the screen. Therefore, they could be said to foster an eminently formalist approach to art, famously described by Viktor Schklovsky as follows: "The purpose of art is to impart the sensation of things as they are perceived and not as they are known. The technique of art is to make objects 'unfamiliar'.... *Art is a way of experiencing the artfulness of an object*" (Schklovsky, p. 20).

The titles addressed in this study typically yield intriguing galleries of characters whose personality traits are studiously integrated with the tone of the worlds they inhabit at practically all times. This rule holds with remarkable consistency irrespective of whether the character is a high-school student struggling to negotiate the legacy of buried traumas or crimes (such as Yuuichi in *Kanon* or Keiichi in *When Cicadas Cry*), an alien princess (e.g., Rin in *Shuffle!*), an android (e.g., Miharu in *Da Capo*) or a reticent fighter (such as Shiki in *Tsukihime, Lunar Legend* or Shirou in *Fate/stay Night*). The approach to characterization repeatedly evinced by the productions here studied reminds us that the worlds to which all of those personae belong are fundamentally very much like our own world even when they appear most bizarre or outlandish. This is, quite simply, because their inhabitants harbor potently human emotions and are entangled in universal human conflicts.

Effective characterization owes much to its combination with a sensitive take on space and its effects on dramatic action. Virtually all of the productions here examined enthusiastically corroborate the proposition that backgrounds play a crucial part in enticing the audience into the world depicted on the screen, regardless of whether they present moments of theatrical grandeur or mundane scenes from everyday life. No less impressive, particularly in the portrayal of urban backgrounds, is the juxtaposition of photorealistic settings with impressionistic and stylized scenarios. Lighting is concurrently accorded an axial role in intensifying or diluting the dramatic impact of a shot or sequence. With the assistance of digital tools, studios have increasingly been in a position to experiment with lighting effects achieved through delicate variations in the stacking and blending of layers. Furthermore, lighting effects are matched by artful chromatic gradations and variations. In the process, light and color alike are systematically blended with natural and architectural features. Abrupt changes in the chromatic and textural properties of a character's field of vision can also be utilized as economical ways of communicating his or her inner state at times of intensified emotional turbulence. Thus, the screen might suddenly become filled with desaturated or monochrome palettes or flooded by disorienting swathes of marks accomplished by computer-generated ink-dripping and crosshatching (to mention merely a couple of examples).

The style adopted for character design in the productions discussed in this study is by no means undilutedly uniform but actually evinces local color and individuality in each. Nevertheless, all of the visual novels and their anime adaptations do share certain common ingredients, above all a preference for the aesthetic principle of "cuteness." In the West, this concept is held to have been introduced by the zoologist and animal psychologist Konrad Lorenz in 1949 as an analytical category of special significance in the field of ethology (i.e., the scientific investigation of animal behavior). In everyday parlance, cuteness is generally associated with infantile or infantilized physiognomies characterized by small bodies with oversized heads and disproportionately large eyes, as well as a pervasive feel of softness evocative of innocence, vulnerability and playfulness. Lorenz, however, sought to go beyond superficial appearances and investigate the emotional implications of cuteness, concluding that childlike forms by and large stimulate nurturing tendencies in grown-ups and hence play a part in the survival of the species. This proclivity is linked with "paedomorphosis" or "paedomorphism" (a.k.a. "juvenification"): namely, the phenomenon whereby adult samples of a species preserve features previously found solely in juveniles. The fascination with infantile shapes was held by Lorenz to be confirmed by many adults' attraction to cute animals and tendency to breed pets distinguished precisely by childlike traits (Lorenz).

The ubiquitousness of the aesthetic ideal of cuteness in the design of many of the characters that feature in the works here examined can hardly go unnoticed. Yet it is worth stressing that cuteness is prevalent in much contemporary anime generally — and not just in anime adapted from visual novels — and indeed in numerous aspects of Japanese art and popular culture, where it goes by the name of "*kawaii.*" In the specific context of Japanese society, the cult of cuteness has incrementally flooded both the fashion industry (e.g., in the guise of frills, ribbons and doll-like costumes) and popular pursuits (e.g., the worship of younger and younger idol singers) since the 1980s. Western entertainment industries have also capitalized for decades on cute icons, as demonstrated by products as diverse as Shirley Temple movies (1930s), *Care Bears* greeting cards (created by American Greetings in 1981 and first painted by the eminent illustrator Elena Kucharik), CG animations in the style of *Happy Feet* (dir. George Miller, 2006), *My Little Pony* toys (produced by Hasbro and introduced in 1983), alongside all manner of fashion items. As the palaeontologist and historian of science Stephen Jay Gould has emphasized, even the Disney empire has relied on the principle of cuteness for its advancement: "Mickey became progressively more juvenile in appearance.... The Disney artists transformed Mickey in clever silence, often using suggestive devices that mimic nature's own changes by different routes. To give him the shorter and pudgier legs of youth, they lowered his pants line and covered his spindly legs with a baggy outfit. (His arms and legs also thickened substantially — and acquired joints for a floppier appearance.) His head grew relatively larger — and its features more youthful" (Gould, pp. 1–2).

In Japan, the passion for cuteness has escalated to endemic proportions, operating as a key marketing force behind the dissemination of a plethora of both goods and attitudes. Notably, widespread attitudes have at times not merely resulted from existing merchandize but rather given rise to particular commercial initiatives. For example, the adoption by teenage girls of a *kawaii* handwriting style to communicate with one another in the 1970s inspired several companies to apply the underlying aesthetics of that initially non-profitable fashion to lucrative enterprises. Visual novels and their transpositions to the animated medium overflow with physiognomies and products — in the form of clothes, props, toys and gastronomic items — immediately evocative of a *kawaii* take on the world. Observing the pervasiveness of the aesthetics of cuteness in contemporary Japan is interesting for anybody engaged in the study of that culture. However, more intriguing still are the sociological import of that trend on the one hand, and its latent connections with earlier phases of Japanese history on the other. These phenomena are not only relevant to Japan but actually impact on global pop culture, since the ever-growing attraction to Japanese goods and vogues in various parts of the world inevitably entails increasing exposure to — and captivation by — the *kawaii* sensibility. Whether the fashion is fuelled by sushi-obsessed food retailers, the deluge of *Hello Kitty!* spin-offs still glutting the market more than three decades since the character's introduction by Sanrio, fashion chains such as *Muji* (officially established with this name in 1983) or indeed anime and manga, it deserves attention as an important component in globalized economies.

As Diana Lee shows, several theoretical explanations have been proffered to throw light on the ascendancy of what she terms "cute power." Some critics argue that it ensues from a "need to be liked" and "accepted in society." These tendencies are, after all, ingrained in traditional Japanese mentalities. Others claim that in embracing an ethos that playfully shuns the imperatives associated with an "austere life in work, family and social responsibility," the promulgation of *kawaii* actually rebels against "traditional values of Japanese lifestyle." A further view, based on an appreciation of indigenous philosophy, holds that the attraction to a cultural trend that "appears to champion" the concepts of "weakness" and "inability" as strengths in their own right is influenced by a Buddhist world view (Lee) — and, to be more precise, the proposition that accepting the self's limitations is prerequisite to any journey of self-discovery. Two related explanations for the *kawaii* boom are supplied in the article "Japan smitten by love of cute," where it is advocated that "Cute is cool in Japan. Look anywhere and everywhere: Cartoon figures dangle from mobile phones, waitresses bow in frilly maid outfits, bows adorn bags, even police departments boast cuddly mascots.... Japanese have come up with nuances of cute and use phrases such as 'erotic-cute' and 'grotesque-cute' in conversation." (It should be noted, in this respect, that anime diversifies its representations of *kawaii* accordingly, drawing clear — though understated — distinctions between the cuteness of a character in a maid outfit, say, and that of a no-nonsense tomboy or a soft–Goth type.) The article cited above then goes on to observe, "Sceptics ... say Japan's pursuit of cute is a sign of an infantile mentality and worry that Japanese culture — historically praised for exquisite understatement as sparse rock gardens and woodblock prints — may be headed toward doom." More magnanimous commentators like Tomoyuki Sugiyama, conversely, maintain that "cute is rooted in Japan's harmony-loving culture." Moreover, current vogues associated with the *kawaii* explosion, such as collecting figurines and other diminutive ornaments as mementos, "can be traced back 400 years to the Edo Period, when tiny carved 'netsuke' charms were wildly popular" ("Japan smitten by love of cute").

The perspective adopted in this book acknowledges *kawaii*'s consumerist dimension, insofar as the fascination with cuteness could be critically regarded as a concession to the dumbing-down proclivities of postindustrial society and attendant promotion of shallow pleasures and undemanding pursuits. However, echoing Lee's argument, the book also proposes that *kawaii* bears intriguing albeit oblique connections with indigenous philosophy. Its emphasis on notions of childlikeness, simplicity and even powerlessness, in particular, is redolent of the attitude to life fostered by Zen Buddhism. Four factors deserve particular attention in this context. Firstly, Zen invites the mind not to hunt for meaning in the information yielded by the world but rather to perceive it for what it is with a childlike disposition. Secondly, and relatedly, Zen criticizes the dominance of reason as a coldly conceptualizing agency in favor of an outlook wherein intellectual and sensuous experiences coalesce. Thirdly, the demotion of reason from the acme of the philosophical hierarchy inspires a profound respect for the concrete dimension of life. Fourthly, Zen promotes an ethos of playful freedom.

*Kawaii* mirrors these positions by encouraging a childlike sensibility and by presenting hard reasoning as quite pointless an exercise, favoring instead a stance in which intellectual engagement and sensory pleasure are intermeshed. At the same time, it celebrates the material as opposed to the abstract side of existence insofar as cute images explicitly eschew metaphysical aspirations. Furthermore, as pointed out at several junctures in this study, the titles under investigation — in all of which *kawaii* plays a role — insistently uphold the value of materiality through their punctilious attention to culinary and sartorial details. Similar emphasis on the inseparability of the intellect and the sensorium and concomitantly on the value of concreteness is pithily communicated by Roland Barthes' writings: "what if knowledge itself were *delicious?*" (Barthes, p. 23). Finally, the aesthetic of cuteness echoes Zen's approach to freedom. Of course, one must be cautious in talking about freedom when assessing what is, after all, a fashion. Nevertheless, *kawaii* does invoke that notion in promoting the idea that visual solace — and, by extension, any form of perceptible pleasure — can be derived from something frankly non-purposeful and non-teleological. The here-and-now is hence prioritized in ways that bring to mind Zen's upholding of simplicity as key to the grasp of reality. As Shigenori Nagatomo observes, this concept is founded on the idea that "a thing-event that is immediately presencing before one's eyes or under one's foot" expresses "its primordial mode of be*ing*" (Nagatomo). In the logic of *kawaii*, this notion is embodied in images that do not seek to find existential justification in anything other than themselves: their graphic terseness confirms this attitude to meaning. This is not to say that a cute icon does not carry symbolic connotations or ideological subtexts; it is, in fact, inevitably bound to do so by its inscription in a culturally sanctioned system of signs. This is, however, a reminder that the image can still be met and appreciated as an ephemeral presence that does not need to be sublimated into lofty abstract ideals. This quality is what is arguably most refreshing about the *kawaii* spirit as it manifests itself in the productions here discussed.

This simplicity translates into playfulness once we as audience feel able to literally *play along* with the images without pursuing transcendental destinations, and even enjoy moments of absurd humor as worthwhile experiences unto themselves — in much the same way as a lot of Zen literature is made especially tantalizing by its use of seeming nonsense and risible paradoxes. Finally, as constructed as *kawaii* images clearly and self-professedly are, they carry an aura of spontaneity: a concept which, in the context of Zen philosophy, is practically coterminous with "freedom" (*jiyuu*). The latter does not connote, as it often does in Western thought, the self's expression of its personal desires released from the shackles of external forces, but rather a force arising out of nothing of its own accord since the self is essentially "nothing." This idea is a corollary of the Zen belief that both organic and inorganic beings share one fundamental attribute: rootlessness. Presenting life as it really is, therefore, means foregrounding its lack of definitive foundations. The time-honored native art of floral arrangement, "*ikebana*," reflects this conviction since it is precisely by severing the living flower from its roots in the soil that the designer exhibits its authentic nature as a transient entity. As Makoto Ueda points out, *ikebana*'s "ultimate aim" is "to represent nature in its innermost essence" (Ueda, p. 86). The word indeed translates as "make flowers live" (from "*ikeru*" = "to live" + "*hana*" = "flower").

The positions outlined in the preceding paragraphs with reference to various sociological interpretations of the cult of cuteness and to Japan's philosophical tradition hopefully illuminate the importance of *kawaii* beyond the boundaries of purely contingent vogues. In looking at *kawaii*'s relationship with tradition, it is also noteworthy, as Natalie Avella persuasively argues in her seminal book on Japanese design, that the cuteness to be found in contemporary anime, manga and videogames informed by related aesthetic tenets is not an isolated phenomenon. In fact, it is part of an ample graphic tapestry in which legions of styles continually collude. According to Avella, what the plethora of interweaving styles to be found in contemporary Japanese culture cumulatively reveals is the composite character of native graphic design as a cauldron of traditional and global influences. While it could be realistically maintained that the progress of modernization in Japan has been far more rapid than it has in other societies, it is undeniable that contemporary Japanese aesthetic principles — with the cult of *kawaii* in a prominent position among them — still value many of the distinctive tenets of an august legacy of seemingly undying potency (Avella).

Central to this cultural inheritance, as intimated earlier, is the reverential attitude to their materials characteristically exhibited by Japanese craftsmen and artists for time immemorial. Following the intrinsic qualities of each material as the guide through which formal and compositional decisions can then be made, Japanese artisans of all sorts prioritize the lessons of nature to anthropocentric tendencies of the kind prevalent in the West. Thus the innate properties of stones, shrubs and water will tell the garden landscaper how best to constellate them into a pleasingly coherent whole. As Yuriko Saito observes, quoting the eleventh-century treatise *Book on Garden Making*, "the scenic effect of a landscape" is best achieved "by observing one principle of design: 'obeying ... the request' of an object." Thus, "the gardener 'should first install one main stone, and then place other stones, in necessary numbers, in such a way as to satisfy the request ... of the main stone....' The whole art ... requires the artist to work closely with, rather than in spite of or irrespective of, the material's natural endowments" (Saito, p. 86). Analogously, the inherent attributes of paper, wood and numerous vegetable fibers will tell the package designer what shapes and sizes are most suitable for a certain wrapper or container. Hence, these materials do not abide exclusively by economic and pragmatic tenets but actually determine, through their inherent attributes, the design of the packages. In a similar vein, the unique flavors, colors, fragrances and consistence levels of various food items will tell the chef how to organize a dish so as to maximize their gustatory and visual potential. According to Kenji Ekuan, the processing and arrangement of different ingredients is guided by the desire to let their essences manifest themselves unimpeded. The preparation of the classic Japanese lunchbox (*bento*), for instance, is underpinned by one vital objective: to collect "normal, familiar, everyday things from nature, according to season" and maximize "their inherent appeal" so as "bring each to full life" (Ekuan, p. 6). Fish will thus be made "more fishlike" and rice "more ricelike" (p. 77). In the titles here explored, both the dietary preferences and culinary exploits of characters as diverse as Momoka (*Touka Gettan*), Kaede and Asa (*Shuffle!*), Ayu, Shiori, Mai and Makoto (*Kanon*), Hayami and Takuma (*H2O Footprints in the Sand*), Sakura (*Fate/stay Night*), Junichi (*Da Capo*), Mrs. Furukawa (*Clannad*) and Sekai (*School Days*) fully demonstrate the validity of this proposition.

Representations of *kawaii* in the productions under examination are subtly diversified and often rendered deliberately ambiguous. For example, Ayu in *Kanon*, Minatsu in *Da Capo II*, and Fuko in *Clannad* are all endowed with infantile traits of an overtly cute orientation, yet are hardly reduced to samples of doll-like fragility, for they insistently come across as plucky, lippy and terse to the point of gruffness. Nanami in *Soul Link*, for her part, exudes childlike innocence, yet turns out to be an imposingly larger-than-life presence. *Touka Gettan*'s Makoto similarly harbors powers of cosmic magnitude despite her ostensible immaturity and correspondingly infantile mien. Rena in *When Cicadas Cry* is a pointedly disturbing instance of multiple personalities, as she shifts repeatedly from a gentle appearance abetted by emphatically girly costumes to the role of a dark, ill-boding agency. Noe from *true tears*, likewise, displays a dewy-eyed mien while also operating as a harbinger of ominous warnings and an utterly unsentimental analyst of human frailty. At the same time, characters that are not overtly portrayed as *kawaii* frequently evince cute undercurrents. Lilith in *Yami to Boushi no Tabibito*, for instance, is a controlling force of immense caliber but is shown to host several infantile weaknesses and hobbyhorses. Saber from *Fate/stay Night* is also a gentle and sensitive young woman at her core, regardless of her literally armored, seemingly inviolable personality and blunt cynicism. The principal female characters in *Utawarerumono*, in turn, are true paeans to paedomorphism — not least due to their mega-cute animal appendages — but acquire graver connotations as the story progressively emphasizes their unique healing and martial skills and self-determination, while also disclosing their nature as genetically engineered beings.

As will be noted at several junctures in this study, the depiction of architectural structures and myriad items of interior decor in a profusion of vivid details is a defining quality of both visual novels and anime adapted from that form. In assessing the importance of character design as a means of regaling players and viewers with stimuli intended to sustain their motivation, it is important to bear in mind that this technical factor is practically inextricable from the execution of architectural settings. One of the most striking features of the productions here explored, in this respect, is their incorporation of a wide range of styles drawn from disparate phases of Japanese history and thereby harking back to numerous traditions, customs and narratives. Throughout, the influence on Japanese architecture of climate, seasonal cycles and geological phenomena is consistently underscored. Thus, many family houses portrayed in traditional styles are shown to be partly raised to allow air to circulate: a design detail dictated by the country's long, hot summers. Wood is also pervasive in the architecture and decor of many shows, which reflects the local preference for a material that adapts easily to shifts in temperature, while also adjusting resiliently to telluric disturbances. Basic construction habits such as the ones just described are ubiquitous traits of the dwellings seen in this book's chosen titles. They indeed feature with striking regularity in shows as diverse as *Yami* and *Myself; Yourself, Shuffle!* and *true tears, When Cicadas Cry* and *Clannad, H2O* and *School Days* — to cite but a handful of illustrative instances.

Among some of the most traditional and ancient types of edifice alluded to in the selected works are tea cottages of the type introduced in the Muromachi Period (1333–1568), when tea ceremonies were especially in vogue. These are enthusiastic celebrations of Japan's dedication to simplicity, evinced by the use of slender structures unencumbered by superfluous ornamentation, and harmony between buildings and the landscaped gardens around them. Another traditional edifice to be noted is the castle: an architectural construct introduced into Japanese society with the ascendancy of feudal lords in the sixteenth century. Time-honored structures such as these are at times interspersed with or even replaced by comparably traditional architectural styles of a decidedly Western derivation. It is therefore not uncommon for the shows (and their progenitors) to invoke old European vogues enshrined either in social reality (*ef—a tale of memories, ef—a tale of melodies* and *Tsukihime*) or in fairytale and lore (*Fate/stay Night* and *The Familiar of Zero*) or in a fusion of the two dimensions (*Aria*). This imaginary admixture serves to remind us that even at their most realistic, the selected productions endeavor to evoke deliberately artificial worlds to be appreciated *as constructs* rather than mimetic reflections of reality as such. Less frequently, yet to memorable effect, the works venture into futuristic territory in the depiction of their settings, echoing Western or indeed global trends. This is most obviously attested to by *Soul Link*, and by the sci-fi segments of *Yami* and *Kashimashi—Girl Meets Girl*.

While buildings such as tea cottages and baronial bastions attest to eminently indigenous sources of inspiration, signs of Japan's exposure to Western architectural influences can also be seen: for example, in the use of brick and stone for both private residences and public buildings such as schools (e.g., Kazami Academy in *Da Capo*) and hospitals (e.g., the ones featuring conspicuously in *Kanon* and *Rumbling Hearts*). These materials were imported into Japan in the Meiji Period (1868–1912). Temples and shrines also make regular appearances, reflecting the legacy of both Buddhism and Shinto. In a typical Buddhist temple, the central pagoda holding sacred relics is surrounded by a main hall, a lecture hall, a bell tower, a repository for *sutras* (i.e., Buddhist scriptures), a dormitory and a refectory. The shapes of Shinto shrines, conversely, vary considerably according to the environment in which they are erected. A path lined with stone lanterns characteristically leads to the highly iconic *torii* gate to the shrine itself. This is guarded by pairs of leonine statues known as *komainu*. A Shinto hall may be temporary, and thus created just for a special occasion, or permanent and modeled on ancient granaries and storehouses. Shrines of various designs are especially prominent in *When Cicadas Cry*, *Air*, *Myself; Yourself* and *Da Capo*.

Modern architecture features in several of the chosen titles, often supplying a succinct means of conveying symbolic contrasts between the hectic urban fabric and the provincial locations in which several shows are set. Although modern styles of Western derivation reached Japan with the Meiji Restoration of 1868, these did not conclusively take root due to the 1880s backlash promulgating a return to traditional models. A more radical reorientation occurred after World War I, partly due to the direct influence of architects such as Frank Lloyd Wright—who, in turn, drew formative inspiration from Japanese architecture itself. This trend continued well into the twentieth century as syntheses of Eastern and Western styles were incrementally elaborated. The typical modern urbanscape depicted in the kind of anime here addressed is replete with all of the standard icons: glass, chrome and neon lights accordingly pervade the ambience.

Moving on to the interior dimension, it is noteworthy that many elements of traditional Japanese interior design are included, with varying degrees of eminence, in both visual novels and their animated progeny. In assessing the classic Japanese house, it is important to remember that interiors were not initially divided into rooms allocated to separate functions. Gradually, self-standing screens (*byobu*) meant to secure limited privacy were introduced, to be subsequently supplanted by room dividers (*fusuma*) and paper-covered sliding doors/windows (*shoji*), still to be found as crucial stylistic features of contemporary homes designed on the basis of traditional templates. Consisting of opaque sliding doors, *fusuma* not only serve to partition a dwelling's interior rooms but also fulfill ornamental purposes, as they are typically painted with some kind of natural scene. *Shoji* likewise have a twofold function, since in separating the inside from the outside, they also provide a source of unique aesthetic pleasure. The translucent mulberry-bark paper covering their lattice frames indeed diffuses the light entering the home in fascinating ways, creating myriad patterns of shadow and brightness.

To most Westerners, the relative openness of the traditional Japanese home will automatically suggest a lamentable lack of privacy. Such an assessment is quite irrelevant, however, for the Japanese — as noted in the segment on recurrent themes and motifs — harbor quite different notions of togetherness and solitude to the ones treasured in the West (and especially in industrial and postindustrial dispensations). Patrick Drazen has commented thus on this important aspects of Japanese culture: "Take half of the population of the United States ... and confine them to the three states on the Western seaboard: Washington, Oregon, and California. This crunch reflects what life is like in Japan. Much of the total area of this island nation is taken up by mountainous land unsuitable for agriculture or commerce, and more green space is lost each year. Consequently, the concept of 'privacy' in Japan has always been very different than in the West. People in Japan have historically lived up close and personal with each other.... In this culture, a person's identity comes from being part of a group rather than just a free-standing ego" (Drazen, p. 28). Furthermore, autochthonous approaches to spatial divisions — be they utterly temporary or permanent but patently unobtrusive — carry psychological connotations by evoking the tenuousness of the barrier between inner and outer worlds, between Self and Other, as will be seen in Chapter 2 with reference to *Touka Gettan*'s take on narrativity.

Several of the anime here studied mirror Western styles in the representation of their protagonists' bedrooms, which are obviously designed to be used by individuals. However, although these exhibit Western-style beds and desks, it is not unusual for the central portion of the room to be occupied by a low table of overtly Japanese orientation (*chabudai*). Concomitantly, emphatically traditional sleeping arrangements consisting of multiple futons laid out on straw mats (*tatami*) can be no less frequently descried, with the accompaniment of the aforementioned screens. While they separate various parts of a house, screens are by definition refreshingly ephemeral since they can be removed to open up space. Inside and outside are not opposites, in this purview, but rather complementary facets of a seamless continuum. This is also borne out by the *engawa* (veranda) as a markedly transitional space. Exterior walls constitute likewise flexible boundaries in the uniquely simple, airy and refined style of the classic Japanese dwelling, since they normally consist of movable sliding panels. At night or in the wet season, wood panels are used, whereas screens of mounted paper replace them in warmer weather. The principal reason behind the proverbial openness of the traditional Japanese dwelling is that whereas in the West, the weight of a building is customarily borne by the exterior and interior walls, in Japanese architecture, it is the pillar that fulfils that function. With one main pillar (*daikokubashira*) sustaining the best part of the load of a classic dwelling, and any additional pillars unobtrusively serving as furnishing adjuncts, the domestic interior feels exceptionally unconfined. This atmosphere is starkly contrasted by the oppressive feel of the tiny and cluttered metropolitan apartments that occasionally appear in the anime as a metonymic encapsulation of urban living.

At all times, the house and the natural environment are conceived of as fluidly interdependent. This aesthetic and ethical stance can be traced back to the Heian Period (794–1185), when complex architectural schemes known as *shinden-zukuri* intended precisely to maximize the dialogue between inside and outside were devised for the elite. Elegant rectangular dwellings connected by long corridors were initially disposed around a landscaped garden complete with a pond. In the Kamokura Period (1185–1333), this model was replaced by clusters of distinct edifices combined under one roof. It is in this phase of local history that the standard for residential architecture still noticeable today was established. The sorts of elaborate designs just delineated are not as prevalent in either visual novels or their televisual transpositions as virtually all of the other architectural elements described in the preceding paragraphs. They are nonetheless echoed in the titles of a more traditional stylistic stamp, such as *Touka Gettan* and *Fate/stay Night*, as well as in the domestic and manufacturing compound central to *true tears*.

Japanese architecture's intimate connection with the surrounding environment is underscored by the article on the traditional indigenous interior published online in the *Yoshino Newsletter*, where it is proposed that Japanese edifices are a natural "response" to the country's "weather, its geography and its harmony with all of those elements," whereas "European structures were built as barriers against the forces of nature" ("Elements of a Traditional Japanese Interior"). The importance of this concept is further emphasized by Daisanne McLane: "Japanese houses have been built to conserve energy and resources, and to harmonize with nature, for more than 500 years." For example, "Inside the *machiya*, Kyoto's 19th-century townhouses, natural sunlight, handmade bamboo shades, and *shoji* paper screens create the illusion of outdoor living in long, narrow city buildings" (McLane, p. 6). Furthermore, "The Five Elements, building blocks of Japanese style, are evident not only in traditional homes, but also in contemporary designs by such architects as Tadao Ando and Kengo Kuma, whose Lotus House is an exhilarating composition of white travertine stone, polished hardwood, water, and air" ( p. 7). Ando himself eloquently corroborates this point thus: "When you look at Japanese traditional architecture, you have to look at Japanese culture and its relationship with nature. You can actually live in a harmonious, close contact with nature — this [is] very unique to Japan" (Ando).

The chapters to follow pursue the ideas advanced in the course of the present chapter by articulating a theoretical model that makes it possible to address visual novels and their animated offshoots in relation to broader debates pivoting on four interrelated categories: narrativity, interactivity, immersion and graphic presentation. The argument proceeds from the premise that visual novels are fundamentally games and that a recognition of their ludic identity is instrumental both in grasping their formal and graphic specificity and in enjoying the challenges they pose. However, in acknowledging the visual novel's gameness, it is no less vital to acknowledge its imbrication with narrativity. A visual novel is not an autonomous story in itself, yet it indubitably accommodates all the raw materials of a potential narrative. These materials become actual stories as the game mobilizes the player's own narrative drives and hence urges him or her to cluster them into coherent (albeit always provisional) stories. The anime adaptations perform a job analogous to the player's own function insofar as one of the primary tasks undertaken by their creators consists precisely of the cinematographical organization of the source games' materials into integrated though by and large open-ended narratives. Therefore, while the anime spin-offs faithfully emulate their ludic models on the stylistic and thematic planes, they concurrently mimic the operations of videogamers intent on a narrativizing act. This places the shows' directors and designers on the level of actively engaged players in their own right. Anime viewers take on the role of second-level narrativizers as they in turn process the stories offered by the shows according to their aesthetic leanings and decoding abilities. It could therefore be argued that three interrelated processes are at stake in the multimedia experiences revolving around a player's interaction with the visual novel, an anime producer's adaptation of the parent game for the screen, and the anime spectator's interpretation of the resulting show. As indicated, pivotal to the particular version of narrativity fostered by the visual novel is the elaboration of multibranching, multiperspectival crisscrossing and intentionally inconclusive yarns evocative of a sense of randomness reminiscent of chaos theory. The deployment of extensive textual passages characterized by explicitly narrative predilections, combined with a passion for genre-straddling, further abet the visual novel's distinctively story-oriented matrix. Anime adapted from visual novels follow closely the parent format in their own diegetic orchestration.

Insofar as its player is responsible for narrativizing the game's elemental ingredients as an active presence by translating their storytelling potentialities into concrete narratives, the visual novel is a markedly interactive experience. This dimension of the source games is also reflected in their anime scions by plots that consistently invite speculation and imaginative interpretation on the audience's part and hence preclude the option of totally passive consumption. Frequent self-referential allusions serving as metacommentaries on the nature of narrative itself strongly encourage the reflective mode. The maximization of both players' and viewers' active involvement often leads to the adoption of immersive ruses that rely heavily in both the games and the anime on plot complexity and character depth, bolstered by meticulously executed designs both for characters and for generic backgrounds of unparalleled lushness. However, immersion never equates to a benumbed state of engulfment in the game's or anime's textual maze. In fact, we are consistently alerted to the constructed stature of the games and of the animated adaptations alike, and indeed encouraged to take pleasure in the artifice *qua* artifice.

# 2

# Parallel Worlds

*The true object of all human life is play.*
— G. K. Chesterton

*A great writer of fiction both creates — through acts of imagination,
through language that feels inevitable, through vivid forms — a new
world, a world that is unique, individual; and responds to a world, the
world the writer shares with other people but is unknown or mis-
known by still more people, confined in their worlds: call that history,
society, what you will.*

— Susan Sontag

Like other types of videogames, visual novels invite reflection on the relationship between the story dimension they articulate in order to proceed textually and the specifically ludic framework on which they depend for their
gameplay. Relatedly, they invoke the arguments put forward by both narratology — the study of narrative structures and of writing and reading modalities —
and ludology — the study of games as dramatic formations of a distinctive kind.
The concept of narrative has played a central role in the humanities for several
decades as the primary vehicle through which both individuals and collectivities organize their patterns of perception and knowledge. Within the realm of
game studies that has grown out of the diffusion of computer-based media, the
importance of narrative has not gone unnoticed. Nevertheless, several ludologists have sought to challenge what they regard as the colonialist appropriation
of their field by narrative theory grounded in the analysis of older, pre-digital
media. In so doing, these authors have tended to emphasize the player's involvement in the shaping of a game as far more pronounced an event than the reader's
involvement in the production of a written narrative.

Narratology and ludology should not, however, be seen as antithetical.
Endeavoring to understand the intrinsic properties of a game as a game within

the context of computer culture does not automatically foreclose the cultivation of narrative theories. As Gonzalo Frasca maintains, the notion that "Ludologists are supposed to focus on game mechanics and reject any room in the field for analyzing games as narrative, while narratologists argue that games are closely connected to stories" and should be studied, at least partially, "through narratology" is the product of "a series of misunderstandings and misconceptions" (Frasca 2003). In fact, Frasca elsewhere proposes, "ludology could be used along with narratology to better understand videogames" and should be seen "not to replace the narratologic [sic] approach, but to complement it" (Frasca 1999).

In evaluating the relationship between gameplay and storytelling, it must also be stressed that RPGs at large are reputed by numerous theorists to harbor potent storytelling tendencies over and above the action-saturated component. Daniel Mackay, for instance, has persuasively argued that whereas several popular games prioritize fighting skills or the accumulation of points and prizes by means of dynamic pursuits, fantasy RPGs resemble an interactive improvisational performance in which players take on a variety of character types and are largely free to define imaginatively the identities of their parts within relatively capacious predesigned scenarios. Therefore, they are accorded the right to weave narratives — which scenarios partly limit but also promote at each turn — that are ultimately responsible for imparting the game with a distinctive formal, aesthetic, social and broadly cultural multi-identity (Mackay). Satu Heliö's writings have been particularly influential in documenting the nature of RPGs as a very specific ludic form guided by "strong narrative aspirations." According to the critic, although there may not be an "actual story" in the game itself in the sense of a free-standing fiction with a neatly mapped-out beginning, middle and end, "there are events, characters and structures of narrativity giving the players the basis for interpreting it *as* narrative." The game, in this regard, strives towards storyness by stimulating "the 'narrative desire' to make pieces we interpret to relate to each other fit in" (Heliö, p. 68). Applying Heliö's argument to the specific domain of the visual novel, it could be suggested that the game per se does not contain an autonomous story in the classic sense of the term. Its arcs and alternate developments only come to form a story if and when players interact with them and string them together through their choices. Yet the game itself does feature all of the ingredients of a virtual or hypothetical story that is capable of coming to fruition through external interventions and is amenable to decoding in essentially narrative terms.

Therefore, the visual novel eloquently attests to the interdependence of the narrative and ludic dimensions. It is clearly an art form that asserts itself as a specific kind of game and could not, accordingly, be adequately understood were one to ignore its ludic status. Yet it also attaches tremendous importance to textuality, emplacing storytelling potentialities as key to its identity. Additionally, while the visual novel partakes of the ludic sensibility in situating the player as an axial agency, it also posits narrative construction as the channel through which players can communicate with the game-text. Thus, narrative construction becomes the ultimate drive directing the game's multidirectional unfolding. In this respect, the visual novel challenges the polarization of narratology as a discipline concerned with the codes underlying the experiences of readers as outside observers, and ludology as a discipline concerned with the codes underlying the experiences of players as internal agents. In assessing how this state of affairs translates into the situation of spectators watching an anime based on a visual novel, it could be suggested that as long as the adaptation is capable of enlisting and then sustaining their interest in the characters, their feelings and their actions, they will perceive the anime story in much the same way players perceive the parent-game story. In other words, if the anime poses questions that stimulate the viewers' imaginations, drawing them into the characters' psycho-terrains, and providing equivocal clues instead of clear-cut resolutions, then it is most likely that such viewers will feel deeply involved in the narrative as active participants. Pivotal to the accomplishment of this effect is a director's ability to weave a fabric out of the threads supplied by the source game that feels unstable and provisional and hence invites ongoing interpretation.

In light of the observations put forward in the preceding paragraphs, the following complementary hypotheses may be advanced: 1. a visual novel asks to be tackled as a game and as a narrative in equal measures; 2. viewers of anime adapted from visual novels undergo an experience akin to the one entailed by playing the parent game if the narrative can ensure their ongoing input in its generation. (The phenomenon of direct involvement is revisited in some detail in Chapter 3 with reference to the topos of player agency, and in Chapter 4 with reference to the phenomenon of immersion. The importance of character presentation is revisited in Chapter 5.) Most importantly, both players and spectators of the kinds here considered are encouraged to address the plausible outcomes of their choices and interpretations *narratively*— i.e., by taking the principle of narrative as the fundamental matrix in the fashioning of human identities, relationships and histories. Hence, they are enjoined to approach the fictional worlds at their disposal as texts knit from disparate story strands that encapsulate allegorically their own real-life situations. Ultimately, regardless of its intrinsic narrative density, the visual novel stands out as a unique expression of narrativity by virtue of its incorporation of legion virtual stories within the boundaries of a single ludic package. This poses an exciting challenge for directors assessing the adaptability of a visual novel into an anime. Such directors will have to judge whether or not a game constitutes viable material for televisual translation principally on the basis of its penchant for magnetizing the audience's narrative urge.

All of the anime and source games examined in this chapter engage with the depiction and exploration of fictive domains wherein parallel realities meet and merge in mutual suffusion. In *Air*, the worlds at stake consist of the reality associated with the present-day character of Misuzu and the mythical reality centered on the ancient princess Kanna. In *Yami to Boushi to Hon no Tabibito*, numerous parallel dimensions are seen to arise from the tomes of a huge library posited as coterminous with the cosmos itself. *Touka Gettan* deals with the theme of parallel existences through a twin focus on the past and present configurations of the imaginary land of Kamitsumihara on the one hand, and the interaction between this realm and its real-world counterpart Kinokuniya on the other. *Shuffle!* portrays the human dimension as a world literally sandwiched between the parallel worlds of gods and demons. In *Soul Link*, finally, two versions of parallelism are offered: one pertains to the coexistence of Earth's civilization with the culture developing on the space station Aries; the other to the simultaneous evolution of humans and the alternate life form known as *sukyura*. In addition, the chapter looks at *Aria* as an anime adapted into the visual-novel format. In this instance, the parallel worlds at play are the fictional configuration of Venice situated on a futuristic version of planet Mars and the historical Venice, existing purely as a corpus of memories and tales.

The parallel worlds portrayed by all of the anime are linked by a key diegetic factor. In *Air*, this consists of the story's emphasis on the aesthetic concept of tragic ineluctability; in *Yami*, of an unrelenting quest; in *Touka Gettan*, of a love capable of transcending not only time and space but logic itself; in *Shuffle!*, of the bridging agency of the human world in relation to its non-human counterparts; in *Soul Link*, of a potent undercurrent of Bildungsroman priorities; in *Aria*, of the concurrently dreamlike and down-to-earth flavor of actual and fantastic spaces alike. Although the recurrence of these narrative patterns based on parallelisms and internal linkages may superficially suggest that the anime themselves are repetitive, this is not truly the case. In fact, considerable local variety at the levels of characterization, settings and cross-generic experimentation renders the shows highly diversified. It must also be observed, as far recurrence is concerned, that this concept echoes a distinctively Eastern cultural heritage that attaches great significance to the systematic utilization of repetitive ritualized acts. This proclivity is instantly noticeable in Japanese theatre, where the actors' objective is not to indulge in originality or extemporization but rather to communicate, by means of highly symbolic iterative motifs, certain recurring states, feelings and ideas. The priority in adhering to this principle is the eschewal of equivocation and ambiguity. The elimination of these potentially destabilizing factors is not intended to inculcate dogmatic views into the audience but rather to propose that the yearning for change is more likely to lead to escapism than to deeper truths. Hence, the methodical return to time-honored discourses becomes a way of intimating that the thirst for constant mutation fails to grasp the existential foundations of performativity by rejecting the old as outmoded, when those discourses actually carry philosophical lessons far more momentous than their contingent dramatic expressions. The notion that the return to the archaic does not merely amount to entrenched traditionalism but in fact operates as a means of conveying ongoing human preoccupations in changing cultural scenarios is corroborated by the chosen anime's commitment to the reiteration of established motifs — with the topos of parallel worlds in a privileged position among them.

\* \* \*

In the *Air* game (2000), the first scenario asks the player to take on the role of the male protagonist, Yukito Kunisaki, as a traveling entertainer in search of a legendary winged girl. The player is given choices that will subsequently determine which of three parallel stories he or she will enter. Each available arc revolves around one of three female characters: Misuzu Kamio, Kano Kirishima and Minagi Tohno. Misuzu is distinguished by a cheerful and highly emotional disposition; Kano is an animal lover inseparable from a puppy named Potato with whom she seems able to communicate; Minagi conceals a caring and scarred personality behind a seemingly emotionless façade. Once the opening scenario, titled "Dream," has reached a resolution, the second scenario, "Summer," is unlocked. This takes the story back in time to ancient Japan, focusing on the personae of Princess Kanna and her loyal assistants Uraha and Ryuuya. Although this scenario does not afford any choices, it elicits the player's active contribution to the narrativizing process by requiring him or her to bridge the gap between present and past events through independent imaginative effort. In addition, it is very entertaining and peppered with erotic jokes consonant with the game's origin in a format aimed at mature audiences. The more overt sexual references were elided from the visual novel for its release as an "All Ages" edition, the version on which the anime itself is essentially based.

In the third and final scenario, "Air," the player is expected to act out the part of a crow named Sora (i.e., "Sky"), deeply attached to Misuzu, who has adopted the bird as a pet. This character is resentful of both Yukito and Misuzu's guardian, her aunt Haruko, whom he regards as enemies. The player-as-crow must decide whether or not to attack the adversaries, which first of all enjoins him or her to assess the girl's relationships with Yukito and Haruko. The final scenario also elucidates the genesis of the myth surrounding the winged maiden Yukito indefatigably looks for. The ending is tantalizingly ambiguous and leaves in its wake a compassionate sense of humanity, sustained by memorable artwork and music. As a ludic construct, *Air* encompasses all of the formal elements described in the preceding chapter, specifically excelling at the subtle handling of its branching points, whereby the choices offered to the player, albeit often quite elementary, yield an engaging sense of pathos. The use of vibrant palettes and superb lighting effects contributes vitally to *Air*'s cumulative ambience. The game's graphic quality in the rendition of myriad settings, complex storyline and elaborate character portraits render *Air* almost addictively replayable. The pursuit of every conceivable path disclosed by certain key decisions engages the player in a self-exploratory psychodrama analogous to the emotional odyssey undertaken by Yukito and his female friends. To categorize the *Air* visual novel simply as a romantic adventure, therefore, would be to do it an unpardonable disservice. In fact, the game supplies a thought-provoking and narrative-oriented text with serious affective undercurrents, peopled with characters some players might find it hard to let go of.

The tensions set up by the *Air* game, both between two parallel worlds and within each of the dimensions it charts, render the potential narrative it accommodates conflict-driven in the way dramatic narrative characteristically tends to be. The player is also caught up in a conflictual situation insofar as moving from one arc to the next inevitably entails confrontation with contrasting options delivering disparate outcomes, on the one hand, and with puzzles of an affective, ethical and epistemological nature on the other. In other words, the player is not solely required to perform certain decisions for the game to advance in concrete terms: he or she must also face the conceptual implications of those decisions. It is from the collusion of particular choices (the practical aspect of the gameplay) and an ongoing evaluation of their possible repercussions (the game's philosophical subtext) that the player may constellate an actual narrative endowed not only with dynamic momentum but also with speculative substance. Once again, action never reigns supreme in the realm of the visual novel, for reflection, abstraction and introspection are instrumental in actualizing its storytelling potentialities. The effort expected of players, therefore, is both performative and intellectual, both game-oriented and narrative-oriented, and thus implicitly upholds the intercomplementarity of ludology and narratology.

*Air*'s admirably orchestrated three-arc structure, with its unobtrusive and multiaccentual parallelisms, makes it crystal clear that for the game to become amenable to narrativization, learning its rules and weighing the behavioral consequences of actions bound by such rules is simply not enough. The player's ability to apprehend the game as a virtual narrative open to concretization requires, in fact, a willingness to build up a cognitive structure that allows the perception of unfolding situations as a coherent story. Although this tendency must ultimately rest with the player, it is initially up to the game itself to promote it. That is to say, for the player to even wish to ideate such a structure, certain elements must be provided by the ludic object from the start. This is where RPGs generally, and visual novels in particular, proclaim their individuality. Indeed, they are designed more deliberately and more systematically than any other kind of computer game to mobilize the player's desire to devise a mold conducive to narrativization by recourse to strategies which, though not coterminous with storytelling moves in themselves, are driven by robust narrative ambitions. Where visual novels are specifically concerned, and *Air* is an outstanding case in point, the key ploys are thematic depth, a wide range of varied emotional experiences, and an approach to characterization eager to supply elaborate psychic histories replete with background information, personality twists, memories and ideals. Thus, players are never merely asked to make progress within the game world. In fact, they are invited to fathom the game's parallel dimensions as opportunities for a rich experiential process. This requires them to negotiate at each turn a bundle of character interrelations in which their own decisions constitute communicative and expressive actions rather than purely functional strategic moves.

The *Air* anime spin-off (TV series; dir. Tatsuya Ishihara, 2004–2005) is heir to the stylistic traits found in the parent game, faithfully perpetuating their impact and indeed enhancing their dramatic scope by disposing them within an explicitly narrative mold. At the same time, the anime smoothly transposes the visual novel's formal strengths into absorbing spectacle, abundantly maximizing the principles of multiperspectivalism and open-endedness within a tapestry where the mundane and the supernatural seamlessly coalesce. The anime blends romantic motifs with mythical and folkloric elements, frequently surpassing the romance dimension in terms of generic emphasis through excursions into disquieting drama (especially, as we shall see, in the movie version of the story). As legend morphs into reality and ancient magic infiltrates the modern world, *Air*'s viewers are treated to a heady journey of loss, love and redemption across parallel dimensions. The supernatural themes are graphically underscored by *Air*'s captivating scenery: azure skies and shimmering waters, in particular, play a decisive role in the lyrical evocation of the flight of time through a multilayered universe wherein a single summer is at once as brief as the "twinkling of a star" and as protracted as "eternity."

In describing the anime (and indeed the source game), it is impossible and perhaps even unfair to avoid poetic images. Both, in fact, are comparable to a wispy summer breeze and a clear blue sky stretching into timelessness, an ethereal filigree artifact and a softly echoing aria. It must also be emphasized, in this respect, that although the scenery is at times so mesmerizingly enrapturing as to verge on the magical, it never altogether ceases to look realistic. This impression owes much to the animation's stunning exactitude, which enables details such as birds, insects, flowers, leaves and even single raindrops to meet the eye with an unparalleled sense of intimacy, especially in close-ups. Additionally, homes are made to look like places where people could actually live, rather than impersonally formulaic stage sets, by means of both close-ups and panoramic takes. Other cinematographical techniques abet the mood, most notably unusual camera angles such as the ones in which some characters are left in the shade, while others stand directly in bright sunlight. Full corroboration for *Air*'s unique realism is provided by its treatment of the crucial temporal jump. This could feel unpalatably abrupt, especially as it leaves the present-day narrative on a cliffhanger, were it not for the well-judged and impeccably detailed depiction of period architecture and vestimentary styles capable of immersing us instantly into the alternate world of Kanna and her associates. The musical score works marvels in bolstering the impact of the visuals throughout, using breezy orchestral pieces for most sequences and punctuating the track with the gentle crackle of cicadas or the murmur of the ocean. The achingly nostalgic insert song used in the climax of the closing installment aptly crowns *Air*'s acoustic range.

In the show, Yukito is introduced in the midst of his travels from town to town in the sole company of a puppet left him by his mother upon her death — poetically described by Minagi as a "physical incarnation of memory" — which he is able to animate without any physical contact and is therefore able to deploy as a form of entertainment to eke out a meager living. However, Yukito's goal as a nomadic thespian is not wholly survival-oriented: it is also the achievement of dramatic excellence in a field some might consider lowly, yet is grounded in time-honored theatrical traditions of both Eastern and Western origins as varied as *bunraku, commedia dell'arte* and various kinds of street performance. It soon transpires, moreover, that the protagonist's peregrinations are not aimless, for he has actually embarked on a quest the purpose of which is to find confirmation for an ancient tale also bequeathed upon him by his late mother. This concerns the winged creature, known simply as the girl "beyond the sky," dreamlike visions of whom punctuate the series. The oneiric motif is consolidated by the presentation of the preternatural girl herself as someone who experiences the same dream time and again. As the plot develops, it is revealed that finding this being — or, at least, establishing the veracity of the venerable tale — is only part of Yukito's mission, as his ultimate task might actually consist of defying fate to prevent the maiden from perishing altogether. The legend's doomed heroine is the aforementioned Kanna, a winged princess deemed to have lived in the remote past whose wings and superhuman powers caused her to be feared by ordinary mortals, held captive and eventually consigned to the sky, where she is sealed in an endless nightmare. Ryuuya, a guardsman in love with Kanna, attempted to rescue her, but in doing so fell prey to a mysterious and incurable disease before he could succeed in his intended aim.

Despite the aura of solemnity issuing from its historical situation in the Heian Period (794–1185), the Kanna-centered arc also abounds, at least in its inceptive stages, with comic relief. Much of this derives from the heroine herself who, not unlike Misuzu, seems rather clueless when it comes to interpersonal dynamics — even though, in the princess's case, this is due primarily to her enforced exclusion from all worldly matters. Kanna's naivety gives Ryuuya plenty of excuses for teasing her, which playfully exposes her spoiled-brat side even as it gradually reveals the mature depth of her attachment to the loyal protector. Ryuuya's own jocular disposition is reinforced by a knack of unexpectedly steering his fluent rhetoric, habitually characterized by inspired metaphors, towards unsentimental sarcasm. The anime explains that winged people, though persecuted in Kanna's times, are magical beings that inherit "the planet's dreams from previous generations, and have imparted pearls of wisdom to the people since the days of old." However, instead of being revered as their powers would commend, they were incarcerated and exploited as weapons in countless wars. Kanna's mother was herself the victim of a curse unleashed by all those "she had been forced to kill over her lifetime," part of which was passed on to the princess. Kanna is reputed to be the last of her kind. Combined with the curse Kanna has inherited from her mother is a further malediction incurred during her flight through the "sacred mountain" in the company of Ryuuya and Uraha. As a result, she is haunted by a recurring sinister dream. Uraha maintains that the day Kanna ceases to experience that vision, "her spirit will descend to the Earth in a reincarnated form. But putting the spirit of a winged being into a human is like pouring the water of the ocean into a small vial. The vial will overflow and eventually shatter. The spirit will not have a chance to heal and she will continue to reincarnate." The show also proposes that Ryuuya, aware that Kanna's ordeal would be renewed every time she was reincarnated, resolved to pass down the tale in the hope that one of his heirs would be able to free the princess's soul.

When Yukito reaches the coastal town where the present-day strands are set, there to find his performance scornfully dismissed by the local kids, he begins to lose heart but his life takes a fresh turn upon encountering the unusual and genuinely airy Misuzu; a girl who might conceivably be connected with the ancient legend. Misuzu's most salient peculiarity is an undiagnosed condition that causes her to fall prey to severe seizures whenever she becomes too close to another human being, even though what she craves most in life is a true friend. However, the baleful side of Misuzu's history is felicitously counterbalanced by her comical clumsiness and puerile fondness for dinosaurs, which results in her uttering the guttural sound "*gao*" (i.e., "grrr") more often than those around her deem desirable or even tolerable. Gradually, Misuzu's condition turns out to be linked, metaphorically if not empirically, with the thousand-year-old curse associated with Princess Kanna. It could indeed be explained, if one were to opt for a mystical interpretation, in accordance with the revelations proffered by Uraha in the Kanna-based arc, and therefore as evidence for the present-day girl's status as Kanna's successor. In the light of this interpretation, Yukito would represent Ryuuya's latest heir. Through this aspect of the story, *Air* brings into play the notion of Eternal Return, which is crucial to Eastern thought's approach to temporality and remembrance, while concurrently engaging with visionary forays into an alternate world. Sad as it is, the *Air* anime never deteriorates into mushiness. This is because Misuzu's ordeal is ultimately invested with the dramatic caliber of true tragedy, especially in its emphasis on the girl's fateful condemnation to solitude. The evolution of Haruko's personality also contributes significantly to *Air*'s gravity. This is most blatantly the case in the later episodes, where Haruko realizes that despite her efforts to distance herself from her charge, Misuzu has become so important to her that she no longer wishes to act merely as a guardian but actually yearns to behave like a real mother — even though she is well aware of the potentially lethal risks this entails.

Besides Misuzu, the series' copiously female cast features Kano and Minagi, as does the parent game. The former is tormented by guilt about her mother's death in childbirth and about the self-sacrificial devotion to her upbringing evinced by her elder sister Hijiri, a proficient physician. Kano, too, is afflicted by a peculiar ailment (the motivating factor behind Hijiri's choice of the medical profession) that since her mother's demise, has periodically caused her to lose control of her body and become temporarily possessed by an older female presence with murderous intent. Eventually, Kano's condition is explained rationally as a psychological disorder associated with her sense of guilt, which she manages to overcome when, with Yukito's help, she realizes that what she should feel towards the departed parent is not guilt but gratitude. Despite this logical explanation, Kano's predicament is allegorically shrouded in myth, as her epiphanic discovery is couched in the form of an oneiric flashback to ancient times — preternaturally witnessed by Yukito, Misuzu and Hijiri with the aid of a magical feather — where Kano and her mother feature as the victims of a curse unleashed by said feather, and the older woman kills herself in order to save her infant daughter from a dire fate as a sacrificial offering. Quiet and elegant, Minagi is presented as the astronomy club's sole member, and more significantly as a tormented personality drawn into a delusional world by despair at her parents' divorce, her baby sister's death at birth and her mother's subsequent descent into paranoia. The chief product of Minagi's self-made parallel reality is Michiru, an impishly chimeric being forged by the girl to cope with her grief as a surrogate for the lost sibling. Equally pivotal is the aforementioned character of Haruko, Misuzu's superficially rough but innerly troubled aunt and adoptive mother.

Bearing the distinctive imprints of the ludic form from which it emanates, the anime presents a character gallery distinguished by a varied array of looks and personality traits (oddities and idiosyncrasies included), which are both thrown into relief and complicated by assorted interactions, subplots and interlocking background stories. Notably, all of the characters appear to be somehow linked to the winged maiden of old. Misuzu's buried memories (literally captured, in the theatrical version, by the image of a box housing mementoes of her mother ensconced in the ground) are complemented by both Kano's and Minagi's haunting pasts and incrementally come to constitute the narrative backbone around which glimmers of a submerged cultural heritage accrue, providing some answers for the enigmas of the present but also ushering in darker mysteries for the future to confront. Thus, the story's overall shape is conspicuously inconclusive and always susceptible to the vagaries of chance. As the show approaches its climax, it becomes clearer and clearer that the quest for corroboration of a time-honored legend is also — or perhaps primarily — a quest for self-exploration and self-understanding.

The *Air* anime replicates the source game's structure by encompassing three arcs. The first focuses on Yukito's interactions with Misuzu, Haruko, Kano and Minagi/Michiru. The second travels back in time to rural Japan and to the tale of Kanna and her friends. The third returns to the present, tracing Yukito's attempt to avert the dictates of fate. In the Sora-related portion of the anime, the crow adopted by Misuzu appears interchangeable with Yukito himself. This is tersely conveyed by both snippets of the voiceover recording the youth's interior monologue and by the scene where, having ostensibly vanished from Misuzu's life altogether, Yukito briefly reappears bathed in preternatural light in Sora's place, endowed with human form. As to the outcome of the male lead's efforts, *Air*'s gloriously open-ended finale suggests that fate is bound to repeat itself once again. This is not sufficient, however, to discourage Yukito from battling on and continuing on his potentially interminable voyage. Cumulatively, the story's multibranching orchestration posits the operations of both personal and collective memories as a pilgrimage through time and space which, like the art of animation itself, defies the laws of both reason and logic — not to mention gravity of the classical ilk. The Sora-based arc offers the show's most exhilarating narrative challenge. The action loops back to the beginning, prior to Misuzu's and Yukito's encounter, and reconstructs in telescoped form several key occurrences dramatized in the course of the episodes placed before the jump to the feudal era. Part of the reconstruction relies on flashbacks but at its most inspired, the diegesis actually dwells on background scenes the original run merely implied. While some of these carry considerable weight, others are ostensibly peripheral, yet all additional footage adds density to the overarching drama. Moreover, certain portions of dialogue already proposed in the earlier installments gain fresh resonance from shifts in perspective and casting. For example, Haruko's account of her relationship with Misuzu, outlining her reasons for the adoption of a distanced and seemingly callous attitude, is now addressed to Sora instead of Yukito — which is consonant with the suggestion that the youth and the crow are ultimately two manifestations of the same basic identity. The new scene imparts Haruko's confession with a sense of solemnity due to its setting in the town's shrine and to the almost ceremonial atmosphere the location silently exudes.

A thirteenth "recap" episode, remapping the narrative with an explicit focus on Misuzu's ordeal, has also been released to crown *Air*'s aesthetic accomplishment. This offers a capsulated version of the anime series, imaginatively edited so as to avoid a mechanical repetition of the exact chronological sequence in which the events were first proposed, and thus evoke a vibrantly vignettish yet panoramic impression. The Summer Special titled *Air in Summer* (TV special; dir. Tatsuya Ishihara, 2005) comprises two installments, both of which are centered on Kanna and her friends, and encompasses a great deal of new material. These include several comic moments emphasizing the princess's amusing unworldliness, a sprinkling of piquant innuendoes and some poignant exchanges between Ryuuya and Uraha regarding grave ethical matters. The most felicitous addition is the portrayal of the guard's background as an abandoned child adopted by a wandering monk, for this offers scope for the representation of a plethora of stunning locations chronicling in a compressed fashion Ryuuya's and his foster father's peregrinations through the rolling seasons. The ending is entirely open as it witnesses the protagonists' progress in their journey without suggesting any obvious destination, and resonates with a far sunnier message than the one elaborated by the main program.

The apportioning of legendary undercurrents to a secondary heroine in the Kano-based arc is a ruse worthy of consideration. The *Air* show, like many other anime here examined, is faithful to the source game in its endeavor to engage the audience as an active participant in the production of the story by stimulating its imagination and interpretative skills; the use of the ancient past alongside the present serves an important role in this respect. Indeed, *Air* could easily have kept its supporting characters squarely within the boundaries of the here-and-now and distinguished Misuzu as the primary heroine by associating her alone with a parallel-world drama. By summoning the mythological dimension in an ancillary arc as well, *Air* steers clear of clearcut hierarchical distinctions between main and supplementary arcs. It thus encourages viewers to establish on the basis of their own perceptions, hypotheses and conjectures which strand should be prioritized at any given stage in the adventure, and how different threads alternately coalesce or diverge within the overarching diegesis. In other words, the anime does not presume to decide on our behalf which components of the story should be considered richer, more multifaceted or deserving of greater concentration. The Minagi-centered arc also uses motifs analogous to the ones articulated in the Misuzu- and Kano-centered arcs, though in less explicitly mythical terms, by insistently drawing attention to the austere girl's fascination with the sky (and, most exuberantly, stars and stardust) and by invoking regularly wing and flight imagery. Most importantly (and confusingly) for Yukito, all three girls are linked by the dream of flying high into the celestial vault. (Minagi is also connected with Kano by her fraught relationship with her own mother, a victim of a severe case of amnesia resulting from her inability to accept her second daughter's death and only capable of acknowledging Minagi's very existence once she has painfully managed to come to terms with her loss.)

*Air*'s generic suppleness is foregrounded by the TV show from its inaugural stages. The opening episode firmly enthrones the proclivity by alternating between jocose and serious moods in the representation of both characters ad dramatic situations. Haruko, for instance, is portrayed as a multidimensional personality capable of shifting in the space of just a few frames from tipsy exuberance to earnestness as she moves from the convivial mode to the meditative one. The tone of the action likewise morphs repeatedly, indulging in farcical zaniness in the sequence where Potato snatches away Yukito's precious puppet, much to the youth's consternation, but quickly shifting gears in the direction of pathos with the shots focused on Misuzu's physical weakness and vulnerability. As Yukito meets Kano and gets a chance to sample her own bizarre disposition, the mood alters again in favor of comedy, as borne out by Yukito's snarky remark: "I wonder if every girl who wears that uniform [i.e., the local school's] is a total whacko." A dreamy atmosphere displaces the levity with the scene where Misuzu beholds Minagi blowing bubbles in a splendid sunset, to be drastically interrupted by the ebulliently clownish martial confrontation involving Yukito and Michiru. The show's

mellow tenor is finally reestablished at the very end of the opening installment, as we are first apprised of Misuzu's fantasies particularly with her sky-
related visions: "I have always had this feeling," she confesses to the
increasingly baffled Yukito, "like there's another me up there."

In 2005, as the TV show was being broadcast on home turf, Toei Animation released a theatrical version of the show, *Air: the Motion Picture*,
directed by Osamu Dezaki. (Please note that the series was released by Kyoto
Animation, as were the 2006 version of the *Kanon* series and the TV shows
*Clannad* [2007] and *Clannad After Story* [2008], two more anime also adapted
from visual novels issuing from the masterful hands of Visual Art's/Key. The
2002 version of the *Kanon* series and the *Clannad* movie, like the *Air* theatrical version, were produced by Toei Animation.) Dezaki's film offers an alternative take on the basic yarn dramatized by the TV series in which the
relationship between Misuzu and Yukito is prioritized and the action's pre-
ponderant timbre becomes decidedly more somber and mature. The romantic component plays a pivotal role in Dezaki's film in the articulation of both
past and present narratives and attendant emphasis on the inextricability of
parallel time zones. Both Kanna and Ryuuya, on the one hand, and Misuzu
and Yukito, on the other, are indeed shown to consummate their doomed
loves in the crowning moments of their respective odysseys. In addition, Misuzu and Yukito's relationship is more regularly and directly compared with
Kanna and Ryuuya's in the film than it is in the TV show. This is accomplished by consistent recourse to intercutting, whereby the action often
switches from frames focusing on the present-day protagonists to their legendary forebears — sometimes with the transitional insertion of a shot of an
ancient painting chronicling Kanna's ordeal of the kind housed in the town's
shrine. The most affecting underlying message, in Dezaki's elegant weaving
of these threads of transtemporal connection, is that just as Ryuuya was the
only friend Kanna ever managed to make in her brief and blighted existence,
so Yukito is the only person ever to forge a close bond with Misuzu in her
own ill-fated life. In both cases, the friendship is predestined to be short-lived
and fraught with a scabrous emotional course.

Flashbacks constructed in the guise of artfully edited montages play a
vital part in recounting the legend of the winged princess — often by means
of delicate allusiveness in preference to explicit statement, in keeping with a
quintessentially Japanese aesthetic inclination. We thus learn by the subtlest
of narrative means about the persecuted girl, held prisoner by tyrannical
authorities that deemed her otherness an abomination, and destined to become
ensnared in an eternal curse by her decision to give her passion free rein.
As Misuzu advances towards the apex of her intractable affliction, her connection with Kanna gains strength and momentum. Although a clinically

realistic explanation for the illness afflicting the present-day's heroine might be adduced, the bond between Misuzu's disease and the world of legend is beautifully and credibly depicted and any hankering for convincing medical data on the audience's part is quietly but conclusively mocked. The *Air* movie is much more explicitly self-referential than the show in foregrounding the materials underlying the final animated frames — e.g., in the form of water-color paintings, rough sketches, character portrayals demarcated by thick outlines and other related visual effects emphasizing the visuals' intrinsic constructedness. Relatedly, the artistic dimension is reinforced as Yukito's own creative quest finds a parallel in Misuzu's desire to undertake a summer project meant to document her town's history and underlying mythology that likewise carries the traits of a quest for artistic self-expression. While attesting to the importance of creative enterprises in visual novels and their anime offspring, this activity also provides scope for an original take on the topos of the relationship between the individual and the community. Moreover, the visual strategies delineated above underscore the medium's eminently material quality. This aspect of the film is further consolidated by the use of images that draw attention to the corporeal dimension of mythology itself in the form of myriad vestiges of the past. These include artifacts recording the ancient maiden's calvary, such as paintings, sculptures and ceremonial accessories. The image of the drummers donning traditional demonic masks, compounded by the thunderous chords issuing from their instruments and the stormy background replete with giant crashing waves against which the performance is set, contributes significantly to this aspect of the drama.

The main characters themselves appear older and graver, while the color schemes are darker, the original drawings are imparted with greater density and texture and the still tableaux based on character and background designs exude an aura of haunting grandeur. Visual effects are pervasively deployed, as are audacious camera angles intended to amplify the pathos of many axial scenes. (Analogous visual strategies, it should be noted, are adopted in the *Clannad* movie, also helmed by Dezaki, which emplaces them as distinctive elements of this director's signature.) The film's duskier tones are paralleled by a much more disillusioned outlook, notably associated with the character of Yukito, than one is ever to detect in the TV show. This is tersely encapsulated by the scene where the male protagonist confesses to Misuzu that despite his profession as a street entertainer, he actually hates crowds — and especially those abounding with seemingly happy families — because he is convinced that people never behave so blithely at home and merely put on their happy masks for the sake of appearances, respectability and a longing to be accepted or even envied by others. The youth's cynically disenchanted perception of his fellow humans is summed up by these words: "I've never met anyone who truly is sincere. It doesn't exist. Everybody's fake — one way or another." Yukito's attitude gradually alters as he becomes closer and closer to the ailing yet optimistically stoical Misuzu and her guardian: "Like the blowing wind," he remarks, commenting on his life thus far and on the unexpected direction he now senses it might be taking. "Unaffected by anything, unimpressed, unseeing. I was supposed to be on that kind of journey. But instead I met a girl named Misuzu and her crazy mother Haruko." Yukito attempts to dismiss these thoughts, reckoning that it is highly unlikely that his existence "is really going to change," yet cannot quite exorcize the "ugly premonition" lurking at the edges of his consciousness that some radical readjustment might indeed be on its way. Intriguingly, as Yukito's inner monologue reaches its culmination, a close-up of a disconsolate-looking Princess Kanna fills the screen.

Loyal to the parent game's studious dedication to detail, the *Air* anime indubitably excels in the area of character design, complementing the distinctive personalities of each member of its cast with highly varied costumes and accessories. Misuzu's unique charm, which issues primarily from her inquisitive spirit and ability to find the most prosaic situations fascinating and latently mysterious, is assiduously enhanced by her simple outfits, be they an austere school uniform or childish pyjamas, a plain summer shift or a dinosaur-themed t-shirt. Minagi's reserved personality is mirrored by a prim choice wardrobe that takes more adventurous notes as she gradually opens up and faces the real world. Michiru's energetic and almost overbearingly playful disposition is appropriately captured by her tomboyish costume and matching whip-like pigtails. As for Kano, the most active of the three key females, frankly no-nonsense comfortable clothes constitute an apposite selection. It is with the transition to ancient Japan that *Air*'s sartorial flair reaches its acme, most notably with Kanna's refulgent royal robes but also, though less sensationally, with Ryuuya's attentively researched uniform and related weapons. A great deal of vestimentary and ornamental details designed to augment the unmistakable individuality of both the characters and their settings are supplied by the artbooks (and viewing companions) *Air on TV* and *Air The Motion Picture*. Both volumes give fans and scholars alike unmatched opportunities to chart the growth of *Air*'s personae and worlds by tracing their graphic evolution from Visual Art's/Key's original artwork; through the rough drawings incorporated in the animation studios' own storyboards and concurrently developing black-and-white character designs portraying the actors from all imaginable angles and in an astounding variety of postures and moods; to the model sheets detailing their psychological and behavioral traits, and finally the full-color frames extracted from the finished animations as well as luxuriously reproduced items of ancillary merchandise such as posters, DVD covers, cards, clocks, sweaters and feather-themed decorative straps.

As the foregoing analysis indicates, *Air*'s engagement with the topos of parallel worlds consistently relies on the interpenetration of the here-and-now associated with the glittering coastal town and the myth-encrusted Japan witnessing Kanna's and Ryuuya's doomed love. From the collusion of the two dimensions, countless opportunities ensue for a sensitive psychological anatomy of intertwined mentalities and histories. Relatedly, both the *Air* series and movie provide a paradigmatic instance of the power held by visual novels and their anime offspring to promote the act of narrativization. They indeed encapsulate events, character interactions and dramatic conflicts within relatively open structures that invite viewers to draw those elements together into coherent narratives on the basis of their own imagination and decoding proclivities. As argued, the principal trigger of the narrativizing enterprise is the discreet invitation to the audience to establish connections between two disparate temporal zones and the actions unfolding in them.

\* \* \*

In *Yami to Boushi to Hon no Tabibito* (literally translatable as "Darkness, the Hat and the Book Traveler"), the theme of parallel worlds reaches an apotheosis as the entire cosmos and the countless dimensions it houses are configured in the shape of a "Great Library" wherein each book corresponds to a different world, and time and space crisscross with kaleidoscopic gusto. The scope for interweaving and multibranching stories, viewed from a variety of perspectives, yielded by this basic idea is immense. In addition, the sheer diversity of the worlds disclosed by *Yami*'s textual matrix offers precious opportunities for the depiction of subtly varied natural and architectural settings, unflinchingly sustained by a refined painterly sensitivity to both color and light. Each world provides a different type of society, with distinctive customs and mores, levels of technological advancement, and mythical heritage combining time-honored Eastern tales (e.g., the story of the "Bamboo Princess," or "*Kaguya-Hime*") and newfangled narratives indigenous solely to *Yami*'s metauniverse.

In this respect, the anime (TV series: dir. Yuji Yamaguchi, 2003) vividly brings to mind Jorge Luis Borges's ideation of the universe as a hypothetical library. In "The Library of Babel," in particular, Borges tersely conveys this proposition with the story's opening words: "The universe (which others call the Library)" (Borges, p. 78). The volumes stored therein appear to consist of words assembled together by sheer chance, yet out of this randomness, meaning periodically emerges. This idea is redolent of the principles of chaos theory outlined in Chapter 1, and hence of one of the guiding mechanisms behind the visual novel and shows based on that format. Borges's philosophy, notably, is also relevant to the productions explored in this study in its emphasis on the nature of narrative as a web of forking roads and multibranching corridors. Where literary cross-references are concerned, it should also be noted that in *Yami*, virtually all of the shots focusing on the Great Library convey the impression that the books themselves, as objects, are sparklingly alive. This motif recalls Umberto Eco's depiction of the mediaeval library central to his novel *The Name of the Rose*, which is indeed described as "a living thing" (Eco 1984, p. 185), wherein the books are capable of interacting and communicating with one another and, at times, even of breeding their own creatures. A deft alternation of prosaic and preternatural occurrences — where legendary pasts and contingent presents coalesce — assists throughout the series' transdimensional richness, allowing disparate generic formulae to meet and blend. Thus, *Yami* supplely engages by turns with romance and comedy, epic and mystery, action adventure and sci-fi (and this list is by no means fully comprehensive). The central proposition animating the show is that a cosmos made of potential texts resolutely explodes the myth of a singular world — as the opening theme song advocates, there are actually "a thousand worlds called 'if.'"

Produced and marketed as an adult visual novel, the *Yami* game (2002) proceeds from the premise that a girl from the ordinary world is taken by a dragon to the realm of a seemingly boundless library where all past, present and future dimensions exist in parallel, stored within its venerable tomes. The player takes the role of a male character who comes from one of the books and has lost track of his route back home. Enjoined by the library's guardians to find the girl, the player explores various book worlds, in the hope of also discovering his own origin in the process. The anime follows a solitary and brooding schoolgirl named Hazuki Azuma as she journeys from world to world with the assistance of Lilith, the Great Library's manager, in search of her beloved and adopted elder sister Hatsumi, who has inexplicably vanished on her sixteenth birthday. Hazuki is introduced to Lilith by a talking parakeet called Ken, a character responsible for much of *Yami*'s comic relief. Lilith herself, in her capacity as custodian of the library-universe, goes by the title of "Yami" and dons a huge hat, endowed with a single blue eye, that enables teleportation from one book world to the next. It soon transpires that Hatsumi is no ordinary human girl but rather the immortal goddess Eve who protects the parallel dimensions, and that she has been migrating for fun from world to world for time immemorial, residing in each for just sixteen years. Lilith, Hatsumi/Eve's sister, resents her sibling's pleasure-seeking disposition, deeming it irresponsible and, worse still, the cause of her own relegation to the library as its appointed caretaker.

Compared with the game, the anime is more explicitly focused on character portrayal and evolving interpersonal relationships, which lends it greater psychological depth. The tension between Hazuki and Lilith, in particular, is conveyed right from the start and contributes vitally to the development of their partnership as they travel from one dimension to the next. Hazuki is so keen on her independence and so utterly absorbed by her commitment to Hatsumi/Eve as to refuse Lilith's help at first—even though Lilith appears to have fallen in love with Hazuki at first sight and to be willing to do practically anything to support her. It is only the pragmatic realization that she will not be able to go world-hopping without Lilith's magical intervention that persuades Hazuki to embark on a somewhat fraught alliance. On the affective plane, the most incisive moments coincide with the dramatization—largely reliant on subtle gestures and expressions—of Hazuki's inner struggle. Consumed by a passion so total and lacerating as to find any relationship beyond her connection with Hatsumi/Eve quite meaningless, the protagonist idolizes her elder sister and accordingly places her on a pedestal as the supreme and unattainable object of admiration, in an almost chivalric fashion. Yet she is also deeply aware of the erotic component of her attraction and feels ashamed by the polluting impact of emotions she deems base on the purity of her love. The treatment of Hatsumi/Eve's own emotions is also noteworthy. Although it might at first appear that Hazuki's feelings are one-sided, the story's unfolding progressively shows that the older girl does reciprocate her sibling's love. Anonymous romantic letters sent to the protagonist succinctly consolidate this idea. Hatsumi/Eve's declaration, at the close of the anime, that of all the people she has met in the many parallel worlds she has inhabited, Hazuki is the one she has loved most dispassionately, enthrones it as a major and at least partially restorative motif.

Even if viewers do not find the anime interesting purely at the romance level, they will feasibly cherish its approach to characterization and welcome not only its presentation of the principal personae but also the extra verve brought into the yarn by a gallery of secondary actors that appear just once in a while. Among the latter, we encounter Gargantua, a narcissistic lunatic who would at first appear to be monomaniacally obsessed with capturing Hatsumi/Eve in order to achieve eternal life. Gargantua is a more complex character, however, than one might initially assume. There is indeed something authentically tragic about his undying attachment to the version of Hatsumi/Eve he has known—namely, a mute girl named Jill who is capable of formidable magic feats and whom Gargantua accidentally stabs to death as he tries to separate her from his childhood friend Ritsuko who, in turn, loves him unreservedly. The plot strand centered on this flawed hero also provides leeway for an uplifting moment of epiphanic redemption at the end of the anime, where Gargantua eventually comes to terms with his guilt-ridden past, has a change of heart, and enters a parallel world with Ritsuko, whose love he is now willing to reciprocate. Ritsuko herself is portrayed as a rich character, combining the traits of a fairytale sorceress endowed with healing powers and the all-too-human weakness of a lonesome and unjustly persecuted young woman. Her reunion with Gargantua marks one of the show's most endearing installments.

Likewise worthy of attention is Quile (a.k.a. Quill), a member of a Stone-Age tribe hell-bent on gory sacrificial rites and possessed by the desire to find ever new deities to which they might devote their overflowing fervor. This world offers opportunities for some stringent parody of religious fanaticism. Also remarkable are Fujihime, a samurai-era incarnation of Hatsumi/Eve who can touchingly empathize with Hazuki's feelings towards her, inspired precisely by her stunning resemblance to the heroine's beloved, even though she clearly shares no part in her past. Additionally, *Yami* excels at the depiction of mythical entities, such as the fox spirits Youko Meirin, a mischievous girl keen on enhancing her demonic powers through Fujihime, and the *sake*-loving mistress of the floating "Space Hall" beyond the flow of time, Tama-monomae. One of the most moving supporting characters is Princess Mariel, seen in Gargantua's and Ritsuko's world as a victim of the rogue's blind greed. Kidnapped and readied for immolation by Gargantua as part of his plan to get hold of Hatsumi/Eve, Mariel kills herself but is reincarnated as Tama-monomae's cheerful maid. Among the actors featuring in more modern or even futuristic dimensions, especially worthy of notice are the cross-dressing intelligence agent Youko Sumeragi, the protagonist of a spy story set in the Russo-Japan war era, and the artificial intelligence Lala who is responsible for leading Earth's former inhabitants through outer space in search of a colonizable planet. In this world, Hatsumi/Eve appears as Lular, a traveler who vanished into the ether on her sixteenth birthday while fixing a component of one of Lala's spaceships — her connection with Hatsumi/Eve is thus implied.

Refreshing forays into the realm of clownish entertainment are supplied by the character of Kogechibi, a four-inch replica of Hatsumi/Eve covered by a one-eyed cloak that only leaves a pair of magnetizing eyes exposed. Kogechibi is distinguished by an addictive passion for fireworks and impressive skill at constructing rockets and launch platforms, which the creature incongruously insists on deploying in the very heart of the Great Library, much to Lilith's irritation. Although the character plays a peripheral role in the anime, the game reveals that the library's guardians splinter as a result of overexertion and that Kogechibi is a shard of Hatsumi/Eve that has popped into being through such a process. The anime's narrator is Arya, a character who can be visualized as a reader sitting amid heaps of old volumes and picking up one or another at random as the plot progresses. The concept of chance is thus accorded once more an important part, in accordance with the lessons of chaos theory. An amusing quirk associated with this enigmatic and silver-haired youth is his tendency to indulge in cosplay, which leads him to select a variety of more or less eccentric outfits over time. This stylistic ruse felicitously complements *Yami*'s flair for constructing parallel worlds, since Arya's adoption of multiple sartorial exteriors mirrors the entire anime's journey across disparate realities.

*Yami* takes a daring stance toward the topos of creative quests by bravely proposing that one may create worlds from scratch by just imagining them. This feat is graphically equated to the act of filling a book whose pages are blank with lands, buildings and characters emanating from the psyche's deepest recesses. Moreover, the act of bringing worlds into being in such a fashion is obliquely compared to the creative roles played by both visual-novel players and anime spectators. This motif is earnestly interwoven with a keen devotion to the concept of textuality — a dimension, as we have seen, axial to the game and its televisual offspring alike. Textuality is most explicitly foregrounded in the conception of the cosmos at large in bookish form. At the same time, it is also thrown into relief by tropes that serve to emphasize the synthetic character of the work as a narrative and performative apparatus. Such tropes include various allusions to the process of storytelling, typically couched in self-referential guise. Thus, it is not unusual for *Yami* to deliver comments on its own style and form, as evinced by the remark that the more one tells a story, the better it gets. The narrator also draws attention to what ought to be considered the most "important part" of an adventure, apologizes for sudden interruptions as a narrative strand is temporarily dropped, and urges us not to get too confused, thus intimating that the narrative weave might be about to take a heady turn.

Also notable, where self-referential gestures related to artistic self-expression are concerned, are the usage of explicitly hand-drawn character sketches with distorted features and dimensions, and the self-dramatizing flourishes on the part of characters keen on taking center stage in the action (ostentatious costume changes and the sudden materialization of numerous props abet this task to spectacular effect). This sustained focus on the narrative weave and its performative potentialities as objects of interest in their own right entails that although *Yami* holds forth plenty of dynamic moments (enhanced by bold camera angles and imaginative visual effects), the storytelling process gains priority. A well-choreographed plot peopled by thoroughly individualized dramatis personae is the memorable outcome of that stylistic choice. *Yami*'s individual stories and side-stories are not always either hugely intriguing or developed in great affective depth. Yet the series is rendered unique by its ingeniously bizarre dedication to cumulative structural coherence. This said, it must also be stressed that *Yami* indulges in a signally episodic and meandering rhythm, according greater power to random ramifications — again reminiscent of chaos theory — than to any teleologically driven progression towards a definitive end. This ploy provides room for an open-ended and multiaccentual finale.

Turning to the handling of recurrent motifs, it is worth noting that the oneiric element enjoys pride of place in the adventure since *Yami* as a whole exhibits the qualities of a dream or otherworldly vision. This is most trenchantly conveyed by the proposition that the same person leads quite different lives in disparate dimensions — which, at base, is what everyone does in dreams (daytime musings included). The topos of individual-community interaction also plays a key part, most notably in the ongoing juxtaposition of the protagonist's intensely personal quest to be reunited with her beloved, and the communal web of relationships engendered by her attendant inveiglement in a transdimensional fabric. Finally, *Yami* shares with several other anime based on visual novels a passion for narrative complications issuing from submerged memories and attendant traumas. Gargantua's repression of all reminiscences surrounding the person of Jill — a defensive denial of his responsibility for her horrific death — offers a particularly absorbing variation on that motif. Also notable is the repression of a childhood legacy of parental abuse, conducive to arrested growth, associated with the side character of Milka. Lilith, for her part, shows no recollection of her creation of the preternatural being known as Seiren. Flashbacks to Hatsumi/Eve's and Hazuki's infancy, in addition, serve to hold *Yami*'s mnemonic tapestry elegantly together. The memory topos reaches its climax in the scenes where Hazuki speculates about the possibility of Hatsumi/Eve having only ever existed in her memories. At one point, she even wonders whether that memory-woven world might have come to be replaced — courtesy of Hatsumi/Eve — by a world in which the cherished girl has never existed at all. This apprehension is reinforced by the suggestion that the heroine harbors vague recollections of tastes and other sensory perceptions associated with her beloved but cannot actually recall Hatsumi/Eve herself: even the snapshot of the two girls seen in earlier portions of the series undergoes a radical metamorphosis as it displays the child Hazuki as its sole occupant.

The visual novel's narrative ambitions, discussed in this chapter's opening segment, assert themselves not just emphatically but even flamboyantly in *Yami*'s construction. Not only does *Yami* offer in bucketfuls all of the key ingredients from which the visual novel may concoct a gourmet dish: it also emplaces the act of narrativization as its focal dramatic drive by proposing that worlds only exist when disparate tendrils of history and lore are braided together into a narrative. The potential and provisional nature of such worlds is persistently underscored by reminders that the process of shaping raw materials into a narrative is an inevitably arbitrary and hence rescindable operation.

* * *

In *Touka Gettan* (TV series; dir. Yuji Yamaguchi, 2007), parallel worlds are woven into the very fabric of Kamitsumihara, the legendary land where the story is set. Not only is this dramatically conveyed by each of the multibranching and intermingling narrative strands comprised by the saga: it is also at one point explicitly stated by the charismatic character of Kikyou, Kamitsumihara's immortal guardian, who describes the land as encompassing multiple "existences." To reinforce the richness of this enigmatic realm, the anime faithfully replicates (and indeed enhances) the source game's painterly opulence, tactile textures and mesmerizingly varied chromatic modulations. It is crucial to note that *Touka Gettan* is sometimes erroneously described as a spin-off of the OVA *Kao no Nai Tsuki* (a.k.a. *Moonlight Lady* or *No Surface Moon* [2001]), adapted from the 2000 visual novel of the same title. The confusion essentially ensues from the fact that the sequel to that game is titled *Touka Gettan ~ Kao no Nai Tsuki II* (2007), which is often shortened to *Touka Gettan*. While the *Touka Gettan* visual novel is related to *Kao no Nai Tsuki* and retains its *hentai* (i.e., sexually explicit) flavor, the *Touka Gettan* anime is not. Thus, where the original visual novel presents graphic depictions of eroticism, the show is fundamentally concerned with foregrounding an elaborate tapestry populated by a large gallery of psychologically complex personae. Therefore, even though it occasionally offers scenes with salty overtones and periodically indulges in fan service, it does so primarily to expose its characters' more or less tortuous psychologies, and by no means more insistently than the average series with romantic connotations.

In the case of Yumiko, the protagonist's adoptive mother and a successful novelist, the narcissistic tendency to flaunt her body in provocative poses and outfits and the incestuous drives that sometimes overwhelm her are portrayed as symptomatic of a pathological childishness issuing from unresolved juvenile traumas. (Yumiko's own mother, Yuriko, was herself drawn into an incestuous liaison with her brother Kiyoharu, which is held partly responsible for Yumiko's morbid immaturity.) Moreover, Yumiko's personality is further complicated, throughout the best part of the story, by the fact that she is possessed by the goddess Juna by who her own admission at times enjoys inhabiting the body of a real human so much as to be carried away by somewhat turbulent desires. However, it is also suggested that due to her traumatic past, Yumiko actually needs Juna's presence to function more or less normally. In the case of the preternaturally gifted schoolgirl Makoto Ikunai, the human-looking host of the formidable Great Dragon, snippets of fan service are deployed as a means of highlighting her disarming innocence. As for Nene Midou, the skillful sorceress who also acts as Yumiko's maid, enticing costumes serve to bring out not only her femininity but also, and more crucially, her magical aura.

Slickly moving from everyday domestic and scholastic contexts replete with lavish representations of both traditional and imaginary cuisine, fashion and design, to baleful scenarios imbued with the darkest of mythological messages (and hence from the secular to the sacred, from the prosaic to the visionary) *Touka Gettan* yields one of the most alluring anime experiences imaginable. Its eccentric diegetic orchestration is largely responsible for the series' overall impact. *Touka Gettan* has indeed been aired backwards, with the final episode therefore constituting the chronological start of the entire adventure. Although the reverse order might at first engender a feeling of confusion in the viewer, it soon becomes exhilarating to embark on each successive episode to discover the causes of occurrences we have already been acquainted with. As explanations are thus systematically postponed, the show's structural constellation turns into a source of pleasure in its own right. Furthermore, *Touka Gettan*'s orchestration brings the audience's own creativity squarely into play, for we are required at each stage to keep in mind how the adventure ends in order to appreciate the events shown in later, yet chronologically earlier, installments. Hence, we must be prepared not only to play along but also to think carefully.

The mechanism of chronological inversion is the principal ruse deployed by *Touka Gettan* to kindle the audience's narrative urge. Most importantly, this suggests that in the experience of time, particularly when this is textually and narratively encoded, chronological linearity matters less than the appreciation of discrete poignant moments and of the flow of affects that they trigger somewhat irrespective of their temporal situation. Such moments may or may not coincide with life-shaping events, but more importantly are treasured by their protagonists as unique. Thus, the occurrences dramatized in the opening segments of the series could be said to warrant diegetic foregrounding to the extent that they hold enduring significance in the psyches of the people who have experienced them, even though they logically take place at the end of the story. This outlook intimates an understanding of life itself not as a teleologically oriented sequential progression but rather as an assortment of concatenated yet relatively independent stages, without prefigured outcomes predicated on the law of causality. Some of these might have witnessed achievements of lasting import. Others might have gone by almost unheeded but still carry an unobtrusive legacy of their own. Therefore, what is truly important is not the objective content of an experience but rather the degree to which it feels relevant to a person at any one point in time. This perspective ushers in the idea of narrativity as a system that ought not to be grasped merely in diachronic terms as the development of particular forms and vogues over time but also, indeed more usefully, in synchronic terms as the body of narratives perceived by a given culture to be cogent to its own situation, regardless of when those narratives were actually composed and circulated.

In shunning the logic of causality, *Touka Gettan* constructs a universe in which everything is intertwined with everything else in both time and space: an elaborate three-dimensional puzzle where truths and facts do not necessarily coincide. Weaving subtle connections between one incident and another, snippets of the past and glimpses of the future, in a labyrinthine story where images are densely layered at each step, the anime charts an erratic epic of the psyche unfettered by the strictures of common sense. At times, this proclivity is so pronounced as to intimate that the overall narrative is deliberately designed not to point towards any obvious destination. In this respect, *Touka Gettan* appears to treat the unfolding of the tale as a process worthy of attention in its own right. Insofar as the show posits the interpenetration of alternate dimensions as axial to the adventure, its foregrounding of the tale as an autonomous process is ultimately inextricable from its focus on the dialogue between parallel worlds. Without such an exchange, the process itself would irremediably come to a halt. In Japanese culture, the interpenetration of different worlds often amounts to the absence of clear distinctions between inner and outer dimensions. This tendency, as seen in Chapter 1, is reflected by indigenous architecture and especially by the usage of flimsy spatial dividers such as *fusuma* and *shojo*—an idea also pursued by Hayao Kawai's study of Japanese fairytales (Kawai 1988, p. 103). In *Touka Gettan*, the idea that disparate planes of being unrelentingly coalesce provides the basis for a conception of reality itself as a flow wherein events are multifariously interrelated at all times.

The story's basic premise is that in Kamitsumihara, potent undercurrents of ancient magic still hold sway. In this alternate world, humans coexist with *youkai*—a term approximately translatable as "demons," although it must be stressed that *youkai* are not incontrovertibly evil or malevolent. This coexistence is not always peaceful and the threat of Earth-shattering conflicts in fact looms large. The plot revolves around Touka Kamiazuma, a member of the clan that has protected the land since its creation, and Momoka Kawakabe, a girl of mysterious origin who unexpectedly comes to reside with the Kamiazumas. The two protagonists' encounter triggers a chain of events that gradually rekindle an old legend with three goddesses at its core — namely, Sei, Juna and Fuu. The forces represented by these deities must be regularly harmonized to maintain Kamitsumihara's precarious balance and prevent the land from falling under the nefarious rule of the *shikigami* (evil *youkai*) seeking to plunge it into total darkness. Retrospective reconstruction of the show's idiosyncratic history reveals that the goddesses came into being as a result of a time-honored ceremony performed by the mythical king Yafutsu, pivoting on two talismanic objects of great significance to *Touka Gettan*'s entire narrative: a mask made of a supernatural substance capable of affecting its wearer in deeply perturbing ways, and a soul-devouring Stone Sword consisting of a fiery blade issuing from a lotus-shaped crystal. As his beloved Sei is about to be sacrificed or forced to marry the king (both options seem tenable), the valiant Isamihiko grabs the Stone Sword to oppose the proceedings and is literally possessed by the weapon, thereby plunging into a paroxysm of murderous rage. The sole survivors of the ensuing hecatomb are the women destined to rise to divine stature: Sei herself, her sister Fuu and Isamihiko's sister, Juna. Blaming Sei as the cause of her adored brother's frenzy and the resulting disaster, Juna goes on passionately hating her until an advanced stage in the adventure. It also transpires that the same ceremony was responsible for the metamorphosis of the original kingdom into the parallel world of Kamitsumihara, for the latter's infiltration by otherworldly *youkai* and hence for the inauguration of centuries of strife.

Thus, the concept of parallel worlds works on two levels: on one of them, Kamitsumihara itself hosts alternate realities; on the other, Kamitsumihara is a world existing in parallel to the ordinary human one (known as Kinokuniya). This is confirmed by scenes set in Kamitsumihara where cell phones do not work, and is most dramatically conveyed by the sequence where Momoka suddenly materializes aboard the train taking other students to Touka Academy when this enters the mystical dimension via a spooky tunnel. Momoka's peculiar provenance is also confirmed by the scene where the girl attempts to enroll at Touka Academy, and although her name does not initially appear to be on the register, it materializes out of the blue just as her status as a "transfer student" is beginning to be questioned. A further parallel world comes into play in the installment where *Touka Gettan*'s diegesis is infiltrated by characters from Yamaguchi's previous hit, *Yami to Boushi no Hon to Tabibito*, discussed earlier in this chapter.

The seminal occurrences revolving around the fatal ceremony are disclosed in one of *Touka Gettan*'s most formally adventurous episodes, the penultimate one. This dramatizes a talk show reconstructing Kamitsumihara's history by means of interviews featuring many characters familiar with Touka and Momoka and thus ties up several loose ends in the yarn. This episode deliberately breaks the regressive timeline by showing events that are chronologically located after the end of the main story (as seen in the inaugural installment). Moreover, it is painstakingly observant of the codes and conventions of the format it follows in both performative and editorial terms and hence stands out as a sophisticated piece of drama in its own right. An exquisite touch is the inclusion of an immaculately detailed 3D replica of Kamitsumihara located within the broadcasting studio, imitating its every environmental and architectural feature. (Note also that when Momoka and Touka appear in snippets of what purports to be archival footage, their eyes are blanked out with masking tape to shield their privacy in genuine documentarist style.) Also notable as an instance of *Touka Gettan*'s formal ingenuity is the episode chronicling Yumiko's life from her very conception out of the incestuous union of Yuriko and Kiyoharau to the painful events of subsequent years. This is very imaginatively presented in the guise of a stage play replete with several theatrical codes and conventions typical of classic Japanese drama.

What is needed to prevent Kamitsumihara from sinking into darkness, beside the goddesses' own powers, is a suitable wielder for the Stone Sword, and it is precisely in this capacity that Touka himself is brought into being. His creator is Kikyou, who employs the Stone Sword and a magical doll of her own making to impart to him a human form. He is thereafter taken into Yumiko's and Nene's care as a member of the Kamiazuma clan, and Yumiko comes to regard him as a substitute for her departed daughter, also named Touka—a would-be Stone-Sword wielder who could not possibly have carried the burden, much as she wished to do so throughout her brief and hapless life. So potent is Yumiko's delusion that at times when the woman's mindset is predominant, the youth is literally visualized as a long-haired girl donning a beautiful kimono. Ultimately, it is only by shattering the land's balance altogether by means of a purification ritual centered on Touka and his weapon that a purer parallel world in which humans and *youkai* no longer have to coexist may emerge and Kamitsumihara can be saved. Unfortunately, this will entail the female divinities' self-sacrificial disappearance. Devoted to the protection of Kamitsumihara, the character of Kikyou (who also plays the part of the Touka Academy Student Council President) is instrumental to the three goddesses' wellbeing and helps Makoto summon the Great Dragon inside her. This results in the girl's performance of a song, intended to abet the cleansing rite, at the "*Joumi* Concert"—an event held annually to prevent Juna's energy from going berserk and disrupting irreparably the land's precarious equilibrium.

As the foregoing reconstruction indicates, *Touka Gettan*'s basic plot is relatively simple, its driving force being the revamping of an ancient legend with Touka and Momoka in the roles of interdimensional catalyzers. What makes the series a steady source of visual pleasure, as well as an intellectually

stimulating challenge, is ultimately the pattern of interrelations among delicately nuanced characters, which it dispenses in generous amounts. (The gargantuan meals consumed by Momoka throughout constitute a comical
correlative for the show's largesse in satisfying even the most voracious viewer's
appetite for entertainment and mental stimulation.) It is therefore apposite
to devote some attention to the key actors in *Touka Gettan*'s varied cast. Touka
himself, as we have seen, is a synthetic being specifically brought into existence for the purpose of bearing the Stone Sword and deploying it at the crucial juncture. The youth's artificiality does not, however, reduce him to a
mere automaton. Though characteristically blunt and unsentimental to the
point of even sounding callous, the male lead is nonetheless portrayed as
deeply caring when it comes to Yumiko, Momoka and the spunky mutt Nero
he temporarily adopts (thereby becoming acquainted for the first time with
the reality of death). Touka often dismisses Momoka's innocent advances by
ungallantly calling her an idiot or protesting that she is pushy and unlady-
like but he never hesitates either to protect her when she is in danger or share
with her enchanting moments of communion with the natural world and its
underlying treasure of dreams and legends. On at least one occasion, Touka
even exhibits the typical attitude of the "knight in shining armor" disappointed by his protégée's oblivion to his valiance, as Momoka shows no recollection of his "cool" display of martial prowess in the face of diabolical foes.

Momoka herself, though she is revealed to embody the goddess Sei and
thus plays a key role in the darker drama at the heart of the show, is endowed
with a sunny personality that contrasts sharply with the hero's gloomy disposition. Additionally, as intimated, she lends the story a facetious touch by
virtue of a seemingly infinite passion for food of all sorts. There are sugges-
tions that Momoka is liminally aware of the painful voyage on which she
embarked upon reentering Kamitsumihara after centuries of preternatural
slumber and that this experience is bound to lead to self-immolation. These
intensify as her love for Touka grows, and much as she wishes to see the land
cleansed of defiling forces and hence return to her shine to sleep for all eternity, she is deeply saddened by the prospect of losing her human form and
hence her love. Momoka nonetheless retains a bright personality consonant
with Sei's commitment to light and harmony, in contrast with her adversary
Juna's devotion to darkness and disruption. This does not mean, however,
that *Touka Gettan* indulges in facile binary oppositions: Juna herself is seen
to be capable of sublime tenderness, as evinced by her romantic relationship
with Kikyou, whom she has known for no less than 1,200 years, and of magnanimous hospitality, as indicated by the sequence in which she invites
Momoka/Sei to her abode for tea. (Earlier, she controlled Yumiko's body to
make her kill Momoka.) Most vitally, it is only Juna's agreement, at Sei's

behest, to forget her hatred for just a little while that ensures her cooperation in the restorative ceremony performed in the story's climax despite her customary preference for violence. Fuu, Momoka's younger sister, is accorded a less protracted period of screentime than either of the other goddesses. Yet, this does not prevent her distinct personality from shining through as a veritable beacon of kindness and self-abnegation. The different strategies adopted in the portrayal of disparate personae bear witness to *Touka Gettan*'s dramatic agility. Just as Kamitsumihara is both a parallel world in relation to the regular human domain and a receptacle of parallel worlds within its fabric, so Yamaguchi's prismatic cast offers something of an ensemble of parallel psychological dimensions through characterization. The aforementioned Yumiko, Makoto, Nene and Kikyou, in embodying a wide range of emotional, intellectual and cultural connotations, contribute crucially to the effectiveness of the show's character gallery as subtle variations on the ongoing interplay between the present-day drama and the parallel universe of myth-wreathed history.

The romance element is largely responsible for *Touka Gettan*'s affective richness and it is therefore important to remember that, as axial as alternate worlds and myriad fantasy themes undoubtedly are, much of the pathos arises from the protagonists' personal interaction and its unfolding from the opening installment to the end — or vice versa, as the case may be. Crucially, the articulation of the romance element adamantly refuses to make any concessions to cheap sentimentalism. This is confirmed by the first episode's final sequence — which also constitutes the culmination of the story as a whole — where Momoka and Touka meet again in changed circumstances. On one plane, the sequence could be read as an assertion of the principle of Eternal Recurrence and the two characters, accordingly, could be regarded as reincarnations of their former Kamitsumihara-based selves in a parallel and patently less legend-imbued reality. The "new" Momoka's determination to confess her love to Touka without hesitating matches the vow she made the night before the fateful *Joumi* concert. However, the series does not unproblematically indulge in the dramatization of a time-defying romance. In fact, the suggestion that Momoka and Touka are characters in a novel penned by Yumiko also makes it possible to view the climax as wholly fictitious — the visualization of a romance author's fantasies. (Yumiko's creative role will be returned to.) Whichever interpretation one chooses, there is something frankly elating about the protagonists' climactic embrace, which gains special force by contrast with the genuine sense of grief emanating from Touka's loneliness in the wake of the cleansing ritual and Momoka's attendant vanishing. The feeling is silently conveyed, and most affectingly by virtue of its sheer wordlessness, by the scene where the youth revisits Momoka's now deserted bedchamber within the Kamiazuma mansion and hugs her discarded, disconsolately empty and inert school uniform.

This scene, and the atmosphere of vacuousness evoked by Momoka's departure generally, brings to mind a theme identified by Kawai as a recurring element in Japanese lore, that of "a woman who disappears"—the tile of the closing segment of an essay devoted by the Jungian scholar to the motif of "The Forbidden Chamber." Such a figure has the power to resist the cultural tendency to suppress women's presence in order to sustain the status quo insofar as she intentionally fades away from the scene, leaving in her wake a deep sense of sorrow (*aware*) and bitterness or rancor (*urami*) that stops her from vanishing altogether from the memories of those she leaves behind and thus perpetuates her latent agency. Crucial to *Touka Gettan*, given Momoka's deliberate choice of a self-sacrificial duty for the sake of positive change in a world threatened by eternal darkness, is Kawai's proposition that in the realm of fairytale, the disappearing woman "is thought to symbolize the urge to bring something new to Japanese culture." Equally crucial, in the context of the anime, is the idea that the woman who has disappeared can be expected "to come back to this world again with a newly gained strength." Thus, "To pursue the woman who disappears from this world sorrowfully and then comes back again" can be regarded as "a worthwhile and necessary task" (Kawai 1988, p. 25). What further prevents the culmination of the adventure from sinking into banal melodrama is its presentation as a piece in the larger jigsaw of vignettes presented in the televisually inaugural but logically final episode. In each fragment of action, the past and the future seem to mirror each other and the present thereby finds itself sandwiched between those parallel and interdependent dimensions.

One of the beauties of *Touka Gettan* for those who wish to write critically about it is that the anachronic arrangement precludes the peril of spoilers. Hence, mapping out the story's temporal scope does not risk impairing the viewer's enjoyment of the anime and can, in fact, assist the task of situating both its principal and its marginal occurrences in a coherent diegetic galaxy. A few points worthy of special attention are highlighted in the ensuing paragraphs. Primary among them is Yamaguchi's unflinching commitment to choreography. This is demonstrated by the show's finale as dramatized in the inaugural installment, where the outcome of the purification rite is not posited as an abrupt tectonic shift but rather as an incremental process. Therefore, we see that several key characters sense that some peculiar events have taken place and that momentous changes are under way. Although these apprehensions tend to engender a general feeling of unease, the personae in question have no clear grasp of the causes of their sensations, let alone their actual manifestations or consequences. It is not until we reach the talk-show episode that we discover the characters have adjusted to their world's metamorphosis in the aftermath of the transitional phase depicted in the opening installment. The idea that the cardinal restorative act has put an end to the alternate world of Kamitsumihara — or at any rate completely sealed it off from the ordinary human dimension — and transferred the cast to the reality of Kinokuya is hinted at through unobtrusive details: for instance, working cell phones that could not have been operational in Kamitsumihara.

Moving on to consider the recurrent themes and motifs characteristic of anime adapted from visual novels, it should first be noted that *Touka Gettan* is pervaded by creative quests for self-expression. Yumiko's role as a professional fiction writer stands out as the most prominent of them. The genre in which she appears to specialize echoes the show's own leanings towards romance. The dissatisfaction Yumiko at one point evinces upon discovering that she has written a happy ending — an unsavory scenario for the vindictive Juna possessing her mind and body at the time — parallels the series' own avoidance of unequivocally rosy resolutions. As argued, the ending proposed at the close of the first episode may be just a fruit of Yumiko's narrative flair and not actually dramatize a genuine reunion of the star-crossed protagonists. It is in the notion that the climax might well be a fiction that Yumiko's creative quest reaches its apotheosis. Also pivotal, where artistic practices are concerned, is Kikyou's skill as a dollmaker, which reverberates with echoes of the Golem-centered legend. Not only is the hero posited as the product of the fusion of one of Kikyou's artifacts with the Stone Sword (as noted); three of the immortal guardian's dolls are also responsible for endowing with human bodies the demons of Ninomiya (a.k.a. the "Princesses of the Second Shrine"), namely the Butterfly Triplets Hibari ("skylark"), Tsubame ("swallow") and Suzume ("sparrow"), so designated for their knack of morphing into iridescent butterflies.[1] As far as Touka is concerned, it should be noted that the creation hence he derives is supposed to have been unfinished, which at least partially explains his self-doubting disposition. The triplets themselves at one stage express their creative urges with the production of *doujinshi*, manga authored by fan artists. The art of music plays a vital part through the character of Makoto, whose unmatched melodic charm proves instrumental in the awakening of the Great Dragon. Furthermore, Makoto has an endearing tendency to pepper her discourse with Italian words used in musical notation, which often leads to delicious malapropisms and hence a modicum of comic relief.

Dreams and visions are likewise important, as most spectacularly demonstrated by the sequences where Yumiko, prey to Juna's vengeful frenzy, revisits the ancient past and specifically the tragedy pivoting on Isamihiko's massacre. Touka, too, returns to that dire point in history whenever he wields the Stone Sword. At these junctures, his body is literally flooded by buried recollections emanating from the weapon itself. Since these visions are also flashbacks to submerged memories, they serve to underscore another recurrent element of the shows here explored. Where the meeting of the oneiric dimension and memory is concerned, an especially intriguing character is Kiyotsugu Kamiazuma, the head of the clan and the Principal of Touka Academy. Cast in the role of Yumiko's uncle, Kiyotsugu is possessed by his brother Kiyoharu's memories due to Kiyoharu's implanting of a shard of the aforementioned magical mask into Kiyotsugu's right eye in the course of a spell of insanity triggered by his separation from his beloved Yuriko. As a result, Kiyotsugu believes that he is actually Kiyoharu and obsesses over Yumiko, whom he mistakes for her mother. (Kiyotsugu does not regain his memories until some time after Kamitsumihara has been cleansed.) Kiyotsugu's son, Haruhiko, is also mnemonically challenged and therefore unable to recall the circumstances in which he suffered a near fatal wound at the hands of the female child Touka during her brief possession of the Stone Sword. Most importantly, the protagonists themselves harbor no coherent memories. Momoka reckons that she only recalls events that have taken place in the past year, yet senses that her mnemonic baggage stretches back in time by 2,000 years, while Touka feels at once that he has only just been born and been alive for a long time. Tied up with the memory topos is *Touka Gettan*'s interweaving of myth, which vividly reactivates the ancient past at each turn, with temporal rhythms redolent of the Eastern concept of cyclicality. In entwining the past and the present, the series draws attention at all times to the inextricability of individual agents from collective networks of relationality, both at the macrocosmic level in the form of Kamitsumihara as a whole, and at the microcosmic one in the form of the communities constellated around the Touka Academy, the Kamiazuma clan and various shrines.

With its deft alternation of moments of apocalyptic foreboding and frank jocularity, epic grandeur and zany comedy, tragic pathos and salacious double entendres, *Touka Gettan* offers a daring experiment in generic diversity. Notably, even characters and situations ostensibly intended to provide sheer comic relief regularly reveal graver connotations. For example, the character of Haruhiko is often deployed as the butt of jokes intended to puncture his rather self-inflated public image as a Casanova, but his tense relationship with his father, beset by an inferiority complex, and his haunting (albeit fragmentary) recollections of the little girl Touka lend his depiction painful undertones. Likewise remarkable is the ongoing feud pitting Shouko Rokujou, Chairman of the "Lotus Association," and the mischievous Butterfly Triplets against each other. Much of the time, their mock-heroic confrontations are just a pretext for fun, but there are occasions where they also serve to throw starkly into relief the darkness surrounding them. Shouko's reckless handling of her snazzy sports car, which she drives through places as inappropriate as school lawns and corridors, yields some moments of undiluted humor. Yet a palpably realistic sense of danger is never far from the scene. Moreover, although the fights and contests in which Shouko and the princesses periodically engage exude carnivalesque exuberance, especially thanks to Shouko's fustian displays of frustration at her recurring defeats, they also strike a wistful chord by hinting at the limited time available to the Triplets in human form. Thus, the action draws attention to the ultimate evanescence not only of Kamitsumihara but also of life itself. Intercutting often proves a useful means of amalgamating and juxtaposing contrasting moods, as evinced by the sequence where the duel involving Touka and Juna in Yumiko's guise is woven with scenes dramatizing the "torture" by recourse to tickling perpetrated by the princesses on the demon girl Yurika, the emissary of a magician's family from a parallel dimension eager to appropriate the Stone Sword and deploy it to their own sordid ends.

As is typically the case with anime based on visual novels, *Touka Gettan* excels in the representation of both natural and architectural settings. As far as nature is concerned, some of the most spectacular effects issue from Yumiko's preternatural influence on the land when Juna's powers animate her. Thus, her determination to have a white Christmas at all costs turns a mild winter day into a phantasmagoria of swirling snowflakes and frosty surfaces, whereas by merely fantasizing about the perfect summer day she causes a whole vast ocean to come into being just outside her dwelling. When Nene invites Yumiko to create a trap (with the intention of ensnaring an enemy), it is enough for the lady of the house to mime the act of digging to produce a fathomless chasm within the Kamiazuma estate. *Touka Gettan*'s seasonal repertoire runs the entire gamut from icily atmospheric mornings through blazing autumnal sunsets to balmy nights, from chilly winds sweeping a barren landscape to ethereally graceful cherry blossoms, from euphoric cascades of light to crepuscular gloom. The effects generated in the process often exhibit almost photorealistic accuracy, without ever compromising a scene's evocative powers to mimesis. Architecture is also peerlessly depicted throughout in the rendition both of mythical locations with no anchor in reality and edifices inspired by traditional Japanese styles down to the tiniest detail. Concurrently, Eastern and Western motifs collude — e.g., in the portrayal of Touka Academy — to engender settings that feel tangibly realistic and fantastic at one and the same time. Priority is regularly accorded to what could be termed an "architectural stance," namely, the formal grid of the frame. What the director frequently appears to have been seeking in the story's interiors is not just atmosphere but also geometry per se. This is most patently attested to by scenes set in Yumiko's elegantly austere tea-cottage writing room, where she is often seen sitting at her desk by the window overlooking the mansion's landscaped garden. These scenes play with the structural motif of interlocking rectangles. Also memorable are empty or barely inhabited rooms oozing with the air of spectral stage sets and silently emphasizing an eerie sense of loneliness. Momoka's bedroom after Sei's disappearance, touched upon earlier, epitomizes this spatial trope with painful poignancy.

An episode that deserves special attention in assessing *Touka Gettan*'s treatment of space is the one pivoting on Momoka's haunting sense of her unreality and gradual discovery of her feelings towards Touka, where a monochromatic scheme is predominantly employed. While the installment as a whole is almost devoid of color, which matches the maturely somber tone of the heroine's reflections, the technique of color isolation is used to throw important details into relief at considerately chosen points. The most spectacular polychromatic explosion occurs in the climax, where Momoka and Touka visit the arid spot held to have once accommodated a gorgeous peach orchard at sunset, and the desolate land appears to burst to life and regain its pristine beauty. A less sensational yet arguably just as memorable scene in which colors are allowed to erupt is the one where Yumiko invites Momoka and Touka to play the "princess game" and presents them with rolls of fabric she has inherited from her mother. These are rendered in traditional Japanese patterns and hues (many of them exclusively indigenous and therefore untranslatable), which incrementally cover the entire floor and infuse the sedate black-and-white setting with a tangible sense of aliveness. The enticing fabrics stand out as artworks endowed with corporeal substance, thus sustaining the inclination to conceive of art as a fundamentally material practice ingrained in Japanese thought. Yumiko's enthusiastic observation that "The names of the colors are lovely" imparts their venerable designations with a solidity of their own, implicitly underscoring the materiality of language itself.

*    *    *

While *Yami* and *Touka Gettan* offer a pair of titles attesting to the stylistic distinctiveness of the visual novel studio Root, a dyad comparably illustrating the individual cachet of the visual novel studio Navel consists of *Shuffle!* and *Soul Link*. Given its focus on a male lead's entanglements with various heroines on the basis of multiple choices, the *Shuffle!* parent game (2004–2005) unsurprisingly contains both allusive and graphic depictions of sexuality. The anime itself, though it periodically plays with innuendoes and hints at erotic preferences of diverse kinds as well as some fan service, has elided the adult component from its repertoire. Fan service itself is so judiciously blended into the drama that it does not feel as though the girls are going out of their way to shower the spectator with eye candy, which would not only have caused the show to pander distastefully to fetishistic scopophilia but also undermined the heroines' overall natures. As anticipated earlier in this chapter, the anime *Shuffle!* (TV series; dir. Naoto Hosoda, 2005–2006) engages with the topos of parallel worlds by dramatizing the coexistence of three domains of being: those of humans, gods and demons. This theme is based on the premise that the discovery within ancient ruins of two doors has led to the opening of the gateway to *shinkai*, the world of the *shinzoku* (gods), and of the gateway to *makai*, the world of the *mazoku* (demons), and caused the two unearthly races to mingle with humans and harmoniously coexist with them.

The basic storyline chronicles the day-to-day life of the human high-school student Rin Tsuchimi as he juggles with the varied personalities, expectations and oddities of an assortment of female characters. The protagonist's positioning as the object of romantic interest for a number of potential heroines lends the drama some of the stylistic traits commonly associated with "harem comedy." In acknowledging this aspect of *Shuffle!*, one should not, however, lose sight of the anime's multigeneric richness and attendant deployment of motifs drawn from the realms of psychological drama, the supernatural yarn and the mystery intrigue. In this respect, *Shuffle!* does full justice to the well-documented penchant for generic diversity characteristic of both visual novels and their televisual adaptations at their best. When we first meet Rin, he is presented as a permanent guest at the home of his childhood friend Kaede, who lavishes almost maternal attention upon the boy and whom he appears to regard as a sister despite Kaede's obvious romantic attachment to her charge. In addition, Rin occupies a very special spot in the heart of Asa, a girl he has known for several years and with whom he has developed a frank and playful relationship that initially appears to preclude romantic options and is indeed more akin to a friendship between boys. Rin's uneventful life takes a bizarre turn when the daughters of the rulers of the god and demon worlds — Lisianthus (a.k.a. Sia) and Nerine, respectively — transfer to his school and he is proudly informed by the royal parents that he is the potential marriage candidate for both girls. To further complicate Rin's existence and the increasingly convoluted relationships into which he is unwittingly roped, a mysterious demon child named Primula installs herself in his and Kaede's home. Through the lenses provided by Rin's both human and otherworldly associations, *Shuffle!* embarks on a sustained exploration of the interplay of individuals and communities at both the mythical level represented by the interpenetrating dimensions described above and at the mundane level epitomized by domestic and scholastic contexts. In so doing, the anime concurrently portrays the interpenetration of the everyday and the legendary, the prosaic and the supernatural.

On all of these coalescing planes, a distinctive atmosphere is conveyed through the painstaking representation of architecture, interior design and natural settings bathed in melancholy rain, radiant sunlight and moody moonlight by turns. Throughout the series, toned-down palettes are employed as an especially felicitous means of expressing a reflective ambience. Deliciously slow pans across empty rooms and their precise decorative details are also a recurring visual trope in *Shuffle!*'s distinctive cachet particularly worthy of note. In assessing *Shuffle!*'s handling of settings and decorative motifs, costumes deserve notice. The characters don numerous outfits throughout the anime which seldom occurs in other shows of its ilk. However, the "look" is not the raison d'être for this aesthetic choice (as is the case, most glaringly, in commercials and fashion plates). In fact, sartorial variety is harnessed to the imperatives of detailed characterization, and each costume accordingly serves to complement the particular facet of a character emphasized by the scene or episode in which it features. Additionally, the quotidian dimension of the story derives considerable realism from the loving depiction of several characters' gastronomic exploits and of the plethora of prandial tools, accessories and embellishments associated with them. These are so flawlessly presented as to raise their performance and status to the rank of an art, in accordance with the genre's sensitivity to its characters' creative urges.

The narrative is bolstered throughout by an emphasis on the importance of memories and their cinematographical articulation by recourse to flashbacks, apparitions and dreams. The princesses' childhood recollections of Rin are posited as key to the entire diegesis from an early stage in the action, while Primula's past and Kaede's juvenile ordeals are gradually woven into the plot as no less significant, and Asa's own childhood is concurrently revisited. Diligently edited flashbacks are instrumental to the disclosure of Nerine's history. We thereby learn that in childhood, the demon princess's body was cloned to create a suitable test subject named Licoris for experiments into the generation of artificial life forms, carried out collaboratively by demons and gods, and that the latter eventually offered up her own life to save Nerine from an incurable illness. Licoris developed a deep bond with Primula—the first successfully engineered artificial being—and endowed her with the most precious reminiscences. In absorbing Licoris's life force and thus regaining her health, Nerine also incorporated the clone's own abilities, feelings and memories. The childhood recollection of her first meeting with Rin in the human dimension turns out to have actually belonged to Licoris, although Nerine declares that in inhabiting the human world as her current self, she has developed her own independent love for Rin. Images from Primula's past are adroitly intercut with these gradual revelations regarding Nerine, acquiring momentum with the disclosure that the enigmatic child possesses magical powers of potentially catastrophic magnitude and that these are only being kept at bay by her possession of human emotions — most crucially, a deep attachment to Rin, and by extension to all those he holds dear. The flashbacks concerning Asa are also interesting as a dramatic experiment with character reversal. For quite a large portion of the story, Asa is quite unequivocally presented as an independent and unwaveringly cheery adolescent, but an unexpected collapse leads her to reveal to Rin that she was once a sickly, somber and resentful child, and that her current disposition is the outcome of hard work and stoic endurance. As these revelations unfold Asa is also increasingly posited as the character who understands the male lead most intimately and dispassionately and is also, in a sense, the only person in a position to give him constructive advice. These elaborate interpersonal dynamics make *Shuffle!* a stirring anatomy of the trials and tribulations ineluctably concomitant with growing up, in this world and in its fictional parallels alike. Thus, even though some viewers may not feel especially attracted to the series' quasi-mythical and romantic dimensions, few genuine anime enthusiasts will fail to appreciate its caliber as a study in subtly modulated character psychologies.

*Shuffle!*'s dedication to affectively capacious personae impacts on both the principal and the side actors, each of whom appears to act naturally within both ordinary and preposterous circumstances. Rin himself refreshingly departs from the harem formula that typically portrays the male lead as a wimp, in fact revealing a multifaceted personality, a proclivity for acting selflessly without coming across as inflatedly generous, and an ability to question frankly his inner states and motives. Rin's closest analogues, in this respect, are the male leads in *Kanon* (Yuuichi) and *Clannad* (Tomoya). As for the female personae, they all have something unique to contribute to the story. At the same time, however, they all share one common trait: the lurking presence of a hidden identity beneath the publicly paraded surface. This does not, it must be stressed, turn them into devious, intentionally duplicitous or manipulative people, but rather underscores with palpable warmth their intrinsic human vulnerability, regardless of their standing as humans, gods, demons or artificial life forms. Just as neither Nerine nor Asa are really what they at first appear to be, so Sia turns out to harbor a split personality. This results from the girl's assimilation into her very being of an unborn twin sister, and leads to an ongoing conflict between a meek, accepting and fun-loving disposition on the one hand and a brash and aggressive makeup on the other. As for Kaede, much as her present relationship with Rin seems to amount to a devotion so unconditional as to verge on self-abnegation, disclosures regarding her past show that matters are not quite so straightforward. Although Kaede relentlessly struggles to convince herself that her dedication to Rin's welfare issues from undiluted love, various flashbacks suggest that it is actually a product of guilt — a feeling triggered by the girl's realization that she has been indirectly responsible for the death of her mother in a car crash (in which both of Rin's parents also lost their lives), and that the boy has taken the blame upon himself in order to rekindle Kaede's will to live at the time of her post-traumatic descent into catatonia. Kaede's guilt, moreover, has been exacerbated by her sadistic treatment of the boy prior to her discovery of the truth about the fatal accident. Kaede's tortuous emotions degenerate first into brutality and then self-hatred as she forcibly endeavors to wrench Rin away from the girl he feels committed to (with grievous consequences), and yet cannot even bring herself to contemplate a life without him and without the bond of servitude she has chosen as a form of self-punishment.

An inevitable corollary of the narrative mold adopted by *Shuffle!* is that the male protagonist will at some point have to choose the girl whose love he is able to reciprocate. However, while many titles dramatizing love triangles (or even squares and pentagons) do not resolve the choice issue until the very end, in *Shuffle!*, Rin makes his decision well before the story is over. This enables the director to maximize the complexities of character development by exploring a relationship in the course of its evolution and not simply in terms of outcomes. Additionally, this ploy intimates that the choice at stake is not merely the singling out of a person from a bundle of characters vying for the hero's attention but also — and more vitally — the choice of a whole way of life and related world view. Just as importantly, Rin's choice is not predicated upon some stereotypical notion of romantic love uncritically absorbed from tradition or the media. In fact, it proceeds from a mature understanding of his genuine feelings, and realization that love has less to do with sentimental infatuation than with mutual respect. (From this, it may be possible to deduce which of the candidates for his heart Rin eventually opts for, even without indulging in obvious spoilers.) *Shuffle!*'s original take on the trope of "choice" also enhances the viewer's narrativizing scope. Indeed, the focus on a relationship's development, rather than merely its inception or its culmination, poses questions about its possible after effects and future ramifications, which it is up to the audience to hypothesize and string together into consistent narrative threads. More often than not, harem anime make it easy to anticipate from a relatively early stage the protagonist's likely choice. The selected girl is normally the one who looks after him, the childhood mate, or else the *tsundere*— i.e., the character type that is initially distinguished by a tough and emotionless demeanor but progressively turns out to be sensitive and innerly troubled. *Shuffle!* eschews this convention, since the girl of Rin's choice displays features of all of those typologies without entirely doing service to the generic requirements of any one of them.

Furthermore, *Shuffle!* delivers an unpredictable dramatic twist as it nears its unraveling, thus offering a novel take on the format it loosely adopts while also hinting at the concept of randomness. This revolves around the exposure of Asa's hitherto occulted association with the demon world, the fatal curse to which this binds her, and Rin's characteristically self-effacing determination to sacrifice everything to ensure her survival. These moments could easily have deteriorated into cheap emotionalism in the hands of a less proficient director. As it happens, they yield touching but by no means mawkish psychological portrayals. *Shuffle!*'s pacing sustains this effect as one of its most remarkable stylistic features. The tempo followed by the first part of the series is so leisurely that some spectators might find the action almost too smooth. Nevertheless, a recurrent emphasis on the incidence of chance and coincidence on the flow of events serves to keep viewers on their toes at all times: easy as things may seem, there is no way to predict what kind of bizarre inflection they could suddenly acquire. A state of creative alertness on the audience's part is thus consistently engendered. In the second part, as the show's pointedly episodic composition and penchant for playful dalliance give way to an edifice of elaborately integrated narrative blocks and a preference for more serious psychological drama, the pace picks up momentum. This is true not only of the explicitly gloomier installments but also of the ones in which amusing motifs are dominant (e.g., the episode in which Rin and Asa take a trip to a theme park absurdly designed to suit the whims of young dating couples).

A subsequent visual novel created by Navel and released in 2004 that has also been translated into an anime is *Soul Link*, to which this discussion now turns.

\*    \*    \*

Set in 2045, *Soul Link* (TV series; dir. Toshikatsu Tokoro, 2006) chronicles the adventures of a group of cadets attending the Central Military Academy stationed on the space base Aries. Their fate takes an unexpected turn as the facility is invaded by the terrorist group "Parallax" and the protagonists remain trapped aboard while the fully qualified military personnel and most civilians successfully evacuate. Matters are complicated further by the appearance within the station of a peculiar virus dubbed "*sukyura*" that enables its disseminator to control the minds of most of the staff and thus turn them into mindless zombies. Leaving Aries alive becomes the sole priority for goodies and baddies alike. In *Soul Link*, individuals and communities are so intimately intertwined that it is virtually impossible to speak in terms of "heroes" and "heroines" in conventional terms. At each step, the social body is indeed foregrounded, with the emphasis consistently placed on the value of solidarity as the key to the retention of humanity and warmth in the face of the most challenging odds. The paramount importance of interaction is effectively reinforced by the dramatization of some quite unforeseeable alliances as the story progresses, which makes distinguishing friend from foe not only arduous but pointless. The enigmatic and uncommunicative Yuu Yamanami, for example, is presented as a passenger on Aries and eventually revealed to be a mercenary appointed by a splinter group within Parallax, who willingly agrees to help the protagonists even though she has no moral obligation towards them. The terrorist Karen Tachibana also ends up on the beleaguered cadets' side, channeling her brimming enthusiasm and tremendous martial skills into their cause.

Another peculiar relationship attesting to *Soul Link*'s commitment to the value of cooperation is the one progressively developing between Gale Lantis, the Parallax leader, and Aya, a klutzy but unremittingly cheerful girl who does not feel in the least intimidated by her hostage status and is quite happy, in fact, to regale her captors with tasty snacks. Her love for Gale is eminently filial and the terrorist's own decision to sacrifice himself for her sake indicates that he fully reciprocates Aya's feelings in an appropriately paternal fashion. (Gale also turns out to have played the part of a surrogate father for the parentless Karen.) At the opposite end of the spectrum stands the character of Cellaria Markelight, who is initially presented as an Academy instructor dedicated to her students' well-being but turns out to be the perpetrator of the onslaught on the base, as well as the perfect *sukyura* being. She indeed consists entirely of mutant self-regenerating cells — her human form having been destroyed by fire years prior to the start of the story — and her objective is to achieve absolute power by dominating the minds and bodies of those who host *sukyura* cells, as well as to annihilate the Earth in the process. Strictly speaking, Cellaria is not so much a human as a simulacrum, whose appearance is comparable to the effect of a large-scale phantom-limb hallucination or delusion. Her disregard of collective welfare is total, and on several occasions, downright sadistic. Whereas Yuu's, Karen's, Aya's and Gale's respective choices emphasize the ethical and emotional benefits to be reaped from the consolidation of communal ties, Cellaria's actions encapsulate the destructive thrust of choices made exclusively in the name of personal self-aggrandizement.

While according crucial significance to communal interactions involving several individuals, *Soul Link* is also capable of yielding sensitive portrayals of one-to-one relationships. The plot strand centered on Ryouta Aizawa, a timid trainee endowed nonetheless with impressive leadership skills, and his friend and colleague Sayaka Nagase excels at blending the tropes of a budding romance with those of a mature professional partnership. The relationship between Ryouta's elder brother Shuhei and his beloved Nao Morisaki offers the most fully developed example of an emotional bond capable of defying destiny and logic. Another intriguing relationship is the one involving Aki Nitta and her elder brother Kazuhiko. Locked in a merry-go-round of constant, petty and fundamentally pointless arguments symptomatic of ongoing sibling rivalry, the two characters actually care very deeply for each other and would not hesitate to put their lives at risk for each other's sake. Flashbacks show that much of the tension results from an unresolved juvenile conflict, leading Aki to look up to Kazuhiko as an exemplar and feel horribly disappointed by the discovery of his shallowness, and Kazuhiko to indulge in vapid socializing meant to sustain his public image when he would have been better off communing properly with his sister. Aki and Kazuhiko are not the only characters whose depiction is indebted to flashbacks. In fact, memories and the legacy of both personal and interpersonal past experiences play a key part in the characterization of several personae. In Shuhei and Nao's case, for example, it is disclosed that the depth of their tie strikes its roots in cherished childhood memories (in which Ryouta, too, features substantially).

The most pregnant of the numerous recollections dramatized by the series revolve around Sayaka, who is haunted by the image of her father's desertion, yet sustained by fond reminiscences of Aya's emotional support and resulting determination never to let her childhood friend down. Sayaka's father, who is introduced in the capacity of a steward employed in the civilian quarters of the Aries station, has been profoundly shaped by memories of his decision to leave his family in favor of work, and indeed resolved to take on his current post precisely to fulfill the promise made to his daughter upon his departure that they would meet again. Yuu's memories of her adolescence in a war-torn society likewise fulfill an important narrative role. In this context, we are also introduced to the character of Shin, a young man from Yuu's past whom she has long believed dead but who turns out to have been in Cellaria's thrall ever since her "cure" of Shin's gravely injured sister—a treatment which, alas, has actually consisted of the girl's transformation into a *sukyura* host and hence amounted to her total loss of humanity.

While memories are accorded a pivotal function in *Soul Link*'s overall diegesis, visions additionally contribute to the show's psychological dimension. Most vital in this regard are the near-hallucinatory perceptions experienced by people infiltrated by *sukyura* cells, who are able to access the minds of other individuals analogously affected, communicate with them telepathically and even direct their movements as though they were mere puppets. Shuhei is the first test subject to challenge Cellaria's plan due to his seemingly innate ability to resist mental manipulation—hence the fiend's determination to use him in order to create a superior entity. Cellaria is eventually defeated by the "child" Nanami Inatsuki found in the Aries storage room in the company of the station's mascot, the alacritous mutt Kuu. Apparently unfamiliar with human language and mores, yet endowed with astounding learning skills, Nanami is revealed to be a hybrid of human and *sukyura* cells and to be the only creature capable of arresting Cellaria's dissemination of the portentous virus. This makes her something of an incarnation of the affects released by the consummation of Nao and Shuhei's love: the couple's metaphorical offspring, so to speak. (It would not seem entirely coincidental, in this respect, that Nanami's chosen designations for Nao and Shuhei should indeed be "mother" and "father" respectively.) Although *Soul Link* does not explicitly deal with mythological or legendary motifs, an element of magic can be detected in this fascinating facet of its plot.

This is maintained well into the show's climax, where Nanami, Nao and Shuhei seem doomed to annihilation as a result of the Aries station's irreversible fall to Earth. However, with the help of an escape shuttle, the seemingly fated trio manages to escape the base after defusing the nuclear missiles intended to bombard the human planet any minute. Ryouta and Sayaka, believing that their friends have perished, attribute the missiles' failure to a miracle — hence, Ryouta does not feel he truly deserves the reputation of an Earth-saving hero, which he has gained since the end of the operation. Nanami's, Nao's and Shuhei's anonymity after their safe return to Earth has been protected by Yuu and Shin, in the justified conviction that humanity might not yet be ready to accept the existence of alien cells, of which the members of the secluded "family" all partake to some degree. However, the finale optimistically indicates that Nanami, Nao and Shuhei are ready at last to rejoin the human community.

In assessing *Soul Link*'s deft orchestration of the interplay of the individual and the collectivity, and of attendant memories as well as contingent crises, it is crucial to appreciate the show's meticulous devotion to the rendition of space. In this respect, one of *Soul Link*'s most salient contributions to the field of visual novels transported to the TV screen consists of its interweaving of narratological and ludological priorities in the rendition of its settings. Both the interiors of the Aries station wherein the bulk of the drama unfolds and the cosmic vistas thrown into relief in the parts of the action devoted to transitions from Earth to Aries and vice versa play an important role in the overall progression of the anime's narrative, thus calling attention to its narratological affiliations. Concurrently, however, they evince the aesthetic influence of computer games set in outer space, and in this respect they throw into relief game mechanics as crucial forces operating alongside storytelling considerations at all times. Ludological tenets are thereby invoked.

Spectators are invited to bring together narrative and ludic prerogatives and thus ponder the import of *Soul Link*'s expansive takes on boundless galaxies, dives into sublime darkness and punctilious representations of space modules, ships, futuristic weaponry and digital microcircuits as both vital aspects of the gameplay and visual stimuli intended to trigger their own narrativizing urges. Both *Shuffle!* and *Soul Link* bear witness to the centrality of narrative desire in visual novels and anime based upon them. The former conveys this idea through an ensemble of relatively open and parallel structures which it is up to the player or viewer to interlink, fashion into a coherent system, and having done so, actually "shuffle" about once again to start afresh. In the latter, narrativity foregrounds itself most powerfully through the acrobatic transformation of a seemingly routine training context of the kind often seen in sci-fi anime (and cinema at large) into the stage of a drama of both private and political proportions wherein disjointed desires, motivations and conflicts gradually coalesce into a prismatic yet holistic ensemble.

\* \* \*

The closing part of this chapter focuses on *Aria*, an anime that has been adapted into a visual novel, assessing its engagement with the topos of parallel worlds and briefly considering the stylistic and narrative features that make it an ideal candidate for such a mediatic translation. To date, the franchise encompasses three TV seasons — *Aria the Animation* (2005), *Aria the Natural* (2006) and *Aria the Origination* (2008), as well as the direct-to-video production *Aria the OVA ~Arietta~* (2007) — all of which have been directed by Junichi Sato. The visual novels issuing from the anime include *Aria the Natural: Mirage of a Distant Dream* (2006) and *Aria the Origination: The Sky over the Blue Planet* (2008). The principal parallel dimensions portrayed in *Aria* are the historical city of Venice, reputed to have collapsed into its watery cradle long before the chronological start of the anime, and the imaginary city of "Neo-Venezia," a settlement founded by humans on the hypothetical planet of "Aqua," a terraformed Mars which is 90 percent mantled in oceans.

The anime charts the daily experiences of three girls training as "Undines" (the appellation of Neo-Venezia's gondoliers). The chief heroine, Akari, is a kindly and unrelentingly positive girl whose optimistic pragmatism contrasts nicely with the main attributes of her friends and colleagues: witty cynicism in Aika's case, and sedate dreaminess in Alice's. This basic cast is complemented by the varyingly charismatic characters of the heads of the three companies at whose behest the protagonists are training: Aria Company, Himeya Company and Orange Planet Alicia, Akira and Athena, respectively). Likewise important are the presidents of those bodies: blue-eyed cats of stupendous intelligence that makes them objects of unmatched respect throughout the aqueous city. The collusion of these various personae is the very soul of the show and persistently foregrounds the value of everyday events — and indeed of each fleeting instant — from one episode to the next. While invoking the parallel worlds of the actual and fictive versions of Venice, *Aria* also dramatizes alternate dimensions in each installment through its sketch-inflected narrative structure. Some parts of Neo-Venezia and its broader environment are caught up in quotidian occurrences and minor dramas; others provide doorways to utterly fantastic territory. Thus, in one episode, the three girls' task may merely amount to guiding a honey-mooning couple through the tracery of canals and facing up to the prosaic crisis posed by the sudden appearance of a dead end. In another, Akari may find herself transposed to the city's near-legendary past and even commune with earlier generations, their dreams and ordeals.

The graphic and formal traits that render the *Aria* shows ideally suited to adaptation into visual-novel spin-offs are multifaceted. Particularly note-worthy is the incidence of chance on the protagonists' adventures, an aspect of the anime that mirrors the visual novel's fascination with the principles of unpredictability and randomness governing a story's unfolding; the adoption of a multiperspectival approach to the diegesis, whereby the three girls' and their mentors' diverse perceptions of events all play important parts; and the articulation of distinct yet intertwining stories akin to a visual novel's arcs. Moreover, *Aria* focuses on several of the themes regularly revisited by visual novels. Most prominent is its emphasis on the relationship between the individual and the community since none of the characters, both principal and supporting ones, is graspable independently of the social formation in which he or she is inscribed. In addition, the efforts put by the heroines into the completion of their apprenticeship as Undines in order to gain the title of "Primas" (professional gondoliers), and ideally aspiring to the position of "Water Fairies" (company leaders) beyond that point, lend their exploits the flavor of creative quests comparable to artistic endeavors. As indicated, past and present coalesce in Neo-Venezia's enchanting arabesque as a futuristic society erected upon the legacy of ancient history and one of its most legendary cities ever. As past and present merge, so do myth and actuality. At the same time, the characters' oscillation between entirely mundane chores and fantastic encounters often invests the action with an oneiric mood. Arguably, it is in its unflinching devotion to the representation of both natural and architectural scenarios that *Aria* makes itself a most fitting object of permutation into the visual-novel format. Regaling the eye with spellbinding tableaux woven from a conscientious synthesis of cell animation and CGI, *Aria* delivers a fluid even metamorphic atmosphere that feels alternately ethereal and plastically tactile, always adopting dexterously modulated palettes ranging from the vibrant to the pastelly.[2]

Aria's unwavering devotion to the evocation of a warm atmosphere, released by the recognition of the value of contingent daily occurrences, is largely responsible for urging the viewer to embark on the narrativizing act. This is because it unobtrusively imbues all of the anime's episodic events (albeit in variable degrees) and hence encourages us to create a sense of dramatic continuity out of what might otherwise stay anchored at the level of fragmentary vignettes.

# 3

# *Returns to the Past*

> *There's no such thing as perfect writing, just like there's no such thing as perfect despair.*
> — Haruki Murakami

> *[A] child that plays.... Why does it play...? It plays, because it plays. The "because" withers away in the play. The play is without "why." It plays since it plays. It simply remains a play: the most elevated and the most profound. But this "simply" is everything, the one, the only.... The question remains whether and how we, hearing the movements of this play, play along and accommodate ourselves to the play.*
> — Martin Heidegger

As argued in the opening part of the preceding chapter vis-à-vis the relationship between ludology and narratology, narrativity constitutes one of the most salient properties evinced by role-playing games generally and by the visual novel specifically. For the game itself to become a narrative, the player's imagination and interpretative skills must be consistently stimulated — hence, it could be argued that it is only through an actively engaged player that the game's storytelling potentialities are actualized. The visual novel, like other forms of RPG, thus disrupts conventional notions of authorship by emplacing the player as instrumental to the genesis of narration and meaning. Interactivity is a key concept, in this regard, and insistently reminds us that games only become games by being played. Anime based on visual novels likewise encourage the audience to piece together plural storylines without dishing out neat answers at many key stages in their development. As Cindy Poremba points out, the author's power in the realm of digital gaming is never absolute for his or her agency is inevitably "instantiated by the player." That is to say, the author's agency exists at a merely notional, abstract state before it is concretized by a player's moves and decisions. In this respect, "the author's relationship to the text of the game is similar to that of the composer, creating the capacity for the occurrence of an experience (that is subsequently 'performed' by a secondary agent)" (Poremba, p. 25). According to Nicolas Szilas, the player's active involvement in the production — and hence realization as a concrete cultural artifact — of a digital game is conducive to the concept of "interactive drama": namely, a "specific kind of drama where the audience can modify the course of actions in the drama, thus having an active role." This art's principal features — all prominent, as we have seen, in the visual novel itself — are "branching," on the basis of which "the user is faced to a choice in the action, and the narrative is different according to user's choices"; "superposed interactivity," whereby "during a global linear path into the narrative, a localized interactive scene occurs" (in the case of visual novels, this could consist, for example, of an especially poignant dialogue or interior monologue assessing the conflicts at hand); and "simulations" — i.e., fictional yet convincing replicas of real-life scenarios in speculative form (Szilas, p. 1).

The level of interactivity afforded by a visual novel depends largely on how it is designed — that is to say, how its frames are spatially and sequentially organized, what sorts of moves it entails, how heavily predetermined its narrative potentialities are, and above all else, how far the game's techniques may compel the player to focus on the ways in which these various elements mesh in sustaining the ludic venture's dramatic momentum. The crucial issue here at stake is the extent to which the emerging game experience in its entirety correlates with the player's own gameplay preferences, motivations and sheer enjoyment. As Richard Bartle proposes, players may be situated in four principal categories according to the play-style, expectations and general proclivities they exhibit with regard to the ludic challenge. "Achievers" aim to accomplish objectives set out by the game; "explorers" seek to discover the minutest features of the game's virtual world; "socializers" use the play context as an arena for interacting with other players; and "killers" draw pleasure from causing harm or distress.

The visual novel partakes, figuratively if not always literally, of various aspects of Bartle's taxonomy. Its player is often driven primarily by the desire to see a chosen path through to satisfactory resolution, which echoes the achiever's mentality. Players keen on replaying the visual novel numerous times in order to discover all they can about its world recall the explorer type. The player's awareness that the visual novel he or she experiences is simultaneously experienced by countless other players in diverse situations makes him or her part of a hypothetical community and hence something of a socializer. (This point is revisited in Chapter 4.) Finally, the "killer" modality is brought elliptically into the equation when a player, having tested alternate possibilities several times, might deliberately choose to play the game in ways that will prove detrimental to the character he or she is enacting. Of the four categories delineated by Bartle, explorers and socializers are the most explicitly interactive ones (Bartle). In assessing the dynamics of interactivity, John Kim's differentiation of alternative play models also deserves consideration. According to the critic, the "drama" model prioritizes the generation of an appealing storyline, while the "game" model is mainly concerned with the nature of the challenges confronting the player. In the "simulation" model, lastly, what matters most is the inclination to face and solve conflicts by treating them as though they were real (Kim). In the visual novel, the first model is overtly invoked by the game's emphasis on a sophisticated handling of textuality. The second comes to the fore with the player's confrontation of some tantalizing decision points. The third pivots on the player's ability (or willingness) to navigate the visual novel's world as a domain akin to his or her own real-life milieu.

The titles examined in depth in this chapter maximize the audience's creative agency, intimating that their stories hold a merely conjectural status until they are fulfilled by the viewers interacting with them. A particularly effective ruse is the deliberate introduction of ambiguous situations open to alternative readings of varying realistic or fantastic varieties. *Kanon* and *H2O Footprints in the Sand* excel in this arena, infusing their yarns with occurrences that cannot be unproblematically deciphered as either totally factual or totally mystical but participate at all times in both concrete and metaphysical planes of existence. *Myself; Yourself* and *true tears* also capitalize on ambiguity by portraying characters whose predicaments elude clear-cut interpretation for a substantial part of the story, insofar as they long remain shrouded in a web of misrecognitions, red herrings and self-blinding obfuscations. *Ef—a tale of memories* and its prequel/sequel *ef—a tale of melodies* take this same trend to daring extremes by interweaving parallel plot strands in such an original fashion, time and again exhibiting an acrobatic penchant for diegetic leaps and loops, as to require the spectator's inventive agency to come forth in its full colors.

All of the selected productions posit their key characters' returns to their past worlds and experiences as integral to the confrontation and resolution of buried traumas. *H2O* locates the origins of its characters' present-day ordeals with lethal disruptions in the social fabric and resulting emotional disorders in individual minds, at times accompanied by severe psychosomatic symptoms. By means of two deftly interwoven arcs, *ef* likewise dramatizes the gradual resurfacing of a direful accident and its impact on various characters' struggles towards self-understanding and mutual reconciliation. In the process, each of the main personae are shown to harbor repressed, submerged or abeyant memories of haunting potency. Both *Kanon* and *Myself; Yourself* capitalize on the evocation of an eerie sense of ambivalence in their respective dramatizations of revelatory pilgrimages to the past. This mood is engendered by their personae's perceptions of the worlds they revisit as simultaneously familiar and mysterious, comfortable and inscrutably dark. This atmosphere gains considerable poignancy from the summoning of the palpably alive genius loci associated with each natural or architectural scenario on display. *True tears* ventures into comparable territory, with special emphasis on the unearthing of lurking affective lacerations revolving around familial and pseudo-familial relationships. In all of the anime, individuals are portrayed as inextricable from their communal networks. At the same time, the interplay of past and present in the actors' current lives runs parallel to the collusion of myth-gilded and secular motifs in the shows' overall diegetic patterns. This often provides opportunity for the infusion of a supernatural element into the narratives. Recurring dreams and visions aptly bolster this aspect of the anime. Here employed as an instance of mediatic migration in the anime-to-visual novel direction, *Kanokon* frames a return to the past consisting of the reactivation of a latent mythical legacy in the prosaic present. This pivots on a legendary creature cardinal to indigenous lore, the fox demon (*kitsune*): an entity that also features prominently in *Kanon*, and makes intriguing cameo appearances in *Yami to Boushi to Hon no Tabibito*.

\* \* \*

The *Kanon* game (1999) takes as its point of departure the return of its protagonist, Yuuichi Aizawa, to a town he has not visited in seven years, harboring no recollection of the time he spent there as a kid. The character gallery features five female types that are all somehow connected with the male lead and his amnesia. The *Kanon* visual novel primarily requires the player to engage with an extensive and densely detailed text consisting of either dialogue between numerous characters or the protagonist's interior monologue. Every now and then, the player is asked to make choices who will affect his or her involvement with five available storylines. The number of threads unspooling in alternate directions, allied to *Kanon*'s textual richness, makes the game lustily replayable. The player assumes the role of Yuuichi as an unsentimental — at times, even cynical — seventeen-year-old high-school student who is distinguished by a tendency to poke fun at the girls he is familiar with in a pleasingly non-chivalric fashion, yet reveals great humanity through his unflinchingly loyal and selfless disposition.

The five girls associated with Yuuichi embody distinctive typologies. Nayuki Minase, the lead's cousin, is an athletic and enthusiastic girl with just one (at least on the surface) endearing foible: namely, an inveterate resistance to waking up in the morning. Nayuki, who lives alone with her proverbially amiable mother Akiko, has been in love with Yuuichi since childhood and must painfully come to terms with his attraction to, and sense of responsibility for, other girls in their milieu. Shiori Misaka is timid, genteel and sickly, while Makoto Sawatari is mischievous and resolutely unsocialized. Mai Kawasumi is so solemnly formal as to appear unapproachable, as well as overly eager to dispense a gentle karate chop to the head of anyone who mocks her in circumstances she deems inappropriate. Ayu Tsukimiya, the key heroine, is vivacious and highly determined, yet haunted by the imperative to seek out a precious object of which she has no clear recollection. Among her idiosyncrasies is the tendency to refer to herself with the masculine first-person pronoun "*boku*," where the feminine "*atashi*," Yuuichi suggests, would be more appropriate. (Please note that a further variation on the first-person pronoun played upon by the protagonists in their banter is "*ore*," the emphatic or boastful form.) Ayu also has a tendency to erupt into the nonsense ejaculation "*uguuu*"—comparable to Misuzu's "*gao*" in *Air* (please see Chapter 2)—out of frustration, aggravation or fear. (In the anime, a further intertextual allusion to *Air* comes in the form of an advert placed on a bus for the brand of extra-thick peach nectar adored by Misuzu in that show. The visual-novel studio behind both *Air* and *Kanon* is economically honored through the cover of the manga owned by Makoto that features the name "Key" in a prominent position.) Yuuichi's relationships with these personae are dramatized across several interconnected arcs that holistically lead to the pinnacle of the pivotal story thread—i.e., the one uniting Yuuichi and Ayu from a traumatic moment in childhood to the present day.

The visual novel was first adapted to the animated medium in 2002 as a thirteen-episode program helmed by Naoyuki Itou. On May 3, 2003, a direct-to-video bonus episode titled *Kanon Kazahana*, also directed by Itou and offering an edited take on the TV show's finale, was released. In the wake of the success enjoyed by the TV series *Air*, Kyoto Animation (a.k.a. KyoAni), the studio responsible for its production, decided to animate a fresh version of *Kanon*. The second series consists of twenty-four installments, was directed by Tatsuya Ishihara (also *Air*'s director in the TV format) and was broadcast in 2006–2007. (Among Western fans, the second show is frequently referred to as *Kanon 2006*.) The 2002 adaptation, produced by Toei Animation, was felt to hold much promise but was met with disappointment by many aficionados of the source visual novel due to its limited scope. This, moreover, was seen to impact adversely on character presentation and development and hence not to do full justice to one of the most vital aspects of the ludic construct at its base. The 2006 release fully attests to KyoAni's artistic stature, consolidating the reputation already established by *Air* and paving the way to *Clannad*. Omni's enthusiastic comments on the new anime's caliber are worthy of citation: "*Kanon*'s visuals and emotional impact" set "a new standard for that type of show, or even for all anime" (Omni).

The remake is partly an endeavor to surpass the first series' limitations on both the affective and the stylistic planes by fleshing out the drama and its personae's psychologies, thereby yielding a dazzling graphic melody nurtured by high-quality animation and cinematography. Both natural settings and various facets of the built environment yield a cumulatively engrossing set in which singular lives dovetail within a multiperspectival mosaic of duties and aspirations. The shift of tone ushered in by the remake also enhances the anime's interactive import insofar as, by delving deeper into the actors and their worlds, the narrative implicitly elicits the audience's participation in the unraveling of its skein to a much higher degree. Thus, the parent game's flair for enlisting the player's inventive impulses is more openly brought to fruition in Ishihara's appeal to the audience's creativity. Furthermore, *Kanon 2006* improves on its predecessor through its orchestration of the various strands so that the characters associated with specific narrative complications make cogent appearances both before and after their individual stories are brought into focus. In blocking the narrative components more definitely and conclusively, the 2002 show exhibited, conversely, a somewhat choppy architecture.

On the stylistic plane, what is instantly evident about the new series is an intentional shift in character portrayal marked by a preference for more mature physiognomies, which invests the anime with greater gravity. In comparison with Ishihara's cast, Itou's feels pointedly juvenile in both appearance and perspective. The only character who retains relatively childlike traits in the 2006 version is Ayu; but this is also, no doubt, the result of a deliberate aesthetic choice. Indeed, this heroine's younger look is logically congruous with her status as the victim of partially arrested development. In addition, it could be explained as a corollary of how Ayu perceives herself within the context of her imaginary existence: in other words, as the body image with reference to which she projects herself onto reality and the lives of other personae. Even in Ayu's case, the range of expressions and emotional variations coursing through practically all of her facial close-ups in the second anime indicate substantially increased psychological depth. It is also worth noting that the Ayu seen throughout the main body of the action always dons a red hairband. Yuuichi supposedly bought the item for her in childhood and although he never got round to giving it to her, he deceived himself into believing that he had to protect himself from reality. The hairband's consistent appearance as one of Ayu's accessories succinctly indicates that the image of the girl inserted into reality conforms with the protagonists' desires rather than empirical facts. The effectiveness of the projection is confirmed by Akiko's remark, at a late point in the series, that her recollections of Ayu always include the red hairband.

Whereas *Air* instantly proclaimed its scenic distinctiveness by recourse to the image of a summery seashore, *Kanon* resorts to a diametrically opposite ambience: the crystalline purity of a snow-blanketed provincial town and its surroundings. The glistening snowy look readily associated with *Kanon* was already cultivated by the 2002 show but in the remake, massively improved animation quality enables it to gather fresh resonance through the inclusion of smooth dynamic effects and dexterous lighting. The ubiquitous snow is not only instrumental to the definition of the anime's atmosphere. In fact, it also operates as an elegant metaphor for the characters' frozen emotions: as the candid mantle gradually thaws, so the actors' defense mechanisms accordingly melt, allowing hitherto repressed affects to surface. Ishihara's pursuit of psychological and atmospheric complexity is abetted throughout by KyoAni's technical excellence. Most conspicuous, in this regard, is the studio's diligent integration of all aspects of the production process from conception to completion. The first stage is the translation of the original into a scenario through the collaborative input of the director and the scriptwriter: it is at this inceptive point in the production process that the anime makers' own narrative urges come crucially into play. On the basis of the scenario, the person responsible for directing the drafting of the storyboards sketches out the anime's general flow. This stage enlists the production team's inventive capabilities in the mapping of the action's structural mainstays, detailing "how a scenario should be turned into pictures" ("A Close Look at an Anime Production House Part 2").

The storyboards also provide the foundations upon which the layouts for the various scenes are designed. These constitute "the blueprints of the scene cuts" and throw into further relief the team's creativity in the constellation of discrete graphic and dynamic elements into a cohesive narrative ("A Close Look at an Anime Production House Part 3"). With the layouts in place, the team's concretization of the source game's virtual story finally starts. It is indeed on the basis of those formal matrices that the drawings supplying the "key points in the flow of actions," as well as their "timing," are produced ("A Close Look at an Anime Production House Part 4"). While the key animation itself is drawn according to the layouts, the in-between animation, in turn, is executed with reference to the key drawings. Backgrounds also come into being as the key and in-between frames are being drawn. Color is then added to the picture by the finisher or colorist. Finally, the scanned key and in-between drawings are combined with the backgrounds and the ensembles are shot. What remains to be done for the anime to be complete is a comprehensive adjustment of the connections between discrete shots, culminating with the photography stage. (This will be discussed later in this chapter.)

As Ishihara has emphasized with specific reference to the requirements of design, a major challenge faced by the production team in creating an anime with a visual novel as its source is the imperative to ideate all manner of elements from scratch. "When the original game is graphic or onscreen," the director has observed, "you have something to consult, but this original is mainly text, so there are a lot of things that don't appear on screen at all. We try to make sure that the props are appropriate to the 'Kanon' world." Character designers encountered a germane challenge in their task, since the source game often offers stationary figures seen from one angle only, whereas the fully animated personae must be visualized from a variety of perspectives with flawless consistency, ensuring that incongruities do not arise in the depiction of diverse facets of their appearance (e.g., hair length) when they are viewed in profile or from the back rather than frontally. Thus, character design demands the same kind of sensitivity to multiperspectivalism one finds in the yarns of both visual novels and their anime progeny. On a broader plane, the early phases of production require the director and his associates to become actively engaged in the making of the story and its interrelations as creative narrativizers akin to players. It is then up to viewers to operate as second-degree narrativizers by piecing together the graphic information at their disposal according to their own decoding and interpretative abilities.

Location hunting and attendant fieldwork also play a cardinal role in the construction of a credible and consistent world. As Ishihara has noted, these tasks were undertaken at the time of the year in which *Kanon* is set — i.e., mid–January — in appropriately snowy regions of Japan. The fact that both the director and scenarist Fumihiko Shimo grew up in cold areas also proved beneficial to the enterprise. The team's primary objective was to infuse *Kanon*'s reality with atmospheric and cultural accuracy by grasping not merely the superficial aspects of snowy places but also the "lifestyle of the townspeople" (cited in "A Close Look at an Anime Production House Part 1"). The anime draws inspiration from a number of actual towns — mainly Moriguchi (Osaka Prefecture), Yokohama (Kanagawa Prefecture), Tachikawa (Western Tokyo) and most importantly Sapporo, the capital of Hokkaido.[1] (It seems worth mentioning that the studio behind the *Kanon* visual novel, Visual Art's/Key, frequently uses real-world locations in its games, even though these do not tend to be explicitly named in their anime spin-offs.)

In structural terms, *Kanon*'s most laudable trait is its exponential amplification of the principle of multiperspectivalism. This arises from a methodical avoidance of stark diegetic compartmentalization, as a corollary of which, as hinted, even when an arc prioritizes a particular persona, it never concentrates unequivocally on that individual but also offers both rapid glimpses and interstitial vignettes of other characters pivotal to previous or later arcs. *Kanon*'s pluridimensional constitution is effectively foregrounded by the early episodes preceding the articulation of distinctive strands. A structural assessment of those installments is therefore beneficial to the understanding of the anime's overall architectonics. Having presented the protagonist's arrival in the snowy town through an astounding synthesis of photorealism and visual poetry, the anime's inaugural segment proceeds to show his meeting with Nayuki, smoothly moving on to the following day's events — namely, his domestic interaction with Akiko and subsequent tour of the town with Nayuki. This portion of the episode also offers a fleeting glimpse of Shiori walking along a pavement, briefly introduces Mai and Sayuri (taking care to highlight the former's animal-loving spirit), makes explicit reference to the hospital destined to carry substantial dramatic weight in later portions of the story, brings in Kaori in the company of the loyal Kitagawa, and then provides a shot of a wild fox anticipating the Makoto-based arc. It is in the course of the tour that Yuuichi also comes into abrupt contact with Ayu and gets to spend some time with her in a local café. Thus, most of the axial personae are economically ushered in through a fluid concatenation of frames. The installment felicitously closes with an oneiric flashback highlighting *Kanon*'s preoccupation with the collusion of past and present through the presentation of a childhood scene set in the shopping mall in which Yuuichi and Nayuki experience situations analogous to the ones seen earlier that day, and Yuuichi then meets a disconsolate Ayu for the very first time and rescues her from staring passersby.

With the second installment, the show builds on the initial impressions evoked by the preceding segment's character introductions, playfully lingering on Nayuki's narcoleptic tendencies and then moving on to Yuuichi's first day at his new school. Another brief scene is devoted to Mai and Sayuri, while Kaori is brought into the narrative as Yuuichi's rescuer when the boy gets lost in the unfamiliar building. After school, Yuuichi bumps into Ayu again and their relationship unexpectedly gains poignancy as Ayu maintains that the youth has finally "remembered" and kept his "promise." Yuuichi, for his part, seems to sense a vague flash of the past puncturing the mist of his amnesia but has no time to dwell on the sensation for Ayu, in an excessively exuberant attempt to hug him, clashes into a tree and thus causes another girl bound to play a key role, Shiori, to collapse to the ground amidst an array of shopping items. No less importantly, the episode inserts Makoto into the action with a verve that will prove central to that character's subsequent portrayal. Thus, the second segment of the anime both consolidates and expands *Kanon*'s character gallery through its agile editing and pace.

The third episode seems mainly concerned with emplacing Makoto as a temporary member of the Minase household and then reinforcing character attributes pertaining to Shiori, on the one hand, and Mai and Sayuri on the other. It is not until the closing portion that a novel plot trigger destined to prove cardinal to the entire narrative is launched — that is, Ayu's quest for an object she holds dear but is totally powerless to visualize. A palpable sense of anguish exudes from these scenes, as epitomized by the frames where Ayu is disquieted by the discovery that on the very spot where she expected to find a small familiar cakeshop, a large bookstore now stands instead. Despite its heightened emphasis on the main heroine, the episode does not fail to make reference to other characters as well right through to the end. Thus, the closing shots are devoted to a wordless moment centered on Mai as she stands alone in a gloomy school corridor at night. The fourth segment of the show capitalizes on the multiperspectival tone established by the preceding installments. The flashback displayed in the opening episode is returned to, with Yuuichi now trying to cheer up the tearful Ayu by buying her some *taiyaki* (her favorite snack) and then meeting up with his cousin outside the grocery store where she has been waiting for him, growing increasingly impatient by the minute due to the boy's failure to keep his promise not to wander off in her absence.

The scene installs another motif bound to recur in *Kanon*: Yuuichi's failure, time and again, to keep his appointments with Nayuki. As the action returns to the present, all of the key characters are accorded appropriate amounts of screentime. Thus, the home-based sequences focus on Makoto, whereas the scenes set in the school fluidly move from Nayuki's athletic training to Kaori, dropping the first hint at the latter's familial troubles. Ayu is accorded center stage once more in the intriguing sequence, set in the shopping district, where she encounters Akiko in Yuuichi's company and the older woman instantly appears to sense Ayu's true identity. Further allusions to Akiko's knowledge of who Ayu might be will be judiciously peppered through the ensuing episodes. (A deliciously understated hint at Ayu's enigmatic status is later supplied by the brief scene set in the hospital where Shiori's doctor suddenly appears to recognize Ayu and to be taken aback by her presence on that spot but politely dismisses her reaction as insignificant.) Equally remarkable are the scenes where Ayu is befriended by the habitually reticent Makoto — which could be seen to suggest that the latter feels some sense of commonality with a person of otherworldly standing due to her own background. (This theme will shortly be addressed.) Finally, the fourth installment accords unprecedented prominence to Mai's quest in the highly dramatic scene where Yuuichi chances upon her in a deserted nocturnal area of their school, to which he has returned to fetch a mislaid notebook.

The story arc revolving around Makoto introduces the girl as the victim of severe amnesia, the sole memory she carries being the one of an unspecified grudge she holds against Yuuichi. Integrated into the Minase household by the unfailingly generous Akiko, Makoto displays quite an irresponsible and uncultured makeup, repeatedly conducive to involuntarily selfish and reckless acts. The marginal but deeply charismatic character of Mishio Amano helps Yuuichi discover the truth behind Makoto's conduct. The girl, it transpires, is not an ordinary human teenager but rather a spirit that has temporarily assumed its current shape for the specific purpose of being with Yuuichi. The entity emanates from a fox cub nurtured by the boy in childhood during a sojourn in the Northern town. The miracle enabling Makoto's embodiment in human guise is inexorably ephemeral and the girl's health is accordingly fated to deteriorate to terminal extremes. In the wake of this unsettling discovery, Yuuichi devotes himself wholeheartedly to Makoto and eventually honors his bond to the doomed creature through an intensely moving private "wedding" set on Monomi Hill, the venue where the fox cub was originally descried.

Mishio featured in the same role in the 2002 version of the anime. Having warned Yuuichi on the basis of her own direct experience about the dangers entailed by his getting too close to a creature like Makoto in that series, Mishio gained fresh prominence in the OVA special *Kanon Kazahana*. Set in Spring, when the actual snow thaws at last and the "windflower" ("*kazahana*") briefly mimics the magic of snow flurries, the bonus episode presents an alternate take on the closing segment of the TV show. Part of the action focuses on what might well prove to be the dawn of a solid friendship between Ayu and Shiori (two characters that did not get much of a chance to interact with each other in the main block of the anime), while also offering a brief sample of Mai and Sayuri's student life abroad as inseparable companions. The crux of the minidrama. however, consists of Mishio's encounter with Makoto in human form on the very hill where the fox cub found and adopted by Yuuichi first came into the world and the fated girl enjoyed her last precious moments with her guardian. Mishio and Makoto play freely in the enchanted scenario of the fleeting *kazahana* season, aware that this miracle cannot last, yet also aware of the indelibility of their mutual devotion over time and space.

The figure of the fox spirit is subject to a radically different — and, on the whole, much more facetious — treatment in the anime *Kanokon* (TV series; dir. Atsushi Ohtsuki, 2008), a show adapted into a visual novel (i.e., *Kanokon Esuii*, 2008) due to thematic and stylistic affinities with some games in that format. In *Kanokon*, the creature is cast as a buxom second-year high-schooler named Chizuru Minamoto who has a pathological crush on the shy first-year student Kouta Oyamada and becomes increasingly determined to fuse with him in order to engender a being of incomparable powers. Chizuru is forward and unruly, harboring beneath the human veneer of an alluring female adolescent the four-hundred-year-old force of a mighty *kitsune*. Her amorous pursuits, which do eventually lead to Kouta becoming the host of preternatural energies, gain vigor and momentum from her rivalry with the two-hundred-year-old wolf deity Nozomu Ezomori, a transfer student in Kouta's class who also feels drawn to the boy. The obvious divergence between *Kanon*'s and *Kanokon*'s respective approaches to the fox-spirit motif economically bears witness to the generic suppleness of anime based on visual novels or indeed adapted into visual novels.

The Mai-based strand unfolds in the immediate aftermath of the previous arc's apex. Realizing that the girl's reclusiveness and despondency — allied to the school council's suspicion that she may be responsible for serious acts of vandalism — are making her quite unpopular among her peers, Yuuichi resolves to escort Mai to the school's annual dance festival. The sequence in which Yuuichi and Mai venture onto the dance floor and soon become the sole focus of everyone's attention shows KyoAni's technical flair at its very best. The sequence is indubitably one of the most beautifully shot terpsichorean numbers in film history and comparable in caliber, though not in style, to the ballroom scene in *Beauty and the Beast* (dir. Gary Trousdale, 1991): a sequence allegedly credited as the first wholly computer-generated animation of color and space in Disney history. The Mai arc contains some adrenaline-pumping action sequences pivoting on the central character's demon-hunting mission that bear witness to *Kanon*'s ability to engage with intense dynamic spectacle even as it foregrounds the emotional and meditative facets of its personae's quandaries. Nonetheless, the action-adventure formula is not merely invoked in order to dispense tantalizing martial drama. More importantly, it serves as a metaphorical means of exploring Mai's traumatized psyche. The demons can indeed be regarded as manifestations of the girl's anxieties and fears: baleful aberrations opposing her benevolent nature and preternatural healing skills that strike their roots in childhood memories connected with her playmate Yuuichi — recollections of which Yuuichi himself has no glimmer at first but which he is eventually, able to help Mai confront and resolve.

The melancholy atmosphere pervading the crowning moments of both the Makoto and the Mai arcs also impacts on the narrative block revolving around Shiori, a girl afflicted by an incurable condition causing her protracted absence from school. The most salient portions of this arc are the installments where Shiori is allowed by her doctor to attend classes for just one week as a special treat, so that she may at least have a taste of life as an ordinary student before the fatal day arrives, and where Yuuichi, for his part, endeavors to arrange a special celebration for what will feasibly be her last birthday. Shiori's sister Kaori, meanwhile, is tenaciously reluctant to admit to her connection with the unfortunate teenager. The avoidance of an explicit face-to-face parting lends the arc a potently open-ended quality, while also problematizing Yuuichi's role as a case of "unfinished business," so to speak. The sensation that the protagonist's achievements are never totally conclusive is indeed one of the most distinctive traits associated with Yuuichi right through to the end of the series.

This feeling of precariousness issues from the lacunae in Yuuichi's psyche and, most importantly, his inability to recall certain key events surrounding Ayu. It is this character, as *Kanon* approaches its dénouement, that comes to be firmly enthroned as the show's main heroine. This role is foreshadowed throughout the earlier arcs, since Yuuichi never takes Ayu totally out of his mind even when he is most deeply embroiled in the other girls' personal odysseys. Additionally, recurring nocturnal conversations between Yuuichi and Ayu set on Akiko's balcony, following the girl's integration in the Minase household as a guest, concisely capture the maturity and depth of their relationship even though the topics they address are quite mundane. Hence, when Ayu's turn finally comes, her emplacement as the axial female persona feels like a logical and cogently prepared outcome, not an abrupt shift of gears. The overall action, in the process, gains considerable coherence from its chronicling of Yuuichi's own journey. Though resolved to adjust to the once familiar but now alien context, the youth is challenged at each turn by the resurgence of morsels of the past that stubbornly elude rationalization. Day-to-day duties as wide-ranging as keeping Nayuki awake, abetting Mai in her imaginary war against demons and taking care of Makoto and Ayu on the domestic front while befriending Shiori in the outside domain, keep him busy. Yet these commitments are not sufficient to exorcize his confusion in the face of the fragmentary recollections that drift back to him unsummoned with no regard for pattern or logic. The protagonist's struggle to recapture his memories is often couched in oneiric terms, and this lends the action a markedly visionary feel even when it deals with prosaic slice-of-life drama.

This aspect of Yuuichi's experience closely parallels Ayu's own ordeal since the heroine herself is persistently depicted as the captive of a seemingly interminable dream. It is through a dream, frustratingly repetitive as it is, that Ayu manages to refrain her memories from "fading away in the eternity of time." It is also plausible that the entire story, in fact, has been choreographed as a visualization of the heroine's dream, and that the Ayu seen throughout the bulk of the anime is an imaginary construct. A gripping allusion to Ayu's chimerical status is the scene where the girl revisits with Yuuichi the clearing in the forest associated with her childhood misfortune and begins to wonder whether she has a right to be there at all or is merely living a lie. Shock turns into panic when, as though to convince herself of her own reality as a flesh-and-blood schoolgirl, Ayu opens her winged backpack only to find it empty. In a last desperate attempt to find the object for which she has been vainly searching all along, she starts digging holes in the ground with the baffled Yuuichi's help, but to no avail. As though sensing that her fantasy can no longer be sustained, Ayu tells Yuuichi that she does not believe they will be able to meet again and vanishes, leaving her words to echo dismally in the boy's mind. At this juncture, Ayu could be said to typify the folkloric figure of the "woman who disappears" theorized by Hayao Kawai and here discussed in Chapter 2 in relation to *Touka Gettan*. Insofar as the proposition that the whole story articulates Ayu's vision is never unequivocally promulgated, *Kanon* asserts itself as a virtuoso exercise in narrative ambiguity. In articulating its branching and overlapping arcs, the series provides no easy answers. It is mainly through this strategy that it brings its viewers' inventiveness into play by inviting them to work out various enigmas and possible solutions on the basis of scattered clues and elusive hints and whispers. Much of the time, it is hard to establish conclusively who is experiencing what or the level of reality at which the experience is occurring.

*Kanon*'s passion for sophisticated interweaving, already attested to by its decidedly pluridimensional take on parallel arcs and their respective returns to the past, reaches its apotheosis in the closing installments. Thus, much as the protagonist may seem totally engrossed in his Ayu-centered quest, this does not preclude his involvement with a variety of characters and their own convoluted searches for understanding and, ideally, emotional closure. This idea is most vividly corroborated by the introduction of a new persona in the penultimate episode — namely, the real Makoto Sawatari after whom the fox spirit's temporary human configuration has been named and ideated. The human Makoto is an older girl whom Yuuichi admired in his juvenile days and whose physiognomy the fox spirit assumes (albeit in a younger incarnation). Amusingly, the human Makoto harbors the same passion for meat buns and bells seen in the preternatural Makoto. Fulfilling the role of an intriguingly unorthodox *dea ex machina*, this young woman rescues Yuuichi as he lies in the snow on the brink of unconsciousness and takes him to her apartment, where she invites him to voice at last the anxieties and fears he has for so long repressed and urges him to honor any promises he has made. This course of action, Makoto implies, is Yuuichi's only chance of overcoming his stultifying sense of frustration. While consolidating its multibranching narrative preferences through its focus on Yuuichi's interactions, *Kanon*'s finale also enables several supporting characters to play their parts as threads in a densely woven tapestry. Yuuichi's exchange with Makoto, for instance, is felicitously intercut with no less transformative occurrences in Nayuki's developmental trajectory. Integral to the girl's epiphany is the realization, achieved with Kaori's help, that by reacting to her mother's possibly fatal traffic accident through self-enclosure in a lonely crypt of pain and silence, she is disregarding Akiko's own ethical lessons — just as Kaori's determination to disavow Shiori's presence to protect herself from the inevitability of her younger sister's illness contravened Shiori's own courageous approach to her destiny. Emerging from her rite of passage, Nayuki is also able to let go of the past, accept Yuuichi's unwavering commitment to Ayu, and embark upon a novel friendship untainted by memories of rejection and loss with her precious cousin. Therefore, no character — not even the protagonist and his beloved — is ever conclusively emplaced as *Kanon*'s sole concern, since emphasis is unremittingly placed on the communal web wherein the personae are knit.

Before reaching its real climax, and hence the acme of Ayu and Yuuichi's ghost-ridden relationship, *Kanon* offers a beautifully choreographed shift of gears, slowing down its pace to depict scenes that deceptively suggest a return to normality. On the surface, the situation suggests that the storm is over, that the various interrelated arcs have arrived at their terminal stages, and that their protagonists are ready to embrace the future at last. With Ayu apparently gone for good, there is nothing left for Yuuichi to do but lay the phantoms from the past to rest and regard his return to old times and places as a closed chapter. While Akiko, fully recovered from her accident, resumes her old life, Mai and Sayuri plan to go to college together after graduating, and Shiori is able to start the normal school life she has yearned for throughout her illness, Yuuichi must come to terms with the painful import of Ayu's parting words. It is with stoical resignation, accordingly, that Yuuichi tells Mai and Sayuri that he does not believe he will ever be able to see his childhood friend again. As shown by a later conversation between Yuuichi and Akiko, the youth is now fully cognizant of the nature of the tragedy triggering his amnesia — i.e., Ayu's fall from a tree to her apparent death seven years earlier before he could give her the iconic hairband as a parting present. This only serves to reinforce his conviction that Ayu is not in this world any longer.

The disclosure that his cherished friend is in fact alive though unconscious jars Yuuichi out of his resigned apathy. Yet it is not sufficient unto itself to redefine reality. The anime's tempo, accordingly, remains deliberate and relatively undramatic, at least in comparison with the sequences set in the forest marking the last moments of Yuuichi's interaction with Ayu and his later search for the lost girl amidst a snowstorm. The seasons roll smoothly by and *Kanon*'s characteristically icy atmosphere gives way to the blossom-laced stirrings of Spring. Gradually, however, the rhythm quickens once more.

This reorientation works most effectively thanks to Ishihara's proficient handling of cinematic irony, whereby the anime's impetus towards a truly sensational rebalancing act is not achieved through overt acceleration of the action but rather through emphasis on the mounting pressure of the dream that has permeated *Kanon*'s diegesis from the start as a symbolic leitmotif and now appears to have actually shaped the anime's entire reality. This zenith is deftly orchestrated and allowed to build to its final crescendo with each of the frames devoted to Yuuichi's peculiar conversation with the comatose Ayu.

While Yuuichi tells Ayu various tales related to the experiences following his return to the town, the girl herself silently participates in the narrative by dreaming that the person she loves is next to her. Yuuichi's stories provide a gorgeously telescoped retelling of all of the anime's most salient moments and culminate with the memory of his reunion with a childhood friend in the dusky streets. This narrative is later paralleled by Ayu's oneiric recollections of her interaction with the town through the changing seasons, where elegant cinematography concisely conveys the transition from fluttering winter snow, through malleable springtime slush and the misty warmth of summer, to autumnal premonitions of the cold weather to come. The show's final segment capitalizes to great effect once again on *Kanon*'s multiperspectival thrust by interweaving Ayu and Yuuichi's ordeal with cogent contributions by other characters, especially Shiori and Mai. The former sheds light on the mystery enfolding Ayu by speculating about a hypothetical "person" trapped in a dream and endeavoring to grant the wishes of the people close to her beloved so as to make him happy. Viewed from this angle, Makoto's temporary assumption of a human body, Mai's emergence from her demon-infested delusion, and Shiori's and Akiko's recoveries could be read as outcomes of Ayu's providential interventions. Mai, in turn, urges Yuuichi to look for Ayu in the past, just as he did for her. Therefore, both Shiori and Mai operate as inspiring forces behind Yuuichi's subsequent actions. Nevertheless, *Kanon* stresses that submerged traumas must be relived and confronted by their victims at first hand and that it is therefore pointless for other characters to attempt to expose them to the truth if they are not yet ready to negotiate it within their own psyches. Thus, it is not until the protagonist acknowledges his self-blinding proclivities that he is able to move forward. Remembering that he never gave Ayu the hairband but merely chose to believe that he had done so in order to prevent his enfeebled spirit from being crushed by the weight of memory, Yuuichi now has his one fighting chance of putting an end to both Ayu's dream and his own wrenching amnesia.

What adds felicitously to *Kanon*'s existential puzzle is the series' multi-generic mold, which allows elements of romance, comedy, the supernatural yarn, the thriller, the ghost story and the mystery drama seamlessly to coalesce. As in *Shuffle!*, the narrative form centered on a male lead's interactions with a number of female characters may bring to mind the "harem" formula. However, also as in *Shuffle!*, the protagonist is not depicted as a stereotypical harem hero (or antihero for that matter). Whereas that type is routinely portrayed as a weak and indecisive fellow, *Kanon*'s protagonist is typically self-possessed and capable of facing his responsibilities towards both himself and others even as he struggles, often vainly, to grapple with a lacunary past and correspondingly perplexing present. Gentle and abrasive by turns, Yuuichi comes across throughout as a sincere and unaffected youth — the sarcastic wit peppering his discourse (redolent of Yukito's register in *Air*) aptly reinforces this impression. While all of the girls endear themselves to the audience without going overboard, Yuuichi himself thus escapes the danger of stereotypical characterization. Kind and accommodating as he almost invariably is, the youth also evinces, like his ludic antecedent, a refreshingly mean undercurrent in his tendency to poke fun at the various females in his life. This facet of Ishihara's method also carries repercussions for the viewers. In evaluating and responding to the protagonist's behavior, they will necessarily have to depend on imaginative interpretations of Yuuichi's surface conduct in relation to his inner feelings and goals instead of simply relying on crystallized generic conventions predetermining their reactions on the basis of a default mode.

*Kanon*'s characters do not only glean complexity from the treatment of major dramatic occurrences but also from apparently marginal details. Ayu's status as a character stranded in a frozen time zone is at one point economically conveyed by the suggestion that she does not know what a cell phone is: when Yuuichi gives her an explanation, she is frankly excited at the thought that one can learn new things with each passing day. Also effective, along similar lines, is Mai's climactic effort to show Yuuichi that she is academically disposed — despite indications to the contrary sprinkled through the story — by donning glasses and proudly holding up a children's book. With Akiko, a habitually open and pragmatic person who would seem to harbor no secrets whatsoever, a jocular hint at mysteriousness is introduced through references to her secret-recipe jam and its ominous reputation. What should additionally be stressed, in assessing the 2006 show's sophisticated character portrayal, is that personae who were accorded only marginal or supporting roles in the first anime adaptation here gain full-rounded identities of their own. This is most blatantly clear in the case of Sayuri Kurata, Mai's sole and deeply treasured friend, as a secondary character whose experiences echo those undergone by the key actors. Sayuri's own past indeed harbors painful recollections, the acceptance of which is integral to her personal growth. The girl's inclination to adopt the behavior of a surrogate elder sister vis-à-vis Mai, in particular, is seen to ensue from her earlier experiences as a real elder sister. Compelled by her strict father to bring up her sickly little brother Kazuya in accordance with sternly disciplinarian codes of conduct, Sayuri did not realize until it was too late that the boy would have benefited much more from a demonstrative and playful attitude on her part than from a routine of monastic punitive restraint. Sayuri's relationship with Mai indicates that she has learned a crucial lesson from those childhood experiences and is hence resolved not to repeat the old mistake.

Another character who hardly transcends stereotypic presentation in the first *Kanon* anime but acquires novel depth in the remake is Kitagawa. Initially associated with the stock figure of the hapless suitor, the youth rises to almost heroic stature as he stands up to the student council in Mai's defense, and indeed takes upon himself much of the blame for the accident believed to have been caused by the girl and providing the grounds for her expulsion. Even personae who already received comprehensive treatment in the 2002 series gain greater complexity in Ishihara's adaptation. Mai herself is possibly the best example. Whereas in the first series it is merely proposed that the demons she hunts are of her own making, in the 2006 anime, Mai's psychological disorder is seen to be rooted in a chain of juvenile experiences depicted with considerable care for a wide range of emotive nuances. At the same time, the supernatural dimension of her mission is interwoven with the realistic portrayal of real-life events associated with a sinister socioeconomic context predicated on the imperatives of rampant urbanization, and by implication the evils of the construction industry plaguing actual Japanese politics for years. (An analogous motif is articulated in *Clannad* through the character of Tomoyo and her struggle to protect an avenue of cherry trees threatened with felling by rapacious authorities.)

The supernatural dimension, for its part, gains poignancy from the infusion into the prosaic here-and-now of time-honored beliefs of an emphatically mystical stamp, where miracles and life-shaping promises, as well as sacrifices, play key roles. Even when it appears to be merely tootling along with inconsequential quotidian chores, *Kanon* is able to imbue its narrative with an engaging emotional drive pervaded by timeless and even metaphysical preoccupations. It is fundamentally up to the spectators to extrapolate these deeper concerns from the actual flow of the narrative. What the anime offers is a set of resolutions that do lend themselves to interpretation as miraculous turns of events: the ostensibly illogical recoveries from terminal conditions and lethal injuries made by several characters are cases in point. Yet, the dramatic and affective sophistication of their treatment hints at more elaborate subtexts. It is at this level that the audience is called upon to delve beneath the miracle-suffused surface of the story and that its creative skills are thereby invoked. These ideas will be revisited in the closing portion of this analysis.

Concurrently, *Kanon* is loyal to both the local values of the visual novel and Japanese culture generally in its celebration of the materiality of expression and cognate notion that all practical activities can be thought of as "art." As in other anime here examined, it is through the discourses of food and cooking that this proposition is most vividly conveyed. The preparation and sharing of meals is central to *Kanon's* diegesis and visual symbolism and works as an excellent means of bringing characters together and consolidating their interpersonal bonds. Moreover, each of the heroines is seen to cherish specific culinary items that soon rise to the status of character markers: the aforementioned *taiyaki* (a sweet bream-shaped filled pastry) in Ayu's case, vanilla ice-cream in Shiori's, *nikuman* (meat buns) in Makoto's, home-made strawberry jam in Nayuki's and *gyudon* (beef bowl) as well as other indigenous recipes in Mai's. In each instance, the respect for their favorite snacks or dishes exhibited by the female personae situates those objects as akin to *objets d'art*. The artistic essence of Japanese gastronomy is beautifully brought out by Sayuri's homemade *bento* (lunch boxes). Featuring all of the indigenous staples — rice, seafood, vegetables and pickles — as well as regional ingredients and items that reflect the season, these attest to the fascination with the visual in their choice of colors, use of elegant patterns and delicately balanced presentation, standing out as artworks within the mundane context of the school lunchtime break. The aesthetic sensitivity to the visual qualities of culinary materials characteristic of Japanese tradition is also evinced by Ayu's gleeful response to the jars of homemade jams populating Akiko's bountiful pantry. The girl is especially enthused by the hues of the products on display, and her reaction is therefore comparable to Yumiko's comments regarding the venerable rolls of fabric she has inherited from her mother in *Touka Gettan*.

The characters' responses to their favorite food items bring to mind the Japanese concept of "*umami*" — strictly speaking, a distinctive gustatory sensation irreducible to any of the four principal tastes (bitter, sweet, sour and salty) but commonly referred to as something of a sixth sense activated by ingredients capable of stimulating the sensorium in deeply affecting, even overwhelming ways. (The word is indeed held to echo the term for "great wave" — i.e., "*tsunami*.") Moreover, the importance accorded by *Kanon* to the varied sensory perceptions accompanying the characters' encounters with their preferred snacks and dishes brings to mind a more generalized tendency, traditionally exhibited by the indigenous approach to meals as situations ideally enlisting all of the senses. In Japanese cuisine, it is the aesthetic appreciation of the whole material and psychological context of a meal, down to details such as the specific sizes, shapes, materials, textures and colors of the various vessels employed, or the attractive disposition of items with a care for textural, formal and chromatic harmonies and contrasts, that engenders pleasure over and above quantity or costliness. (For example, to evoke a sense of formal balance while also honoring the principle of asymmetry pivotal to Buddhist thought, food items with sharp angles are placed on round vessels and circular items on square or rectangular ones.) Seasonally inspired garnishes are likewise valued, with cherry blossoms floating on clear soup or carrots shaped like maple leaves lyrically marking the advent of Spring or Autumn. All of these values are ardently upheld by numerous anime here examined, with *Touka Gettan, Fate/stay Night* and *Da Capo* in the front ranks.

*Kanon* could therefore be regarded as a true paean to two of the main tenets traditionally treasured by Japanese art and aesthetic theory highlighted in this study's opening chapter: namely, the celebration of the material dimension of all art objects and practices, resulting in a methodical exposure of the interrelationship between human activities and artifacts, and the unmatched sensitivity to the peculiarities of their media evinced by Japanese artists and craftsmen over the ages. Underpinning both of those principles is a further aesthetic criterion, underscored by Joan Stanley-Baker in her comprehensive evaluation of Japanese art, according to which feelings of harmony, calm and equilibrium are paradoxically achieved by the deliberate promotion of a sense of discordance. Thus, the overall impression of peace communicated by many Japanese works ultimately emanates not from a taming of diversity and conflict but rather from a focus on "nuances of emotion" evocative of "tension" through the handling of "texture, color, form and space" and capable of expressing balance through "asymmetrical" distributions of all of those elements (Stanley-Baker, p. 10). Concurrently, "the human qualities of imperfection" are intimately "built into the artwork" (p. 11), and even unpolished aspects of the creative act which much Western art seeks to efface in the name of mimetic perfection are honestly revealed — e.g., "rough edges, fingerprints or chisel marks" (p. 13). In *Kanon*, these ideas are reflected in the assiduous emphasis laid by the visuals on tangible objects, the practical activities entailed in their production, the characters' inseparability from such objects and activities, and the distinctive properties of the materials involved. The reverential attitude to materials evinced by these attitudes and responses to art is redolent of a world view influenced by Shinto beliefs. In this tradition, a spiritual essence is believed to dwell in all natural phenomena and forms, as well as in man-made objects grounded in an appreciation of natural substances. Therefore, all corporeal entities in principle deserve the designation "*kami,*" spiritual forces. Most importantly, objects can be seen as the abode of powerful energies that continually foster genesis and development and hence shun any notion of perfection as a permanent (or indeed truly attainable) condition.

All life forms are in a process of constant becoming. Objects which, like culinary products, are by definition ephemeral and thus caught up in a cycle of ongoing transformation epitomize that process.

While paying homage to indigenous tradition with reference to the language of food, *Kanon* also evokes aspects of Japan's artistic heritage in its handling of backgrounds, where echoes of ancient representational trends can be detected. Above all, the natural settings are often redolent of the visual style and thematic repertoire associated with Heian landscape painting, *yamato-e*. (This term designates specifically Japanese painting as opposed to imported painting, which goes by the name of *kara-e*.) Flourishing in the eleventh and twelfth centuries, this art lay the foundations for several aesthetic ideals destined to become hallmarks of native art over time, and still noticeable in contemporary sensibilities. Where *Kanon* is concerned, the Heian legacy oozes through in the guise of environmental elements pervaded by a distinctively Japanese preference for imagery that is at once shimmering and subdued, sublime and unpretentious. In the process, a predilection for abstract modalities of expression makes itself felt.

Like *yamato-e*, *Kanon*'s artwork is replete with places and seasonal effects imbued with poetic connotations that invariably strike a balance between magnificence and intimacy. Therefore, mighty trees and humble shrubs are repeatedly juxtaposed, as are forbidding skies and snow-kissed folds, rushing crests and tranquil slopes, racing and overhanging cloud banks, waves of turbulent dynamism and pockets of hush stillness. The layering of forms contributes significantly to this visual mood. Chromatic and textural effects redolent of *yamato-e*'s combined use of ink and gold or silver paste also feature, while the handling of compositional rhythms evokes that art's reliance by turns on minimalist inkwash intended to suggest subtle atmospheric gradations, and long curving lines alluding to emotively expansive spaces. *Yamato-e*'s blend of economy of line, accomplished by means of abbreviated shapes, and palpably unctuous brushwork is concurrently revamped in *Kanon*'s settings. As these effects coalesce, the viewer is drawn into the picture as a physically absent yet kinaesthetically involved participant. We are hence taken on somersault flights requiring us to dive and soar, be plunged into the picture one moment and hurled skyward the next. Especially notable in this respect are the scenes related to Ayu's accident that recurrently punctuate her endless dream, where we are enjoined to contemplate the situation both from the ground, where Ayu lies inert registering her final impressions before the descent into unconsciousness, and from a bird's-eye perspective associated with Yuuichi, kneeling or standing next to her, and past Yuuichi, with the sky framed by the treetops looming over him.

At the same time, both the anime and the visual novel behind it corroborate Stanley-Baker's propositions regarding the essence of Japanese art in their representation not only of intimate domestic contexts but also of the wider urban and natural domains in which they are imprinted. This is demonstrated by their persistent tendency to underscore the vibrant energy and related feeling of emotive tension issuing from the coexistence of disparate shapes within a single scenario. It is not uncommon, for example, for the aura of provincial tranquility exuded by the familiar shops and their comfortably mundane wares to be punctured by undercurrents of dissonance or even agitation. This is paradigmatically borne out by the sequences where Ayu, in flight from an irate *taiyaki* street vendor, slams into Yuuichi and the latter is then attacked by a feral Makoto who claims that she bears him a grudge. Even more striking in this regard is the climactic scene in which the austere stillness of the nighttime forest is ruptured by the sense of unrelenting anxiety animating Ayu and Yuuichi's pursuit of a vital yet unknown goal. In all of these frames, feelings of strain and inharmoniousness are evoked primarily by the artwork's emphasis on subtle affective nuances.

As in the template presented by Stanley-Baker, however, discordant forces still manage to coalesce in studiously designed tableaux capable of conveying an overall impression of structural equilibrium through the interplay of their visual planes. Often, scenes evocative of a feeling of tension depict the tide of unrest preceding an action as more dramatic than the action itself, capitalizing on the value of anticipation and an event's dynamic potentialities as no less significant than the contingent explosion of energy. This preference is embedded in Japanese art and can be traced back to the style of the handscroll paintings ("*emaki-mono*") brought into vogue in the twelfth century by works such as the illustrations for the time-honored courtly romance *The Tale of Genji* created by Lady Murasaki Shikibu. A sense of imperfection is simultaneously communicated by situations wherein each object and each accompanying move implicitly or explicitly call attention to the human actors' foibles and insecurities. Ayu's winged schoolbag epitomizes this idea, being at once stylishly and realistically crafted and empty, devoid of its intended function due to its owner's peculiar condition.

The artbook *Kanon Visual Memories* offers a wealth of architectural, sartorial and decorative details documenting the extraordinary richness of characters and locations alike. In its punctilious documentation of *Kanon*'s architectural fixtures, in particular, the book throws into relief the anime's distinctive take on space. This evinces a focus on a concept theorized by Henry Jenkins — "spatiality" — to designate the architectural stance adopted by proficient game designers in their efforts to construct consistent worlds (Jenkins, p. 3). Spatiality provides a context for the emergence of narratives from particular configurations of the built environment. Spatial design, Jenkins argues, has been a major priority for game creators for a long time and can be traced back to the conception of pre-digital ludic situations such as board games. These tended to focus principally on "the design of spaces, even where they also provided some narrative context. *Monopoly*, for example, may tell a narrative about how fortunes are won and lost ... but ultimately, what we remember is the experience of moving around the board and landing on someone's real estate." Thus, the "narrative experiences" yielded by such games depend to a considerable extent on "the structuring of game space" itself. Moreover, the prioritization of spatial properties could be seen to hark back to "a much older tradition of spatial stories, which have often taken the form of hero's odysseys, quest myths, or travel narratives. The best works of J. R. R. Tolkien, Jules Verne, Homer, L. Frank Baum, or Jack London fall loosely within this tradition" (p. 4). In extending this line of argument from the realm of gaming to that of animation, it could be suggested that the creators of a show that places considerable emphasis on location — as *Kanon* clearly does in accordance with the source game's own preferences — are also engaged in the production of spaces conducive to the emergence of narratives in which space itself is not merely a setting or backdrop but a vital storytelling force in its own right. In this regard, their endeavor facilitates the genesis of what Don Carson describes as "environmental storytelling" — i.e., a set of techniques whereby "The story element is infused into the physical space" and this, accordingly, "does much of the work of conveying the story the designers are trying to tell" (Carson).

Spatiality, as a function of *Kanon*'s narrative, is inseparable from temporality, since space is not a fixed given but rather a permutational ensemble shaped at each step by the particular rhythm, pace and tempo of the action, as well as by the specific time zones occupied by different characters at each stage of its development. For example, the symbolic space accompanying Ayu's oneiric monologues is defined by the rhythm of her meditations as a predominantly static reality matching the sense of stagnation the heroine experiences throughout her recurring dream. By contrast, the spaces associated with her frantic quest are rendered intensely mobile by the very pace of her increasing sense of urgency. In the Mai-based arc, the nature of space alters depending on whether it accommodates the girl's hyperkinetic battles in the present zone or her retrospective explorations of childhood scenes bathed in an atmosphere of semimythical timelessness. In addition, temporality is affected by the ways in which the viewer's experience is structured in terms of his or her part in the story-making venture — that is to say, how strategies designed to foster interactive involvement impact on our grasp of the narrative. Thus, when interactivity pivots on puzzle-solving tasks, the action's tempo might slow down in accordance with our need to ponder the implications of particular twists in the diegesis. Alternately, the tempo might increase at times when we are induced to feel so intimately caught up in the action as to wish to advance as rapidly as possible towards a climax or reorientation. Our perception of space will comparably vary depending on whether we move so deliberately through the anime as to take in every single nook of its map or rather proceed so nimbly as to absorb its cumulative structure but not necessarily its minutiae.

In focusing specifically on the temporal dimension, it must first be recognized that the anime encodes meaning at two main levels and that to each of these corresponds a distinct time scale. At one level, we are asked to focus on the temporal structure of the form in which the anime is represented as a series of episodes. This provides a cinematic continuum that does not mirror the linear order in which the events surrounding Yuuichi and his friends occur but rather moves fluidly between the past and the present. In this respect, reconstructing the actual sequence in which events have taken place rests with our own inventive efforts. At another level, our engagement in the shaping of the story as we interpret its occurrences and act upon them by stringing them together according to largely personal choices makes the anime's temporal structure a markedly performative construct. In this scenario, viewers can choose to prioritize certain narrative ramifications over others, to allow certain quests to remain open and help other quests to reach completion, to adopt certain possible interpretations and marginalize others, as though they were actors working imaginatively on their allocated parts.

Thus, one may choose to prioritize the ramifications pivoting on Makoto's metamorphosis over Mai's fights, allow Ayu's dream to assert itself as an effective miracle-working quest or a forever inconclusive journey, embrace the situation depicted in the finale as satisfyingly reparatory or else view it as merely one possible outcome out of legion alternatives. In the process, spectators must rely consistently on character interpretation and take their understanding of the personae's choices and actions as cues on the basis of which composite dramatic roles may be extrapolated. Therefore, in interpreting the characters, we adopt their moves as the raw materials for the ideation of dramatic roles of our own making. Taken in tandem, spatiality and temporality abet the task of turning the anime's multifarious situations into a narrative form that conforms (however loosely and precariously) to a particular structural pattern. The nature of the specific patterns adopted by different audiences will spring from their personal predilections, motivations and experiences but in all cases, the anime itself can be seen to supply a set of fictive units and a repertoire of possible behaviors that remain amenable to diversified forms of large-scale narrative organization right through to the close of the series.

As it nears its resolution, the story becomes increasingly somber, dispassionately recording the escalation of Yuuichi's mood from unrest through consternation to downright anguish. Baffled by Ayu's abrupt disappearance and cryptic parting worlds, the youth at first struggles to piece together the fractional pointers at his disposal with only one frustrating certainty: the fact that his memory blocks remain intractably solid even in the presence of those minor revelations insofar as he still misses the critical linkages among them, and any conscious awareness of the exact nature of the tragedy that took place at the time of his last visit to the town. This canopy of darkness reaches the culmination of impenetrability with the cinematographically audacious shift of tempo accompanying Yuuichi's epiphany just two installments away from the end (i.e., in the final portion of the twenty-second installment). At this point, the hitherto pensive atmosphere gives way to an almost brutal impression of impetuousness. Even the most saturnine of viewers is unlikely to remain utterly unaffected by such a twist.

However, even as the narrative grows darker and denser, *Kanon*'s visual style never relinquishes its delicately crafted texture and correspondingly refined mood. It is tempting, in this respect, to think of the anime as paperthin — not in the sense that it yields shallow or insubstantial entertainment but in the sense that its graceful, almost ethereal elegance brings to mind the unique beauty of *origami* and the rarefied purity of the hand-crafted paper (*washi*) deployed in its traditional execution. Considering *Kanon*'s aesthetic of refinement, its choice of music — the most aerial of arts — as a structural mainstay could barely be more apposite. This motif is sustained by the employment of musical terms as key components of the show's episode titles — e.g., overture, introit, partita, caprice, serenade, divertimento, fugue, fantasia, berceuse, requiem, intermezzo, waltz, trio, concerto, sonatina, oratorio, nocturne. Most important is the use of Johann Pachelbel's *Canon in D major* as the accompaniment for especially poignant moments, including the exchange between Ayu and Yuuichi in the coffee shop where they shelter in the first episode.

The philosophical relevance of the canon as a musical composition is captured by Sayuri's words in the scene where she sits in the same venue with Yuuichi, and Pachelbel's *Canon* is again playing in the background. [2] The boy, who is aware of having heard the music before but does not know what it is called, asks his companion for enlightenment and Sayuri explains that a canon repeats the same melody a number of times, allowing the beauty of its harmony to emerge little by little. This is a fair description of that type of composition, where a contrapuntal structure is typically used in which a dominant melody (*dux*) leads to one or more imitations of that melody (*followers*) played in a different voice. However, Sayuri's words matter less as an academic account than they do as an existential comment on the experiences and relationships at the heart of the anime itself. Indeed, it is by chronicling the day-to-day unfolding of parallel lives as they develop gradually — and often almost imperceptibly — that *Kanon* provides a dispassionate anatomy of the human struggle towards harmony. Just as each repetition in a canon harks back to the inceptual melody as its substratum, so the characters invariably revisit the past as the stepping-stone to any constructive change. The structural organization of the canon as a piece of music whose overall impact and coherence depend on the cultivation of incremental change through the reiteration of a key motif, and hence on the accumulation of impressions in a coral-reef fashion, finds a parallel in the process of anime production. Just as the repeated melodic elements come together in the climax of the composition, so the visual elements conceived over the process of production come together in the photography/CG stage. As stated in the final segment of the aforecited documentary devoted to KyoAni's technical procedures, in this phase, the "animation data created in the finishing process and the backgrounds created in art design are combined" to produce the complete picture through the deployment of "various camerawork" ("A Close Look at an Anime Production House Part 8").

In inviting its viewers to decipher its underlying mysteries on the basis of elusive clues, *Kanon* compels us to play a game akin to the one played by the original visual novel's users. At the same time, it requires us to pay heed to the storyness of the enterprise, consistently reminding us that in playing the decoding game, we are both receiving and producing a narrative construct, insofar as the decoding never happens in a vacuum but rather in a dense fabric of serpentinely unfurling events. Furthermore, while we as spectators engage interactively with the show's enigmas, the enigmas themselves interact with one another to form a patterned narrative structure. In other words, as game-playing and story-making drives coalesce, so do rhythms of interactivity involving the dialogue between the audience and the anime on the one hand, and the anime's internal dynamics on the other. (Interactivity takes place both *between* viewers and animated scenes and *within* the animated scenes themselves.) In the process, *Kanon* also throws into relief the anime's textual dimension per se and the audience's engagement with the codes and conventions on which that dimension relies as intercomplementary faces of the interpretative venture. In interacting with *Kanon* as though they were playing a puzzle-solving game, yet grappling with the internal interactions of its constituent parts as storytelling events, spectators are at liberty to explore and understand the show's imaginary world as a dynamic textual object amenable to diverse readings. Nowhere, arguably, are interactivity and narrativization more vibrantly yoked together.

If the anime were merely expecting to be consumed in a passive fashion through the reception of what is displayed on the TV screen at any given point, there would be no involvement on the audience's part in the production of the story. By positing its materials as variably interpretable riddles, *Kanon* precludes the option of acquiescent consumption, enjoining us to grasp how those riddles are construed and pursued by its designers. This is not to say that in order to interact meaningfully with the anime we need to possess knowledge of all the techniques deployed in its making. In fact, it is largely by *not* having full access to or a total grasp of that information that we are free to devise ways of interacting with the series of which its creators did not think upon designing it. In this regard, interactivity unencumbered by peripheral data liberates possibilities that the anime merely implies: it turns its world into a galaxy of possible worlds akin to the ones theorized by some groundbreaking contributions to modern physics. This perspective brings to mind a concept invoked by Julian Kücklich in his discussion of computer games, inspired by the writings of the constructivist thinker Ernst von Glasersfeld: "viability." This designates a situation in which a person is able to operate within a space that he or she cannot actually perceive but can nonetheless grasp as a hypothetical map, elaborated through experience. While a real map leaves precious little to the imagination and even less to unpredictability, constructs based on viability engender "nontrivial machines" — i.e., devices or strategies capable of producing "unpredictable results" (Kücklich).

This argument can be extended from computer games to anime like *Kanon* that also work towards the maximization of outcomes beyond incontrovertible prediction, thus intimating that no reality is amenable to objective representation, and anything one might call a world is only ever a process of incessant meaning-production, or semiosis. Considering the textual maneuvers through which viewers are enabled to interact with the anime, it should be noted that there are elements that help viewers recognize and even identify with what they perceive on the screen: for instance, certain forms of visual and verbal language that can be quite straightforwardly pinned down as established conventions of the medium or a category thereof. However, what allows *Kanon* to be perceived as entertaining, and even more importantly suspenseful, is its creators' erection of some resistance to the audience's efforts to solve the show's mysteries. In other words, certain ingredients are brought into the cocktail the purpose of which is precisely to elude instant recognition at face value. These are responsible for making *Kanon* pointedly rewatchable and recall comparable ruses utilized in the making of visual novels to render them replayable. What is fostered, in both cases, is not the audience's ability to unravel the anime at the first attempt but rather a developmental trajectory whereby decoding skills are incrementally expanded with each viewing. In this fashion, we are little by little rewarded by the discovery of fresh territories with which to interact and enabled to regard this discovery as a form of narrative evolution unto itself. Thus, interaction and narrativity become consummately interdependent. At the same time, the anime provides something of a speculative template containing the building blocks which other shows might subsequently adopt or refer to for inspiration, thus advancing a playful process of recreation and innovation. For example, some of the foundational components used by *Kanon* in its articulation of the various characters' psychological journeys (such as the drama of oneiric self-projection or the plight of an austerely inaccessible persona) are adroitly revamped by Ishihara's next series, *Clannad*, with tantalizing variations.

\* \* \*

The *Myself; Yourself* game (2007) dexterously handles several of the thematic preoccupations and stylistic codes characteristic of its format, excelling in the depiction of settings distinguished by a unique visual poetry. The plot pivots on the protagonist's return to his hometown, Sakuranomori, from which he was wrenched away by his parents' business obligations five years earlier, his interactions with his former childhood friends in circumstances that feel genial and uncanny at once, and the narrative ramifications spawned by these encounters. The anime adaptation (TV series; dir. Tetsuaki Matsuda 2007), for its part, tackles the return-to-the-past topos most dispassionately, couching the recuperation of occluded memories as a confrontation of multilayered psychological abrasions. As these are progressively exposed, the viewer is invited with increasing explicitness to participate actively in the narrative-making enterprise. Key to this aspect of the drama is the character of Nanaka Yatsushiro, a girl whose entire personality appears to have radically altered in the aftermath of the fire that killed both of her parents, destroyed her childhood home and, it eventually transpires, was initiated by Mr. Yatsushiro himself, driven insane by the discovery that Nanaka was not his biological daughter but the issue of an adulterous liaison. Once gentle and caring, Nanaka appears to have become unremittingly somber, defensive and uncommunicative in response to the disaster. In gradually charting the events leading to Nanaka's metamorphosis as the anime unfolds, *Myself; Yourself* brings the audience's creative skills into play insofar as it does not dish out clear-cut explanations up front but rather discloses its riddles deliberately and with a galvanizing measure of intelligently interposed red herrings that call for active interpretative involvement. Vital to this process of incremental disclosure is the realization that Nanaka's ordeal has been rendered especially exacting by the absence from her life, throughout those shocking experiences, of her childhood friend Sana Hidaka, the story's protagonist.

Sana's own crippling memories, the exact causes of which are left undisclosed until the show's climax, are nimbly interwoven with Nanaka's. In the boy's case, the disturbance lies with his subjection to ruthless bullying and his resulting suicide attempt, blighting the time spent in Tokyo after leaving Sakuranomori. Like Yuuichi in *Kanon*, in returning to a town he has not visited since childhood Sana inaugurates the recovery and acceptance of repressed memories and hence embraces the possibility of emotional restoration. However, whereas Yuuichi does so unwittingly, at least at first, Sana deliberately returns to the old town in the hope of transcending the state of stultifying inertia in which he has sunk since his self-destructive act. Sana's return to his provincial roots after half a decade spent in Tokyo amidst much psychological turmoil proves salutary not only for the youth himself but also for the childhood friends he left behind as a kid. Initially, convinced that the town has not altered significantly since his departure, the protagonist must incrementally recognize and negotiate the many things that have in fact changed, not merely in the location itself but also — and more disturbingly — in the lives of his old mates. In so doing, Sana is released from the dusky crypt of his personal pain and enjoined to put his troubles to one side in order to help the other characters address, and hopefully resolve, their emotional turbulence. The opportunities for interaction between the individual and the community afforded by this narrative maneuver are numerous and proficiently managed through a multiperspectival approach to the drama.

For both Sana and Nanaka, the arduous march towards catharsis is punctuated by flashbacks, triggered by the sight of either blazing light or blood, which gain the pathos of veritably apocalyptic visions thanks to adventurous cinematography and disorienting chromatic shifts. As the audience progressively pieces these initially baffling images together to establish their collaborative contribution to the diegesis, its inventive capacities are again summoned. While some of the contents delineated above may on the surface sound soap-operatic, the style — both dramatic and pictorial — in which they are presented invests them with unique affective density and enables the show to bypass formula-driven limitations. An especially felicitous touch, working as both a narrative catalyst and a connective thread, is the symbolic encapsulation of Nanaka's predicament in her inability even to touch a violin in the wake of the arson affair, even though up to that point playing the instrument had been her main asset and source of pleasure. Importantly, her farewell gift to Sana prior to the boy's departure from Sakuranomori in childhood was an incomplete composition which she then vowed to finish and play for him when they would meet again. It is not until the very end of the drama, by which time Nanaka has fully regained her memories and reappropriated much of her original personality, that we see her playing the violin in public and executing the old piece, complete at last — a composition appropriately titled "Myself; Yourself." The musical motif binds Nanaka and Sana throughout, as demonstrated by the idea that although the boy is no longer able to play the piano as he used to when younger and has forgotten every single song he ever knew, he still remembers clearly the melody written by Nanaka years earlier.

Secondary personae, consisting primarily of Sana and Nanaka's school friends, also harbor painful recollections. The twins Syusuke and Syuri Wakatsuki, for example, are haunted by memories of their departed mother and of the happy events surrounding her kindly and sparkling presence, rudely obliterated in recent times by their father's remarriage to a lax and predatory woman, as well as by the man's total insensitivity to their needs and preparedness to sacrifice their welfare for his political success and financial gain. Comparably troubled is the character of Asami Hoshino, a seemingly generous and sympathetic girl who in fact is so persecuted by the memory of her rejection by Syuri as to indulge in vindictive sprees of noxious violence and consequence. Some of the most touching reminiscences are associated with the figure of Yuzuki Fujimura, the homeroom teacher of Sana's class. Playful, outspoken and dauntless in the face of the most reactionary scholastic authorities when it comes to advancing her students' rights, Yuzuki lives with the baggage of a lonely childhood in which she was routinely left to fend for herself. Her past experiences have not, however, embittered the young woman but rather urged her to support those in need with the same alacrity with which she was able to sustain herself in childhood. The memory of a little boy — who turns out to have been a younger Sana — she once met in a playground in her high-school days and endeavored to cheer up with a gift of caramel candy economically summarizes Yuzuki's disposition.

The anime's subtle treatment of materials that could easily have yielded trite situations in the hands of a less conscientious studio owes much to its assiduous integration of stylistic and graphic elements typical of the visual novel at its best. Plot depth, carefully modulated character presentation and interaction, and an unflinching devotion to well-balanced structural ramifications are especially noteworthy. It should also be noted, in assessing the show's relationship with the parent ludic format, that the anime offers various instances of self-reflexivity as its characters are periodically seen in the act of playing videogames and, at one point, what is unmistakably a visual novel. Last but not least, *Myself; Yourself* sparkles with engrossing landscapes and townscapes. In the representation of the natural habitat, the series sometimes recalls different facets of traditional Japanese art. On the one hand, the rural scenery in Sakuranomori's immediate vicinity brings to mind fourteenth-century Zen ink painting in its flair for evoking multifarious vegetation

by recourse to minimalistic lyrical strokes. On the other hand, the hypnoti-
cally enrapturing crystal formation hidden deep in a mountain cave which
Sana at one point reveals to Nanaka (as though to seal their bond in the presence of a preternatural witness) resonates with visual echoes of the twelfth-
century style known as *onna-e* (i.e., "feminine painting"). This mode is
characterized by a tendency to communicate intensely private emotions
through subtle compositional devices, traces of which can be detected in the
anime's scene. The integration of a solemn sense of stillness and pulsating
energies is particularly remarkable and accomplished largely by recourse to
the synthesis of thickly applied layers of color with limited gradation and delicately drawn, fluid lines whose grace is augmented by their interspersal with
touches of gold pigment.

The degree of meticulousness courted by the production teams behind
*Myself; Yourself* is borne out by the modeling of many of its backgrounds on
real-world locations. The fictional countryside bordering the Pacific Ocean
in which the bulk of the anime is set, for instance, is closely based on
Wakayama Prefecture (Kansai region) and its distinctive environmental attributes. The devotion to topical accuracy evinced by both the visual novel and
the televisual adaptation is also shared by the light novel centered on the same
basic story, penned by Takumi Nakazawa like the anime's own scenario and
published in serial form in 2007. The natural habitat is also the object of serious thematic treatment, with Syuri's endeavor to save a nature park doomed
to be erased to make room for a grand town hall (a project helmed by her
power-hungry father) resulting in drastic life choices for both the girl herself
and for those around her — and, most acutely, her twin brother Syusuke, with
whom she relates in almost romantic terms.

The principle of tension seen to play an important role in *Kanon* is also
effectively brought into play in this anime, particularly through the depiction of architectural and environmental contrasts between provincial and metropolitan settings. The former are typically characterized by an emphasis on
stylized visual motifs evocative of a mood of contemplative tranquility even
as they harbor the seeds of discord and turmoil beneath their seemingly quiet
façades. The latter foreground sensations of kinetic disquiet punctuated by
flashing shots of a hectic, unreflective, and by implication uncaring and atomized lifestyle. Nowhere is the big city equated to notions of glamour or mon-
umentality. The anime's primary setting, in turn, is rendered most memorable
by its taut and terse lines, diffuse lighting and warm textures: namely, which
have been mainstays of Japanese art and design through the ages. While the
natural scenery exudes a sense of spontaneous exhilaration, the provincial
urban context itself is never totally divorced from a keen appreciation of
nature's beauty as the quality to which all man-made constructs should look

for inspiration. This lesson is not promoted, it must be stressed, for the sake of mimetic accuracy but rather in the understanding that such beauty is ultimately inextricable from life itself.

* * *

In *true tears* (TV series; dir. Junji Nishimura, 2008), the return to the past takes quite a different diegetic guise, as it does not actually entail any geographical transitions or relocations but rather occurs entirely at the introspective level. The past is thus strenuously revisited on the internal stages of the key characters' psyches and their contradictory desires. By extension, the audience is encouraged to engage dialectically with the developmental curves traced by the protagonists' experiences by focusing on their psychological import rather than their kinetic component. The anime shares little with the visual novel of the same title, released in 2006, in terms of either cast or storyline. Nevertheless, it partakes of the parent game's psychological and emotional preoccupations, as well as its interweaving of various personae's individual experiences into a colorful and sensitively orchestrated dramatic tapestry. Moreover, the anime echoes the *true tears* visual novel's utilization of multiple plot lines that are at least potentially open to diverse resolutions, thereby drawing the audience into a tantalizing interactive process. Like several other visual novels, the *true tears* game requires the player to engage with extensive textual passages recording either dialogues or intimate thoughts. The game's storyline is divided into weeks and at the beginning of each week, the player is given the choice to select any three days of it. Depending on the days picked by the player, different events take place.

This ploy helps *true tears* capitalize on two crucial aspects of the visual-novel format. First, it throws into relief the player's centrality as a creative agency largely responsible for the shaping of the narrative, since the course of the story hinges on that agency's decisions and is bound to alter quite radically in their light. Second, it conveys the aleatory essence of the experience since the nature of the events with which players are presented as a result of their choices is fundamentally predicated on sheer chance. To experience all of the available concatenations of events (or at any rate, as many as possible), players will have to experiment with disparate choices. This guarantees the visual novel's high level of replayability. An especially intriguing strategy resides with the game's employment of so-called "tear points." These indicate how each of the heroines associated with specific occurrences is being treated. If the number of points in question exceeds the total of eight, the resolution of that heroine's arc is made inaccessible in the course of that particular play-through. In other words, tear points operate as something of a notation system showing the player how his or her decisions at designated stages in the game are affecting the dramatic viability (or "survival," so to speak) of a specific female character and of the plot stream related to her. The invitation to take the story in widely diverging directions with each successive replay of the game is therefore not merely tempting but also forceful. Relatedly, the butterfly-effect implications of the player's moves, selected weekly schedules and resulting actions at the given junctions can hardly be underestimated. Viewed from this angle, the *true tears* visual novel constitutes a celebration of chaos theory.

In terms of its affective content, the resulting anime yields a broad range of personality types, inner conflicts and attendant efforts to overcome them by confronting the past's onerous bequeathal. Most importantly, in this regard, the show consistently draws attention to its characters' struggle to develop emotional resources that will enable them to become more resilient in the face of adversity, without in so doing degenerating into cold or callous people. At the same time, the anime emphasizes that while it is vital not to lay the blame on others for one's unhappiness, uncritically censuring oneself for everybody else's pain is no less deleterious an ethical stance. Learning how to reconcile the often discordant dictates of the moral mind and the longing heart is hence pivotal to the show's dramatic trajectory. The narrative of *true tears* dwells on several and partly interdependent returns to the past. A major instance of such an undertaking revolves around the male lead, Shinichirou Nakagami, a high-school student and accomplished artist, and relies on two recurrent motifs: the youth's efforts to encapsulate both long-standing and recently formed memories in his drawings and accompanying stories, and his childhood recollections of his fellow student Hiromi Yuasa, an orphan who has moved into Shinichirou's household following her father's demise. Hiromi's own personality, in turn, is haunted by memories of Mrs. Nakagami's revelation that she is actually her own husband's daughter and therefore Shinichirou's half-sister. Although this baleful disclosure is eventually exposed as a lie, or at least, he poisonous fruit of a misunderstanding bred by mindless jealousy, it has a profound impact on Hiromi's psyche that proves conducive to pathologically discordant patterns of behavior. Thus, while at school the girl appears unremittingly vivacious, amiable and confident (largely due to her popularity as a talented athlete), at home she is characteristically brooding and reserved. This conduct is a corollary of her awareness that although she has loved Shinichirou since an early age and senses (rightly) that her feelings are reciprocated, there cannot be any legitimate future for the two of them as a couple.

A further introspective parable is traced by the development of an eccentric and disarmingly frank girl named Noe Isurugi (to whom the protagonist becomes emotionally attached at one stage in the drama and from whom he derives crucial artistic inspiration) and her constant regression to the memory of her grandmother's demise, at which point she claims to have "given away her tears." Noe's inability to cry is obviously the outcome of a realistic mental disturbance, but its dramatization as an almost supernatural occurrence imparts the story with a mythical flavor. Finally, *true tears* portrays the return to the past experienced by Shinichirou's childhood friend Aiko Endou, a slightly older and proverbially feisty girl who feels deeply drawn to the protagonist but agrees to date his mate Miyokichi Nobuse—if anything, in the hope of getting closer to Shinichirou himself. Aiko concisely revisits the past in the form of a flashback recording that rather infelicitous decision.

Anime viewers ill-disposed towards love triangles may automatically assume that *true tears* is not for them. However, were they willing to engage with this series even they would probably find, that it tackles its materials in a radically innovative fashion, thereby circumventing stereotypical generic limitations, despite a handful of concessions to commercialized repertoires. The eschewal of generic stereotypes confirms this proposition. The three heroines' depictions, moreover, escape fossilized typologies in that they do not conform to the letter with the standard models of the impenetrably solemn adolescent, the cute bimbo, the tomboy or the *tsundere*, even though they accommodate elements thereof, and this invests their characterization with a commendable sense of sagacity. The series' stylistic distinctiveness issues primarily from a top-quality screenplay and a markedly deliberate pace. The latter specifically bears witness to the anime's aversion to gratuitous coups de théâtre. This aspect of *true tears* is further consolidated by the avoidance of implausible plot twists, angst-ridden separations or oversentimentalized reunions, hyperbolically jocular interludes and unpredictable climaxes. Inviting us to focus instead on the characters' thoughts and feelings as these unfold over well-structured dialogue and stream-of-consciousness introspection, the show evokes an overall mood of delicate balance, mellowness and quietude even when it engages with distressing or suspenseful situations. Both script and tempo enable *true tears* to delve into is characters' minds with unparalleled depth and deliver convincing personalities even in the representation of secondary actors.

For example, the protagonist's best friend transcends the formulaic approach that blights so many anime characters cast in that role (who often amount to cardboard and luckless Don Juans) thanks to an elaborate psychological makeup. Shinichirou's father, likewise, does not simply come across as the practical guy keen on hiding from domestic conflicts behind the shield of a newspaper (even though he is at times superficially associated with that character type). In fact, he shows himself capable of overcoming his flaws by letting go of his nepotistic tendencies and honestly addressing his family's assorted tensions and dramas. Mrs. Nakagami, for her part, forges a positive bond with Hiromi, and in so doing not only overcomes her own selfish and proprietorial instincts but also helps the girl explore hitherto untapped wells of emotion. What is more, all of the key personae appear to have learned some vital lessons by the time *true tears* reaches its dénouement. The male lead succeeds in facing up to his anxieties and doubts instead of running away from them, when he bravely acknowledges that up until now responsibilities have been forced upon him rather than chosen by him and that the time to make his own decisions has come at last. His choices, moreover, convincingly attest to the boy's maturation. They show that in adopting a certain course of action and cultivating his honest feelings, he does not blind himself to their painful implications. Thus, while his separation from Noe is an inevitable concomitant of Shinichirou's pursuit of his genuine preferences, he can still feel sorrow at the parting and sense that in looking at the girl, his heart still "wavers." (According to Mr. Nakagami, it is the feeling that one's heart is wavering that triggers the only authentic tears.) Hiromi comes to acknowledge her own solipsism and propensity towards jealousy, thereby developing a more flexible disposition. (This is literally confirmed by her hard-won ability to do the box splits after years of diligent stretching.) Aiko gets over Shinichirou and resolves to embark on an honest relationship with Miyokichi. Noe's case is somewhat more problematic since the resolution of her plot strand is left intentionally open to interpretation. For one thing, it is not incontrovertibly clear whether or not she has regained the ability to cry and thus overcome her affective impasse (though a hint at tears does crown the closing frames situated after the ending proper). What seems incontestable, in any case, is that Noe has learned to accept sadness without dogmatically equating it to weakness. As these developmental processes unfold, the inextricability of personal and collective dramas is effectively underscored.

Sophisticated scriptwriting and the adoption of a rhythm that enables the characters to evolve and reveal themselves according to a credible momentum are constantly boosted by high production values. While the artwork itself is ideally suited to the communication of the anime's atmosphere, dynamic sequences — most notably Hiromi's baseball games — are fluidly animated, technically accurate and superbly lit. In addition, 2-D and 3-D elements are seamlessly synthesized. The anime's top-notch cinematography also deserves close attention, especially in the handling of intensely lyrical frames capturing the glittering ocean, the dancing snowflakes, or the seagulls presiding over the coastal setting like guardian deities of sorts. Equally worthy of notice is *true tears*' handling of its architectural and natural sceneries. Among the former, the most impressive are Shinichirou's family residence and the surrounding edifices devoted to physical training, manufacture and commerce. These communicate a distinctive preference for an approach to design governed by clarity and harmony of the kind found in ancient architectural compounds wherein aesthetic principles of meditative tranquility and care for unobtrusive ornamentation are never wholly sacrificed to the pragmatic imperatives of functionality and usefulness. In a sense, this is a corollary of Japanese art's avoidance of stark adversarial contrasts between decoration and function, beauty and practicality, whereby no element is either simply ornamental or simply serviceable. Even more modest locations such as Aiko's family diner or the tiny flat into which Hiromi moves in her emotional journey towards independence are rendered with passionate attention to both overall mood and individual details. Natural settings are most useful in chronicling the principal actors' developing feelings by suggesting subtle parallels between the seasonal cycle and inner states. Thus, the characters' gradual awakening as they progress further and further along their personal pilgrimages is mirrored by the transition from a honeyed autumn through a forbidding winter to the stirring atmosphere of spring.

Among the recurrent motifs found in visual novels and their anime offshoots, particularly prominent throughout *true tears* is that of the creative quest. The picture book the protagonist creates in the course of the story, centered on the chickens Raigomaru and Jibeta, serves as an allegorical fable of Aesopian resonance commenting unobtrusively on both Shinichirou's innermost feelings and his interactions with Hiromi and Noe. Furthermore, this almost dreamlike and magical story-within-the-story incrementally gains autonomous aesthetic power: so much so that at times the style used in Shinichirou's watercolor paintings spills over into the main body of the action, and several shots endowed with special pathos are rendered in an analogous mode. (A comparable ruse is adopted, incidentally, in the most pregnant moments of Osamu Dezaki's films *Air* and *Clannad*.) Tradition, and through it the legacy of a legendary past, is also invoked with the preparations and eventual staging of an annual festival replete with symbolic connotations at the levels of performative, sartorial and culinary conventions of a pointedly indigenous stamp.

\* \* \*

The analogy between the central story and the drama of artistic creation set up by *true tears* is also a key component of *ef—a tale of memories* (TV series; dir. Shin Oonuma, 2007) and *ef—a tale of melodies* (TV series; dir. Shin Oonuma, 2008). But where *true tears* is so delicate and restrained stylistically as to seem to make no concessions to artiness, *ef* sonorously declares its experimentative thrust right from the beginning. Positing the animation itself as integral to the series' narrative content through indefatigable formal play and technical adventurousness, Oonuma intersperses the regular footage with monochrome frames, hand-drawn sketches, character silhouettes wherein portions of the actors' surroundings appear to flow, stylized representations of environmental motifs such as snowflakes or raindrops, artfully edited photographs, and recurrent shots of a sky in virtually perpetual motion enriched by all manner of textures. Solarization, desaturation and color separation are also deployed to great dramatic effect in the more allusive moments and offer a striking contrast with the photorealism of numerous backgrounds and props. Daring cinematography is likewise noteworthy, with unorthodox framing, the insertion of apparently random shots and off-kilter camera angles featuring conspicuously among the show's most distinctive traits. A further stylistic feature of *ef* that deserves attention is the show's intertextual allusion to other anime, including two of the series here discussed in the final chapter: *School Days* and *Clannad*. Where settings are concerned, one of *ef*'s most original features lies with its location in a town, Otowa, said to have been destroyed in the war and rebuilt from scratch only to be razed to the ground once more by an earthquake. Following the second catastrophe, Otowa was rebuilt in an eminently non–Nipponic fashion, and this gives the animation a unique opportunity to experiment with the depiction of a wide range of meticulously detailed urban sceneries of European derivation, with elements of Palladian, Baroque, Gothic and Romanesque styles harmoniously coalescing in an enticing architectural blend. It is by means of its unique technical composition, above all else, that *ef* magnetizes the spectator into intimate involvement with the action's building blocks as the raw materials of a sophisticated narrativizing process. As we shall see, *ef*'s technical daring extends to the second series with undiminished gusto.

The visual novel behind *ef—a tale of memories* and *ef—a tale of melodies* is a two-part package titled *ef—a fairy tale of the two* that effectively comprises two games. The first anime is an adaptation of the whole of the first game (i.e., *ef—the first tale*, 2006) and the first half of the second game (i.e., *ef—the latter tale*, 2008), while the second anime is an adaptation of the second half of the second game. The visual novel's gameplay uses a set of predetermined scenarios containing alternative courses of action and interaction. The player is given the option of taking on the roles of four possible protagonists (two in each tale) and hence relate to different heroines according to the part he or she chooses. As with other visual novels here examined, a significant portion of the player's task consists of engaging with elaborate textual passages, though the computer graphics accompanying each scenario concomitantly provide scope for the aesthetic appreciation of stunning pictorial imagery as a source of pleasure of autonomous standing. Decision points also hold considerable importance insofar as a "wrong" decision on the gamer's part, in the logic of the game, may prematurely lead to a so-called "bad end." When this happens, it is necessary to regress to an earlier stage in the ludic process and make a different, hopefully more favorable choice. The software company responsible for *ef*'s execution, Minori, was eager to engender a visual product akin to a film and therefore utilized strategies not regularly encountered in games of that ilk — e.g., plenty of animated shots taken from disparate angles and off-center images reminiscent of those found in "event" computer graphics, which give the impression of filmed action, rather than customary straight-on images of characters situated in the middle of the screen of the kind one tends to see in less adventurous visual novels. These techniques, in their cinematographical daring, foreshadow the emphatically experimental character of the anime itself.

Like other anime here explored, *ef* proficiently transcends the limitations of the romance genre. Its treatment of the love dimension uncommonly realistic, and touches of comedy and ebullient action elegantly enrich its generic recipe. Thus, technical innovation is fittingly matched by bold attempts at genre-straddling. *Ef* fundamentally consists of two parallel and at first relatively independent arcs held together by a link situated in the past and by the traumatic recollections this enshrines. The twin sisters Kei and Chihiro Shindou have been wrenched apart by a tragic accident, resulting in Chihiro's mnemonic impairment at the age of twelve, and lead separate lives. As their emotions evolve amid tortuous relationships, internal conflicts and societal duties (attesting to the ongoing interplay of individuals and groups), the bond between the two characters is progressively explored and their shared past brought to light by means of alternately harrowing and poetic flashbacks. The girls' connection is consolidated through the character of their common childhood friend Hiro Hirono, now an aspiring manga artist relentlessly rebuked by Kei for skipping classes to pursue his vocation. While the tomboyish but inhibited Kei competes for Hiro's romantic attention with Miyako Miyamura, an exuberant girl who also turns out to harbor lacerating memories, the reclusive and bookwormish Chihiro discovers hitherto unsuspected emotions after meeting the gentle Renji Asou at an abandoned railway station.

Afflicted by a form of amnesia that curtails her memory span to no more than thirteen hours at a stretch, Chihiro has persistently dreamed of writing a novel but has been prevented from fulfilling this desire by her peculiar condition. Bravely confronting the elusive phantoms of Chihiro's psyche, Renji embraces a singular quest: enabling the girl to achieve her goal at any price. This requires considerable persistence on the youth's part, since Chihiro's initial response to the suggestion that they work together on her project is extremely defensive. Even when the girl gives in and even lends Renji the notebook containing her embryonic ideas, her helper's task is made arduous by Chihiro's inevitable propensity to forget who he is from one day to the next — unless, that is, she writes about him in the diary she keeps to retain a hold, albeit tenuous, on the passage of time. As Chihiro and Renji work on the novel and the girl overexerts herself to the point of catatonia, Kei becomes increasingly determined to "erase" Hiro from Miyako's memory and Miyako herself develops a morbid dread of being abandoned by the manga author, which would cause her to relive the trauma of neglect suffered upon her parents' relinquishment of their duty towards her. The climax of the Kei/Hiro/Miyako strand is predominantly realistic, whereas the resolution of the Chihiro/Renji arc is tinged with more symbolic nuances. Its most pathos-laden moments are the sequences in which Chihiro tears out the diary pages hosting information about Renji and disperses them through the air — an emblematic gesture communicating her conviction that her relationship with the boy is doomed. Renji's reaction to this destructive act is no less dramatic, as he alacritously sets out to collect as many fragments of the scattered pages as possible and to return them to their author, as though to heal the imperiled bond and shore up the precarious edifice of Chihiro's memory at the same time. The interweaving of the two arcs is rendered especially original by Oonuma's handling of their emotive tempo in such a way that the two stories are never at the same level. Thus, at any one point in the action, one of the heroines may seem in total control of her lot, while another is tentatively tootling along and the other teeters on the verge of psychological disintegration. This strategy enables the series to maintain its overall momentum and affective density throughout.

Through Chihiro, *ef* articulates one of the most poignant creative quests ever, while concurrently emphasizing the importance of artistic self-expression through Hiro's aspirations. The presentation of Chihiro's budding narrative in the form of almost surreal visions (a strategy also employed by *Clannad* in relation to Nagisa's dramatic ambitions) imparts the anime with a potently oneiric feel. This aspect of the program is fuelled by the introduction of enigmatic side characters (bound to play axial roles in the second *ef* series) endowed with otherworldly stature, whose agency imbues the here-and-now with a timelessly legendary flavor. Himura is one of these figures and his role appears to be that of a rather disillusioned advisor who has experienced an ordeal akin to Renji's in his own lifetime, though a connection with Hiro's experience is also suggested. More enigmatic still is Yuuko, a mystical woman who features in one of the stained-glass windows of the church housing some of the most markedly symbolic sequences and who makes several appearances throughout the story as something of a catalyst, bringing together various actions and their affective import.

In articulating the theme of the creative quest and the related topos of artistic self-expression, *ef* frequently delivers animated exchanges in which various characters put forward their divergent opinions regarding concepts such as aesthetic quality, personal motivation and critical reception. Hiro and his schoolfriend Ryosuke, for example, at one stage argue quite passionately about the extent to which artists should follow solely their vision regardless of audience expectations and mainstream trends, or else endeavor to meet the requirements of their cultures and times. Ryosuke is particularly troubled by the clash between his yearning to make experimental films of an Impressionist ilk and the more orthodox objectives of other members of the Film Club, which ultimately leads to his departure from it. Chihiro and Renji, for their part, engage in a probing conversation regarding the difficulty of evoking narrative moods that adequately match the symbolic and emotive attributes of the characters and are thus capable of eliciting comparably apposite responses from the reader. When Renji notes that Chihiro's protagonist comes across as "cute" in one sequence, the girl is disappointed since her primary goal was to engender a pervasive atmosphere of "unease" and "discomfort." In the Chihiro/Renji arc, the centrality of storytelling and reading as concurrently thematic and structural concerns is firmly established by the camera's supple intercutting of scenes recording the main action with shots narrating Chihiro's novel. The latter are at times literally situated within arty borders redolent of picture frames: this device suitably mirrors the portrayal of Chihiro's protagonist as a painter in her own right while also echoing self-referentially the visual novel's formal deployment of screens within the screen.

*Ef*'s self-reflexive proclivities are supported by the animation's persistent foregrounding of textuality through an emphasis on the materiality of language. This is characteristically borne out by the sequence in which Miyako sends Hiro increasingly agitated messages following his failure to turn up for their date. As the girl's anxiety escalates, fuelled by her dread of disappearing once again from the heart of a loved one in the way she disappeared from her disaffected parents' hearts in childhood, the screen is rapidly filled by lines of text. Evenly and legibly distributed at first, these degenerate into a tangle of crisscrossing and scrambled characters that bear no resemblance to comprehensible sentences and thus replicate the paranoid turmoil afflicting Miyako's psyche. In the scene's climax, the text is methodically blotted out to symbolize the girl's own fear of being expunged from Hiro's memories. Another sequence where the materiality of language is explicitly underscored revolves around Chihiro and her creative apprehension: "The obstacle," the girl candidly admits, "is that I can't finish writing in one day.... I forget memories and details. The story, setting, and even my impression of the characters change." The culmination of Chihiro's revelation is effectively rendered by shots where the background fills with twirling fragments of sentences and even individual typographical items in different fonts, alternately superimposed, assembled and disassembled across the screen. Writing is also used in the scenes showing various aspects of Chihiro's story, with its distinctive protagonist, setting and props, where extensive portions of text scroll over the background, cut across the visuals or flash intermittently through the frames. The visual novel's dedication to the emplacement of textuality as a principal aspect of its graphic makeup is here explicitly echoed.

*Ef*'s characters are some of the most resolutely anti–stereotypical anime personae portrayed in the medium in recent years. Chihiro's convoluted personality deserves special consideration in this respect. While her *raison d'être* is a dream she has harbored since she was twelve, and its realization would plausibly be vital to her self-fulfillment, she cannot help but wonder what might become of her life once the dream has reached its fruition. The girl's approach to this dilemma is dispassionately logical, though her logic is at times flawed. On the one hand, she is stuck with her twelve-year-old self, which would appear to preclude any chances of development. Furthermore, she only knows who she is from one day to the next, insofar as yesterday's Chihiro tells her who she is today through her diary and its disturbingly cold taxonomic entries. In other words, the present self is the product of a narrative created by a past self-more specifically, by a systematic return to the past undertaken by purely textual means. On the other hand, Chihiro subliminally longs for recognition by both herself and others as an autonomous being, deeming this achievement indispensable to future development. Regression and progression are thus posited as intercomplementary facets of the character's broken forays into a submerged life curve. Chihiro's creative quest, in this perspective, encapsulates the girl's latent urge to move on. Writing the novel might be a frightening prospect, yet failure to do so would amount to self-negation. Moreover, compelling analogies between Chihiro and her fictional heroine are insistently proposed. Adopting a rationale that feels almost creepy in its unsentimentally pragmatic, indeed clinical take on the story, Chihiro's novel mirrors the style used in the diary. At the same time, just as Chihiro depends on her diary to preserve a modicum of existential continuity and coherence, so her protagonist, seemingly alone in the world, must learn everything from a library. (Please note the tangential connection with *Yami*.) The fictive girl only encounters humans in the guise of pictures and portraits, some of which she executes herself and with which she is invariably dissatisfied.

While Chihiro is outwardly timid, yet stoical, her twin sister appears confident and plucky but likewise conceals quite a different inner self. Kei is in fact intrinsically insecure and excessively dependent on how others, and principally Hiro, perceive her. Even her confidence ultimately boomerangs and turns out to be her worst enemy. For one thing, Kei has always taken it for granted that her destiny is to be bound to Hiro for life, and it is not until the door literally closes on her that she comes to appreciate the vapidity of her dream and the importance of Hiro's own desires. (Having lived her whole life to please and impress the childhood friend, Kei closely resembles *Shuffle!*'s Kaede.) In the portrayal of Miyako, *ef* again emphasizes the fallaciousness of superficial impressions. The fun-loving and ostensibly independent girl whose frankness occasionally borders on audacity and is quite simply unstoppable as long as things are going her way, retreats into a colorless and silent vault of grief the moment fate refuses to yield to her desires and the specter of emotional rejection raises its dismal head once again. The psychological realism pervading Miyako's depiction arguably makes her *ef*'s most tantalizing persona, even though viewers may favor the more lyrical flavor of the Chihiro-centered arc. The male protagonists are also proficiently portrayed, with Renji coming across as principled yet naive and Hiro as more mature yet indecisive.

From what has been said in the preceding paragraphs, it will not be surprising to see the word "memories" installed at the titular level of the show. If Chihiro longs to abide in someone else's memories and Kei struggles to hold on to memories of her past connection with Hiro, Miyako, for her part, is terrified of vanishing again from the memory bank of a loved one. It could also be argued that the anime's treatment of the mnemonic dimension is symptomatic of a broader preoccupation with temporality at large. This theme is explicitly foregrounded by the Chihiro-based thread, as the girl is literally stuck in time, forced to relive the same thirteen hours over and over. With Kei, time is also intractable due to her tendency to waver between the past's hazy promises and unrealizable future goals, which effectively disables her from living in the present. A poignant flashback to Miyako's past shows that in her case, time stopped when her parents forsook her and color itself evaporated from her life. The sand washing away all traces of human presence from the shore — one of the anime's leitmotifs — epitomizes *ef*'s concern with temporality as the erasure of dynamism and progress when people bow to its dominion rather than attempt, however haphazardly or unsuccessfully, to take it into their stride. All of the characters, ultimately, appear to experience an eerie sense of disconnectedness from the world. This, it should be emphasized, is a topos frequently elaborated by visual novels and anime based upon them. *Ef* stands out, among other things, as an especially well-wrought anatomy of that theme. The lack of connection felt by its characters cannot be dismissed as basic adolescent angst for it actually evinces the magnitude of an existential condition of metaphysical proportions. (What is more, it is presented as a key feature of adults — no less than of the young protagonists particularly in the second series.) It indeed emanates from a radical sense of "not belonging" grounded in the impression that the world as such is unreal. This perception, in turn, issues from the realization that so-called reality offers no plenitude, no lasting or reliable satisfaction since its interplaying facets — practical situations and abstract ideas alike — are fundamentally constructs, not natural givens.

Like the first series, *ef — a tale of melodies* exuberantly proclaims its uniqueness at the technical level, deploying originally all of the animation strategies seen in *memories*, alongside numerous collages combining full-color frames, monochrome cut-outs and textual elements. An important symbolic motif introduced early in the show that offers considerable latitude in the execution of intriguing visual effects is the mask. While this image resonates with traces of indigenous traditions, given its pivotal part in many aspects of Japanese ritual and drama, the specific masks portrayed in *melodies* (both in photorealistic and in stylized modes) explicitly recall Western trends, mainly of Venetian derivation. This is quite consonant with the setting's markedly European feel. Masks do not only serve as visual props amenable to technical experimentation, however. They also function as a key component of one of the show's abiding thematic preoccupations: namely, the tension between reality and illusion. The character of Shuuichi Kuze at one point opines that as people grow older and get used to adopting various roles that may not coincide with their authentic mentalities, masks become incrementally more real than the identities underlying them. The logical and deeply disquieting corollary of this proposition is that masks might eventually conceal not a presence but an absence, not a true self but the void left behind by the self's disappearance into a gallery of fictitious personae. (An imaginative parallel between the world of the series and the essence of RPGs is here obliquely called forth.) The theme is echoed by the show's setting, through which the second series imparts a novel twist to the situation already presented in *memories*. *Melodies* indeed proposes that the city of Otowa actually consists not of one location but rather of two urban conglomerates situated in Japan and Australia, which could be regarded as mirror images of each other — one city being real and the other fake, though they are superficially identical. This idea reflects the visual novel's proverbial passion for multiple perspectives, while also engaging with a philosophical concern that is never too far from Japanese thought and cultural output.

*Melodies* operates as both a prequel and a sequel, portraying events from the early lives of characters seen only in their adult roles in *memories* — i.e., Yuu Himura, Yuuko Amamiya and the aforementioned Kuze — and moments from the lives of Renji, who is still attached to Chihiro, and his mother Sumire situated after the end of the first show's story. These characters are revealed to inhabit the Australian version of Otowa and are currently hosting the sprightly Mizuki Hayama, Sumire's niece, a character redolent of Miyako from the first series. To the same temporal scale as Yuu's and Yuuko's belongs Nagi Hiromo, a character not seen in the first anime, who would appear to be Hiro's sister, though she actually looks like the spitting image of Kei. The relationship between Yuu and Yuuko is accorded special prominence as it transpires that they were both raised in an orphanage, which the girl was able to leave at a relatively young age upon her adoption by the Amamiya family, but which would be Yuu's sole home till adolescence. Having endeavored against the odds to become independent and build a promising future for himself, resulting in his receipt of a prized scholarship and admission to the exclusive Otowa High School, Yuu is hell-bent on burying the past and the haunting memories engraved all over its substance. Most troubling among them is the phantom image of his beloved sister Akane, lost in baleful circumstances, which keeps resurfacing in the youth's nightmares. As is often the case in anime adapted from visual novels, the themes of memory and dreaming are jointly invested with pivotal diegetic significance. When Yuuko suddenly reenters Yuu's life ten years after their separation, he is only too keen on keeping her at arm's length and tersely enjoining her to stay out of his life, since to Yuu the girl epitomizes the very legacy he is resolved to consign to oblivion. Profoundly devoted to her first and enduring love, Yuuko is not easily persuaded, however. In fact, she is determined to help Yuu forget the bad times and "erase" his traumatic recollections. In her resolve, Yuuko recalls Kei from the first series, although Yuuko's intent is benevolent whereas Kei's was bitterly adversarial. Another parallel between the two anime is articulated through the character of Himura, who warns Mizuki about the dangers entailed by her possible emotional involvement with Kuze, in much the same way as he warned Renji about his connection with Chihiro in *memories*.

Analogies such as the ones delineated above bear witness to one of the most salient structural preferences evinced by visual novels and their anime adaptations. As noted, both forms are habitually characterized by a penchant not only for ramifying narrative potentialities but also for overlapping story arcs. The most striking link between *memories* and *melodies* pivots on the character of Yuuko and on the supernatural element central to her role. In the second series, it is disclosed that the Yuuko recurrently seen in *memories* acting as a source of inspiration and encouragement for other key personae at times of uncertainty and fear is an otherworldly presence enabled by a transient miracle to inhabit the Japanese version of Otowa. The "real" Yuuko, in fact, perished in a car accident when she was merely an adolescent — a tragedy that put an end to both her fraught romantic relationship with Yuu and a history of unspeakably harsh abuse at the hands of her foster brother. In articulating this unsavory theme, *melodies* is most effective in its avoidance of crude ethical binaries. Thus, while blaming the Amamiya heir for his ill-treatment of Yuuko, whom he resents for being alive at all while his real sister died in the same earthquake that killed Akane, it also intimates that Yuu is partially responsible for Yuuko's misery due to his rejection of the girl when, as a kid, she longed for him to regard her as a younger sibling in her own right. Other notable links between *memories* and *melodies* consist of scenes set either on the school roof or in the church, intended to mark special moments in the story.

Just as *memories* revolves around two parallel stories, deftly moving from one to the other in the space of single installments, so *melodies* interweaves the Yuu/Yuuko arc with the present-day events pivoting on the relationship between Kuze and Mizuki. In the process, three interrelated temporal zones are brought into play. These encompass the period coinciding with Yuu's and Yuuko's childhood in their shared days at the orphanage; the events set in their high-school days, situated approximately ten years after the earlier period; and the current developments with Kuze and Mizuki at their center, and Renji, Chihiro, Sumire and Himura (among other characters) in secondary roles. These are separated by a gap of a further decade from the high-school times. A moving connection between the Yuu/Yuuko and the Kuze/Mizuki strands serving to strengthen the link between past and present occurrences is provided by the revelation that Mizuki is the teenage version of an orphan child befriended by Yuu and Yuuko, and thus rescued from a state of tragic loneliness, in their time as high-school students. Kuze is also seen briefly to meet the little girl and to tie a side ponytail on her, destined to become one of Mizuki's most memorable physical attributes.

Like *memories*, *melodies* contains several self-referential gestures consonant with the pointedly formalist commitment to the exposure of artifice evinced by the show's animation techniques. The most remarkable examples are the devotion to the art of drawing exhibited by Yuu as a kid — an activity which, though underpinned by tremendous talent, the youth appears to have forsaken by the time he has entered high school; Nagi's exploits as a painter, with nude self-portraiture of questionable propriety in the scholastic context in a perspicuous role; and Kuze's internationally acclaimed caliber as a professional violinist — a skill marred by a rare form of neurosis, deemed terminal, which playing the violin aggravates to paroxysmal extremes. The inextricability of Kuze's entire being from music is underscored by graphic analogies between the workings of his heart and the inner mechanisms of the metronome, rendered in stylized ensembles of cogs and wheels. The device itself is perceived as a living agency by the disturbed musician, to the point that at one stage, he equates it to an actual human being. One of the principal messages regarding creativity promulgated by *melodies*, and voiced explicitly by one of Yuu's mentors (and Yuuko's adoptive brother), is that once you allow yourself to get involved with art, in whatever form, there will be no way out. This is an ominous proposition, unequivocally presenting artistic skill as a curse more than an uplifting vocation.

*Melodies* plays with generic admixtures of the kind often seen in the titles here studied. Although the overall mood is somber, and imbued by turns with a wistful apprehension of unfulfilled yearnings and an atmosphere of foreboding, moments of delicate humor periodically lighten the tone. This is testified, for example, by Yuuko's playful claim that the bullying to which she is routinely subjected at school, which many would find downright distressing, is only a case of "medium-level" persecution, and not therefore, a genuine cause for concern. Even when grave drama does not actually give way to lightheartedness as such, the show's tenor might unexpectedly lift thanks to the instillation of a disarming sense of innocence into the darkest of scenes. A case in point is the sequence where Kuze, determined to put an end to his torment, sets his violin and its case on fire on a moonlit beach, and Mizuki athletically leaps onto the scene out of nowhere to prevent the mishap. The sheer elan and selfless spontaneity exuded by the girl's actions, aptly complemented by the surrounding scenery's palpable dynamism, imparts what could have otherwise degenerated into tragedy with a vestigial glimmer of hope.

On the stylistic and figurative planes, *melodies* is rendered especially memorable by a recurring topos alluded to by its very title: that is, the relationship between narrative and music. More specifically, given its status as an eminently visual narrative, the show makes sustained albeit discreet reference to the connection between the visual arts and music. Music-based images abound throughout, both in the form of realistic representations of Kuze's violin and in the guise of symbolic backgrounds displaying pentagrams with notes floating about the music sheet as though to evoke a feeling of emotional unrest. (These are merely two illustrative instances out of numerous, imaginatively diversified allusions to the Apollonian art.) The link between the visual arts and music is pithily captured by Mizuki when she states that with Kuze's deterioration, his memories are losing their "colors." (These words recall Miyako's assertion in the first series that her world has been drained of color following her parent's desertion.) In consideration of the anime's intensely European setting, it seems legitimate to assess its elaboration of the relationship between the visual arts and music with specific reference to Western perspectives on the concept. It is notable, in this regard, that the pictorial realm overlaps with sculpture and architecture to the extent that both kinds of three-dimensional arts feature pervasively in painting, as both *memories* and *melodies* corroborate in their studious renditions of monuments and edifices. At the same time, painting could also be said to join hands with literature — and most pronouncedly poetry — in its cultivation of lyrical motifs. Again, Oonuma's shows confirm this hypothesis through their assiduous pursuit of poetic imagery at the levels of both graphic symbolism and verbal language.

However, nowhere is the kinship between different art forms more potent than in the connection between the pictorial and the musical sensibilities. In the West, the bond can be traced back to the furthest reaches of art history, with Greek vase painting as an illustrious ancestor and both medieval and Renaissance painting as worthy successors. The church appearing ubiquitously in both *memories* and *melodies* echoes several aspects of the latter traditions. More importantly still, the pictorial domain and music tend to share a common lexicon, as works issuing from both are frequently designated as compositions. Colors, moreover, have notes and harmonies, while sounds can be visually described as warm or cold by analogy with hues. In the West, it was in the nineteenth century that music and painting came to be more closely aligned from a theoretical point of view than had ever been the case before. This historical detail is worthy of notice in the present context due to the obvious preference exhibited by the anime under scrutiny for motifs associated with that period. The proclivity is demonstrated by both the representation of its more traditional settings and the experimental manipulation of its materials in ways that recall avant-garde artistic movements as varied as Symbolism, Impressionism, Lettrism and Art Nouveau. In *melodies*, music's influence is adroitly deployed on several occasions to help the visuals approach the threshold of abstraction. Concurrently, the musical score itself is infused with painterly effects that make it possible for the audience to visualize its import. Therefore, the show comes to the fore as a bold foray into musical pictorialism and pictorial musicality at once.

* * *

Faithful to the gameplay style typically associated with visual novels, the *H2O Footprints in the Sand* game adopts a storyline comprising different scenarios centered on distinct characters and related opportunities for varied interaction. What is most distinctive about the *H2O* visual novel is the utilization of two modes of gameplay predicated on one of the story's axial themes: the male lead's visual impairment. The "Blindness-Effect" mode is shaped by the character's condition whereas the "Normal-Effect" mode removes that element from the gameplay. In the Blindness mode, while the protagonist is able to imagine the appearance of the characters around him, he cannot discern colors. This impacts on the artwork, which is accordingly presented almost entirely in a black-and-white palette, and imbues the action with a wistfully oneiric feel. As the lead's disability is progressively overcome in the course of the game, that graphic strategy is set aside and he is able to perceive realistically the world he inhabits. In the Normal mode, chromatic distortion does not occur at any stage in the drama. What the player might find most tantalizing in interacting with the package as a whole and replaying it several times to sample all its possible plotlines and directions is the fact that it is possible to switch back and forth between the two modes even within a single play-through.

The plotline comprises three blocks. In the first, the characters' initial encounters and introductions are dramatized. Titled "Post Chapter," this serves to establish *H2O*'s diegetic premises and enables the protagonist not only to meet the heroines destined to prove essential to his laborious Bildungsroman but also to begin to discover their distinctive personalities. In the second, the focus is on a separation and a reunion. Proceeding from the assumption that the lead has been away from the game's principal setting for several years and only very recently returned to it, this block, titled "Reunion Chapter," chronicles the boy's fresh encounters with the girls from the past and progressive realization that each of them has somehow changed due to events of which he holds no knowledge or else no recollection. One senses increasingly that many secrets are buried in the past of the location revisited by the protagonist, and that he too has occluded many important facets of his own past. In the third block, "After Game," players make choices dictating with which of the available heroines they will experience the rest of the adventure. Once players have made their selection of the key character meant to accompany them for the remainder of the game, the story incrementally advances towards a pertinent climax.

The first two parts constitute the bulk of the visual novel and emphasize assiduously the thematic centrality of the past and the multifold mysteries embedded therein by being structured as a flashback experienced from the protagonist's perspective and containing approximately fifty smaller flashbacks highlighting aspects of both the boy's and his friends' lives. In each block, the experiences, thoughts and feelings of singular personae are interwoven with societal mores and the tenacious legacy of traditions ingrained in the local community. Concomitantly, present-day occurrences are led back to a hidden (and not seldom ugly) communal inheritance of simultaneously historical and legendary stature. Some visual novels, especially those based on adventure-oriented scenarios, locate the text at the bottom of the screen, leaving the rest of the area open for the game's graphic materials. *H2O* enthrones textuality as a more pivotal function of the gameplay insofar as the text fills the entire screen, placed in a transparent shaded box. It is possible, however, to hide the text to view the images unhindered and hence appreciate in its own right the game's enticing artwork at the levels of nature and architecture alike. Furthermore, although *H2O* is a predominantly serious, at times even harrowing drama, it evinces the visual novel's characteristic passion for generic suppleness by incorporating twinkles of comedy enhanced by CG artwork that portrays the key personae in a superdeformed style.

The anime *H2O Footprints in the Sand* (TV series; dir. Hideki Tachibana, 2007) marginally departs from the parent game's narrative pattern, using a mold more consonant with its own medium's formal codes and more suitable for serial presentation. In a nutshell, it develops from the premise that the sightless protagonist, Takuma Hirose, has decided to return to his hometown, Sawai, to recover from an illness, and that in gradually getting to know the girls at his new school, he has a chance to heal his personal wounds, yet must also confront their society's dark forces. Before he can truly recover, Takuma must be scarred once more by ghastly events that force him to accept reality instead of retreating into fantasy. Although Sawai comes across from practically the very first frame of the series as a lush paradise replete with alternately sublime and bucolic sceneries, this tranquil veneer conceals crimes of tragic proportions. The inaugural hint at Sawai's lurking darkness is offered in the presentation of Hayami Kohinata, a seemingly strong and determined girl who does not hesitate to help Takuma out when he gets lost on his way to school just after his arrival, but instantly proceeds to distance herself from him and soon turns out to have deliberately cut herself off from the rest of the class. Her isolation is pithily encapsulated by Hayami's choice of residence deep in the mountains, in a secluded spot which townspeople are enjoined never to visit. However, not all of Sawai's bleakness is so overtly foregrounded for some of its most disquieting secrets actually underlie characters that initially appear to be perfectly well-adjusted and comfortable with their environment. A case in point is Hinata Kagura, the president of Takuma's class: a scatterbrained but more significantly generous and sunny girl who tersely disregards hierarchy despite her belonging to a highly influential family within a rigidly stratified community. Hinata treats Takuma in a concurrently amicable and respectful fashion from the start, without her conduct seeming in the least forced or etiquette-driven.

Notwithstanding blatant differences in their characterization, Hayami and Hinata are revealed to be linked by a deplorable chapter in Sawai's submerged history, the disclosure of which will eventually play a key diegetic role. Flashbacks gradually show that the two girls were once close friends but Hinata's grandfather, the head of Sawai's most prestigious dynasty, objected to this relationship due to Hayami's lowly status, and with the help of several villagers engineered the destruction of her parental home by fire. While putting an end to the friendship, this nefarious action also resulted in Hayami's ostracization as a pariah. This is borne out by her constant and unrestrained bullying by various classmates and her relegation to the remote spot mentioned earlier, where she lives alone in a ramshackle home between two old buses. Hayami's own family turns out to have abused their power in the old days, which confirms that beneath the surface of rural tranquility evinced by Sawai course noxious waves of prepotence and hatred. Takuma restores Hayami and Hinata's friendship, but the burden of ancient feuds survives as a threat to the entire community's welfare. At the time of the summer festival, this ominous baggage fully resurges in an outburst of unmotivated resentment, leading the villagers to burn Hayami's makeshift residence. Hinata's predicament is no less agonizing. It indeed transpires that her real name is Hotaru, and that following her elder sister Hinata's demise the Kagura family decided to pretend that Hotaru had died instead. The grotesquely arrogant reason behind this identity swap was that Hinata was deemed a paragon of virtue and charm, whereas Hotaru was looked down on as a timid underachiever, and a family as powerful as the Kaguras could not possibly countenance the thought of divulging to the villagers that the survivor was the weaker sister.

The magnitude of Hotaru's ordeal is emphasized by her grandfather's merciless behavior, which is at first limited to verbal reprimands but degenerates into physical brutality as the girl refuses to comply with his mendacious self-aggrandizing schemes, The old man clearly has no regard for his heir's emotional welfare, his sole concern being the establishment of a link with the prestigious Hirose house, Takuma's own lineage — for the benefit of his clan's future. Hotaru, despite her notoriety as a gauche and mousy second-rater, actually exhibits admirable resilience in her efforts to comply with her ancestor's wishes, even though this causes her great distress. Takuma, whose sensitivity develops exponentially from one day to the next as he attempts to tackle Sawai's inveterate prejudices and enmities, seems to be the only character capable of seeing Hotaru's conduct for what it truly is: that is to say, a bravely but painfully enacted charade. In this respect, the anime could be said to play with a key element of the source medium in a self-reflexive fashion, insofar as role-playing is clearly no less vital to the visual novel as a form than it is to Hotaru's actions. The girl's brave decision to declare her true identity in public in defiance of the despotic elder's orders provides some of the most memorable moments of elegantly orchestrated drama.

If Hayami and Hotaru/Hinata stand out as multifaceted personalities, no less notable is Otoha, arguably the most enigmatic of the young females with whom Takuma interacts. Unwaveringly positive and distinguished by a knack of appearing unexpectedly in all sorts of places, Otoha describes herself as "the spirit of the sound of time" and seems to be visible only to the protagonist — which is ironic, given the boy's condition — while the other characters are oblivious to her very existence. For Takuma, Otoha plays the role of a spiritual guide redolent of the magical creatures accompanying the protagonists of many narratives in the dream-vision tradition going back to Classical times and the Middle Ages, and could be seen to emanate from his own troubled psyche. *H2O* offers one of the most sensational instances of the return-to-the-past topos in its climactic episode, where Takuma is compelled by Hayami to recall that his mother committed suicide, and is told by Hotaru's grandfather that the Kohinata family is to be blamed for the tragedy — something which the boy's own uncle reluctantly confirms. In light of these disclosures, Takuma notices that his vision is blurring again and loses the ability to see altogether after beating Hayami unconscious to give vent to his frustration. While the protagonist's blindness symbolically captures his repressive drives, as a result of which he is unable to face up to his memories and embark on the path towards genuine self-understanding, it also leads to his conviction that he was never able to see and that everything he ever experienced was therefore chimerical. At one point, he even opines that the entire village and its population might merely consist of an "illusion." The trauma is so potent as to cause Takuma to regress to an infantile state and start believing that Hayami is actually his mother. Paradoxically, it is precisely in the midst of his psychological disturbance that Takuma is able to remember at last that his real mother did not actually kill herself but perished in an attempt to save a life. The discovery is triggered by Hayami's own death as she crosses the railroad tracks to aid a child in danger.

In a dénouement that some viewers will find heart-warming and others simply preposterous, we see Takuma in Sawai at an older age, in full possession of both his vision and his mature mentality, building a windmill. Following an apparition of Otoha, who seems younger than ever before and cryptically alludes to having had to convince the "Spirit Council," a fully grown Hayami is seen walking up the hill as though she had come back to life. This deliberately ambiguous ending remains open to interpretation. The more cynical (or simply more down-to-earth) viewers will feasibly maintain that Hayami is an apparition akin to Otoha, concocted by Takuma's still delusionary brain. The more romantic spectators and those who do not feel uneasy about the supernatural — which is, in any case, less neatly separated from reality in Japanese tradition than it is in the West — will probably choose to believe that Hayami has actually returned. It is worth noting that while Otoha appears at the end in a childlike form, suggestive of the character's timeless standing, Hayami features as an adult, which could be taken as evidence for her actual reinsertion in the here-and-now. This nebulousness is complemented by an additional grey area in *H2O*'s diegesis: that is, the unresolved question of whether Takuma has been blind throughout up to his climactic awakening to the truth concerning his mother's demise or whether he did at one point regain his vision (perhaps courtesy of Otoha) only to lose it again in the face of the shocking discoveries outlined above. One possible interpretation is that Takuma was never able to see but was at one stage so keen on seeing that he was able to deceive himself into believing that he could. This was a time when the boy wished to open himself up to the world and other people, and thus accept life for what it was. Takuma loses his sight again when he clams up in the aftermath of the traumatic revelation about the Kohinata family's responsibility for his mother's death. As Otoha puts it, Takuma's "eyes can open when he thinks through life, and becomes ready to accept everything." However, "everything is sealed along with the darkness when he resists." It is principally through its undecidables that *H2O* harnesses the spectator's creative energies to the production of a coherent albeit intentionally ambivalent narrative construct.

Heir to the source game's keenness on flashbacks, the anime deploys that same strategy quite tenaciously. Its treatment of retrospective visions eloquently consolidates the proposition, endemic to anime scholarship, that the effectiveness of such scenes depends vitally on the concatenation of apposite timing, diegetic relevance and symbolic imagery. Takuma's mnemonic odyssey is punctuated by the flashback of the railway crossing associated with his mother's death couched as an oneiric recollection Hayami also experiences periodic visions, most prominently in the form of a childhood memory of Hotaru attempting to cheer her up with a candy intended to flood her mouth — and hence her soul — with happiness. An especially felicitous deployment of the mnemonic component is the scene in which Hayami revisits the site of her parental home, now amounting to no more than an assortment of charred wood, and picks up a fragment of crockery. As the girl beholds this paltry vestige of a once prosperous household, recollections accrue around it, mushrooming first into an image of a whole plate carrying Hayami's favorite dish, sweetened omelette, then into a picture of the building around it, its furniture and myriad accessories, and in a climactic position, into a vision of the Kohinata family at their dinner. The effectiveness each these visual memories accumulate in the course of mere instants is proficiently complemented by the camera's drastic displacement of the pleasing illusion and uncompromising return to reality. The theme of memory is also beautifully articulated in the sequence from the last episode where Hayami walks around Sawai at night before leaving for Tokyo with Takuma and experiences flashbacks to various moments in the story in which she retains her normal appearance while other personae feature as phantasmatic presences, issuing a golden aura expressive of the sense of warmth Hayami associates with their recollection.

The anime is also loyal to the visual novel's penchant for infusing the here-and-now with legendary motifs, as shown by the scenes in which the protagonist is told that an "evil monster" known to have terrorized the village in days gone by lives on the other side of the town's suspension bridge and that the location is therefore considered taboo by all sensible people. The tale, absurd as it may sound, is not totally fictitious. In fact, it constitutes a mythological distortion of a harsh social reality, since the person residing in the proscribed area, Hayami, represents the last descendant of a powerful family indeed notorious for its ruthless conduct. The recurrent use of the theme of creative quests in visual novels and anime based upon them is again corroborated by *H2O*. This production engages with the topos in three forms. Two of these revolve around Hayami and specifically her artistic skills as the creator of windmill toys of numerous shapes (an ability she decides to share with Takuma) and of meticulously finished *yukata* (lightweight cotton kimonos) for the annual town festival. A further expression of the theme is associated with Hotaru, whose only manifest talent as a child was the ability to draw engaging visual narratives. Forced by her tyrannical grandfather to forsake her art (deemed by the patriarch a menial pursuit) Hotaru revisits the last work she produced prior to her assumption of Hinata's identity once she has courageously exposed the lie and declared her true name. Titled "Tale of the Spirit of the Sounds of Time," the story provides a dramatization of the Otoha-based plot strand *in nuce*, positing the Spirit in question and a character dubbed the "Promised One"—which is also the title given Takuma by Otoha—as the agents capable of helping the village people "settle their differences." Like *Myself: Yourself*, *H2O* conveys the tension between the countryside and the city as loci of discordant effects. However, in *H2O*, even the transition to Tokyo reveals a passion for an overall atmosphere of old-fashioned mellowness congruous with the mood yielded by the rural sequences. It thus reinforces the feeling of *mono no aware* (a compassionate grasp of the evanescence of life and beauty) already established by the preceding country-based action. In both kinds of setting, the melancholy awareness of ephemerality is thus enthroned as a leading motif and gracefully deployed to convey the formidable affective energies and the waves of psychological turbulence raging beneath even the calmest of surfaces.

In their treatment of the return-to-the-past theme, a refined sensitivity to the narrative potentialities of space generally and urban space in particular. In this respect, they undertake what Kevin A. Lynch has described as "the deliberate manipulation of the world for sensuous ends" (Lynch, p. 116). Both the game and the animation designers behind the selected titles deal with the ways in which people use the spaces they construct and the sorts of scenes they stage therein with a perseverant focus on the elements that render them narratively memorable and hence affectively significant. In so doing, they intentionally refrain from predetermining entirely the functions and meanings of the locations they produce, implicitly subscribing to Lynch's contention that "a landscape whose every rock tells a story may make difficult the creation of fresh stories" (p. 6). They therefore embrace an aesthetic that imparts city space with what the eminent urban planner terms "poetic and symbolic" potential, establishing "a sense of place" that "enhances every human activity that occurs there, and encourages the deposit of a memory trace" (p. 119). The mnemonic component highlighted by Lynch is also, as we have seen, of cardinal importance to the shows here studied. The allusive, rather than conclusive, settings on offer amplify our sense of interaction with the game or show and thus explicitly invite us to contribute to its story-making thrust. The narrative itself may be arrayed on the basis of the characters' movements through the spaces they inhabit. Alternately, it may emerge from the memories embedded in those spaces. In both instances, the spaces offered by the anime and the visual novels at their roots emplace the animation or the game designers at one level and the viewers or players at another, as interactors with spaces loaded with storytelling potential, and thus directly invoke their narrativizing skills, according them the role — to cite Jenkins's incisive expression — of "narrative architects' (Jenkins).

# 4

## Epic Exploits

> But how many kinds of sentence are there...? There are countless
> kinds: countless different kinds of use of what we call "symbols,"
> "words," "sentences." And this multiplicity is not something fixed, given
> once for all; but new types of language, new language-games, as we may
> say, come into existence, and others become obsolete and get forgotten....
> The rules of language games are not unchangeable laws. There is a
> continuous evolution not only in how many language games there are,
> but evolution, too, as to the kind of language games there are. Here the
> term "language-game" is meant to bring into prominence the fact that
> the speaking of language is part of an activity, or of a form of life.
> — Ludwig Wittgenstein

> Role-playing games are theoretical in a non-traditional but thrilling
> way. Players are both actors and audience for one another, and the
> events they portray have the immediacy of personal experience.
> — Janet Murray

As seen in Chapter 3, visual novels earnestly encourage players to give
vent to their creativity in the production of the game as an interactive narrative. It is here proposed that they concurrently endeavor to draw players
into their universes in an eminently immersive fashion. The sheer tangibility
and lushness of their settings, allied to intriguing character dynamics, serve
to lure us into the game's virtual reality with magnetic intensity and an almost
physical sense of participation. Whereas involvement can simply amount to
highly concentrated attention, immersion is so seemingly corporeal an experience as to affect a person's entire perceptual apparatus and thus verge on a
feeling of non-mediation — i.e., the sensation that one has actually entered
the world created by the computer instead of just using a computer. The
immersive process engages both the mind and the body as complementary
agencies. Resolutely eschewing Cartesian dualism with its stark separation of

the mental and physical domains as realities governed by different laws, the process of immersion invoked by the works under scrutiny posits those realities as mutually sustaining at all times. In this respect, it brings to mind Maurice Merleau-Ponty's proposition that the human subject is always situated in a physical environment, and becomes aware of itself through its body's interaction with that environment rather than through a purely mental exercise. Four interrelated ideas central to Merleau-Ponty's "phenomenology of perception" are especially relevant to the present context. Firstly, perception requires action since, in perceiving the world, we do not simply receive its stimuli in a passive fashion but actually shape it through "a communication or a communion" (Merleau-Ponty, p. 320). Secondly, perception is always embodied because it depends on our corporeal reality and on the totality of our senses. Thirdly, perception leads to the formulation of interpretations about the world that are defined by prior experience "in the form of a horizon" (i.e., certain perceptual habits) enabling us to impart a contingent experience with "significance" (p. 22). Fourthly, perception utilizes external tools that tend to become assimilated to the body as parts of its own reality.

The ludic and cinematic productions here studied closely reflect these concepts. They corroborate the hypothesis that perception requires action by involving us as creative agents in the production of meaning. In so doing, they also demonstrate that perception is always embodied insofar as the ways in which we immerse ourselves into a game or show depend on how we position ourselves physically in relation to it, and how we deploy the whole of our sensorium in the process. Indeed, the visuals' tactile qualities, the myriad atmospheric effects evoked by the backgrounds in tandem with the acoustic effects unleashed by the musical scores, and the olfactory and gustatory impressions conveyed by the representation of everyday objects and materials clearly show that sight is by no means the sole vehicle at work. Synesthesia further enriches the perceptual experience in numerous instances. The chosen works simultaneously suggest that certain sets of possible responses, incrementally built up through experience, help us formulate particular interpretations as we play or watch. The greater our familiarity with a specific genre, format or style, the wider the repertoire of decoding strategies available to us. Finally, the devices through which we communicate with the work, such as the technological interface, are so integral to our patterns of perception and interpretation as to become akin to organs integrated within our very bodies. Our association with particular technological devices impacts crucially on our communion with the contents of a game or an anime. The medium here becomes akin to a material — that is to say, something that can be manipulated and molded into something else, such as a dramatic stage, a receptacle for stories or a matrix for the genesis of psychological explorations. Given the formal, dynamic and graphic qualities of the works here studied, a grasp of the medium's contribution to the expression of such qualities is of paramount importance. It is not especially useful, on this point, to concentrate on the representational peculiarities of a specific game or show, since this approach would only yield contingent insights into isolated cases. In fact, it seems far more fruitful to adopt the stance promulgated by Rudolf Arnheim in his study of media-related properties, where emphasis is laid on the concepts of shape, form, balance, space, color and movement (Arnheim). Such categories clearly go beyond the contingencies of a singular product insofar as they draw attention to universal design criteria.

Thus, they invite a shift of focus towards *abstraction*—a tendency that has pervaded Japanese art for time immemorial—since abstraction characteristically aims to expose realities that are not explicitly available in the world's external manifestations. In indigenous art, the urge for abstraction is embedded in long-lasting cultural and philosophical values. This is attested to by Shinto's preference for clarity and simplicity of expression, as well as by the emphasis on intuitive directness and clear-cut design habitually evinced by Zen-inspired black ink painting, where the world's intricacies are conveyed by a few minimalist strokes. Calligraphy has also evolved over time into an expressive form of abstract drawing, while the terse functionalism ingrained in traditional architecture and interior design overtly incarnates a germane predilection for compositional rhythms of an abstract ilk. Most crucially, where the dynamics of immersion are concerned, the kind of abstraction promoted by traditional Japanese arts and crafts requires the viewer to enter the work as a creative party, and thus fulfill a role comparable to that of the artist or artisan. The viewer is expected to harbor a commodious disposition towards the object, embrace it generously, and never shrink from the interpretative effort it demands. Relatedly, in communing with the object to formulate an interpretation of it, the viewer must also be always open to the possibility of fresh associations of ideas issuing form the object itself. In this regard, a work endowed with (at least partially) abstract qualities is worth just as much as what the viewer is able or willing to put into it.

Through their emphasis on the structural and chromatic aspects of the image as autonomous values rather than mere accessories, the anime bring to mind the Russian artist Wassily Kandinsky's views on abstraction. For Kandinsky, music is the ultimate art form insofar as it is under no obligation to use tangible objects as its referents. All of the shows here examined appear inspired by an aesthetic longing to emulate music in their search for rhythms, principles of composition and chromatic ploys that can impel the spectator into an immersive experience quite independently of the material circumstances in which they are inscribed. Thus, while we are asked to appreciate the intellectual and emotive import of specific situations (often through a focus on a frankly slice-of-life modality), those are never unequivocally prioritized over the formal quest per se. Furthermore, there are numerous occasions when they deliver visuals that are very much figural in the sense that they show recognizable and convincingly rendered people and environments, yet cannot be classified as naturalistic in the sense that they seek to imitate external forms accurately or mimetically. The most striking illustrations of this proclivity are the sequences — of which there are several in the anime here studied — that endeavor to capture oneiric visions and flashbacks. In addition, there are many scenes where the affective or kinetic impact of an action is presented in highly stylized ways, rather than in a documentary or reportorial vein, by recourse to pure color and form. At the same time, the tendency towards abstractism manifests itself blatantly in scenes where the animation's technical aspects are foregrounded as protagonists in their own right. Kandinsky's ideas are also pertinent to the present context in virtue of their celebration of the specificity of materials in a manner that echoes directly a staple of Japanese aesthetics referred to in both Chapter 1 and Chapter 3. "The artist must not forget," Kandinsky maintains, "that each of his materials conceals within itself the way in which it should be used, and it is this application that the artist must discover" (Kandinsky, p. 154). Abstractism will be returned to in the closing part of this chapter.

As Marie-Laure Ryan argues, in order to grasp the concept of immersion adequately in the context of digital culture, it is important to assess it in relation to other forms of interactivity. These include: "Internal/External" interactivity, where the player either "projects himself as a member of the fictional world" or "situates himself outside the virtual world" as its controlling force; "Exploratory/Ontological" interactivity, where "the user is free to move around the database, but this activity does not make history nor does it alter the plot" (exploratory modality) or else is allowed to perform "decisions" that "send the history of the virtual world on different forking paths" (ontological modality) (Ryan, p. 6). Although the visual novel is eager to immerse the player in its world, achieving this objective mainly by enlisting his or her interpretative powers to the solution of multilayered riddles, it simultaneously invokes the other types of interactivity described by Ryan. Indeed, it fulfills the requirements of the internal typology by encouraging players to place themselves within imaginary domains, and those of the external typology by enabling them to affect those worlds' contingent histories through their actions. Concomitantly, it keeps players in a purely exploratory role as long as it requires them just to engage with lengthy portions of text, yet encourages an ontological stance at crucial decision points where the course of diverse arcs can be altered.

In appraising the concept of immersion, it is important to acknowledge that while the feeling of being sucked into the world of the game is a very personal sensation, it also constitutes a collective phenomenon to the extent that it implicitly brings together an unquantifiable number of players individually engaging with the same ludic construct in diverse situations. Thus, even though players pursue their activities separately, the experience of immersion somehow binds them in a communal web. Since such players are not actually in competition with one another, the ludic mode is not of the kind described by the illustrious game theorist Anatol Rapoport as the "zero-sum" game, where the interests of different players are irreconcilable. In fact, it closely resembles the "non-zero-sum" game, where the interests of different players at least partly coincide (Rapoport). It is also noteworthy, as Craig A. Lindley has emphasized, that prior to "the advent of computer games," the "study of gameplay" had "historically been the study of competitive systems" involving "little or no story context." As computer games developed, and their association not only with gameplay criteria but also with narrative issues gradually emerged, the principle of "competition" could no longer be unequivocally elected as the sole focus of attention (Lindley, p. 1). In terms of game theory, moreover, the visual novel is especially close to the game category designated by Roger Caillois as "alea," or game of chance, due to its association with the concept of randomness, as discussed in Chapter 1 with reference to chaos theory. At the same time, its incorporation of proliferating narrative branches of potentially disorienting intensity recalls the "ilinx," or game inducing vertigo (Caillois).

According to Nicholas Yee, when players choose to value the sense of commonality engendered by their implicit association with a group of (unknown) fellow players, they enter a ludic category ruled by the principle of "relationship." The factor distinguishing this play modality from other forms of gaming is the players' wish to establish meaningful connections with other players and even feel that in learning about the game world, they might simultaneously learn something useful about interpersonal dynamics in real life. For Yee, the relationship-driven mode differs substantially from "immersion" as such, where the objective is to become so fully enmeshed in the fictive construct as to identify wholeheartedly with its characters, insofar as it encourages players not only to try out alternate parts but also to imagine background histories for them (Yee). On that point, it could be said to emulate the task typically undertaken by performers trained in Method Acting. According to Mike Pohjola, the modalities theorized by Yee create scope for further speculation about three possible attitudes towards narrative within a game. The concept of passive reception posits the audience as the mere recipient of a preordained story, whereas active performance enables the player to enact a character role within a story. With "immersion" proper, the distinction between player and character is supposedly elided and the two agencies merge in a composite persona (Pohjola). The visual novel participates in all three typologies insofar as passive reception gains priority in the reading phase, whereas active performance takes over through character enactment, and immersion becomes dominant when role-playing is so intimately and pervasively experienced as to acquire the quality of physical impersonation. It should also be noted, in looking at immersion, that in absorbing players into their fictive worlds, these games do not, however, blind us to the markedly constructed character of the ludic domain. In fact, they consistently call attention to their inbuilt artificiality by laying bare the devices deployed in their production, mirroring a resolutely antimimetic ethos consonant with Japanese art and aesthetic theory. In anime adapted from visual novels, audiences are likewise alerted to the medium's constructedness. In the process, they are drawn into both private and collective quests and asked to contemplate a variety of ethical issues that prompt them to wonder how they themselves might tackle those and other analogous real-life challenges.

The exploits dramatized in the productions tackled in this chapter genuinely deserve their designation as epic enterprises insofar as the quests their characters seek to accomplish and the knotty riddles they thereby confront call for a steadfast dedication of heroic proportions — even though, time and again, the characters might be driven by murky urges that threaten to taint the nobility of their goals. In *Tsukihime, Lunar Legend*, the pivotal quest engages its protagonists in an epic struggle against demonic forces that seem capable of eroding the concept of humanness itself by tampering with the natural order in feasibly irreversible ways. Interwoven with this exploit of global magnitude is an intensely personal search for self-understanding predicated on the onerous reappropriation of a suppressed psychic and dynastic legacy. *Utawarerumono* also intertwines an adventure of planetary dimensions straddling the remote past, the present and a postapocalyptic future with an individual pilgrimage to the restoration of abeyant knowledge and its harnessing to the construction of an alternate and ideally fairer world. Both *Tsukihime* and *Utawarerumono* bring into play a number of motifs drawn from established mythological systems of overtly epic resonance: vampire lore, in one case, animistic Japanese traditions in the other. *Fate/stay Night* likewise derives many of its narrative ingredients, terminology and character types from a well-known corpus of legends associated with the Arthurian epos. In articulating its own, highly original, take on the myth of the Holy Grail as a quintessentially quest-driven component of that Western heritage, the anime simultaneously dramatizes the impact of duties enshrined in the ancient past on the mundane lives of present-day people, as the pull of epic grandeur takes over their ordinary identities and societal roles. *When Cicadas Cry* arguably offers the most complex variation on the topos of the epic exploit here examined since none of its characters is unproblematically presented as heroic. Yet, in endeavoring to unravel the many enigmas clustered around the cult of an ominous deity, this anime proclaims more sonorously than any of the other aforementioned titles the broadly cultural and political relevance of its adventure to real-life vicissitudes. Indeed, the mythological component is persistently brought into collusion with the imperative to expose a web of corruption and iniquity, and in so doing, challenge the authority of fate itself.

*   *   *

*Tsukihime, Lunar Legend* and *Utawarerumono* offer two germane variations on the topos of the epic exploit centered on the concept of reincarnation, while conclusively employing temporal dislocation as their key diegetic ploy. *Tsukihime* is set in the present but harks back to a half-forgotten folkloric heritage. *Utawarerumono*, conversely, comes across as a tale steeped in a mythological past redolent of the ancient civilization of the Ainu, Japan's indigenous people, yet turns out to be a sci-fi drama staged in a postapocalyptic Earth's distant future. This strategy enables both anime to yield a vibrant generic mix and a correspondingly varied tone, ranging from an utterly unpretentious slice-of-life atmosphere to the heroical grandeur of full-fledged epos. At the same time, the collusion of disparate time zones and related generic formulae gives leeway for an unconventional synthesis of the earthly and the supernatural conducive to a variety of interpretations, intersecting yarns and narrative perspectives. The visual novel's distinctive style is thus explicitly mirrored by both shows.

The *Tsukihime* game (2000) follows Shiki Tohno as a second-year high-school student who returns to his family estate after an eight-year absence. The decision to reinstate the youth as a legitimate member of the Tohno household results from his sister Akiha's ascent to the role of the family's new head. The prim girl's resolve to assert her authority initially places Shiki in the position of something of an inmate within the mansion, but little by little Akiha's icy surface melts to reveal an affectionate and troubled mentality. The anime deftly fleshes out Akiha's contorted personality, attesting to the immense potential for sophisticated character portrayal—rooted in a sustained narrativizing effort—evinced by anime adapted from visual novels. The conflict between Akiha's ascetic behavior and her delight in Shiki's companionship is most notable. In the source game, Shiki slowly unearths his buried past while also becoming entangled in a chain of exploits carrying momentous repercussions. Adopting the visual novel's characteristic gameplay, the storyline presents the player with choices of variable magnitude.

While decisions to do with the protagonist's perceptions of and relationships with other personae tend to impact radically on the direction of the game, more marginal moves lead to correspondingly minor adjustments to the ludic flow. Each of the two available routes — namely, the "Near-Side Route" and the "Far-Side Route" — prioritizes a different set of heroines with whom the player may interact.

In the anime *Tsukihime, Lunar Legend* (TV series; dir. Katsushi Sakurabi, 2003), the legendary dimension is supported by an elaborate terminology, a grasp of which will feasibly assist the viewer in his or her experience of the narrative. The figure of the "Vampire" is pivotal and comprises two categories of creatures: "True Ancestors" (a.k.a. "Primordials"), namely, pure-blood vampires that do not physically require blood in order to survive, yet yearn for the substance and must channel most of their powers into suppressing the predatory drive; and "Dead Apostles" (a.k.a. "Proselytes"), vampires that were once human and need to acquire blood on a regular basis to prevent their weaker DNA from deteriorating. A True Ancestor that surrenders to the blood-drinking urge and eventually goes insane is dubbed a "Demon Lord." The "Dead" are mindless bloodsucking drones under the aegis of the Dead Apostles. A Vampire's ability to alter reality and even summon alternate locations goes by the name of "Marble Phantasm." Within *Tsukihime*'s logic, "magic" and "sorcery" often coexist, yet carry substantially different connotations, since the former can be related to tangible albeit illogical causes such as necromantic practices, whereas the latter transcends empirical reality altogether. A "Psychic" is a human being endowed with preternatural abilities without the assistance of non-human blood. A "Demon," conversely, is a human who hosts an element of non-human blood and is bound sooner or later to lose her or his sanity and become a lethal agent through a phenomenon known as "Inversion Impulse."

As in the parent game, the protagonist is Shiki Tohno, a youth endowed with a special power dubbed the "Mystic Eyes of Death Perception," which he is held to have acquired as a result of a near-fatal injury sustained at a young age. This enables him to perceive the threads that run through all people and objects, the "death lines," and the "points" where those lines intersect and more ominously enables him to annihilate both living and inanimate entities by cutting through lines or by stabbing related points. This sinister faculty can be kept at bay as long as Shiki wears some special glasses he has received from a mysterious lady. *Tsukihime* encourages immersion mainly by enabling its spectators to perceive the world in which it is set directly through the eyes of its protagonist. Since the character views his surroundings very differently depending on whether or not he is wearing the special glasses, the spectators' own perceptions alter drastically depending on whether they see *Tsukihime*'s reality as an ordinary environment or else a baleful otherworld crisscrossed by an intricate proliferation of esoteric marks. When the latter modality is predominant, the picture's blatantly non-figural orientation suggests a leaning towards abstraction consonant with the theoretical positions outlined in this chapter's opening portion. Shiki's life is relatively normal, though beset by spooky flashbacks and visions, until the day he encounters a woman to whom he feels inexplicably drawn and inadvertently kills her — only to soon discover that his act has not in fact put an end to her life because she is not a human but rather the Vampire princess Arcueid Brunestud. A True Ancestor created for the purpose of exterminating creatures of her ilk that have succumbed to their bloodsucking impulses, Arcueid did not initially need blood, but became attracted to the element when the immortality-seeking priest Roa tricked her into drinking blood concealed within a rose, at which point the villain also rose to the status of one of the mightiest Apostles ever to have walked the Earth.

Before long, Arcueid draws Shiki into her lifelong battle against Roa, a being rendered especially hard to destroy by his infuriating knack of reincarnating ad infinitum. Roa's latest incarnation prior to the current one (revealed in the show's climax) was Ciel, a character who features as one of the protagonist's senior school mates but is actually an employee of the "Burial Agency," a shadow branch of the Vatican staunchly committed to the elimination of heretics and notorious for its unmitigated ruthlessness. Ciel's personal raison d'être is the desire to eliminate Roa in order to atone for the sins she committed while her body was being possessed by the villain. Shiki's embroilment in this epic struggle increasingly forces him to confront not only unpropitious supernatural forces ostensibly incompatible with his ordinary domestic and scholastic milieux, but also a tangle of secrets that have shrouded his own life since childhood and have been consigned to the uttermost depths of amnesia. Simultaneously, a bizarre and multifaceted relationship develops between the youth and Arcueid, turning what might at first have appeared a bond of servitude into mutual respect and affection. As the Tohno family skeletons come crawling out of their cupboard in a series of shocking blows and Shiki begins to piece together the dark shreds of his dormant past, it becomes incrementally obvious that the relationship between the protagonist and the extramundane princess stands little chance of enduring the burden of their respective inheritances.

*Tsukihime's* storyline affords ample room for forays into light-hearted territory, as evinced by episodes that feature classic set pieces typical of romantic and comedic anime. A case in point is the installment where Shiki and his motley crew of friends visit an amusement park and a typical Japanese hot spring (the renowned *onsen*). Moments of domestic warmth, such as the scene in which Shiki's habitually severe sister allows the youth to own a TV set despite her deep dislike of noisy objects and popular culture as a whole, are especially touching. Nevertheless, the show's prevalent tenor is quite tenebrous, as evinced by many of its settings, lighting techniques, chromatic effects and acting style. The anime abounds with formulae derived from Gothic literature, including architectural elements, such as the emphatically Victorian design of the Tohno mansion, and thematic leitmotifs, particularly in the guise of variations on violence based on a more or less morbid fascination with blood. The overall mood is intensely redolent of an Edgar Allan Poe tale or even poem. Refreshingly, though, the vampiric heroine is clad in a perfectly ordinary sweater-and-skirt combination rendered in light hues that departs drastically from the Goth, Neo-Pagan or Mock Medieval vogues often alluded to in the representation of costumes designed for analogous supernatural beauties.

The hub of *Tsukihime's* riddle, exposed in the finale, is itself quintessentially Gothic, consisting as it does of a particularly harrowing case of identity swap (a motif already seen in *H2O Footprints in the Sand* and also, as will be shown, utilized in *When Cicadas Cry*). This is predicated on the idea that the Shiki Tohno we have been following through the main body of the narrative is not actually a Tohno by blood but rather a foster child whose real family name is Nanaya. The true Shiki Tohno, driven mad by a genetic abnormality triggered by experiments undertaken by his family that entailed the absorption of demonic blood, is said to have stabbed the adopted Shiki to death in childhood and to have subsequently been locked up in a cellar by his father to be prevented from indulging in further outbursts of blind violence. Akiha was able to bring the victim back to life by instilling part of her own life into his being. The miracle-oriented aesthetic often embraced by visual novels and their anime adaptations is here evident. Unfortunately, Akiha's generosity eventually extended to her biological brother despite the bestial state into which he had by then descended, and this led her to release the deranged Shiki from his dungeon — which resulted in her father's slaying. In the series' climax, the real Shiki Tohno is presented as Roa's present incarnation. The plot gains an ironic twist at this juncture as we discover that the reason for which Ciel was originally conveyed by her employers to the protagonist's town and school was precisely that the Church deemed Roa and Shiki Tohno to be one and the same person. What they were not aware of, however, was the crucial identity substitution.

Relatedly, the mnemonic dimension is emplaced as axial to *Tsukihime's* diegesis by the disclosure that following the stabbing incident, the male lead lost his memories and accepted the fallacious explanation of his condition proffered by the adults around him as the consequence of a major car crash.

After reinstating him within the Tohno household, Akiha endeavored to protect him from knowledge that might lead to irrevocably crippling traumas. Her plan was carried out with the connivance of the twin maids Hisui, a cold girl equipped with the ability to imbue others with life-sustaining energies, and Kohaku, a cheerful girl innerly tortured by vestiges of a tragic past of exploitation and abuse. Hisui and Kohaku stand out as secondary but outstandingly rounded characters, posited as the complementary sides of a psychological dyad as tormented by the specters of history as the principal personae themselves. Although it is highly doubtful that Akiha does Shiki a favor by perpetuating his ignorance, the girl's strategy allows the anime to engage in a subtly realistic anatomy of psychological unrest. This is thrown into relief by Akiha's shift from a glacial to a kindly attitude, compounded with a schizoid oscillation between a perception of the protagonist as more real a sibling than the treacherous Shiki/Roa, on the one hand, and an attraction to the lead suffused with romantic affects that strike their roots in infancy on the other.

* * *

The *Utawarerumono* game (released for different platforms in 2002 and 2006) fuses elements typically found in visual novels with features of the strategy RPG. Heavily reliant on a linear story, it does not offer any significant choices conducive to alternate outcomes. In fact, the bulk of the game is quite straightforwardly played out as a sequential narrative, although strategy RPG battles take place at certain crucial junctures. Their layout is relatively undemanding (though the DVD-ROM version of the game, unlike its CD-ROM counterpart, does encompass variable difficulty levels) and hence simply requires the player to move, attack or take no action. Strategy is here clearly posited as a priority over design. With each battle, points can be won that enable the player to gain levels. The package does not, however, allow for what videogaming fans normally describe as "leveling up." In other words, the player cannot replay particular battles multiple times in order to gain further levels before confronting the next fight.

The *Utawarerumono* anime (TV series; dir. Tomoki Kobayashi, 2006) is essentially a war saga centered on a mysterious man whom a village girl named Eluluu finds in a forest, seriously injured, garbed in a mask he appears powerless to remove and, most importantly, utterly oblivious to his origins. Having recovered thanks to Eluluu's grandmother's unique healing skills and adopting the name of the girl's deceased father, Hakuoro, as his own, the hero takes it upon himself to unite the villagers in a bloody insurgence against the tyrant who rules over the region, then rises to the status of emperor of a newly formed extensive country and devotes his life to the preservation and prosperity of the land — which inevitably leads to an unending chain of grue-some fights involving warriors from numerous tribes and cultures. As shown, Roa's knack for reincarnating repeatedly supplies *Tsukihime* not only with a convenient structural mainstay but also with a connective thread capable of bringing together all of the key characters even though their personal paths, destinies and concomitant exploits might at first seem separate or even mutu-ally irreconcilable. In *Utawarerumono*, in turn, the topos of reincarnation impacts directly on the anime's protagonist and ultimately explains his arcane and literally larger-than-life stature.

The series' backstory, disclosed by means of sporadic flashbacks increas-ingly interspersed with the present-day action as the show nears its culmina-tion, is of vital significance to an adequate grasp of its hero's nature and the exact scope and purpose of his veritably epic quest. Significantly, the hero-ical element, is captured by the title's literal meaning — namely, "the one being sung" — whereby the ancient art of verbal storytelling specifically designed to celebrate the deeds of great warriors and rulers (*chanson de geste*) is explicitly evoked. Hence, the backstory deserves some attention at this stage. This pro-poses that in our current age, an archaeologist chances upon a fossil shaped like a deformed beast that embodies the forgotten deity "Witsuarunemitea." The archaeologist is killed by a scientist who deems the discovery far too dan-gerous for the times, and as he dies, his blood comes into contact with the fossil, enabling Witsuarunemitea to awaken. The god infuses the dying man with new life and adopts him as its new receptacle. Having been frozen for a long time, and thus gaining the nickname "Iceman," the archaeologist even-tually reemerges many years into the future, still attached to Witsuarune-mitea in the guise of a mask, in a subterranean research base where he is being routinely investigated as an ancient human sample while the world above has turned into a postapocalyptic wasteland.

Seeking to enlist the Iceman's DNA to the production of synthetic humans in an effort to repopulate the planet, the facility's scientists engage in countless experiments, but only a few specimens survive successfully. Among them is the beautiful Mikoto. Having learned that the researchers intend to seal him once more in cryogenic sleep for the purpose of later inspec-tion, the Iceman flees the base with Mikoto, who eventually bears his child. When the fugitives are captured, Mikoto is dissected as the first artificial human to have given birth and thus a uniquely valuable object of study. As the Iceman is about to be refrozen, the man's fury and despair are so potent as to resuscitate Witsuarunemitea. The deity itself, driven purely by blind rage, splits into two entities, one of which yearns for destruction and one of which longs instead only to be annihilated. While the postapocalyptic Earth gradually regains a population, new countries are formed and fresh power struggles develop, Witsuarunemitea's warring sides continue to vie for supremacy until the day a massive earthquake, unleashed by their martial vigor, grievously disrupts the planet once more. In the wake of this calamity, the half of Witsuarunemitea seeking to be destroyed is found by Eluluu in the forest in the shape of *Utawarerumono*'s hero. The dark drive at the heart of the godly substance whence Hakuoro emanates courses through his character for the duration of the saga, affording room for a searching and nuanced psychological portrayal. A wrenching sense of loss defines the protagonist's personality far more memorably than the paraphernalia of military leadership with which he is incrementally associated as the epic unfolds.

The events dramatized in the series are set in the aftermath of the chain of baleful occurrences delineated above. It is not until the penultimate installment that Hakuoro conclusively remembers the circumstances in which he was first appraised of his status as a test subject on the verge of being frozen and was able to escape the underground base with Mikoto (who is physically identical to Eluluu, incidentally). In the same episode, the hero also recalls his true name and his association with a mysterious divinity, at which point (quite appropriately) he morphs into a formidable monster representative of one of Witsuarunemitea's warring halves. The final installment builds on this dramatic transformation, devoting a substantial portion of its action to the ultimate fight between the god's two facets. In the course of this titanic confrontation, where the two sides concede that worldwide misfortune has been triggered by their insatiable pride, an intensely affecting flashback revisits Hakuoro's past in some detail, chronicling his romantic relationship with Mikoto, the lovers' capture, the young woman's dissection and the hero's own descent into insanity. While Hakuoro manages to contain the destructive half, this victory comes at the inevitable price of his departure from the world he has come to love and respect, and most painfully from his beloved Eluluu — who will always go on loving him as a "man" despite his supernatural status, and hence will always be waiting for his return.

The anime's cast is exceptionally large and an attempt to outline it comprehensively in the present context would be more likely to obfuscate matters than to elucidate truly pivotal elements in the diegesis. What is here worth emphasizing, however, is the immense range of opportunities for crisscrossing tales and plural points of view the anime's extensive character gallery affords at each turn. At the same time, *Utawarerumono*'s extensive personnel affords precious occasions for a multifaceted elaboration of the relationship between individuals and communities. These are consistently presented as inextricably interwoven in both momentous military exploits and prosaic domestic affairs. In the latter context, the theme of the creative quest also makes an important appearance: Eluluu's identity as both a singular person and a member of her tribal society is indissociable from the genuinely artistic flair with which she handles medicinal herbs and ointments, thus perpetuating a time-honored legacy she has inherited from her grandmother Tsukuru, after whom Hakuoro's new empire comes to be named.

All of the key motifs recurrently found in visual novels and anime based upon that ludic format feature prominently in *Utawarerumono* even though, as noted, this series does not constitute a straightforward adaptation so much as a mediatic hybrid. Alongside the two elements discussed above, oneiric and visionary experiences also play an important role, especially in the progressive disclosure of the protagonist's mystifying background. Also crucial is the cognate theme of amnesia, as noted in the opening part of the discussion. Additionally, supernatural forces are persistently invoked by *Utawarerumono*'s mythical component, particularly in the dramatization of the hero's relationship with the ancient god. The show's depiction of its almost invariably opulent and chromatically evocative settings also deserves attention. Built spaces are lovingly depicted throughout, regardless of whether they capture a lowly rural hut or a sumptuous urban palace. Realism here coalesces with abstract (rather than figural) presentation in order to evoke the affective significance of particular locations. This strategy bears witness to an underlying tendency towards abstractism as the style most suited to the visible communication of essential emotions. Where the rendition of the natural environment is concerned, *Utawarerumono* excels at the presentation of luxuriant and uncontaminated forests. It is indeed quite unsettling to find out, at the end, that these locations do not pertain to a semi-mythical past but rather to a dystopian future wherein they have slowly come back to life following centuries of inhospitable barrenness. Analogously disorienting is the discovery that despite his preternatural appearance and power, Hakuoro is the only authentic human character out of the entire prismatic cast. The surrounding personae are evidently humanoid, rather than unproblematically human, insofar as they are endowed with all manner of furry ears, tails, wings and other outlandish attributes. While the folkloric atmosphere pervading the narrative makes it tempting to explain those features as corollaries of the characters' fictive status, the story reveals that their composite constitution actually results from their genesis in complex scientific experiments undertaken to create a substitute for Earth's extinct humanity. Other bizarre creatures such as the lizard-like beasts employed in the capacity of horses, the "Woptar," consolidate the mythical feel.

In assessing *Utawarerumono*'s distinctive landscape, one can hardly fail to notice the show's heavy reliance on digital technology in the rendition of its mammoth battles. In this respect, the anime pays homage to the visual novel's penchant for CGI intended to enhance certain scenes' dramatic import, while also evoking the cast-of-thousand aesthetic, facilitated by the use of increasingly sophisticated synthespians, in the domain of live-action cinema. Whereas at times the computer-generated effects come across as even more fluid and elegant than the regular animation itself, at others they feel blatantly artificial and formulaic: most notably, in the sequences that deploy scores of nameless and fairly nondescript massed troops in the background with a named and individualized character acting as the jewel in the crown in the foreground. The anime concurrently provides a tantalizing generic mix, whereby the preponderance of martial formulae and conventions does not preclude the parallel elaboration of a sensitively orchestrated romance. Even the most somber installments in which the doom-and-gloom atmosphere of the classic war saga might initially appear to dominate unchallenged the anime's entire stage will at some point allow room for emotive moments emphasizing unobtrusively Hakuoro's and Eluluu's evolving feelings and long- ings. The extent to which *Utawarerumono* might or might not be deemed effective in its promotion of the ethos of immersion will depend on intensely personal aesthetic preferences. For the show to draw the viewer intimately into the action, a passion for combat-heavy spectacle abetted by state-of-the-art digital tools is a *sine qua non*. If such a predilection indeed obtains, then *Utawarerumono* could undoubtedly be said to offer no less immersive an expe- rience than the most advanced arcade game or even VR simulation.

*   *   *

The *Fate/stay Night* franchise started life in 2004 with a visual novel marking the studio Type-Moon's commercial debut following a period of merely hobbyist activity. This had culminated with the self-published game *Tsukihime*, with which *Fate/stay Night* shares a commitment to well-defined character designs and a compellingly spooky atmosphere. The game encom- passes three branching storylines: *Fate*, *Unlimited Blade Works* and *Heaven's Feel*. The three potential yarns diverge at crucial decision points and their res- olutions vary according to player interaction. The *Fate* scenario prioritizes the character of Saber, whereas *Unlimited Blade Works* pivots on Rin and Archer, and *Heaven's Feel* focuses on Sakura. The anime consists of a commixture of those alternate scenarios, with a distinctive preference for the events drama- tized in the *Fate* arc. A sequel titled *Fate/hollow ataraxia*, often regarded as a side-story rather than a real narrative development, was released in 2005. This game features new characters alongside returning personae, including the protagonist Shirou. A fighting game also based on the franchise, *Fate/ Unlimited Codes*, was launched in 2008.

The TV series *Fate/stay Night* (dir. Yuji Yamaguchi, 2006) proceeds from the premise that seven mighty magicians named "Masters" periodically embark in epic confrontations with the objective of obtaining the "Holy Grail"—a ritual object deemed capable of satisfying any conceivable wish. In their exploits, Masters are aided by reincarnations of legendary souls known as "Servants," or "Epic Spirits," all of whom vaunt highly refined supernatural skills and distinctive secret weapons dubbed "Noble Phantasms." The wars are held to have taken place over the past two centuries, normally every six decades. However, the current conflict seems to have begun prematurely since the most recent Holy Grail War only came to an end ten years prior to the present adventure. Masters and Servants are locked together in an inevitable partnership, for Servants alone are entitled, as intrinsically spiritual entities, to retrieve the precious vessel, which only materializes in its proper form when one single Servant remains on the battlefield.

Masters control Servants by means of three "Command Seals" engraved on their bodies as stigmata by the will of the Grail itself. When the power of one of these emblems is invoked, the Master is able to issue an order to a Servant, which the latter has no choice but to obey even if it runs counter to his or her personal desires. Should the Master do so, however, he or she will lose one precious Seal. Additionally, a Seal may be activated to enable a Servant to carry out a particularly momentous exploit. When all three Seals are used up, Servants are at liberty to disobey their Masters and even turn against them. Alternately, if a Master were to perish, a Servant could elect a new Master. In the case of a Servant's demise, a Master has the option of picking an alternative (masterless) Servant or else may seek the protection of the Holy Grail War's impartial supervisor, typically an emissary of the Roman Catholic Church. Given that Servants alone can obtain the coveted prize, defeating Masters is not, necessary, strictly speaking, in order to win the tournament. Nevertheless, insofar as Servants are proverbially hard to defeat, killing the Masters responsible for preserving the Servants' presence as viable combatants is deemed by many contestants a worthwhile pursuit unto itself. It is also noteworthy, in this respect that since the Holy Grail is considered capable of granting the wish of its retriever, a Servant might choose to seek fulfillment for his or her own personal yearning rather than passively comply with his or her Master's goal. In the course of the particular conflict dramatized in *Fate/stay Night*, the following Master/Servant partnerships obtain:

Shirou Emiya: "Saber"/Arturia Pendragon
Rin Tohsaka: "Archer"
Kirei Kotomine: "Lancer"/Cuchulainn and "Gilgamesh"
Illyasviel von Einzbern: "Berserker"/Hercules
Shinji Matou: "Rider"/Medusa
Souichirou Kuzuki: "Caster"/Medea
"Caster": "Assassin"/Kojirou Sasaki

The protagonist, Shirou Emiya, is a fledgling mage whose wizardly potential has not yet developed past an ability to sense intuitively the underlying structure and design of all manner of objects. In truth, Shirou is so talentless a practitioner as to lack even the most elementary skills, such as controlling the elements. At one point, his classmate Rin Tohsaka, a proficient Master herself, unceremoniously describes the protagonist as only "technically a magus," and in fact an "unbelievably inept" specimen of that ilk. The main action encompasses merely a two-week stretch in the life of its protagonist, having economically depicted his background with the opening installment's pre-credit sequence. This shows that ten years prior to the present narrative, Shirou was caught in a fire that annihilated a large part of his city and its inhabitants, including the boy's own family, and was rescued as he lay dying in the smoldering debris by a man who would thereafter adopt him as his son and sole heir: the skillful mage Kiritsugu Emiya. Having died without realizing his ideal — namely, to act as a "Champion of Justice" for the powerless and the vulnerable — Kiritsugu has bestowed his dream on his foster son. When the series begins, one clearly senses that Shirou feels deeply frustrated by his lack of powers that could plausibly benefit others, finding scarce solace in his ability to fix domestic appliances and reinforce all manner of inanimate objects thanks to a knack of mentally "tracing" their interior circuitry. Before long, however, he is unwittingly flung into the very heart of the current Holy Grail War as a key contender — even though he has never thus far been aware of the existence of any such thing, let alone the likes of Masters and Servants. Shirou's troubles begin when he inadvertently witnesses a duel involving the Servants Archer and Lancer and is hastily executed by the latter, who is eager to safeguard the war's secrecy at any price. Shirou is resuscitated by Rin with the aid of a powerful heirloom but Lancer does not concede defeat and hounds the boy to kill him again — and more conclusively this time. Just as Lancer is about to inflict the fatal blow, Shirou unknowingly summons the Servant named Saber — a loyal and powerful warrior attired in an alabaster armour — and is saved by her.

An important development occurs when Rin realizes that Shirou is magically illiterate, so to speak, and resolves to introduce him to the magician currently responsible for overseeing the Holy Grail War, Kirei Kotomine, who also happens to be her legal guardian much to the girl's chagrin. Kirei discloses some crucial information regarding the recurrent tournament and Shirou's prospective part therein. Firstly, he reveals that supervisors are meant to prevent Masters from being so driven by their greed as to start butchering one another blindly. The Holy Grail itself is said to choose the seven Masters and to determine the summoning of their relative Servants, which intimates that humans have virtually no control over the situation and therefore could not, put an and to the cycle of wars even if they wished to do so. Relatedly, once a person has become a Master, he or she cannot simply walk away from the appointed task. In fact, the only way of putting an end to the conflict is obtaining the ultimate prize — an entity which, it is also stated at this stage, has the power to enable its winners to reinvent their past and hence rid themselves of its burdens. It concurrently transpires that Servants might suck the souls of harmless humans as a means of enhancing their preternatural powers. At the time of the previous Holy Grail War, Kirei avers, the prize was touched by an unworthy man, as a result of which the disaster witnessed by Shirou in his childhood ensued and the conflict then came to an inconclusive end. This confirms the hypothesis that the Holy Grail has a will of its own, which implies that even if Masters were to try to end a war, they would be powerless to do so if the prized relic refused to abet them. (The saga's climax will show that Kirei himself was responsible for triggering the fire through his reckless pursuit of the Holy Grail, while Shirou's adoptive father, Saber's Master at the time, endeavored to stop him from attaining his goal and indeed managed to destroy the prize.) Shirou is at first unwilling to join the fray but eventually accepts his involvement in the hope of preventing the occurrence of another cataclysm analogous to the one seen ten years earlier. His chance of truly ascending to the ranks of a "Champion of Justice" might have come at last.

Rin remains cooperative in the episode where Shirou and Saber are attacked by Illyasviel von Einzbern (a.k.a. Illya), a young Teutonic aristocrat endowed with an angelic mien and unmatched wizardly abilities, who has journeyed to Japan specifically to take part in the Holy Grail War, along with her Servant Berserker. In the course of this fight, it is up to Shirou to rescue Saber from what could easily amount to a death blow, thus incurring serious injuries in turn. Rin chooses to assist him in his recovery but does not forget that she and Shirou are supposed to be enemies — a reality of which she forthrightly reminds the protagonist the following day by attacking him unexpectedly at school. The fight is brought to an end by the appearance onto the scene of yet another baleful Servant, Rider. In order to pinpoint the entity's master, Rin and Shirou decide to establish a temporary truce.

Shirou initially endeavors to prevent his tutor and self-appointed guardian Taiga Fujimura and his schoolfriend Sakura Matou from discovering that an otherworldly lady has installed herself as a member of his household — a spacious samurai compound executed with punctilious attention to architectural detail, which the protagonist has inherited from his late adoptive father. Eventually, however, Shirou chooses to introduce Saber to his earthly acquaintances in the conviction that, regardless of her epic status, she is also a human being deserving civilized treatment and not an inanimate tool. Saber, for her part, is annoyed by the realization that she cannot assume the incorporeal form that would be both more convenient and more suitable for a Servant of her stature insofar as Shirou's powers, being as yet inadequately developed, do not supply the energy she needs to absorb so as to accomplish that goal. Nevertheless, Saber invariably employs a deferential register whenever she addresses her "boss." To begin with, she only does so in accordance with an old-fashioned regard for hierarchy ingrained in her historical and legendary origins and not without a lingering dose of resentment. This affective tension expresses itself in two guises. On the one hand, even though Saber takes her obligation towards Shirou very earnestly, she is quick to lose her temper when he adopts a protective attitude towards her, thereby treating her as though she were an ordinary, defenseless girl. This is evinced by Saber's reaction when Shirou blocks Berserker's onslaught by acting, she asserts, in a fashion ill-suited to a proper Master. On the other hand, while she is characteristically courteous, Saber adamantly rebukes attitudes on Shirou's part that she deems coterminous with foolhardiness and naivety. Therefore, although Master and the Servant putatively strive towards a shared aim, they occasionally find themselves at loggerheads. It is not until the anime is well under way that Saber begins to sense that she is assisting a Master she can be genuinely proud of and not a clumsy novice. Indeed, Shirou eventually appears to possess magical powers far greater than those of many of his colleagues in both the current Holy Grail War and previous contests of its ilk.

Following Shirou and Rin's discovery amidst a profusion of enrapturing occult symbolism that Rider's Master is Sakura's elder brother Shinji, a narcissistic and pompous student who comes from a family of powerful sorcerers but has inherited no magical abilities whatsoever, *Fate/stay Night* enters its first sustained spate of explicitly martial scenes. These unleash a plethora of poignant complications, marked by Saber's nocturnal duel with the Servant Assassin in the spellbinding setting of the monumental flight of stairs leading to the Ryuudou Temple, on which she embarks against Shirou's wishes; the tragicomic training sessions undertaken in Shirou's *dojo*, where his epic associate endeavors to prepare the youth for battle with only scarce success; Shirou's capture in a potentially lethal trap generated by Rider; and Saber's first visible deployment in the fight against Rider of her Noble Phantasm, the legendary Excalibur, through a performative flourish of unparalleled intensity and elegance. In the aftermath of that fight, the relationship between Shirou and Saber reaches fresh levels of affective intimacy as they become progressively able to share dreams. Each of them thereby learns aspects of the other's past. The fascination with both the oneiric realm and the theme of memory typically evinced by visual novels and their anime adaptations is here reflected by a twin focus on dreams and recollections as germane threads of a single mesh. A subsequent onslaught of ebullient dynamism comes with the sequences where Saber, Rin and Archer go looking for Shirou after Illya has captured and imprisoned him in the deceptively fairytalish castle where she resides, with the intention of making him her Servant. The dynamic acme of this segment of the anime indubitably lies with the sequence highlighting Archer's deployment of a volley of stylishly implacable combat techniques and subsequent defeat at the hands of Berserker amidst flashes of brutal beauty. The sheer visual power and narrative starkness exuded by these sequences might suggest that tense, grisly and protean action is *Fate/stay Night*'s raison d'être.

However, even in the midst of this often hyperkinetic chain of battles, the series remains faithful to the parent format's preference for placidly reflective moments focusing on the characters' churning emotions. This is suggestively evinced by the conversation between Shirou and Illya set in a melancholy park, where the girl discloses her personal background in a deeply moving vein. More notably still, the action scenes are interleaved with situations that highlight the meandering course of the relationship gradually forming between Shirou and Saber, where moral imperatives alternately merge and collide with as yet inchoate romantic leanings. The tough, notoriously standoffish and unsentimental Rin also comes to reveal deep wells of emotion and to harbor inner conflicts of grave consequence. Some of the most harrowing scenes coincide with the events unfolding around Shirou's rescue from Illya's fortress, where Archer meets his end and Saber's powers are severely impaired. The authentic sense of pain exuded not only by Rin's reaction (which attests to the depth of her bond to Archer) but also by her companions as they struggle to flee the seemingly invincible Berserker, is sufficient unto itself to speak volumes about the overall anime's emotional richness. It should also be noted, in this regard, that throughout several portions of the series, touching moments are likewise yielded by the portrayal of Sakura as an outwardly timid but in fact influential agent in the saga as a whole.

Shirou and Saber's partnership witnesses a rebalancing of power as the youth realizes that he alone has the ability to replenish the Servant's waning strength in the wake of the battle against Berserker by utilizing his own very particular brand of magic. Thus, he gives the depleted Saber part of his own magical circuit: a feat he accomplishes thanks to the intensified powers he has developed after swallowing a formidable jewel supplied by the increasingly supportive Rin a few installments earlier. The sequence in which Shirou telepathically accedes to Saber's very core indulges quite sensationally with computer-generated graphics, rendered in a style that overtly brings to mind the aesthetic features of adventure videogames, particularly in the depiction of the Servant's inner self in the guise of a 3D articulated dragon.

Shirou's comments on the experience, and specifically on how it has left him with the warm feeling that he and Saber are now more closely connected, carry tasteful erotic undertones. No less portentous is Shirou's subsequent tracing of a sword strong enough to vanquish Berserker. The anime gradually builds up to its climax over the last third of the saga. The entry into this segment is marked by the episode in which the incidents that have been plaguing the city for some time rapidly escalate and the population becomes prey to mass comas. These are revealed to emanate from the absorption of innocent souls by an utterly unscrupulous Master/Servant pair: the pseudo–Master Souichirou Kusuki (one of Shirou's teachers) and his Servant Caster (who has actually slain her true Master and summoned Assassin as her own Servant). The complete lack of moral restraint characterizing these two actors reaches a peak with Caster's capture of Sakura with the intention of using her as a sacrificial victim and exploiting her latent power as a magus to summon the Holy Grail. The strategically coordinated maneuvers deployed by Saber, Shirou and Rin to defeat their foes and free the hapless girl offer some of the anime's most striking instances of flawless intercutting and editing. Their narrative culmination is equally remarkable in unexpectedly ushering into the action the gold-armored Servant Gilgamesh as the protagonists' savior.

However, Gilgamesh soon reveals his true colors as a ruthless adversary and possibly the most formidable enemy yet. As Shirou and Saber desperately struggle to fend off his onslaught, the youth's magical powers reach their apotheosis with the tracing of a sheath for Excalibur that enables him to repel the attacker. Interlaced with these effervescent combative exploits are the sequences devoted to the elaboration of Shirou and Saber's tortuous liaison, especially in the segments where the youth acknowledges the true nature of his feelings towards the epic being and asks her out on a date as though to pretend, albeit ephemerally, that they are just ordinary teenagers. It is both delicately amusing and moving to see Saber display expressions characteristic of an innocent young girl not immune to blushing. Also memorable, in this regard, is the scene where Shirou openly states that he wishes Saber to remain by his side once the war is over in a capacity quite different from her current one. The real coup de theater comes with the disclosure that Kirei is Gilgamesh's Master and that his goal is to destroy Shirou so as to eliminate the last obstacle on his way to the Holy Grail. In their final battle, Shirou and Saber combine their powers to outdo Kirei and Gilgamesh in a magisterially choreographed sequence, staged once more in the enthralling setting of the Ryuudou Temple. Having destroyed the Holy Grail in compliance with Shirou's desire, Saber vanishes — though not without grasping her last chance to admit her love for Shirou. As shown in the coda, the Epic Spirit manages to go back to her original epoch and homeland, where she dies peacefully after enjoining Sir Bedivere to return Excalibur to the Lady of the Lake. The dramatic peak of the history of the "King of Knights" is marked by some deeply affecting lines of dialogue that eloquently confirm the anime's textual worth and accordingly deserve appropriate citation:

> ARTURIA: Bedivere ... I was just dreaming for a moment ...
> BEDIVERE: Dreaming, Sire?
> ARTURIA: Yes. I rarely have dreams. It was an invaluable experience.
> BEDIVERE: In that case, please rest without worry, Sire. If you close your eyes again you will surely begin the dream where you left off.
> ARTURIA: Continue the dream? Is it possible to continue the same dream?
> BEDIVERE: Yes, I've done it myself many times, Sire. You just have to want it enough.
>
> ...
>
> ARTURIA: I'm afraid my slumber this time will be a very long one. [*Arturia closes her eyes and falls into a deep sleep.*]
> BEDIVERE: Are you dreaming now, King Arthur? Are you still dreaming the same dream?

Expressive nuances in Bedivere's mien suggest that the knight might be simply humoring the dying ruler out of sheer compassion. Yet it is hardly deniable that the exchange also hints at an intriguing alternate take on Saber's experiences in Shirou's world and their possible extension beyond the show's boundaries.

Rapid action sequences, such as the ones revolving around Saber's battles with Rider or Assassin, Archer's duel against Berserker, and most spectacularly Saber and Shirou's joint efforts in their climactic confrontation with Gilgamesh and Kirei, invite kinaesthetic immersion in their moment-by-moment development, encouraging us to respond swiftly and intuitively to their tactical contents. Reflective and dialogue-dominated scenes, by contrast, call for cerebral immersion, urging us to use our powers of observation, speculation and deduction to ponder intently the anime's patterns of action and interaction, and to configure possible paths to the resolution of its mysteries. However, what ultimately holds the entire structure of *Fate/stay Night* coherently together does not lie so much with the pleasures yielded by either its strategic moves or its mental challenges as with its ability to capitalize on narrative immersion. This type of immersion comes into play when audiences truly begin to care about the characters and what happens to them within an artfully unfurling story. The skills needed by animators to accomplish this goal are quite different from those needed to create either kinesthetic or cerebral immersion, and depend above all on the smooth integration of thought-provoking dialogue, vibrant interrelations and a solidly constellated plot.

*Fate/stay Night* demonstrates that a fundamental means of fostering immersion is analogy. This principle helps animators bring ideas to life with palpable immediacy and sustain their development over a protracted period of time. While enabling diverse aspects of the anime to communicate particular concepts, analogy concurrently supports both characterization and plot construction. The series embraces the proposition that an idea might be interesting in itself, yet fail to be genuinely engaging if it is not communicated in a fashion to which the audience can relate. To make ideas engaging in the series, Yamaguchi and his team deemed it necessary to resort to visual and dynamic elements that are capable of enlisting the viewers' senses by involving not only thinking but also feeling — not only the mind but the body, too. Those elements include various forms of language (both verbal and non-verbal) and action, and analogy is arguably one of the most effective of them all. As Ellen Besen explains, analogy sets up a "correspondence" between a "theme" expressing "certain characteristics" of a work "abstractly or figuratively" and a "vehicle" expressing those same characteristics "physically or literally." In other words, the vehicle "translates the theme into a physical form." The emphasis on corporeality intrinsic to the dynamics of analogy is what renders such a mechanism ideally suited to the facilitation of immersion. In ideating ways of endowing a theme with material presence so as to give the audience a seemingly physical reality into which it can immerse itself, animators face a major challenge. Isolating the essential core of their theme is of paramount importance, in this context. One route at their disposal is the generation of "symbols" that "can work on a private or public level" (Besen 2003a). In *Fate/stay Night*, the relevant thematic kernel consists of the quest for harmony in a world recurrently and unendingly riven by discord. This idea is thrown into relief at an early stage in the anime, where it is shown (as indicated) that the last Holy Grail War had devastating consequences and that Shirou, a lucky survivor, may now be the key to preventing an identical disaster from marking the current conflict. The principle of analogy is employed in order to translate the show's axial preoccupation into tangible symbols. These are persistently buttressed by the vast repertoire of ritual objects, accessories, sartorial attributes, icons and emblems associated with Arthurian lore. Yet, since that legacy is imaginatively appropriated, there is also plenty of room for fresh symbols to come to life — for example, in the design of costumes inspired by vogues of different provenance.[1]

Relatedly, the available symbols operate on both the public and the private planes. They are public insofar as they issue largely from a corpus of shared and collectively recognized knowledge. The advantage they hold, in this respect, is that they are straightforwardly identifiable even by audiences that have had no academic experience of Arthurian literature but rather encountered the relevant epos through any of the legion forms of popular entertainment indebted to its discourse in varyingly distorted guises. However, those same symbols can also work at the private level for this very reason, since the specific ways in which they might resonate with individual spectators will depend on those spectators' personal experiences of exposure to their properties. (Clearly, a viewer who has plodded for years through hefty medieval tomes will relate to the symbols differently than a viewer who has gained familiarity with them via Hollywood, comic books, commercial novels or musicals.) At both the public and the private level, what secures the endurance of the Arthur-centered epos over the centuries is its translatability into symbols that feel pertinent to the here-and-now. John Matthews' observations on the subject are worthy of notice here: "how are we to account for the vast interest to be found in Arthurian literature today, an interest embracing both the academic and the common person? The answer may lie in the possibility that there is more of interest to the human being than his own circumscribed range of personal experience and the limited collective experience of the society in which he finds himself. Man has a sense of wonder and he seeks to look beyond the confines of the everyday. Marvel-filled literature enables him to do this and provides him with the stimulus which his imagination craves" (Matthews, p. 23). In the specific case of Yamaguchi's anime, it is the contingent relevance of the materiality of analogical symbolism to both individuals and groups that maximizes opportunities for immersion as an immediate participation in the anime's reality. The public and private dimensions are tied together in *Fate/stay Night*'s narrative by the language of magic, since as Besen inspiringly maintains, the ability to "make the internal, external; the abstract, concrete and the invisible, visible" is "powerful magic indeed" (Besen 2003a).

It is also noteworthy in evaluating the anime's utilization of symbolism for analogical purposes that even though Arthurian lore plays a key part, other legendary motifs and figures are also invoked. As intimated by the Master/Servant pairs outlined earlier in this analysis, Hercules, Medusa and Medea feature amongst the Servants, thus bringing Greek mythology into play. At the same time, Assassin harks back to a legendary swordsman associated with samurai culture, while Gilgamesh echoes Mesopotamian tradition, and Cuchulainn springs from Irish mythology. Moreover, Archer is posited as a Servant who does not originate in any recorded epic personage but rather fulfils an independent role as a promoter of the principle of the creative quest: a vital aspect, as argued, of both visual novels and their anime adaptations. Archer could indeed be seen as an adult version of Shirou that has succeeded in perfecting the tracing skill over time and eventually translated it into a true art in its own right, thereby gaining the stature of an Epic Spirit. Shirou's exploits, in comparison with Archer's creative flair, still belong to the league of menial labor. The connection between Archer and the protagonist is not implied until an advanced stage in the adventure. To begin with, Rin's Servant is actually seen to nourish adversarial feelings towards Shirou, sarcastically referring to the unusual Master as a "clown" and cynically dismissing his idealism as vapid, naïve and delusional.

The privileged status accorded to Arthurian tradition in Yamaguchi's anime, allied to its experimentative reconceptualization of some of its mainstays, is most forcefully conveyed by its portrayal of Saber's history and personality. The story's backdrop reveals that Saber's real identity is that of Arturia Pendragon, daughter of the British monarch Uther Pendragon — in other words, a fictional adaptation in female guise of the legendary King Arthur. Believing that his subjects would not accept a woman as the legitimate heir to the British throne, Uther decided not to divulge Arturia's existence and entrusted her instead to the care of the magician Merlin and the knight Sir Ector. Upon Uther's death, the country precipitated into a phase of great turmoil and Merlin resolved to emplace Arturia as the new ruler — a status to which she might ascend, according to the wizard, if she succeeded in drawing a ceremonial sword from the slab of rock in which it was embedded. The girl accomplished the sanctioned task quite effortlessly and thereafter proceeded to lead the country from her stronghold in Camelot with the assistance of the Knights of the Round Table and under Merlin's assiduous guidance, thereby taking Britain into an era of peace and prosperity.

In one version of the legend, the weapon drawn from the rock is referred to simply as the "Sword in the Stone" and is differentiated from the sacred sword Excalibur and its magical scabbard, said to have been proffered by the Lady of the Lake. In another version, the sword drawn from the rock and Excalibur are deemed to be one and the same. From the point of view of *Fate/stay Night*'s diegesis, the difference between the two versions is immaterial. What matters is that the weapon endows the wielder with immortality in battle and an unaging physique. Despite her commendable performance as a monarch, Arturia was innerly tormented throughout her reign by feelings of inferiority and inadequacy, and by divesting herself of all visible personal emotions to establish the image of a selfless ruler, eventually came to be blamed for an inherent lack of humanity. By and by, the land descended into civil strife and Arturia herself was lethally wounded. Escorted to a blessed isle by Sir Bedivere, one of her most trusted followers, Arturia instructed him to return Excalibur to its place of inception. Although the anime does not explicitly mention this point, it is also intimated by the game's backstory that just before drawing her last breath, Arturia is supposed to have expressed the desire to become an Epic Spirit so as to be able to lead a different life in which a worthier ruler might govern Britain in her place. The version of Arturia we see in *Fate/stay Night* under the professional designation of "Saber" is precisely the Epic Spirit that thenceforth came into being, and in accordance with the ancient monarch's dying wishes seeks to retrieve the Holy Grail as a means of rewriting history. (In the visual novel's various versions, Saber's quest meets diverse conclusions.) All of the background figures mentioned above, it must be emphasized, strike their roots in Arthurian lore.

In assessing *Fate/stay Night*'s debt to Arthurian tradition, it is important to acknowledge the anime's imbrication with the aesthetic of "neomediaevalism," a concept ushered in by Umberto Eco in his essay "Dreaming the Middle Ages" (Eco 1986). In its broadest sense, the term designates the rediscovery of mediaeval material in both academic circles and the domain of popular culture as the repository of ideas and icons metaphorically applicable to a variety of historical contexts and philosophical debates. For Eco, the contemporary attraction to the Middle Ages is by no means driven purely by fantasy. In fact, it entails an acknowledgement, however subliminal, of that epoch as the moment of inception of several key discourses and structures underpinning the Western world, including modern languages and the capitalist economic system. Furthermore, the intersection of medieval tradition and popular fantasy proposed by Yamaguchi's anime and the visual novel behind it mirrors a widespread fascination with medieval themes not just in popular culture generally but in the realm of computer games in particular. The ubiquity of the neomedieval trend in the field, which frequently extends to quite unexpected occasions and venues, is picturesquely captured by Eddo Stern's description of the people attending the *39th Annual Renaissance Pleasure Faire* (San Bernardino, California, 2001): "The creatively anachronistic Renfaire crowd is comprised of a colorful band of jolly Anglophiles, mediaevalists, woodworkers, elves, druids and wizards selling handmade crafts, performing jousts, drinking mead and offering an all out sun-beaten Californian version of new-age virtual reality" (Stern, p. 258).

In the gaming domain, medieval elements of Celtic and Gothic derivation often mesh with motifs drawn from Tolkien, Wagner, and of course the world of Camelot and its legendary leader to conjure up mock-historical, magic-imbued realities. According to Stern, in order to fathom the reasons for the immense popularity of medieval (or pseudo-medieval) motifs, it is vital to grasp the relationship between "magic and technology" as a concurrently historical and philosophical phenomenon. That relationship originates in a peculiar "mix of power, religion, science and art" (p. 259). Nowadays, Stern contends, "technology operates to realize what was previously in the hypothetical realm of magic. There is definitely some connection in the way both magic and technology create a sense of wonder as they seem to expand upon the notions of what is or has been feasible in the realm of the real." Appropriately, Stern cites A. C. Clarke's famous dictum — "any sufficiently advanced technology is indistinguishable from magic" — to corroborate his thesis (p. 260). Therefore, in assessing the revival of medieval themes and imagery in works like *Fate/stay Night* (in both its ludic and animated incarnations), it is important to bear in mind that fantasy-driven entertainment is not the sole objective. In fact, even the appetite for nostalgic antiquarianism can serve to alert us to the relevance of magical fabulation to the present and its both overt and covert ideologies.

The invocation of a medieval heroic fantasy — traversed by echoes of the *chanson de geste*, the troubadour lyric and the early picaresque novel — is essentially the channel through which a contemporary narrative aims to communicate its no less contemporary aesthetic goal. Ultimately, this amounts to the story's yearning to narrate as an autonomous agent and thus immerse its viewers in its flow as a self-determining and self-referential construct. The story never relinquishes its connection with reality, with the moral requirements of the here-and-now, and hence with the intractable density, opacity and fragmentation of things as they are. The generic and thematic contaminations, reversals, hybridizations and relocations in which *Fate/stay Night* thereby indulges are, in this light, to be understood as means to an end and not as ends in themselves. The medieval material is not harnessed to the ideation of a purely fictive dimension but rather brought into play as a presence, a vehicle for the expression of a desire to speak to the present about the present. Any danger of the anime sinking into consolatory nostalgia is counteracted by a scintillating sense of irony whereby correspondences between the past and the present never become pretexts for an uncritical worship of the past. In fact, they function as reminders of the inevitable fractures and discontinuities we must always face whenever we attempt to make sense of the present world with reference to times gone by.

*Fate/stay Night* is also sensitive to the importance of understanding intimately and putting to maximum advantage the specific properties of its medium in order to advance its immersive strategies. According to Besen, some of the most distinctive attributes of the medium of animation to be take into account are "caricature," the tendency to "simplify and exaggerate"; "movement," the medium's prime form of communication; "fantasy," the principle through which the medium can "achieve magic"; and "reality," the principle through which animation can construct "an alternate world" (Besen 2003b). *Fate/stay Night* uses caricature in several ways. The most explicitly distorted persona is Taiga, a character so hopelessly clumsy and impulsive as to verge on the farcical despite the disarming purity of her intentions. However, caricature is also more discreetly deployed to highlight aspects of the protagonist's personality: while Shirou, mostly comes across as a fully rounded character endowed with a range of intelligently modulated psychological nuances, his portrayal as a would-be "Champion of Justice" lends his presentation a stylized flavor. Likewise, Saber is mainly depicted as a multifaceted, divided mentality, but gains caricatural connotations from her association with a stiffly formal register and often inflexible disposition. Her gargantuan passion for food further contributes to the caricature-oriented dimension of her makeup. Thus, while with Taiga simplification and exaggeration come overtly to the fore, with the principal actors they constitute supplementary yet dramatically effective ingredients.

*Fate/stay Night*'s commitment to the language of motion is exuberantly conveyed by its action sequences and especially the fights referred to earlier in this discussion. At the same time, the anime sensitively integrates the dynamic component with static elements intended to enhance its atmosphere and to foreground its stylistic range in the contexts of both interior decor and large-scale architecture. Indeed, it could be argued that although the show's character designs offer intriguing aesthetic achievements (particularly in the depiction of the Servants), the settings often function as the real protagonists. The provincial city of Fuyuki where the bulk of the adventure takes place is meticulously rendered throughout, exhibiting the same devotion to details in the representation of its bland office buildings and its comely residential areas, of Shirou's austere samurai compound and Shinji's lavish Victorian mansion, of the imposing Ryuudou Temple's unmistakably Oriental attributes and the Western-style church from which Kirei oversees the Holy Grail War. Most memorable, where settings are concerned, are Illya's forbidding castle and the tenebrous woods surrounding it, where spectral moonlight and drifting mist provide apposite environmental equivalents for the shadowy history underlying the tournament and its occult imagery. If static elements aptly complement the series' kinetic dimension, acoustic elements — and in particular Kenji Kawai's alternately stirring and haunting soundtrack — play no less axial a role in consolidating *Fate/stay Night*'s distinctive mood. Thus, understanding the significance of movement as one of animation's structural mainstays means grasping not only the principles of movement per se but also their interplay with stationary visuals and auditory effects. As for *Fate/stay Night*'s relationship with both fantasy and reality, the foregoing analysis ought to have provided appropriate insights into the anime's scope in that matter. What deserves attention, at this stage, is the effectiveness of the four components (i.e., caricature, movement, fantasy and reality) in fostering immersion.

Caricature is especially useful in enriching the viewer's relationship with a character insofar as it visibly highlights that character's salient attributes in an eminently stylized and therefore instantly identifiable mode. At the same time, it helps animators cultivate one of Japanese art's most inveterate tendencies — namely, the desire to expose the intrinsic artificiality of images — by preserving a modicum of aesthetic distance. Indeed, while caricature can draw us to an actor more immediately and palpably than realistic portrayal, it also throws into relief the persona's constructedness. Moving onto the next category outlined above, it could be argued that the coalescence of dynamic, static and acoustic elements is instrumental in creating a comprehensive experiential environment for the audience to enter and participate in. Where animation's relationship with fantasy and reality is concerned, immersion comes overtly into play with the evocation of fictive realms through which the medium is capable of both absorbing us magically into a parallel dimension and inducing us to entertain fresh perspectives on the concept of reality itself. It is worth stressing that the "alternative worlds" conjured up by animated cinema do not, as Besen comments, "come from nowhere," but are actually established in a consistent and conscious fashion: animators "need to ultimately move from anything being possible to a logical, coherent structure in which only certain, well-defined things (some real, some not so real) are possible." That is to say, they "need to give those worlds some rules" (Besen 2003b). As shown in some detail earlier in this discussion, rules are of paramount significance in the world of *Fate/stay Night*, since the complex set of codes and conventions underpinning the Holy Grail Wars, alongside the specific vocabulary and symbolism on which they depend, provide the backbone of its entire diegesis. In the orchestration of the four fundamental factors delineated in the preceding paragraphs the focus, is the search for a range of opportunities that may inaugurate "a whole hidden 'what if' world for the storytellers," and for a framework wherein such a range of opportunities "both builds the platform and provides the strategies for a meaningful, multileveled show" (Besen 2003c). *Fate/stay Night* pithily validates these propositions by translating a wholly hypothetical proposition into the bedrock of a consummately prismatic narrative and performative event.

The show's dramatic tension reaches its apex with the conflict between Shirou and Saber regarding the latter's future, where incompatible emotional and ethical priorities sorely clash. Saber wishes to deploy the Holy Grail to go back in time in order to ensure that her country enjoys the leadership of a worthier monarch. Haunted by her failure to fulfill her public duties in days gone by, the spirit is locked in her previous existence, and hence in the injunction to redress its evils. Shirou in vain encourages Saber to think about her humanity, maintaining that making things better does not automatically equate to rectifying the past but should also be a matter of addressing how one may progress from the present towards a consciously chosen future. After all, Shirou is not merely promulgating an abstract lesson but speaking from experience, since he too once chose to ignore his fellow humans and think solely of his own survival, and has had to accommodate that legacy within his psyche in order to move on. Therefore, Shirou affirms that even if the Holy Grail were to allow him to return to the past and alter it, thus expunging the humiliating memories of his desertion of the people perishing all around him at the time of the previous war, he would not take that option. For the boy, learning how to live with one's feelings of shame and guilt is a vital part of the march towards maturation and self-understanding. Retaining his painful recollections, instead of seeking to erase them, enables him to prevent them from becoming meaningless and hence honor their lesson and stoically embrace the pain they bear. This segment of the narrative fully bears witness to the anime's penchant for psychologically complex characterization, as well as to the essence of its moral message. Moreover, in foregrounding the topos of memory at a climactic juncture, it fittingly echoes the show's ongoing preoccupation with that theme, made clear from the very start by Shirou's flashback to his rescue and adoption and by Rin's recollection of her father's departure from the Tohsaka family mansion, as well as by Archer's remarks concerning the haziness of his memories beyond his summoning by Rin.

As the series progresses (and most pointedly in the climactic installments), *Fate/stay Night* offers a paradigmatic illustration of effective narrative and dramatic immersion through its inspired integration of the mytho-historical and personal levels. Had the series limited itself to the articulation of the former, *Fate/stay Night* might have required an interest in Arthurian lore (though, as noted earlier, not necessarily scholarly expertise in the area) in order to function immersively. If, on the other hand, it had operated purely as a private drama, it could hardly have aimed to engage the viewer's whole sensorium by means of what is ultimately a beautifully orchestrated but by no means unprecedented romance. The collusion of the two dimensions, however, makes the anime not only unique but also highly rewatchable. Indeed, it is largely thanks to its generic amalgam, bolstered throughout by exciting action, serious psychodrama, an intricate backstory, complex character interactions and unpredictable twists and turns, that the series yields a truly magnetic experience, capable not simply of keeping viewers on the edges of their seats but also of drawing them thence into the screen's alternate reality.

The theme of the seemingly inept magician actually harboring powers of unrivalled magnitude, addressed above with reference to Shirou Emiya, is also utilized as a pivotal motif in *The Familiar of Zero* (TV series; dir. Yoshiaki Iwasaki, 2006), an anime adapted into a visual novel in 2007 with the title *The Familiar of Zero: Goblins of the Spring Breeze Concerto*. The protagonist, Louise de la Vallière, is a second-year student at the prestigious Academy of Magic in the kingdom of Tyrsing. In summoning her familiar (a task traditionally assigned to all students in her cohort), she accidentally brings forth an ordinary teenager from Tokyo named Hiragi Saito who has no grasp whatsoever of the peculiar world to which he has so suddenly and inexplicably been transposed. Louise's act contravenes both common practice and the dicta of respectable magical performance, but this hardly surprises her tutors and peers. Indeed, the girl is so proverbially hopeless as an aspiring magician as to have gained the nickname of "Louise the Zero," due to her inability to master any of the four common elements. (In this world, wizardly power is measured according to the number of elements one is capable of controlling, the titles "line mage" designating the practitioner that can only handle one element, at one end of the spectrum, and "square mage" the one that can handle as many as four, at the opposite end.) What is not revealed until the climactic moments is that Louise is actually a "Gandalfr"—a magician of the "void" (the fifth element)—and hence the most powerful and rarest of all recorded sorcerous types. The unusual familiar, accordingly, little by little displays preternatural abilities of his own. Set in an alternate universe characterized by a stylistic pastiche that brings together elements from various phases of European architectural and vestimentary history (with Renaissance, Neoclassical, Rococo and Victorian motifs in special prominence), while also unobtrusively paying homage to indigenous traditions, the anime clearly matches the visual-novel mold's appetite for polydimensional schemata. In addition, its palpably textured and chromatically exuberant fictional environments, allied to a passion for multilayered adventures and nuanced character typologies, make *Zero* an ideal candidate for translation into that format.

\* \* \*

One of the most frankly experimental anime of recent years is undoubtedly Chiaki Kon's two-season TV series comprising *Higurashi no Naku Koro ni* and *Higurashi no Naku Koro ni Kai*—i.e., *When Cicadas Cry* and *When Cicadas Cry—Solutions*. Also known in the West as *When They Cry—Higurashi*, the anime is hereafter referred to simply as *Higurashi* for the sake of succinctness. The two *Higurashi* TV series were released in 2006 and 2007, and complemented by the OVA series *Higurashi no Naku Koro ni Rei* (*When Cicadas Cry—Gratitude*), directed by Toshifumi Kawase, in 2009. Several *Higurashi* games covering different arcs of the original series were released between 2002 and 2006. Further arcs have been thereafter created in videogame, manga and anime format in order to develop the initial adventure in alternate, multi-forking directions. The original game, providing the primary source of inspiration for the two TV series examined in depth in the ensuing pages, comprises eight arcs, four of which are designated as Question arcs and four as Answer arcs. At the beginning of each, the player is

offered an enigmatic poem by someone known simply as Frederica Bernkas-
tel (possibly an adult incarnation of the heroine Rika Furude) meant to reveal,
albeit cryptically, elements of the storyline to follow. One of the most distinctive aspects of *Higurashi*'s gameplay is the use of "tips" that allow the
player to read supplementary information designed either to consolidate the
setting's societal traits or to provide clues to the mystery's solution. Among
the former type are relatively straightforward descriptive entries, such as the
one telling the player that the scene is a small place with just one school where
kids of various ages share the same classroom and teacher. Among the latter,
are more tantalizing snippets of information alluding to the dark history of
the village where the story takes place, such as excerpts from newspaper arti-
cles about the crimes occurring therein over time.

In the anime, the Question arcs present concatenations of varyingly
bizarre and mystifying occurrences which the Answer arcs recapitulate from
alternate perspectives with more or less drastic diegetic changes, offering partial solutions but also positing fresh enigmas of their own. The artbook *When
They Cry/Higurashi Character and Analysis Book* does a great job in bringing
out the show's multiperspectival approach by recourse to frame-assisted dia-
grams that illustrate the interactions unfolding in individual arcs, with a focus
on the characters conferred centrality within their dramatization. The 2006
anime encompasses the four Question arcs and the first two Answer arcs; the
2007 sequel covers the remaining two Answer arcs, prefaced by an anime-
exclusive segment. Set in June 1983, the story develops in the context of the
fictional rural village of Hinamizawa (modeled on the real-world village of
Shirakawa, Gifu, a World Heritage site). As in the visual novel, the village is
so diminutive as to accommodate just one school in which kids studying for
disparate grades share a single classroom and one tremendously versatile tutor.
Superficially tranquil, Hinamizawa labors under a baleful curse associated
with its legendary deity and patron, Oyashiro-sama. Leading up to the main
story, for the four previous years one person has met a violent death and
another has vanished without trace on the night of the Wataganashi ("Cotton-Drifting") Festival, held annually to honor the god. At first, it would
appear that the villagers unproblematically believe that the curse results from
Oyashiro-sama's anger at plans to build a dam that would leave Hinamizawa
totally submerged. Yet, it is also gradually intimated that the grisly deaths
and mysterious disappearances may actually have been engineered by
Hinamizawa's three "great families," helmed by the Sonozaki clan and its
*yakuza* connections, who conceivably have their own vicious reasons for wanting the old superstition to be perpetuated. One thing is clear: all manner of
scandals, allied to rampant corruption, underlie the dam-construction project and the staunch opposition put up by the local protest group to induce

its cancellation. Age-old privileges, feuds and conspiracies based on tyrannical abuse and persecution accordingly emerge but for a substantial part of the story it is practically impossible to ascertain where illusions end and stark facts begin. The story's protagonist is Keiichi Maebara, a boy who has recently moved to Hinamizawa with his parents after growing up in the big city. Although ostensibly endowed with natural charisma and an easygoing disposition that enable him to make new friends quite effortlessly, Keiichi ultimately turns out to host malevolent ghosts of his own. These surface as his otherwise uneventful life becomes increasingly embroiled with Hinamizawa's tenebrous secrets and crimes.

In two story arcs, the male lead is seen to fall victim to murderous paranoia. Yet his ultimately ineradicable inner strength and unfailing trust in the value of friendship allow him not only to own up to, and thus negotiate, his own checkered past, but also to play an axial part in the mystery's solution. In the course of the story, Keiichi interacts with five main heroines and a number of supporting characters that deserve some attention, at this juncture. Character portrayal is indeed one of the anime's principal ingredients and strengths. All of the main female characters are vividly individualized, and not just by recourse to distinctive hues that could easily be dismissed as formulaic "color-coding." Rena Ryuuguu, for example, might at first come across as an unproblematically light-hearted *shoujo* type with an addictive passion for all things "cute"—including many objects and situations which her friends deem quite unpalatable—and for treasure hunts in the local garbage dump. In fact, Rena is quite a serious person and endowed with powers of observation and logical deduction enabling her to perceive aspects of the overall *Higurashi* riddle that go unheeded by the others in the group. Moreover, her traumatic family history, pathological reactions conducive to destructive and suicidal actions, and obsession with Oyashiro-sama impart her portrayal with unmatched psychological density. The storyline that emplaces Rena as the principal culprit is, accordingly, particularly harrowing. Mion Sonozaki, Keiichi's oldest mate and the class president, is likewise multifaceted. A bossy tomboy on the surface, she harbors a secret girlish side and related romantic proclivities. Much of her pluck results from her appointed destiny as the Sonozakis' future head. As the story progresses, we learn that she is actually her twin sister Shion but that she was mistaken for Mion as a baby and hence branded with the clan tattoo intended to seal her fate. The twin sister that actually goes by the name of Shion in public, removed by the family to a private boarding school but resourceful enough to escape and return to live near her hometown, is superficially quite different from the future Sonozaki head but has a very close relationship with Mion and retains a flair for swapping places with her—most notably in the arcs where hatred for the great families, which she holds responsible for the disappearance of her beloved Satoshi Houjou, leads her to multiple murder under the assumed identity of her sister. In fact, the public Mion is the only character that does not at some point fall prey to nefarious psychosis.

Another good instance of duplicitous personality is Satoko Houjou. Energetic, mischievously playful and renowned for her knack for setting traps, Satoko is arguably the most grievously traumatized of all the characters. As her sinister side gradually emerges, we learn that she was actually responsible for her parents' putatively accidental death and that her excessive dependence on her elder brother Satoshi has played a significant part in the boy's own psychological decline. Although Satoshi himself in not present in *Higurashi*'s present-day scenario as an active character, since he effectively spends its entire time span under heavy sedation in an underground area of the local clinic, his background influence supplies the key to the actions of several other personae. Revered by the Hinamizawa population as the heir of Oyashiro-sama's shrine and the *miko* ("shrine maiden") in the annual festival, Rika Furude is the most vital piece in the *Higurashi* puzzle, having lived for over one-hundred years by the time the anime's sixth arc unfolds and witnessed the cycle of events conducive to the story's present zone several times. While she retains a childlike physique and voice, indulging in nonsense words and onomatopoeic effects, she is at core a troubled adult and her real voice is solemn and even intimidating. Rika is inseparable from her alter ego Hanyuu: a meek, easily frightened and nervous girl decked in deliciously traditional gear whom only Rika perceives and converses with until the day she materializes — at an advanced stage in the narrative — as a mysterious "transfer student." A nice touch to the Rika-Hanyuu relationship is the idea that their senses are interconnected. Thus, when Rika is in a bad mood and wishes to take it out on the wimpish Hanyuu, she imbibes large amounts of wine, which the Furude heir is very fond of and quite able to tolerate while her double abhors it. Another felicitous detail of the partnership lies with its emphasis on frank and unadorned human feelings: although Hanyuu is supposed to be a reincarnation of the formidable Oyashiro-sama, Rika sees her and treats her just as a close friend and Hanyuu herself responds in the same vein without any hierarchical expectations.

Among the adult characters, the most unconventionally endearing is Detective Kuraudo Ooishi, a veteran resolved to unravel the Hinamizawa puzzle before his retirement so as to avenge a close friend. Often rough and uncouth, yet sustained by an unflinching belief in the values of loyalty and cooperativeness, Ooishi is unintentionally instrumental to the genesis of the paranoia afflicting the characters designated as culprits in various arcs by seeking their assistance in the investigation. Other important grown-ups in the series are Miyo Takano, a nurse at the Hinamizawa clinic who harbors a morbid interest in the Oyashiro-sama cult and seems to derive sadistic satisfaction from using her thorough knowledge of its blood-soaked substratum to make others uncomfortable or even downright terrified. As the plot evolves, she turns out to be the mastermind behind the recurrent crimes and to be driven solely by the consuming desire to take her revenge on the many people that derided her adoptive grandfather's research. Takano is often seen in the company of the character of Kyousuke Irie, the head of the Hinamizawa clinic, who has been roped into the woman's plan with only partial knowledge of its full scope. Irie's portrayal eloquently attests to *Higurashi*'s psychological subtlety. Though highly respected in the community and keenly devoted to the well-being of each of its members (but especially Satoko), the physician is also invested with a comical side that manifests itself as a parodically perverse fascination with maid outfits and Lolita-style cuties. A further character recurringly seen in Takano's company is Jirou Tomitake, officially a freelance photographer who visits Hinamizawa regularly (and invariably around the annual festival) who also holds an essential connection with Miyo's research and the organization behind it. Finally, the young police detective Mamoru Akasaka deserves notice as a character through whom we acquire much valuable information regarding Hinamizawa at the time of the "Dam War" in the first season, and whose development into a highly competent professional in the second series places him in the position of a central force within the cumulative unraveling of the mystery and the redefinition of Rika's seemingly inexorable fate.

While the concept of the community is insistently (indeed somewhat dogmatically) upheld by the locals as the guarantee of mutual support, it repeatedly shows its true face as a cover designed to conceal unspeakable evils. It is not until a relatively advanced stage in Season 2 that the community is genuinely posited as a source of strength for its members. Even the head of the Sonozaki clan, the formidable "granny" Oryou, shows herself capable of magnanimity eventually, whereas the real culprit turns out to have been ruled solely by unscrupulous self-interest. This shift gains great dramatic prominence in the sequence of events surrounding the epic efforts enacted by Keiichi, his friends and ultimately the whole of Hinamizawa to put an end to Satoko's abuse at the hands of her uncle Teppei. At first unwilling to lend her support, Oryou is eventually so impressed with Keiichi's determination to save Satoko and with the actions and rhetoric he deploys to this effect that she pulls out all the stops to abet him, using her authority to instruct the entire population of both Hinamizawa and the neighboring town of Okinomiya to join the youth's ranks and personally persuading the Mayor to take the decisive steps in advancing the protesters' cause. Finally, Oryou even welcomes the infusion of fresh air into Hinamizawa's stale atmosphere, though she generally detests outsiders, and prophetically alludes to the role to be played by a valiant youth from the outside world (supposedly Keiichi himself) in the town's regeneration. Rika, also emphasizes the male lead's unique role when she states that the previous versions of Hinamizawa that did not contain this character were the worst of the alternate worlds she ever experienced. However, the special value accorded to Keiichi does not make him a stereotypical hero so much as a versatile dramatic catalyst.

In chronicling the history of an idiosyncratic, twisted or even putrescent community, *Higurashi* abounds with quite horrific scenes of violence. Yet it never wallows in gory spectacle for its own sake. In fact, the creepy build-up to moments of brutality plays a more crucial part than the gruesome component per se, and the sheer sense of sadness permeating many of its principal sequences prevails over sensationalism. The Latin root of "horror" (i.e., "*horrere*" = "to shiver" or "to bristle") is thus elliptically invoked. Pathos-laden instants of introspection and crippling anxiety contribute significantly to the drama's overall mood, allowing the pace of the action to slow down and the audience to be drawn into the characters' psyches with their manifold fears, doubts and ghosts. Their memories — or pathological dearth thereof — frequently come into play as the agents responsible for the actors' ubiquitous unease, resurging unexpectedly at key points in the yarn despite sustained attempts at repression or obfuscation. In several of the sequences devoted to the depiction of violence, realism tends to give way to images which, while not overtly stylized, prioritize structure over content. Clashing planes and tortile lines in particular are used to evoke a rampant sense of tumult that exceeds in pathos even the blood-spattered frames. At their most memorable, such sequences communicate an impression of sculptural density, as though they had been not so much drawn on a canvas or a computer screen as carved out of wood blocks. One almost senses the latent presence of the artist's chisel attacking the wood and thus releasing a demon eager to dictate the shape and rhythm of the composition.

The first Question arc, *Onikakushi-hen* ("Spirited Away by the Demon Chapter"), adopts as the main focus of attention the character of Rena, a student who is supposed to have settled in Hinamizawa only a year earlier, even though she, unlike the protagonist, is originally from the village. Rena is almost invariably friendly and cheerful but harbors a dark past. This is hinted at by Detective Ooishi, who reveals to Keiichi that the girl was responsible for acts of vandalism and assault while residing in the town of Hibaraki, to which she had moved upon leaving Hinamizawa a few years earlier, and that neurological assessments indicated that she felt haunted by Oyashiro-sama. The hyperconfident Mion also betrays sinister undertones as it transpires that her relationship with Ooishi has been so hostile that she has been seriously tempted to kill him and only refrained in the knowledge that the officer is just one year away from retirement. These disclosures are not overtly foregrounded, however, since Hinamizawa initially appears to enjoy a peaceful and jovial atmosphere. It is in the wake of the annual festival and the crimes attendant upon the event that the anime's mood radically darkens and Keiichi falls prey to mounting paranoia concerning the town's ominous secrets. This eventually deteriorates into undiluted insanity, as a result of which the youth beats Rena and Mion to death, deeming them intent on planning his murder, and claws out his own throat with his very fingernails.

In the second Question arc, *Wataganashi-hen* ("Cotton-Drifting Chapter"), Mion takes center stage. Keiichi's unlawful penetration of Oyashiro-sama's shrine in the company of Shion, Tomitake and Takano allegedly paves the way to a chain of ghastly deaths and inexplicable vanishings. Once again, the protagonist has good reason to fear for his own life. Mion appears to take responsibility for several of the crimes that have beset Hinamizawa over recent years, and indeed for the misfortunes marring the current summer, attributing at least part of the blame to her role as heir to the village's most powerful dynasty. It is only when the anime reaches this segment's alternate retelling in the first Answer arc that it fully transpires that at this stage, Mion is actually Shion — even though a cryptic hint is at one point dropped by the criminal herself, while Detective Ooishi raises more openly the possibility of an identity substitution in the arc's closing part. (Ironically, when Shion claims to be Mion, she is telling the truth if one bears in mind that the twins' identities were swapped shortly after their birth.)

Question arc 3, *Tatarigoroshi-hen* ("Curse-Killing Chapter"), pivots on Satoko, who is portrayed as the victim of dire abuse at the hands of her thuggish uncle Teppei, with whom she has been forced to live following her parents' tragic demise. While in the early stages of this grievous cohabitation the girl could depend on her elder brother Satoshi for comfort, the boy's disappearance in conjunction with the murder of Teppei's wife has left her utterly alone and vulnerable. It is suggested that Satoshi has actually been responsible for the homicide, perpetrated to put an end to his aunt's own abusive conduct. However, the official truth disseminated by Hinamizawa's prestigious clans is that the woman was killed by a psychopath. Keiichi embarks on his own vengeful act by beating Teppei to death with Satoshi's baseball bat, but his efforts to free Satoko are bafflingly inconclusive. Although the youth has vivid recollections of the crime and we actually see him carry it out in detail, his friends later claim that at the very same time he was putatively killing and burying his victim, Keiichi was actually attending the Wataganashi Festival in their company. No less disturbingly, when the makeshift grave in which

Teppei is supposed to have been buried is dug up, no signs of a body are to be found. It is at the close of this arc that we are supplied with the first explicit account of the "Hinamizawa Disaster": the tragedy officially triggered by a "gas leak" in which practically all of the villagers lose their lives. In this rendition of the catastrophe, Keiichi is said to be the sole survivor.

The fourth Question arc, *Himatsubushi-hen* ("Time-Wasting Chapter"), is a prequel set five years prior to the story's main events. It chronicles Detective Akasaka's investigative trip to Hinamizawa, his attempt to reconstruct the incidents surrounding the anti-dam protest — in spite of hints at the locals' hostility — with Detective Ooishi as his sole ally, and his encounter with Rika, this segment's heroine. The same arc also works as a sequel in its closing portion, dramatizing a meeting between Akasaka and Ooishi taking place years after the main story's conclusion, in which we learn that Akasaka's wife incurred a fatal accident at the time of the young investigator's visit to Hinamizawa: an event to which Rika alludes in a delphian fashion in one of her early conversations with him. It is also at this point in the arc that Akasaka tells Ooishi about Rika's prophetic foreshadowing, in a chilling amount of details, of the crimes that would take place for five consecutive years around the annual festival and culminate with her own murder. As the anime moves onto its Answer arcs, all of the key events presented in the Question arcs are reproposed in a new light.

The first Answer arc, *Meakashi-hen* ("Eye-Opening Chapter"), offers an alternative take on the events shown in the second Question arc through the eyes of Shion with some variations. The idea that Shion has swapped places with Mion and retains the latter's assumed identity while perpetrating her own crimes, which is merely hinted at in the second Question arc, is pivotal to this subsequent dramatization of the same basic occurrences. Moreover, the reason behind the criminal's actions is more clearly depicted as a manic resolve to avenge a lost love. Shion believes that her family is directly responsible for brutally tearing her away from Satoshi due to the Sonozakis' hatred of a family they regard as no more than a bunch of traitors due to the Houjous' backing of the dam project, and will stop at nothing to exact her revenge. It should be noted, however, that just as the source visual novel deliberately refrains from dishing out overt or concrete answers for a substantial component of its unfolding, thus stimulating the player's own creativity and interpretative skills, so the anime (or at least the best part of the first show) withholds clear explanations. Thus, while the romantic element can to some degree be accepted as the trigger for Shion's actions, there are also more ominous allusions to her clan's power-driven role in the cumulative Hinamizawa ordeal. For one thing, at this stage it is assumed that the Sonozakis are responsible for divulging the rumor regarding the identity of Satoshi's aunt's slayer as a frenzied drug addict so as to pretend that Satoshi has been spirited away rather than run away to avoid prosecution, and thus maintain the intimidating fabrications associated with the Oyashiro-sama myth. In fact, Satoshi has been surreptitiously appropriated as a medical test subject.

The occurrences dramatized in the second Answer arc, *Tsumihoroboshi-hen* ("Atonement Chapter"), echo those presented in the third Question arc, placing Rena in a position akin to Keiichi's in the earlier segment and likewise emphasizing her escalating mistrust of her friends. In Rena's case, the obnoxious Teppei features again as a victim, this time alongside his mistress and partner in mischief Ritsuko, Rena's father's exploitative lover. In cahoots, the two characters flaunt a notorious record of blackmailing, gambling and badgering. An interesting variation on the diegetic pattern thus far established by the series is introduced in this arc by means of a flashback in which Keiichi suddenly remembers beating Rena and Mion to death (thus harking back to the first Question arc) and seeks to gain their forgiveness. The youth appears to hold memories of an alternate Hinamizawa reality of which none of the other actors — with the notable exception of Rika — holds any conscious awareness or recollection. The second anime series will shed light on this conundrum, revealing that different versions of Hinamizawa have obtained over time. Each of them has contained a chain of events destined always to culminate in the same baleful Wataganashi night, its grisly deaths and Rika's immolation in their wake. Rika herself states that Keiichi's flashback is something of a "miracle." A post-credit scene offered at the end of the first show paves the way to this disclosure through Rika's remark on the inevitability of her replaying time and again the same "endless June." The quintessentially Eastern concept of Eternal Return or Eternal Recurrence is here invoked. At the same time, the anime's "infinity" could be interpreted as a self-reflexive comment on the exponentially prodigious replayability of the visual novels at its root. (The recurrence topos will be shortly revisited in some depth.)

The provisional explanation supplied by the first anime season is that the cycle of deaths coinciding with the Wataganashi Festival — and eventually brought to an end by the extermination of Hinamizawa's population — has been caused by the Three Great Houses, led by the Sonozaki Estate. Their goal, it is averred, has been to revive Oyashiro-sama's cult and reestablish primitive customs dating back to the days when the village was still called "Onigafuchi" (literally, "demons' abyss") — i.e., a series of murders and sacrificial disembowelments. A plot of veritably global immensity that surpasses by far even the most iniquitous dynastic machinations in both its Machiavellian scheming and sheer horror is gradually exposed as the anime develops further. However, at this stage in the adventure, the potential truth disclosed by Rena following her perusal of Takano's notebooks is that when the clans found out that Takano was close to unveiling their plan, they quickly resolved to eliminate her, making Takano and Tomitake's deaths the nub of the fifth and climactic Wataganashi horror. If the families' dark secret were to be publicly exposed, this explanation maintains, Oyashiro-sama's divine credentials would be exploded.

Undoubtedly, beneath the terrifying surface of Hinamizawa's assassinations and disappearances, there lies a rather flimsy faith. Its only foundational rule appears to be the injunction for the autochthonous people never to leave the village and for outsiders to keep out of its boundaries. To sustain this dubiously isolationist creed, a myth of more imposing proportions has come into being. This promulgates the belief that wild demons at one point emerged from the town's marsh and that Oyashiro-sama dealt with these invaders by giving them human form and thus enabling them to coexist with the original villagers. The truth — at least as disclosed by the first season — is that what actually rose from the swamp was a powerful virus responsible for a peculiar contagious disease capable of driving the infected specimens berserk. Oyashiro-sama, in this version of history, was not a god but a doctor of sorts who could deploy preventive measures to stem contamination. If a person contracted the disease and attacked another person, he or she would be killed alongside the victim. In the legend, it was said that the intestines of designated individuals must be eaten for ritual purposes. In the alternative version of the truth provided in the second Answer arc, the tissues extracted from fatalities of the virus are said to have been used to produce a rudimentary vaccine enabling humans and bacteria to become mutually compatible and live on.

The revelations put forward in the first season's concluding arc are elaborated upon in the early part of the second season. This opens with an installment set in 2007, ideated specifically for the anime, that echoes several motifs dramatized in the preceding segments both visually and thematically. This episode indicates that the Hinamizawa massacre is believed by many to have been the result of an alien landing, and by others to have been a bioterrorist act accidentally triggered by the three great families' research into the production of a powerful virus capable of sustaining the rekindling of the Oyashiro-sama legend. This portion of the story is distinguished by an especially extensive use of descriptive and speculative dialogue that works very effectively in conveying its reflection-oriented mood, as well as in capturing the source game's textual slant. The melancholy feel issuing from the abandoned paths and crumbling buildings, combined with the intoxicating abundance of vegetation able to propagate unfettered by human hands, contribute vitally to the segment's pensive rhythm. The aged Ooishi and Akasaka evince memorable facial expressions evocative at once of a mature resignation to the vagaries of fate and a bittersweet empathy with a world gone forever. The close-up of Ooishi's face as he looks at the luscious environment through the car window on his tour of Hinamizawa with Akasaka poignantly encapsulates the cumulative mood of this part of the action.

The first actual arc of Season 2, *Yakusamashi-hen* ("Disaster-Awakening Chapter")—was also created expressly for the anime and does not strictly speaking constitute either a Question or an Answer arc. In fact, it knits together moments from the four Question arcs and intersperses them with novel information that both harks back to the previous Answer arcs and foreshadows those to come. From the inceptive stages of this segment, Rika acquires unprecedented centrality as the sorrowful side of her childlike character comes to the fore, thus disclosing a spilt personality. In this arc's finale, the anime offers a graphic portrayal of the Hinamizawa Disaster's immediate aftermath that mirrors directly the presentation of the same tragedy at the end of the third Question arc. This time around, Satoko is held to be the only named survivor. However, the child is not allowed to enjoy this privileged status for long since the parties keen on concealing the real causes of the holocaust rapidly dispose of her.

A crucial turning-point in the disclosure of Hinamizawa's real dark history is the opening part of the third Answer arc, *Minagoroshi-hen* ("Massacre Chapter"). In a splendidly choreographed sequence combining magisterial handling of compositing techniques and graceful lyricism, Rika delivers a monologue in which close-ups of her face and full shots of her infantile body feature in conjunction with multifaceted shards of rocklike material displaying fragmentary images of the other characters selected from various parts of the show. Through Rika's poetic exposé, we learn that over the decades, she has experienced countless versions of Hinamizawa invariably set in June, 1983, each time reliving approximately the same temporal span. With each successive reincarnation the world around her alters, however marginally at times, and the way different people act within it accordingly varies. All of the stories dramatized in previous arcs could therefore be regarded as flashbacks to alternate configurations of this "endless June" and of the crimes, tragedies and emotions embedded therein. Directly addressing the viewer with such self-referential subtlety as "You, the witness at my side," Rika points out that despite their contingent variations, all of the sequential Hinamizawas share certain fundamental rules. One of them is the recurrence of states of terminal paranoia conducive to brutal actions. The cases which the monologue explicitly refers to are Keiichi's from the first Question arc, Shion's from the first Answer arc and Rena's from the second Answer arc.

Rika is eager to emphasize that all of these people are, at root, "affectionate and kind. And yet, when the cogwheels of fate are out of gear, they become overwhelmed by unrealistic beliefs, and begin to use destructive, violent force." No less crucially, the perpetrator of these "atrocities" changes from world to world due to "arbitrary causes." The pertinence of chaos theory to this situation as a dramatic stimulus of great potency is worth noting. Another key rule is the repeated occurrence of Tomitake and Takano's murders, soon followed by Rika's own execution. A further unchanging development is that whenever Teppei returns to Hinamizawa, he will again start abusing his niece. The ostensibly unceasing emergence of worlds governed by unchanging rules is not, Rika contends, "coincidental." Chaos theory is again elliptically hinted at in this portion of the monologue since, as indicated, this system does not preclude the existence of relatively regular factors even within a scenario of apparent randomness although these are, by and large, empirically indiscernible.

At this point in the series, Rika also asserts her firm conviction that the reiteration of particular elements across disparate worlds results from their shared origins in "someone's strong desires." However, while the girl has sampled several other dimensions and therefore possesses "knowledge that others do not," she still has no clue to the identity of the force that sanctions her death, let alone its reasons for doing so. The tenacious endurance of this enigma is of pivotal significance to *Higurashi*'s overall diegesis, insofar as it enables the story to pursue diverse leads and engage in alternative speculations concerning an extensive spectrum of incidents without this strategy coming across as gratuitously dilatory. If not even the axial character is in possession of all the pieces in the puzzle, it is only natural for all of the other actors — and by extension the audience — to fumble in the dark and harbor suspicions that may well prove incorrect. There is one thing, however, that Rika knows for sure: her resolve "to break through the labyrinth of fate, and reach a happy future."

Following this informative monologue, we enter the next Hinamizawa. Hanyuu here makes her first visible appearance, even though it has been incrementally suggested throughout the anime that Rika has a latent counterpart. This time around, Rika enters Hinamizawa in early June, which means that she has very little time at her disposal before the next Wataganashi Festival to bring about any variations on the established pattern of events that might transform her ceaselessly reenacted destiny. Rika's lack of time (reminiscent of Momoka's predicament in *Touka Gettan*) intimates that her powers are dwindling. Although on this occasion Keiichi does not seem to carry any recollections of previous Hinamizawa realities, which dashes the hopes raised in Rika's heart by the climax of the second Answer arc, the youth staunchly declares his determination to oppose fate when Rika states that one has no choice but to accept what has already been decided, and soon manages (albeit unknowingly) to introduce changes into the endlessly repeated June-1983 history. At one point, he even appears to sense subliminally a feeling of familiarity with the situation in hand, even though he is convinced he has never experienced it before. While Keiichi dismisses the uncanny sensation as a déjà vu, Rika maintains, "There's no such thing as memories that 'couldn't have existed.' If you remember it, then it's something that actually happened." In the wake of this assertion, Keiichi recalls the anime's first world quite vividly, yet notes that it feels like a "dream." As is often the case in visual novels and their animated offspring, memories and dreams are thus seamlessly synthesized. Rena's psyche is also able to reach back into a previous world through a recurrent nightmare in which she murders a woman hell-bent on exploiting her dad — the baleful incident at the core of the first season's concluding segment. By confiding in Mion and then confronting her deluded father, Rena can avoid translating the haunting vision into a reality, which breaks the tragic loop dramatized in the earlier arc. Shion likewise faces up to a nightmare of her own in which she kills both her sister and Satoko, as she did in a previous Hinamizawa incarnation, by sharing her sinister dream with Mion. In both Rena's and Shion's cases, the willingness to share one's pain with a loved one proves instrumental to the characters' defiance of a seemingly preordained and ineluctable course of action.

Now Rika has grounds on which to hope that her own sealed fate might alter and that she might thus transcend her entrapment in eternal childhood. What the anime seems to be advocating here is the necessity to withstand fate's unyielding dictates as the sole viable means of avoiding the blind repetition of the same hideous mistakes time and again. Exhorted by Keiichi to stop using the word "fate" as if everything was already "determined," Rika herself comes to conclude that "Fate is something we can change ourselves." This brave confrontation of temporality at large is shown to be the prerequisite for the unveiling of the actual mastermind behind Hinamizawa's baneful history, which in fact occurs in the third Answer arc. In rapid succession, various key characters reveal themselves capable of performing choices and actions that depart from the customary trajectory and thus of driving a wedge between the spokes of destiny's wheel. This ability results precisely from an abeyant readiness to recall tiny fragments of other versions of Hinamizawa. The protagonists do not actually achieve their goal at the end of the "Massacre Chapter," and instead of breaking through the labyrinth of fate, they must endure a crushing defeat at the hands of the indomitable and increasingly deranged Takano. Nevertheless, they do leave the arc having discovered what they will need most in order to sever the shackles of Eternal Return in their next reality — which will also feasibly constitute the last manifestation of Hinamizawa in June, 1983, and the springboard from which they might move forward.

The key is their retention of the memory of the true culprit's identity. The third Answer arc is also diegetically axial insofar as it includes Rika's explanation of the village's ordeal on the basis of the "Hinamizawa Syndrome," a condition conducive to paranoia, delusional fears and bestial conduct. All Hinamizawa residents host the virus but can generally tolerate it unless they are subject to severe stress or leave the village, while outsiders possess no defenses against its onslaught. Thus Satoko, who turns out to have caused her parents' death due to her manic conviction that they intend to kill her, falls prey to the disease as a result of anxiety bred by parental ill-treatment. Rena and Shion are beset by the syndrome (as indicated by the arcs to which they are central as culprits) when they return to Hinamizawa after a period of absence. Keiichi, for his part, precipitates into psychosis (as seen in the first Question arc) simply due to his status as a non-native.

People have known about the virus since ancient times (even though it was only brought to global attention at the time of the Second World War) but have attributed it to a curse rather than to physiological phenomena. The existence of the Hinamizawa Syndrome has not been publicly divulged to avoid spreading panic since no cure is yet available, but more ominously because there are parties keen on exploiting it as the basis of a biological weapon. The "Irie Institution," headed by Takano, is said to have been established precisely to develop this type of armament. Dr. Irie himself, however, is oblivious to the intended aim of the enterprise, honestly believes he has been appointed to create a cure for the syndrome for military purposes, and has indeed found a way of suppressing even the most advanced symptoms through injections. The Irie Institution is sponsored by a secret organization known as "Tokyo" that comprises numerous influential politicians, financial experts, government officials and military personnel. Insofar as its plan flagrantly contravenes the "Biological Weapons Convention," the organization uses fierce special troops dubbed "Yamainu" ("Mountain Hounds") to guard its secrecy at any price. The key agent in the handling of the indigenous disease is Rika: as the latest female descendant of the Furude dynasty, she perpetuates the legacy associated with women of her lineage over many generations by hosting from birth the inceptive pathogen known as "Queen" which makes her the current "Queen Carrier." This person has the power to curb the virus and thus prevent its mass eruption. Rika's elimination, accordingly, would inevitably lead to a veritable hecatomb. All along, Tomitake's mission has consisted of preventing the Hinamizawa Syndrome from exploding — or to put it in Takano's own words, to "defuse" the "bomb" symbolized by the disease. It is not until Takano is about to inject him with a Level-5 version of the virus — which is bound to unleash its terminal, self-destructive symptoms — that Tomitake realizes the enormity of the crime she intends to perpetrate. Doctor Irie is another naive fatality of Miyo's delusional plan. Ultimately he merely supplies a convenient scapegoat for the Yamainu, who dispose of him at Takano's behest and divulge the rumor that Irie himself has caused Takano and Tomitake's deaths to prevent them from exposing his misappropriation of funds for the clinic.

Upon entering the new Hinamizawa in the fourth Answer arc, *Matsuribayashi-hen* ("Festival-Accompanying Chapter"), neither Rika not her friends appear to hold any conscious recollection of Takano's role in the town's misfortunes, unwavering resolve to validate her theories at the cost of the village's very survival, and unscrupulous appropriation of the Oyashiro-sama legend in order to attain what she insanely considers divine stature. The characters' mnemonic failure would seem to entail their powerlessness to apply the lesson learnt at the end of the foregoing arc to their current situation. Yet this is not quite the case, since even if their collective memory is still lacunary, it is subconsciously able to trigger Hanyuu's climactic materialization. The creature therefore features for the first time in the story as an embodied presence despite her essential status as a preternatural force: namely, a guardian deity devoted to the protection of the region that has contributed vitally to the dissemination of the Oyashiro-sama cult. Furthermore, the entity is said to be personally responsible for the creation of the endlessly repeating June of 1983 as a means of preventing Rika from being conclusively slaughtered. In the finale of the "Massacre Chapter," it was suggested that the characters' recent efforts to defeat fate had been ineffectual due to Hanyuu's failure to join their ranks as an active participant rather than an impotent onlooker. The final arc dismantles this residual obstacle and emphasizes Hanyuu's centrality by making her responsible for revealing once more that were Rika to be killed, the Hinamizawa Syndrome could spread and Hinamizawa's inhabitants would meet a dismal end by asphyxiation to be prevented from reaching the terminal stages of the disease.

This is exactly what Takano aspires to as a means of sensationally proving the veracity of her foster grandfather's research and hypotheses concerning the Hinamizawa Syndrome, fulfilling her dream of perpetuating his legacy while also vindicating his reputation as a scientist and no less crucially taming at last the manic desire to be valued, caused by the loss of her parents and hellish entrapment in a sadistic orphanage, that has persecuted Miyo since childhood. What Takano does not know is that her plan is actually being exploited by warring factions within "Tokyo." Indeed, the death of the organization's leader, and Takano's key sponsor, Mr. Koizumi, means that his antagonists now stand a chance of gaining supremacy: if the theories surrounding the disease could be discredited, Koizumi's own repute would be questioned, which would create scope for a radical reallocation of power and resources. Hence, Takano is fundamentally a pawn in the hands of much larger and darker forces than she could ever have suspected. If her own research into the Hinamizawa Syndrome could be seen to lead to a scandal of cataclysmic proportions, this would provide a brilliant pretext for a drastic rearrangement of the corporation's internal hierarchy.

These developments demonstrate *Higurashi*'s standing as a complex, sophisticated and dispassionate anatomy of political intrigue and financial sleaze capable of transcending the limitations of scores of shows in the mystery and horror molds. The political dimension is additionally brought into play in the magisterially staged sequence in which Rika, pretending that the plot revolving around Takano of which Hanyuu has informed her is the basic scenario for a manga she is writing, asks her friends for tips meant to help her keep the story "consistent." Mion, arguably due to her association with a family well-versed in matters of corruption and organized crime, excels at the game and meets the challenge with a seasoned strategist's flair. The sequence is also important insofar as it foregrounds the role played by collaborative creative enterprises within both visual novels and anime based on them as concurrently pragmatic and speculative quests. A further self-reflexive touch lies with Hanyuu's reference to her and Rika's current experience as the "game" of June, 1983. As noted, the first season closes with a very telling post-credit sequence in which Rika makes a sibylline allusion to the "endless June." Season 2 also comes to an end with a post-credit sequence of deep relevance to the anime's thematic and structural handling of the wheel of fate. This features a grown-up incarnation of Rika and an infantile version of Miyo, where Rika enables the little girl to make a choice that effectively reverses her destiny and allows her to embark on a life in which she does not lose her parents at an early age and therefore does not need, ever to come into contact with research regarding the Hinamizawa Syndrome.

A schematic reconstruction of *Higurashi*'s timeline extrapolated from the foregoing analysis (here included on the assumption that spoilers are no longer a danger at this stage) discloses the following sequence of interrelated events.

[*Hinamizawa's ancient past:*]
- The mighty priestess Hanyuu is born. Choosing to act as a receptacle for all of Hinamizawa's sins and offering herself up as a sacrificial victim, Hanyuu becomes a deity connected with the cult of Oyashiro-sama and retains a place within the Furude family.

[*Decades immediately preceding the main story:*]
- Dr. Hifumi Takano discovers the Hinamizawa Syndrome and resolves to make it the object of his lifelong research. His late pupil Tanashi's only child, Miyoko, endures hellish abuse in an orphanage following

her parents' death in a traffic accident, until she is rescued by Dr. Takano. The scientist's work is ridiculed, which leads to his foster granddaughter's obsessive resolve to perpetuate his quest, thereby changing her name to Miyo Takano and advancing the project with Mr. Koizumi's bounteous funding.

• The twin sisters Mion and Shion Sonozaki are born. The real Shion is accidentally marked with the demon tattoo intended to distinguish the great family's legitimate heir and hence becomes the public "Mion," while the real Mion is sidelined by the Sonozakis and becomes the public "Shion."

• Rika is born in the Furude clan as its eighth successive female and reveals herself able to see Hanyuu.

• Reina Ryuuguu leaves Hinamizawa.

• The dam project is launched by the Japanese government and the Houjou family, its principal supporter, becomes the object of widespread hatred.

[1978:]

• Detective Mamoru Akasaka is sent to Hinamizawa to investigate the protest against the dam construction in conjunction with the kidnapping of the Minister of Construction's grandson, carried out to boycott the project by the Yamainu personnel, though it is at one stage intimated that the Three Great Houses are actually behind the act. The dam operation is abruptly discontinued but Rika predicts that direful events will follow every year at the time of the Watanagashi Festival for years to come and that these will include her own death.

[1979:]

• The project manager supervising the construction of the dam is driven insane by the Hinamizawa Syndrome and attacks his coworkers, thereby causing their retaliatory reaction. This culminates in his dismemberment and the dispersal of the severed limbs. In order to further her research into the Hinamizawa Syndrome, Dr. Takano abducts one of the dam workers involved in the gruesome affair, who is reputed to have contracted the disease and thus constitutes a suitable live specimen. Detective Kuraudo Ooishi is personally affected by the murder since the manager was like a second father to him, and makes the solution of the crime his raison d'être as he advances towards retirement.

• Rika's father reveals to his wife and daughter that the girl is pivotal to the future of the Hinamizawa Syndrome due to her special status as Queen Carrier. Rika thereafter offers to operate as Dr. Takano's test subject in the hope that a vaccine may be formulated.

[1980:]

- Affected by the indigenous virus, Satoko Houjou develops the delusional fear that her parents intend to kill her, as a result of which she pushes them off a viewing platform while on holiday. The woman's body is never found. The Houjou kids are adopted by their aunt and uncle and subject to persistent abuse. When Satoko is taken to the local clinic and her condition is diagnosed, Rika persuades Dr. Kyousuke Irie to try an experimental medicine on the girl. Satoko, however, is told that she is acting as the test subject for potentially groundbreaking vitamins.

[*1981:*]

- Mr. Furude, a priest who provided the Houjous with protection at the time of their harassment, dies suddenly of mysterious causes and his wife drowns herself. As with Mrs. Houjou, so with Mrs. Furude: no conclusive corporeal evidence is obtained. In actual fact, the Yamainu are responsible for both deaths, requested by Dr. Takano to stop Rika's parents from interfering with the research undertaken on their daughter.
- Blaming herself for her parents' divorce, Reina Ryuuguu starts hurting herself and, having narrowly escaped rape, gives vent to her repressed anger by bludgeoning her tormentors. When she accidentally hears Hanyuu's voice, she becomes convinced that Oyashiro-sama's curse has fallen upon her.

[*1982:*]

- Reina returns to Hinamizawa and changes her name to Rena.
- Shion runs away from boarding school and relocates in Okinomiya. She thereafter meets Satoshi Houjou and falls in love with him. The youth, for his part, is so grievously unbalanced by his domestic situation as to start believing that Oyashiro-sama is after him. For Satoshi, as for Rena before him, Hanyuu's voice has much to do with the genesis of this obsession — though in fact the preternatural girl is struggling to apologize to them for the dire destinies in which they have been ensnared, feeling tangentially responsible. In a fit of blind rage, Satoshi murders his aunt and shortly after exhibits some of the Hinamizawa Syndrome's advanced symptoms, at which point Dr. Irie intervenes by relocating him to the clinic and deploying him as an additional test subject. To explain Satoshi's disappearance, some people maintain that he has transferred to another school and others that he has run away, but the dominant opinion seems to be that he has been spirited away.

[*1983:*]

- This is the key year in the story since all of the anime's principal arcs constitute alternative versions of the events surrounding the Watanagashi Festival held in June, 1983, where Rika fulfils her ceremonial duty as a *miko* by performing a ritual dance of awe-inspiring beauty. The characters of Jirou Tomitake and Miyo Takano feature as victims in all of the available variations. Other characters are also shown to meet hapless ends but the identities of these additional fatalities alter according to which character is employed as the specific arc's focal point of reference. The climax, in all versions, is marked by Rika's violent death, the catastrophe triggering the Hinamizawa holocaust and the village's official isolation.

[*2007:*]

• Detectives Ooishi and Akasaka meet again in a desolate and crumbling Hinamizawa and interview an adult and dismally unhappy incarnation of Rena Ryuuguu.

*Higurashi* is one of the most boldly innovative of the anime here studied at the levels of both cinematography and narrative. The former relies consistently on unusual camera angles meant to intensify succinctly a scene's dramatic impact. The latter capitalizes on a ubiquitous atmosphere of ambiguity that makes it practically impossible to distinguish between heroes/heroines and villains. This mood is heightened by *Higurashi*'s generic mélange, whereby baleful prophecies and zany comedy coexist on numerous occasions. At the same time, the gentle pastoral feel of many scenes is deftly juxtaposed with either laconic or strident references to each of the protagonists' dark undercurrents. Even within the more clownish moments, one finds hints at the heroines' secret and at least potentially malevolent tendencies. In an early installment, for example, the male lead accuses his friends of hiding secrets and even intimates that they are "evil" in the innocent context of a card game wherein the girls shamelessly resort to cheating. Before long, Keiichi will have reason to question the girls' honesty over much graver matters. Another good example is the game of "Zombie Tag" played by Keiichi and his friends in an early episode of Season 2, where ludic enthusiasm escalates into a paroxysm of horror-laced frenzy — even though, felicitously on this occasion, the punishment ultimately amounts to no more than team-tickling.

*Higurashi*'s flair for generic acrobatics is confirmed by the five-episode OVA series *Higurashi no Naku Koro ni Rei*. This opens with the one-installment *Batsukoishi-hen* ("Shame-Exposing Chapter"), a piece of slapstick revolving around Keiichi's coincidental acquisition of some "popularity swimming trunks" and the incrementally preposterous strategies deployed by the rest of the customary *Higurashi* cast to remove the bewitched item from his body. Irreverently indulging in parody and pastiche by turns, the installment capitalizes on a mismatch between the various actors' registers, expressions and body language, which are consonant with their roles in the original story's more serious moments, and the trivial absurdity of the situation, distorting the very concept of "epic exploit" into a paean to mock-heroic farce. With the OVA's transition to the second arc, *Saikoroshi-hen* ("Dice-Killing Chapter"), the tone alters drastically as the narrative grows darker and more tense. In this three-episode segment, Rika is transposed to an alternate world in which the dire recurring events chronicled in the main series never take place and yet the girl, now friendless, must endure the burden of loneliness in exchange for a crime-free world. Eventually, Rika must decide whether to stay in this parallel reality or commit a sin that will enable her to abandon it. The final, one-episode arc *Hirukowashi-hen* ("Daybreak Chapter"), adopts again a lighter tenor, though this time in the direction of myth-imbued romance rather than zany comedy. Rena's swallowing of a mysterious charm endowed with portentous powers in the course of one of her legendary treasure troves, constitutes the crux of the adventure.

Where visual ambiguity is concerned, it is also noteworthy that while both natural and architectural backgrounds are invariably detailed and pictorially tactile in their richness, the character designs for the key personae often come across as stylized. (Supporting characters — e.g., Takano, Tomitake, Ooishi — are on the whole more realistically portrayed.) The young female actors' facial features in particular are sometimes intentionally flattened, and chromatic symbolism might initially abet individuation more than actual physiognomic traits. When expressions are overtly or even bizarrely distorted, as is routinely the case in highly charged sequences, the abnormality of the actors' affective states gains special pathos precisely by virtue of their ordinary miens' drastic departure from the norm. Some of the techniques proficiently used to signal mental disturbance are asymmetrical distributions of somatic attributes, deformations effected through grotesque wrinkles and pouches, the blanking of a character's customarily glossy eyes to vacuous expanses of gelatinous white or dull color, and the contraction of the pupils into feline slits. Thus, *Higurashi*'s artwork is able to lead the audience along with its apparently familiar images and suddenly defamiliarize its perceptions through torridly original shards of dread. The show's mixed tone is already evident in the opening theme of Season 1, where mellow chords and deliberately discordant notes coexist and the visuals fluidly oscillate between idyllic charm and connotative horror. There is something forbiddingly eerie about the graphic incongruity conveyed by the tension between the joyfulness of the colors employed and the glacial rigorousness of the formal arrangements. Flowers play an especially important role, alternating between a candid celebration of natural beauty rendered with stunning accuracy and an exposure of the uncanny forces lurking behind even the most innocuous of forms. Accordingly, one moment the eye is regaled with photorealistically familiar and reassuring shapes. The next, the delicate petals and leaves are depicted in a coldly stylized mode as multihued geometric elements that are alternately assembled and disassembled like the slivers in a kaleidoscope.

The anime's ambiguous personality owes much to Kon's maximization of the principle of multiperspectivalism, as a result of which most of the characters, depending on the circumstances, shift between sanity and lunacy, operating as beneficent forces in one arc and agents of chaos in the next. At all times, however, *Higurashi* refrains from indulging in such mutations merely for the sake of ostentatious spectacle by intimating that behind even the most reckless actions there lie cogent and believable reasons. For example, when Rena morphs from a compassionate and innocent *shoujo* into a cleaver-wielding maniac hellbent on outwardly pointless bloodshed, her motivations are not random but grounded in a convincingly charted history of both private and collective disturbance. Relatedly, the anime seeks to exploit to maximum effect the speculative thrust of the parent game, and indeed of all visual novels at their most accomplished. In doing so, it posits each arc as a "would-if" schema and proceeds, from that premise, to explore what sorts of divergent decisions characters might plausibly take in different contexts, pursuing each hypothetical option to its logical albeit unpleasant conclusions. These strategies allow *Higurashi* to transcend the limitations of less analytical horror yarns, where characters tend to be defined at an early stage on the basis of crystallized attributes, and hence portray its actors as continually amenable to redefinition, layering and expansion. Even after repeat viewings, spectators may feel that the show is playing tricks with their heads through its protean character portraits and attendant perspectives on the evolving action.

The *Higurashi* franchise foregrounds several stylistic elements that are firmly embedded in the foundations of Japanese aesthetics. Most prominent among them are the predilection for elegant lines, subtly juxtaposed swathes of bold hues, and adventurous approaches to composition and perspective. Simultaneously, the anime bears witness to the endurance of traditional values in contemporary forms of indigenous cultural production, which suggests that time-honored trends are still respected today. This is demonstrated by homages to a wide variety of artifacts and practices rooted in Japanese tradition, from screens and shrines to calligraphy and rituals. Some factors are explicitly highlighted, the Furude Shrine and festival-accompanying performance no doubt offering the principal examples, while others are unobtrusively sprinkled through the mise-en-scène: e.g., the paintings adorning the Sonozaki mansion and parts of the Furude compound or the banners bearing diverse calligraphic styles used to advertise the anti-dam campaign.

*Higurashi* also brings to mind native woodblock prints in its use of vivid colors that do not seek to emulate accurately the chromatic range of the real world but aim instead to individuate succinctly both characters and locations, to underscore moments of intense drama, and to bring out the tactile qualities of both natural forms like flowers and leaves and manmade objects such as clothes, dishes and toys. The influence of the woodblock print can also be detected in the anime's maximization of the dynamic properties of space. The composition often relies on powerful diagonals in order to infuse otherwise static settings with energy and vibrance. The geometric lines deployed to energize the inanimate components of space are at times further enlivened by their integration with imaginary lines defined by character interaction as a web of crisscrossing verbal exchanges or wordless glances. In the process, cadenced feelings of activity and intimacy seamlessly coalesce and the viewer's eye is invited to travel not only across the space of the frame but also beyond it. Yet the artwork's attention to detail ensures that there is always sufficient material for the eye to dwell upon and hence precludes hurried visual processing. It is often through the intimation of movement more than through the differentiation between figure and ground that the sense of space is created. When lines converge over a conflictual scenario, a feeling of confinement is conveyed that schematically intensifies the impression of menace. Viewers may even sense that the threat is about to erupt into their own space through the screen, as though this were a door inadvertently left ajar beyond which darkling passageways unwound in unknown directions.

A major homage to tradition is the massive statue of Oyashiro-sama accommodated within the forbidden sanctum of the Furude Shrine. The sculpture paradigmatically encapsulates a fundamental tenet of Buddhist and Shinto philosophy, described by John Reeve as a collusion of "Serenity and turbulence, spirituality and slaughter" (Reeve, p. 22). The great statue's disarming poise conveys an impression of imperturbable clam even though, as the anime incrementally stresses, it emblematizes the tumultuous forces coursing through both Hinamizawa's external reality and it inhabitants' inner worlds. At both levels, one senses an unpretentious urge to point towards an understanding of reality as a process of continual flux, as impermanence (*mujou*), and hence partaking at all times of everlasting cycles of birth, death and rebirth. At first sight, Oyashiro-sama could well be a version of the classic Buddhist figures found in ancient temples and intended to welcome the faithful to eternal happiness in the Pure Land. The degree of concentration evinced by the statue on essential details unencumbered by excessive ornamentation forcefully transmits its spiritual ascendancy. However, like several representations of the Indian guru Daruma, reputed to have founded Zen Buddhism, the image of Oyashiro-sama harbors discordant connotations in a single body, which makes him akin at once to a "death-dealing knife" and a "life-giving blow" (thirteenth-century Chinese poem cited in Reeve, p. 27). In this regard, Oyashiro-sama also recalls religious figures from Buddhist art in which ferocious attributes and weapons are deployed to suggest baleful powers that are not meant to contradict but rather complement in a dialectical fashion the deities' supposedly compassionate natures. The icons displayed at the gates of temples and shrines (the Furude compound included) likewise evince harrowing traits while serving as devoted guardians.

Thus, it could be argued that while *Higurashi* echoes traditional Japanese art in its treatment of composition, perspective and color, it is in the use of images evocative of disquietude and unruliness that the anime elliptically captures one of the most tantalizing facets of indigenous culture. As in many of Akira Kurosawa's movies, and indeed in the actual history of Japan in the Middle Ages and early modernity, any promise of balance is threatened by lurking disorder. It is in festivals, a ubiquitous aspect of Japan's traditional culture for time immemorial, that the passion for extremes finds one of its most tangible and graphically rich expressions, granting symbolic centrality to distorted, macabre and portentous figures that are redolent of the vengeful ghosts (*yuurei*) with which Japanese lore famously pullulates. It is no coincidence, in this context, that *Higurashi* should choose a traditional festival as its diegetic pivot in the dramatization of age-old strife.

As proposed, the tension between harmonious and tempestuous drives pervades the fabric of Hinamizawa as a receptacle of societal turmoil that nonetheless comes across as a natural sanctuary of tranquility. In the depiction of outdoor settings, this mood is thrown into relief by the consistent incorporation of visual references to the four elements, whose balanced interaction is held by Japanese art and ritual as aesthetically pivotal. (As a spiritual practice, the Tea Ceremony epitomizes this idea.) The illusory serenity issuing from Hinamizawa's sceneries is fully demonstrated by the artwork's employment of subtly modulated textures and hues, filtered sunlight and half-veiled moonlight. It should also be noted, on this point, that the anime's liking for settings that deliberately leave some aspects unseen mirrors a vital ingredient of Japanese art: namely, a preference for approximation, adumbration, inconclusiveness and incompleteness, allied to a deep attraction to the inscrutable components of aesthetic experience. Nancy G. Hume vividly illustrates this idea as follows: "When looking at autumn mountains through mist, the view may be indistinct yet have great depth. Although few autumn leaves may be visible through the mist, the view is alluring. The limitless vista created in imagination far surpasses anything one can see more clearly" (Hume, pp. 253–254).

Whereas the imposing statue of Hinamizawa's patron echoes the aesthetic principle of *yugen* as a valorization of eternal and incorruptible forces that defy empirical observation, the sense of simplicity exuded by rustic forms recalls the notion of *wabi*, and the portrayal of partially shrouded vistas hints at the related concept of *sabi* as a fascination with the imperfect. As for the best-known mainstay of Japanese aesthetics, sensitivity to the ephemerality of beauty, pleasure and life itself known as *mono no aware*, this could barely find more memorable an expression than in the punctuating sound of churring cicadas. The melancholy beauty of the garbage dump in which some of the most significant scenes are set reflects at once the principles of *wabi/sabi* and *mono no aware* in variable atmospheric and lighting conditions. Even in its most turbulent moments (e.g., the rain-battered nocturnal sequences chronicling Keiichi's abortive "execution" of Teppei and its aftermath), *Higurashi* never fails to communicate the lyrical beauty of nature through dream-like compositions and through the shimmering drizzle of golden tinges imbuing the landscape. Therefore, the artwork gently records, frame after frame, the essence of its world's seasons and creatures while also hinting at the symbolic vocabulary underlying Japanese art's depiction of flora and fauna.

*Higurashi*'s landscapes — especially the panoramic vista of Hinamizawa as seen from the Furude Shrine grounds — echo early Japanese paintings and their penchant for a hazy and magical atmosphere originating in poetic imagery more than in documentary accuracy. The mountains surrounding the village act as powerful symbols for all natural forces that mock human fragility through their engulfing presence as not merely geological but also spiritual formations: importantly, mountains are held by Shinto to host some of the most influential *kami*. Yet, as noted, the fictional setting is based on a real-world location and this can be felt by simply observing the artwork's devotion to details. Thus, the coalescence of stylization and naturalism characterizing the portrayal of Hinamizawa aptly mirrors the duplicitous narrative significance attached to the village as both something of a paradise on Earth and a locus of intractable turmoil. A recurrent element is the emphasis on the simultaneously comforting and threatening agency of Hinamizawa vis-à-vis its dwellers. This discrepancy parallels Japanese art's simultaneous cultivation of quiet grace and kinetic tension. The frequent scenes set by the water mill encapsulate both sides of the village since they inspire a soothing sense of serenity, often bathed in aureate twilight, even when they witness exchanges alluding to harrowing events.

In *Higurashi*, the phenomenon of immersion works in two ways. On the one hand, the anime ushers in a type of immersion infused with metaphysical undertones by drawing us not simply into one definite time zone but rather into a potentially interminable cycle of recurrence of overtly Eastern derivation. On the other hand, the overabundance of riddles — rendered exponentially elaborate and even befuddling by their presentation from kaleidoscopic perspectives — palpably draws the audience into the story in what could be termed the detection mode. At this level, we are obliquely enjoined to attune ourselves to the figures of the two investigators included in the cast, who come to operate as our intradiegetic avatars. Focusing on the latter modality, it is noteworthy that *Higurashi* articulates various forms of detection at different stages in its exuberantly multiperspectival diegesis. In so doing, the anime, brings to mind alternate modalities of what Tzvetan Todorov has famously termed the "typology of detective fiction." On one plane, *Higurashi* recalls the classic "whodunnit" insofar as, like this subgenre of detective fiction, it develops consistently "not one but two stories: the story of the crime and the story of the investigation" (Todorov, p. 159). Since, due to the show's numerous variations on a core set of events, the same character might feature at different junctures as the criminal and the investigator (professional or amateur as the case may be), the two basic strands postulated by Todorov proliferate into a tangle of forking narrative paths. In each alternative configuration of the crime-centered story, however, the anime deploys the key narrative devices associated with it by the structuralist champion — namely, "temporal inversions and individual 'points of view.'" These strategies, in emphasizing that "the tenor of each piece of information is determined by the person who transmits it" from his or her angle as he or she assesses past occurrences with hindsight, iconoclastically proclaims that "the author cannot, by definition, be omniscient." Where the story of the crime abounds with literary conventions of the kind just described, the story of the investigation in the whodunnit is deemed by Todorov to adopt a relatively "neutral and plain" style to suggest that its function is essentially to operate as a "mediator between the reader and the story of the crime" and therefore is not, keen on devices that might render matters "opaque." *Higurashi* is never unproblematically transparent in style even in the solution arcs, yet it is undeniable that as it enters the unveiling mode, it becomes willing to deliver facts and details that are merely adumbrated in the mystery-laden arcs.

The second category theorized by Todorov, the "thriller," is also invoked by the anime in its cultivation of the two "forms of interest" associated by the Slavic commentator with that subgenre: "curiosity" and "suspense." The former "proceeds from effect to cause: starting from a certain effect (a corpse and certain clues) we must find its cause (the culprit and his motive)." The latter traces an inverse trajectory "from cause to effect: we are first shown the causes, the initial *données* (gangsters preparing a heist), and our interest is sustained by the expectation of what will happen, that is, certain effects (corpses, crimes, fights)" (p. 161). In *Higurashi*, curiosity is stoked by the story's insistent emphasis on the opprobrious results of what is at first held to be Oyashiro-sama's curse and attendant interest in their motivations. Suspense, on the other hand, becomes especially conspicuous in arcs that map out the devising of a crime. (The Shion-based question arc is a particularly good example of this approach). Finally, Kon's work could be said to conform with Todorov's third modality, "the suspense novel," wherein aspects of both the whodunit and the thriller can be found. Like the former, the suspense novel works with enigmas that evoke "two stories, that of the past and that of the present." Like the latter, it seeks to kindle the audience's interest not solely in "what has happened" but also "what will happen next" (p. 164). *Higurashi* consummately satisfies this formula insofar as it intermeshes the past and the present at each turn precisely in order to maintain a delicate equilibrium between chains of events that have already come to pass (and have indeed done so an incalculable number of times) and events emerging therefrom — likewise in perpetuity unless the Eternal-June pattern is broken.

Most relevant to the current discussion is the anime's use of the dynamics of detection as a major means of drawing the audience into its narrative in an immersive fashion. In the face of *Higurashi*'s undecidables, viewers are confronted at least potentially with a number of intercomplementary tasks. Each of these is connected with a formal characteristic of the show itself (and by implication of its ludic wellhead). According to the game designer Chris Crawford, all computer games evince four key features: "representation," the portrayal of a portion of reality in a subjective mode; "interaction," the acknowledgement of and reaction to a player; "conflict," the tension between a player's effort to accomplish a goal and the obstacles put in his or her way by game mechanics; and "safety," the guarantee that the player's actions will not impinge negatively upon the real world (Crawford). As a subset of computer games, visual novels partake of all of these attributes. So do anime adapted from them, and *Higurashi* is a case in point. Furthermore, a particular task corresponds to each of those characteristics. Firstly, viewers are required to evaluate *Higurashi*'s deliberate lacunae as essential ingredients in the representation of a particular world with defining aesthetic and ethical prerogatives. Secondly, in undertaking this analytical job, viewers must take into consideration the ways in which the diegesis enjoins them to perform certain interpretative choices and, as a result, takes shape in response to those choices. The narrative, in other words, is not a solidified sculpture but a malleable substance. Thirdly, viewers must accept that their decoding acts are never likely to lead to verifiable answers, for a tension will always subsist between the solutions they arrive at and the insoluble questions that go on resisting univocal explanations even after the answer arcs have been thoroughly examined. Fourthly, viewers are given the reward of knowing that whatever solutions they may believe to have reached, these will only carry contingent weight within the remit of the viewing experience in which they have participated, and therefore never preclude renegotiation in the way real-world events (lamentably) tend to do.

As the interrelated tasks delineated above are carried out, the anime's narrative repeatedly invites us to ponder the strategies through which its diverse textual components are linked to one another in such a manner that no incident can be assimilated as a complete occurrence, for disparate items connect, albeit obliquely, with other details and clues. Thus, the narrative recalls a digital hypertext: a system of language which, as George P. Landow has emphasized, brings to mind the poststructuralist conception of language as a fundamentally unstable and decentered galaxy of signs (Landow, pp. 33–34). As far as the phenomenon of immersion is specifically concerned, *Higurashi*'s elaboration of a fluid semiotic structure yokes together a number of factors. Jesper Juul's study of ludic dynamics seems especially useful in addressing at least some of those factors. While Juul is fundamentally interested in computer games, his observations are also pertinent to the type of watching experience entailed by Kon's show — which after all proceeds at least partly from assumptions established by its antecedent's gameplay. According to Juul, the key elements involved are "empathy and identification," as the underpinnings of a "player's relation to the character he/she controls"; "desire," namely, an urge to play that translates into a yearning for "narrative"; "death," as a function of "the acquiring of knowledge"; and "repeatability," i.e., the possibility of experiencing a game several times as a potentially "inexhaustible work" (Juul, p. 43). In watching *Higurashi*, these elements are brought into the equation quite explicitly as functions of immersion.

Where Juul's first category goes, it must be stressed that the anime does not automatically assume that all spectators will relate to one single character as the key focus of their attention but rather opens up plural interactive avenues by means of an extensive cast of well-defined personae each of whom constitutes, in principle, an available point of privileged reference. The audience's opportunities for psychological immersion are thus numerous and wide-ranging. Desire is an even more relevant category in the context of the show, due to its specifically narrative component. If the desire to perceive a text as a narrative leading to a resolution is a common trait of all sorts of viewing, playing and reading experiences, it is bound to acquire additional resonance in the watching of a show that assiduously encourages the constellation of its building blocks into a coherent narrative and yet at the same time obstructs the path to neat unraveling through its pronounced appetite for riddles. In this respect, the desire fostered by Kon's anime could be said to be less a desire for results, completion or explanation, than a desire to engage with the story as an ongoing process. The show makes us wish to focus not so much on its likely (or appetizing) outcomes as on its structure, on the mechanisms through which its world develops both in accordance with and in flagrant contradiction of the expectations it might have raised. Therefore, what we are actually asked to immerse ourselves into is not some edenic promise of plenitude but a forever provisional narrative framework driven by the dynamic performance of multiple interpretative choices. The nature of the show as a mobile organization of meaning is thereby thrown into relief. It would be cogent, on this point, to speak of "structurality" in preference to "structure" insofar as the notion of structurality captures more faithfully the idea of the anime as a text in constant motion and not a sealed product. This understanding of structurality is indebted to Jacques Derrida's writings, and specifically *Writing and Difference* (1978), where he proposes that structures have been traditionally predicated upon the existence of stable points of reference that somehow transcend the endless "play" of language. Conversely, Derrida, promotes structurality as the mechanism that only keeps systems together in precarious and ephemeral ways, perpetuating their dynamism and hence recognizing their self-dismantling thrust.

In Juul's model, death is imbricated with knowledge in the sense that in both computer games and stories, according to the critic, when "a fictive person dies," the player or reader is granted "a kind of bonus: additional knowledge on death" (p. 52) — that is to say, a knowledge which the character itself does not or cannot possess. In *Higurashi*, the possibility of death — or, more elusively, disappearance — looms large over the entire plot. At the same time, the narrative hold of that theme is exponentially amplified through ambiguity. Concepts of presence and absence, of aliveness and inertia, bypass empirical verification in the anime, since it is frequently hard to determine who is truly present or alive in a literal sense at any one given juncture. At various stages, different characters could be seen as figments of the imagination and hence presences made of absence even in scenes where they appear most zestfully alive. Moreover, the degree to which they are actually in control of the situation or merely its casualties remains largely a moot point. Moving on to Juul's last category, repeatability, *Higurashi* could be regarded as a prime example of the kind of show that lends itself to multiple explorations precisely by virtue of its unswerving cultivation of structural openness to variable detection exercises. In addition, the anime posits itself as markedly rewatchable in the way mythical narratives are repeatable. According to Eco, this attribute of the mythical proceeds from its engagement with universal preoccupations rather than purely circumstantial incidents (Eco 1979). In its methodical investigation of philosophical issues of great resonance, and above all the relationships between presence and absence, life and death, reality and illusion, *Higurashi* evidently tackles universal concerns even at its quietest and most mundane. Thus lending itself to repeat viewings, the anime exhorts us to interact with its ambiguous world in an incremental fashion, revealing more and more of itself each time and yet ushering in fresh conundrums in the process.

As noted at several junctures throughout this study, both visual novels and their anime spawn abound with artistic attributes. These can be immediately observed in the quality of their graphics and their handling of color, form and space, and are further amenable to critical evaluation with reference to relevant aspects of Japanese art which they deliberately or coincidentally echo. The two main titles explored in this chapter, *Fate/stay Night* and *Higurashi*, are no exception. Nor could it be claimed, in all fairness, that they are overtly more artistic than some of the other productions examined in the book as a whole. In fact, some would argue that the aesthetic merit of the titles emanating from Visual Art's/Key's unmatched genius (*Air*, *Kanon*, *Clannad*) surpass both *Fate/stay Night* and *Higurashi* where artistry is concerned. However, *Fate/stay Night* and *Higurashi* arguably exhibit a more explicit preference for abstraction than virtually any of the other productions here studied. While this does not, in and for itself, make them more commendable as works of art, it does attest to a dedication to the status of the work as a consciously constructed ensemble of signs since abstractism is the art form that most blatantly declares an artifice's independence from empirical reality.

In *Fate/stay Night*, that disposition is most characteristically borne out by combat scenes in which chromatic values, light effects, linear and multidimensional patterns and loving attention to the most conceptual geometrical aspects of the overall mise-en-scène gain precedence over naturalistic portrayal. Straight, curved and zigzagging lines traced by the characters' movements at times mirror and at others contrast with the shapes of their natural and architectural surroundings to evoke the oscillation between harmony and dissonance at the heart of the anime's diegesis. As the battle sequences progressively grow in intensity and urgency, lines and shapes gain a sense of universal potency that economically symbolizes a world on the verge of destruction. Jagged masses upon which splinters of light intermittently burst are used to heighten that impression at carefully chosen points, while slanting rhythms of motion push dynamism to the brink of restlessness. Yet paradoxically the sense of a well-conceived scenario of compositional balance, punctuated by impeccably orchestrated martial moves, invests even the most frantic sequence with structural rigor. Saber's climactic annihilation of the "poisoned chalice" firmly enthrones the anime's appetite for abstraction as one of its most enduring stylistic assets. The tension resulting from the action owes more to the abstract organization of the graphic elements than to the cinematic content per se. The use of myriad esoteric symbols across the fabric of *Fate/stay Night*, that hold the power to absorb disparate audiences into a multilayered deciphering enterprise further amplifies its penchant for abstraction.

In *Higurashi*, abstract attributes tend to come to the fore in the more openly crime-oriented scenes depicting either the crimes themselves or their alternately retrospective and anticipatory staging in a character's mind. Nonfigurative patterns, explosions of full chroma, solarized figures and furiously crisscrossing, clashing or splintering lines and planes feature quite regularly. Moreover, even the grisliest of scenes tends to be imbued with gestures towards abstractism that subordinate sensationalism to aesthetic refinement. Concurrently, facial distortions signaling states of heightened psychic activity are sometimes rendered in so stylized a fashion as to verge on abstraction. At times, bold strokes and brilliant hues deceptively convey sensations of ecstatic joy when the affects coursing beneath them are in fact dominated by ravaging horror. In the representation of both actions and states of mind of these kinds, shapes meet in violent, headlong combat, evoking images of chaotic rage that allude to the sense of cosmic conflict underlying the anime as a whole. Thus, even though *Fate/stay Night* and *Higurashi* are not, by any stretch of the imagination, autonomously classifiable as more valid objets d'art than other anime here addressed, they could be said to foster the partnership of anime and an understanding of art at its least mimetic — or, to phrase this differently, at its "artiest." (It may be due to this aspect of their makeup that the two titles are occasionally reputed to appeal to audiences who are not as a rule drawn to anime.) In proclaiming their constructed status and thus problematizing the notion of immersion even as they advocate it, the two productions invite reflection on a broader issue: namely, the artistic significance of anime of the type explored in this book, and in the case of anime adapted from games generally, of the ludic constructs behind them.

As emphasized in previous chapters, both visual novels and their anime heirs cast their recipients in the role of active performers — i.e., agents directly responsible for meaning-production. They thus posit the playing or viewing experience as an artistic performance: an activity aiming to concretize a virtual or potential story in accordance with particular aesthetic proclivities and skills that transcend the ambit of strictly competitive or utilitarian priorities. Both visual novels and the anime adapted from them should be regarded as art, in that respect, insofar as they provide contexts that promote the deployment of artistry on the part of players and viewers. (Considering the technology-based character of the works involved, the concept of art they invoke vividly brings to mind the old Greek term for "art"—"*techne*.") In the case of games which, like visual novels, contain or even afford precedence to elements other than rules (complex graphics and characterization, plot threads, dialogue), there can be little doubt as to the appropriateness of assessing their worth according to aesthetic criteria. Since those elements are not only inherited but exponentially maximized by their animated adaptations, an even smaller margin of doubt should obtain in evaluating the anime themselves as art. Nor should one be discouraged from addressing the games and related animations as artworks by the claim that such products strike their roots in mass entertainment. As Janet Hetherington contends, it is not unusual for art to look at everyday objects seemingly devoid of artistic value as apposite points of departure, and the contemporary gaming industry could well be taken as a relevant springboard: "Andy Warhol first took everyday things and raised them to a new level of artistic awareness in the 1960s.... Today's artists are again looking to pop culture for inspiration, and videogames are providing that inspiration" (Hetherington). According to Lorne Lanning, it is on this basis that videogames (and, by implication, adaptations therefrom) may be cogently considered artworks "to be seen and judged by the artistic merits of the creators and not by the commercial success that is all too often mistaken for quality in our mass-market medium" (quoted in Hetherington).

In his influential volume *Principles of Art* (1938), R. G. Collingwood criticizes mechanically reproduced art due to its putative inability to be "con-creative"—that is, to encourage a collaboratively creative relationship between authors and audiences—and attendant inclination to render audiences passively receptive (Collingwood). As Aaron Smuts maintains, contemporary videogaming contests that argument through its persistent cultivation of immersive and interactive strategies. Videogames, the critic stresses, are the "first concreative mass art." Their specifically artistic status is lucidly borne out by their creators' devotion to "traditional aesthetic considerations familiar to animators, novelists, set designers for theater productions and art directors for films." The imbrication of visual novels (and related anime) with filmic strategies can be situated in a broader scenario of mediatic dialogue insofar as the creators of contemporary ludic packages frequently endeavor to make their products appear more cinematic through the incorporation of "full-motion video sequences called cut-scenes" that exemplify their makers' desire to "situate their work in the tradition of cinema. For such reasons, any historical theory of art that admits film as an art form would most plausibly admit video games."

Smuts also draws attention to specific connections between videogaming and animation that are even more overtly pertinent to this study's emphasis on the synergetic cooperation between the visual novel and anime: the evocation of the actors' patterns of motion, according to the critic, is a notable design task wherein game designers "share goals with animators." Therefore, it can be argued that any position that recognizes the artistic standing of animation would also have to take notice of the status of many videogames as art objects of comparable merit (Smuts). Thus, just as cinema has gradually evolved from the collusion of theatre and photography, videogames have been fuelled by the twin impact of cinema and animation. Since, as this study illustrates, certain videogames are also increasingly becoming fonts of inspiration for animated shows, we might well be witnessing an intriguing case of cross-pollination that is not predicated on a one-way transition from a source (or an original) to its outcome (or descendant), but rather allows for ongoing movement from one party to the other.

# 5

# *Journeys of Self-Discovery*

*If you give people nothingness, they can ponder what can be achieved from that nothingness.*

— Tadao Ando

*There are ... two interpretations.... The one seeks to decipher, dreams of deciphering the truth or an origin which escapes play.... The other, which is no longer turned toward the origin, affirms play and tries to pass beyond man and humanism.*

— Jacques Derrida

The depiction of their personae's physical attributes and complex mentalities is pivotal to the articulation of visual novels in supplying their players with affective and graphic stimuli capable of engendering immersive experiences of the kind assessed in the foregoing chapter. This proposition is advocated by Petri Lankoski and Satu Heliö, who maintain, "An important tool for setting up motivations and goals for the player are well-defined characters with distinct natures and needs. Those will create the basis of conflict in the game" (Lankoski and Heliö, p. 311). Furthermore, "The consistency in character motivations and game structure is prerequisite for players to perceive a game as logically whole" (pp. 312–313). The visual novel typically extends the principle of character centrality from the protagonist to its entire cast and this strategy is largely responsible for conferring the form with unique psychological richness.

Much character interpretation will feasibly occur at a subliminal level, yet guide the player's attitude towards not only the character per se but the game as a whole, insofar as it will impact crucially on the sorts of decisions the player might be inclined to make at any given juncture. Thus, the characters' desires and objectives implicitly shape the player's own. In the anime here explored, character presentation plays an equally significant part. Ironically, some of the most striking results are achieved when a show does not go out of its way to come up with groundbreaking designs but rather seeks to convey diversity and novelty through sedate modulations of established codes and conventions as well as popular typologies, in accordance with Japanese art's passion for recurrent stylized motifs. As often highlighted in the course of the foregoing analysis, both the videogames and the animations they have spawned enhance character appeal by situating their actors in worlds replete with environmental, architectural and decorative elements. Yielding luscious backgrounds brimming with minute details and dramatic lighting effects, such settings indicate that the game or anime creators are more than willing to channel extra effort into something that might not have any direct or significant influence on the plot but will circuitously support it in a symbolic fashion. At the same time, they serve to complement the characters' psychological orientations, as well as their distinctive dynamic attributes and eccentricities. Hence, character portrayal and the graphic execution of settings capturing both nature and man-made habitats can be seen to fuel each other.

As to the fountainhead of ludic enjoyment, it is mainly our ability to distance ourselves from the characters' experiences that enables us to perceive even unsavory developments, such as the failure to undertake a quest to successful completion, as potential sources of delectation. Pleasure would be unlikely to be felt, in such a case, if we were to identify with a character so totally as to experience his or her inadequacies as our own. This does not, of course, altogether foreclose the possibility of an intelligently measured modicum of character immersion coming into play. The perspective on this issue embraced in this book concurs with Petri Lankoski's proposition that the ways in which players experience role-playing games and interact with them depends largely on the setting up of "goals" and the attendant emergence of "emotions" driving the desire to achieve such aims. "Goals," the critic maintains, "are the very basis of character immersion and emotional experience. As a player evaluates the character's goals meaningfully and takes them as hers in the game, she is able to experience 'shared emotions'—to feel what the character would feel in the situation." While stressing that goals are "important," Lankoski believes that "habitus" holds no less axial a role as the "framework for understanding events and decision-making" (Lankoski, p. 140).

To elucidate the concept of habitus, Lankoski cites Pierre Bourdieu's contention that habitus develops as particular "conditions of existence" lead to the formulation of "different definitions of impossible" or "probable" and hence "cause one group to experience as natural or reasonable practices or aspirations which another group finds unthinkable or scandalous, and vice versa" (Bourdieu, p. 78). Thus, habitus could be regarded as the force influencing people in their understanding of objectives and in their choice of certain courses of action in consonance with the beliefs and mores of their specific societies. By embracing particular ideals and developing emotions that help us conceive of routes feasibly conducive to their realization, we propel ourselves into the characters' own tasks. Yet, insofar as we are continually aware that those objectives are fabricated ploys created by game designers and animators in order to sustain a ludic or viewing process, we simultaneously retain a sobering knowledge of artifice and corresponding aesthetic distance.

In the specific case of Japanese visual novels and their anime brood, a sound appraisal of character presentation requires some appreciation of its relationship with broader developments in the domain of indigenous graphic design and of the myriad styles interacting therein. Such a necessity is thrown into relief by the characters' intimate relationship with numerous objects, reflecting both traditional customs and contingent vogues, that serve to complement not only their environments but their psychologies as well. The interplay of characters and objects is dramatized in virtually all of the titles explored in this book but is highlighted at this specific juncture due to its overt connection with the design principles underlying the execution of both actors and settings, and hence with the ideation of worlds capable of motivating players and viewers alike in their pursuit of narrative coherence. What is instantly notable about the objects with which characters tend to interact is a distinctively Japanese tendency to meld native elements with Western influences, as a result of which local traditions simultaneously adapt to and distinguish themselves from foreign imports. While Western styles are adopted, they tend to be imparted with a Japanese flavor. Simultaneously, local trends from the past are revamped and given a contemporary feel.

According to Sarah Lonsdale, in recent decades there has been a growing inclination to revisit traditional domestic styles. This, Lonsdale avers, is largely attributable to the economic and broadly societal pressures spawned by the failure of Japan's "bubble years of the 1980s," and the attendant recognition of the necessity to pursue a new model "driven primarily by cost consciousness" (Lonsdale, p. 6). This is not to say that rediscovering time-honored indigenous trends is coterminous with the simple desire to save money. Rather, it bears witness to a maturely refined approach to design and production that no longer prizes lavish accumulation as the supreme objective but is actually concerned with the development of environments and lifestyles consonant with today's realities. The current proclivity to revisit the past not merely out of antiquarian reverence but also to explore and savor its pertinence to the present is emblematically demonstrated, as Junichirou Tanizaki has noted, by "The recent vogue for electric lamps in the style of the old standing lanterns": a corollary of "a new awareness of the softness and warmth of paper" attesting to a "recognition that this material is far better suited than glass to the

Japanese house" (Tanizaki, p. 13). The cultural specificity of the substance in question is confirmed, according to the critic, by the fact that "Western paper turns away the light, while our paper seems to take it in" (p. 17).

The anime here studied document the reorientation towards the past in the representation of a vast repertoire of everyday objects — including garments, household accessories, school equipment and toys — that resonate with autochthonous notes. They do so not by parroting the old in an uncritical fashion but by making it relevant to the present with reference to global sources, while concurrently honoring aesthetic values of internal provenance. Thus, the shows echo Japan's inveterate predilection for simultaneous adjustment to and self-differentiation from the West, at the same time as they attest to the cultivation of older styles in light of fresh cultural imperatives. The sartorial domain provides a couple of apposite examples of the two attitudes outlined above. School uniforms, ubiquitous in the selected works, bear witness to Japanese design's adoption of Western influences through most of the outfits worn by female students, where the native passion for cuteness is overlaid with components such as sailor blouses and hats, pleated tartan miniskirts, thigh-high stockings and floppy socks, or even quasi–Victorian mantelets, muffs and flapping collars. For boys, a more Oriental design tends to be used, resulting in conceptual stark lines, sober hues and classic mandarin collars.

The revival of traditional styles to suit the requirements of a changing world, conversely, is signaled by a passion for the *yukata*, appreciated by women and young girls as a fashion item in its own right even though traditional festivities and events such as fireworks displays may provide the contingent pretexts for their donning. On a broader plane, indigenous traits can be seen to impact on everyday clothing of fundamentally Western orientation as this is more or less overtly infused with a sense of respect for materials and textures that attests to a deeply embedded commitment to the autonomous value of the designer's medium over and above its practical applications. In several outfits worn by female characters, in particular, the devotion to the intrinsic properties of different fabrics results in temerarious combinations of functional and whimsical details. The tactile properties of materials are also alluded to, and the ultimate roots of all art and design in the realm of nature are underscored through the utilization of hues immediately redolent to organic forms such as plants and animals, earth and water.

The tendency to bring together national and Western elements of design is also manifest in the objects filling the anime's domestic interiors, where Western-style furnishings such as sofas, tables and chairs coexist harmoniously with quintessentially Japanese materials: paper, straw, bamboo, clay, cypress and pine, for example. As with clothing, the materials employed in the home exude a sense of palpable immediacy that underlines the undying influence of natural substances in the culture's artisanal and artistic pursuits. The custom of removing shoes in the doorway, insistently foregrounded in the shows, attests to the local respect for materials and the desire to enter into intimate communion with their sensory qualities without the interference or interface of artificial barriers. The same message is conveyed by the endurance of traditional furnishings such as seats consisting simply of cushions (*zabuton*) that express the proclivity to live close to the ground, and thus by implication to the dwelling's natural substratum. Kitchens and their equipment, featuring pervasively in the chosen anime, provide a paradigmatic instance of cultural cross-pollination, insofar as they may come across as Westernized spaces in their overall look, and yet on closer inspection reveal their origins in age-old native layouts through the depiction of shelves for the storage of cooking vessels and of utensils hung from the walls. Thus, interiors could be said to mimic at the microlevel the broader reality of Japan's metropolitan settings as syntheses of Western-style roads and blocks on the one hand, and traditional neighborhoods retaining the atmosphere of small communities on the other.

Concomitantly, Japan's reverential attitude to materials is corroborated by the representation of household items rendered distinctive by the very substances employed in their production. Thus, even though objects made by recourse to Western substances like plastic make regular appearances, no less attention is devoted to goods of traditional derivation. These involve ancient techniques such as the manufacture of metalwork, bamboo craft, mother-of-pearl inlay, both glazed and unglazed stoneware, items based on the art of wood-bending (*magemono*) and, most memorably perhaps, lacquerware reliant on the native *urushi* (i.e., "lacquer tree"). As John Reeve explains, the crafting of lacquer "began in prehistory as a way of waterproofing wooden objects such as bowls and protecting fragile objects like combs." However, these pragmatic considerations were soon superseded by artistic goals as it became obvious that the technique lended itself to the evocation of unique impressions. For instance, "by applying many layers" of resinous *urushi* sap (usually colored black or red), "it is possible to cut through them to create sculptural effects." In addition, the utilization of "gold foil or gold dust (*makie*, 'sprinkled pictures') and mother-of-pearl" could lead to a stunning sense of multidimensionality (Reeve, p. 54).

All of the aforementioned skills are laborious and hugely diversified, and still reflect a legacy that strikes its roots in an unwavering dedication to top-notch workmanship and to a regard for the natural world as the receptacle of all-pervasive spiritual energies. Among some of the most distinctively Japanese items featuring in varyingly prominent or ancillary roles in the outdoor and indoor settings of the shows here explored there are several time-honored objects. These include *chochin*, paper lanterns with both commercial and ritual functions, and *shimenawa*, sacred straw ropes associated with the Shinto tradition to which paper streamers (*gohei*) are customarily attached for ceremonial purposes. (The art of *origami* is held to have found inception in this practice.) Also evident are the *furoshiki*, square pieces of cloth used as extremely adaptable and eco-friendly carriers, *washi* (handmade paper), *mizuhiki* (decorative paper cords), *noshi* (folds of white and red paper attached to gifts as tokens of friendship), *jubako* (tiered boxes with often exquisite ornamentation and lacquer coating used to store food prepared in advance for special occasions), *pochi-bukuro* (small gift envelopes bearing beautiful patterns such as flowers or the animals from the Chinese zodiac) and, of course, the proverbially iconic *hashi* (chopsticks) and *hashi-oki* (chopstick rests).

Japanese design also places great emphasis on the inextricability of legion material objects from a plethora of both traditional and contemporary patterns and symbols. This firmly enthrones the centrality of visual forms of expression in Japanese culture at large — an aesthetic preference borne out by the emphatically pictorial character of the written language as not merely a conceptual system of signification but also a corporeal reality. The passion for emblems and stylized figures typically finds expression in the ethos of *kazari* as a delight in ornamentation. This does not automatically result in either gaudiness or affectation, however, for even manifest beauty (*en*) and flamboyance (*hade*) are tempered by the principles of artless simplicity (*soboku*), gracefulness (*reiyou* or *yuu*), propriety (*ga*), understated good taste (*jimi*) and unadorned charm (*karumi*) grounded in an appreciation of even the most prosaic of forms (*hosomi*). Patterns and symbols thus acquire a perceptible and vibrant life of their own as catalysts for rich interactions between abstraction and embodiment, rhythm and substance, form and matter. The pervasiveness of this principle is confirmed by the fact that those objects belong to quite disparate categories: fashion, interior design, gardening, cuisine and, no less importantly, the art of packaging and the underlying practices of wrapping, tying, tucking and folding for which Japan has been renowned the world over for centuries. Inspired by the basic tenet that "small is beautiful," indigenous design spares no effort in the execution of even the tiniest of containers, possibly accommodating seemingly insignificant contents, to the highest standards.

While emblematic ornamentation is no doubt a distinctive feature of Japanese design, no less important is the artisan's effort to match the geometric or organic properties of the visual elements employed to the shape of the object. For example, a pattern containing a wave or a whirlpool adopted to decorate a porcelain bowl may use the curve of the vessel itself to suggest the dynamic qualities of the water motif. Analogously, the swelling forms of persimmons or lotus petals may be maximized by their application to the domed portions of a lidded jar. At the same time, even the most conceptually refined forms tend to be imparted with an aura of aliveness. Prehistoric clay sculptures were already allusively animated through the infusion of animal or quasi-anthropomorphic attributes to mere cylindrical pots. More recent instances of decorative pottery (and matching textiles) yield a marked sense of implied animateness in their exquisite amalgamation of chromatic and linear elements. So do designs adorning Edo-Period writing-boxes in which black lacquer and eggshell are combined to evoke interlocking shapes redolent of M. C. Escher's optical art. The sensitivity to the distinctive material properties of diverse substances, related products and crafts, allied to the fascination with decorative patterns and symbols, are aspects of Japanese design that have attracted many Western artists — including painters such as Édouard Manet, Edgar Degas, Henri de Toulouse-Lautrec, J. A. McN. Whistler and Pierre Bonnard, as well as composers such as Claude Debussy and Benjamin Britten and architects like Frank Lloyd Wright — as sources of inspiration unfettered by the classical conventions of European aesthetics. This point deserves consideration, when assessing contemporary anime, insofar as it provides an apposite backdrop to the West's increasing interest in that particular art form. At the same time, it offers a poignant instance of those rhythms of cultural cross-pollination which, as observed, have for long inhered in the development of Japanese design.

The productions addressed below harness their sophisticated portrayals of characters and settings alike to a common goal: the delineation of psychological expeditions tracing an individual's maturation or deterioration. Several of the chosen anime evince recurrent traits. Both *Clannad* and *Da Capo*, as well as their respective sequels, pivot on their personae's laborious efforts to negotiate their current circumstances vis-à-vis old scars on the one hand, and prospective challenges on the other. In *Clannad*, *Tsuyokiss* and *White Album*, this task is couched in the guise of a creative quest that posits artistic self-expression as coterminous with the pursuit of self-understanding. The acceptance of the ineluctable imbrication of one's personal ambitions with intersubjective requirements is cardinal to all the narratives elaborated in the aforementioned shows, as it is to *To Heart*—a germinal intervention in the history of the visual novel's translation into anime. The imperative to face the present and the responsibilities it carries is likewise central to *Kashimashi — Girl Meets Girl*, an anime subsequently adapted to the visual-novel format. The transition from juvenile expectations to the realities of adulthood also constitutes the diegetic and psychological core of *Rumbling Hearts*. Like *Clannad* and *Tsuyokiss*, however, this anime also deploys creative aspirations as the means of upholding the undying value of dreams conceived in childhood and indefatigably treasured in the face of adversity. With *School Days*, the journey of self-discovery acquires a murky twist, as its potential pleasures disintegrate altogether to disclose a resolutely dystopian scenario of both private and social malaise. Thus, the works here studied engage with both the uplifting and potentially constructive sides of their developmental voyages and the dark, intractably malignant demons stunting their characters' maturation. Anime's resolute rejection of stark binaries thereby openly declares itself in these anime as an ensemble of intercomplementary odysseys.

\*   \*   \*

*To Heart* (TV series; dir. Naohito Takahashi, 1999) may not constitute one of the most challenging or engrossing titles among the anime here explored on either the thematic or the narrative planes. Nevertheless, the seminal role played by the source game (originally published for different platforms in 1997 and 1999) as the first of its ilk to experiment with tropes destined to become central to the visual-novel medium can hardly go unnoticed. Nor can its establishment of the journey of self-discovery as one of the form's most inveterate preoccupations. In the anime, this is articulated through the reflections shared with the audience in a quasi-diaristic style by the female protagonist, Akari Kamigishi, while she and her mates (primarily her childhood friend Hiroyuki Fujita) cruise, plod or amble through a year of high school. Endowed with a distinctively painterly feel that alternates between the tactile realism of furnishings and props and the dreamy gentleness of watercolor backgrounds, *To Heart* attributes great value to distant memories and their undying influence on people's lives. This idea is overtly communicated from the start through a flashback to Akari's and Hiroyuki's childhood and consolidated by the girl's assertion that although she knows that life is a process of unending change, she still holds onto the belief that her friendship with Hiroyuki will withstand the erosive agency of time and survive unscathed. Various complications will test Akari's idealistic conviction before the story is over, contributing vitally to her self-exploratory trajectory.

As the anime series develops, the firm commitment to an interpersonal bond involving two individuals extends to other personae and plot threads as well, delivering a warming sense of solidarity. For example, Akari and Hiroyuki are quite willing to offer the mysterious Serika Kurusugawa, the sole member of their school's "Occult Research Society," their assistance and friendship despite the somewhat ominous nature of her interest and of the esoteric ceremonies this entails. Similarly, it is through their and their friends' encouragement that the feisty but inexperienced first-year student Aoi Matsubara finds the strength to engage in strenuous martial training and accept a daring challenge that might pave the way to the realization of her most cherished ambition. What is more, Aoi learns that even defeat is a palatable outcome as long as her conduct can gain her the respect of her opponent, while doing one's best is the ultimate ethical goal and one's friends' disinterested support the supreme reward. As indicated later in this chapter, this theme is also tackled in *Tsuyokiss*. In both anime, moreover, a clear sense of the motivations and goals driving not only the protagonists but also the supporting cast plays an essential role in shaping and directing the audience's own objectives and most crucially, the desire to instantiate the show's multifarious contents as a harmonious narrative ensemble.

The paramount value of the kind of esprit de corps promoted by *To Heart* is pithily captured by Akari's gnomic comment at the end of the Aoi-centered segment of the show: "The feelings of those who work hard always find a way to reach others." *To Heart* features several formulae to be found in both visual novels and anime based upon them. Above all, Hiroyuki is emplaced as the unorthodox hero at the center of a multibranching narrative woven around various girls with whom his life might, become entangled for disparate and not always incontrovertibly logical reasons. Accordingly, chance plays more substantial a part in the advancement of the action than either choice or design. This aspect does not make Takahashi's program especially memorable, let alone unique. Yet it is undeniably handled with endearing sensitivity to the real feelings flowing beneath the superficially conventional diegesis. It is in this approach to its subject matter, more than in any stylistic flourishes, that the anime triumphs over several other titles adopting a cognate structure and becomes truly deserving of acknowledgement as a foundational contribution to the visual novel/anime synergetic interplay.

*     *     *

*D. C. - Da Capo -* (TV series; dir. Nagisa Miyazaki, 2003) might initially evince tonal similarities to *To Heart*, yet also bears witness to the extent to which the visual novel has progressed since the launch of that seminal production by delivering an altogether richer and more psychologically convoluted narrative weave. The generic suppleness typically evinced by visual novels and their anime adaptations manifests itself in two main guises in *Da Capo*. On the one hand, a shift in dramatic emphasis in the direction of increasing seriousness is notable in the course of the first season. On the other hand, an effusive juggling of spirited and meditative moments immediately characterizes the transition from the first anime to its sequel. The reorientation of *Da Capo*'s tenor is rendered especially poignant by its setting in an apparently magical crescent-shaped island, Hatsunejima, where cherry trees bloom all year long and a comparably magical breeze nourished by all manner of more or less scary and enticing legends beckons the protagonists towards the promise of novel encounters and adventures.

Like other visual novels studied in this book, the *Da Capo* game (2002) offers a moderate amount of digital interaction, opting instead for a style of play that prioritizes the user's engagement with text-based conversations and inner monologues. At certain key points, multiple choices that allow the narrative to develop along alternate plot lines (of which there are six pivotal ones) are made available. Replayability is thus guaranteed. *Da Capo* elaborates several themes and motifs also found in other titles here explored. Like *Air*, it introduces the topos of characters who are somewhat cursed by their preternatural abilities with Jun'ichi Asakura (the male lead), a youth endowed with a knack for peeking into other people's dreams, and Kotori Shirakawa, a girl capable of reading other people's minds. Through a self-referential flourish on Miyazaki's part, Jun'ichi declares from the very start that while in a "novel" or in a "game," his skill might be considered "cool," to him it is actually a bane. Being an unrefined visionary, a "mage lacking in knowledge," the boy can look into others' oneiric experiences but is powerless to intervene and is therefore destined to feel intense frustration whenever he is faced with a person in need or in distress to whom he cannot reach out. In a sense, Jun'ichi's talent is merely a form of unwitting voyeurism.

The character himself is often beset by troubling dreams, and as the story progresses, he has reasons to wonder whether the dreams he considers his own are really products of his unconscious or rather external visions into which he has inadvertently wandered. For example, when Jun'ichi experiences a dream revisiting his first encounter with the character of Sakura Yoshino in childhood, he wonders whether the images truly belong to him or rather emanate from the girl's psyche. Sakura later reveals not only that the dream was indeed hers but also that she was aware that Jun'ichi was witnessing it. Kotori likewise derives scarce solace from her mind-reading faculties since most of the time she would rather not hear echoing around her head the lewd fantasies of her school friends, who consider her Kazami Academy's "idol." Ironically, however, Kotori feels even more uncomfortable when her powers suddenly evaporate, as she realizes that telepathy has been her means of getting along with people and avoiding conflict, which she dreads due to a traumatic infancy. It is with Jun'ichi's help that the girl comes to grasp the value of not knowing what others think (and desire) insofar as lack of knowledge is the force that urges people to find things out by themselves and to accomplish goals autonomously: although, as the youth puts it this prospect might seem intimidating at face value, it is actually "fun."

In the handling of the oneiric dimension, *Da Capo* also foreshadows *Kanon*, and particularly Ayu's ordeal in that story. Like both *Kanon* and

*Clannad*, moreover, *Da Capo* deploys the type of the comatose girl lying inert in a hospital, yet mysteriously able to conduct a parallel life in the outside world, in the arc centered on Miharu Amakase. (The image of the unconscious female in an alternate configuration, will also be seen to play an axial role in *Rumbling Hearts*.) *Da Capo*'s use of a hybrid character in the person of the cat-girl Yoriko Sagisawa anticipates *Touka Gettan*'s incorporation of an analogous creature through Nene's sister, Kaya, while also bringing to mind the fox spirits featuring in *Yami to Boushi to Hon no Tabibito*, *Kanon* and *Kanokon*, as well as the numerous cross-genetic beings that populate *Utawarerumono*. The theme of quasi-siblings caught up in a problematic liaison is central to *Da Capo*, as shown by the protagonist's relationship with the character of Nemu, and looks forward to both *Shuffle!* and *true tears*. On the generic plane, *Da Capo*'s gradual descent into darkness finds a partial heir in *School Days*, though Miyazaki's series offers redemptive options truculently foreclosed by the later show. Finally, the importance of promises and seemingly miraculous phenomena in the cumulative diegesis relates *Da Capo* to several other anime addressed in this study while also abetting its distinctive articulation of simultaneously personal and communal journeys of self-discovery.

The esoteric element is firmly emplaced as a vital ingredient of *Da Capo*'s thematic mix from the opening installment with the introduction of the aforementioned Sakura, the descendant of powerful magicians and Jun'ichi's childhood friend, who returns to her hometown from the U.S. after a six-year-long absence and instantly claims a prominent role in the lives of both the lead and his adoptive sister Nemu — much, it must be stressed, to the latter's resentment. Curiously, Sakura's physical appearance does not seem to have altered in the least since the time of her departure from Hatsunejima. The girl may at first seem to incarnate the stereotype of the cutely obnoxious immature female but hints of an enigmatic promise binding her to Jun'ichi since infancy lend her character portrayal a vaguely ominous feel. With the introduction of the telepathic Kotori, the supernatural strain acquires further resonance within *Da Capo*'s overall melody. The subsequent introductions of Miharu in the form of a sophisticated android (as the real girl lies unconscious following her fall from a tree) and of Yoriko the hybrid consolidate that facet of the series. Two less overtly outlandish yet still attractive characters are Moe and Mako Mizukoshi, two sisters employed by the narrative largely to celebrate the culinary arts. Intriguingly, Moe and Mako not only give vent to their passion for all sorts of *nabe* dishes (casseroles or stews) in the privacy of their home but also through a BBQ idiosyncratically located on the school roof at lunchtime. Moe's disconcertingly detailed descriptions of the salient qualities of each ingredient provide touches of comic relief, yet also attest to traditional Japanese artists' and artisans' deferential stance towards their materials and desire to bring out their unique natural properties instead of harnessing them to anthropocentric imperatives.

Once again, the show's reliance on a male protagonist's interactions with several heroines recalls the "harem" format. As in other anime here examined (notably *Shuffle!* and *Kanon*), however, *Da Capo* turns out to be more concerned with the unfolding of mysteries embedded in the peculiar land where it is staged and with the secrets harbored by most of the anime's personae than with multiple romances. Accordingly, as intimated earlier, the plot incrementally gathers dramatic momentum through the infusion of tense and grave complications into its inceptive framework. In the first season, this makes itself patently felt just past the halfway mark. However, discreet allusions to somber subtexts are scattered throughout the narrative at an earlier stage. The story arc centered on Miharu is a blatant case in point. This indubitably provides scope for comic relief, especially in the scene where Jun'ichi is instructed by his homeroom teacher to look after the robot and keep its status a secret. Yet it is also pervaded by an unsettling sense of foreboding, since Jun'ichi's tutor unscrupulously states that the artificial version of Miharu is fundamentally an experiment whose fate is as yet undecided, which implies that the creature might be the subject of callous exploitation.

Furthermore, while the action exudes an exuberant mood of innocent fun with the sequences emphasizing the idea that everything the robot encounters is new to her and hence a source of undiluted excitement, it concurrently underscores her vulnerability and weakness — not least due to her proclivity to malfunction severely whenever she is overstimulated by the environment and its wonders. Also affecting is the synthetic girl's desire to become so realistically akin to her human prototype as to truly deserve the friendly treatment she is receiving from all those who are oblivious to her true nature. This undercurrent of sadness strikes pathetically touching chords in later scenes where the robot states that she is well aware that when the real Miharu eventually recovers, she will have to give up the world she has come to know and love and thus lose the people she holds dear. The arc's dramatic impetus reaches its culmination as the robot, endeavoring to emulate the human Miharu's personality down to the minutest detail, starts searching for the girl's memories inside her own head. Unfortunately, the human Miharu's mnemonic heritage has not been programmed into the her artificial double, and the effort therefore rapidly and inexorably leads to the creature's demise.

The arc based on Yoriko also combines comedy and a wistful mood of quintessentially Japanese orientation. The situation leading to the kitten Yoriko's assumption of a human appearance, the girl's rescue by Jun'ichi from a gang of abusive kids, and her subsequent emplacement as an inept maid within the Asakura household is absurdly carnivalesque. Nevertheless, it oozes with a genuine sense of warmth in the scenes emphasizing Jun'ichi's selfless disposition, as well as in those focusing on Yoriko's heartfelt shame at her lack of domestic skills. As with Miharu the android, so with Yoriko the hybrid, memory acts as a powerful motivator. In Yoriko's instance, this is disclosed in the climax of the plot strand devoted to this heroine, where Yoriko states that she has endeavored throughout to "make wonderful memories" with Jun'ichi and his friends for the sake of the owner of the kitten whence she herself emanates, Misaki: an agoraphobic girl haunted by unfulfillable long- ings who has shut herself off from the world altogether. Both Miharu the robot and Yoriko the cat-girl are ultimately doomed by the withering of the giant cherry tree dominating Hatsunejima since their shared desire for uplift- ing memories is prevented from fully coming to fruition when its preternat- ural power to grant people's most unrealistic wishes is exhausted. The plot strand with Moe at its center similarly conveys an amalgamation of sheer zaniness, especially in the sequence where Jun'ichi is enjoined to capture a duck which the Mizukoshi sisters intend to use as the staple of one of their proverbial dishes, and austere solemnity, particularly in the depiction of the palatial Mizukoshi residence and the overwhelming regard for tradition it silently imposes. *Da Capo*'s ambivalent mood is confirmed by the installment in which Nemu is stalked by a "mysterious poet" determined to win her heart at all costs. Although the episode finds a felicitously humorous resolution when the besotted pursuer is revealed to be the victim of an innocent mis- understanding, there is something authentically creepy about the insistence with which he follows Nemu's every step and hacks into her computer, con- ducive to a fear on the girl's part that comes across as entirely convincing.

Sakura initially seems more inclined to indulge in infantile pranks that in necromancy. However, it incrementally transpires that she has been endowed with baleful magical powers from an early age (possibly even from birth) and that these have at times resulted in unintentionally lethal actions. It is in order to curb these faculties that Sakura has preternaturally contrived to remain a child. The girl's formidable abilities pivot on the giant cherry tree referred to earlier, which is said to have been planted by her grandmother, and its capacity to grant everybody's wishes. Sakura's powers reach their cul- mination when she realizes that she has been responsible for the mysterious condition afflicting Jun'ichi's beloved Nemu, whom she bitterly resents due to her special place in the protagonist's heart. At this point, she seeks to make amends by killing the tree and thus putting an end to its magic — even though this entails the rescinding of all previously fulfilled wishes and hence the dis- solution of the spells that have enabled the likes of the android and the cat-girl to live out their dreams. Sakura's counteractive measures are for a while curtailed by her inability to let go of the past as a corollary of which Nemu, after a brief recovery, descends into an even more serious illness accompanied by amnesia. It is not until Sakura manages to take her own desires out of the agenda altogether that Nemu can return to normality and her relationship with Jun'ichi be allowed to flourish unimpeded. The intensity of Sakura's inner conflict is magisterially conveyed in the climactic frames where the animation lingers on her deranged facial expressions and body language, redolent of some of *When Cicadas Cry*'s most disquieting moments.

The dramatization of *Da Capo*'s supernatural subtext owes much to the recurring appearance of the cat-man garbed in gear one would readily associate with the hard-boiled detective genre or even film noir, whom Sakura dubs "Fushigi-san," which translates as, "Mr. Mystery." This enigmatic figure features in some of the show's most surreal and dreamy sequences — i.e., the ones where Kotori spends a day by an entirely deserted and mesmerizingly beautiful shore, where Sakura dines at a traditional restaurant exuding lore-encrusted charm, and where Moe explores the Hatsunejima marine fauna before setting off in an oarless dinghy under mercurial skies of breathtaking splendor. The creature also appears behind the window of the haunted house Mako and Nemu enter to shelter from torrential rain after the girls have identified the abode's ghastly nature and made a most inelegant escape. Further sightings occur in the sequence where Yoriko temporarily leaves the Asakura home at night and enters a visionary world teeming with cats of all kinds that culminates with her balletic encounter with a handsome stranger, and in the sequence where Nemu, Mako and Moe wind up in an enchanted forest complete with Alice-in-Wonderland tricks.

The unobtrusive ubiquity of Fushigi-san's image is reinforced by *Da Capo*'s assiduous inclusion of other visual motifs that echo the cat-man's physiognomy. Among them are the pet Utamaru (an organic, yet glaringly toylike, entity), the logo adorning Nemu's schoolbag tag and the picture on the robot Miharu's T-shirt. These examples bear witness to the anime's devoted portrayal of small everyday objects regardless of their putative pettiness, in a fashion redolent of traditional Japanese culture, as seen in the early portion of this chapter. One of the entire series' most memorable segments is the installment where the girls team up to find Fushigi-san, whom they deem benevolent despite his bizarre physique and stealthy manner, and roam the island for a whole day. This temporal setting is important, as it enables the camera to register myriad atmospheric and chromatic changes in a compressed style and thus regale the senses with a panoply of opulent effects. Appropriately, when the heroines eventually locate the elusive character, he has just boarded the ferry that will take him away from Hatsunejima for good. Bathed in a sublime sunset, the scene emits a quintessentially Japanese feeling of nostalgia.

One of *Da Capo*'s most distinctive attributes is its formal orchestration. The first seven episodes are accompanied by "image songs," i.e., music clips performed by the main female characters' *seyuu* (voice actors). Although these sequences do not advance the plot in any obvious ways, they play an important role in supplying insights into the various personae's psychology, behavior and goals, which serves to stimulate the audience's interest in the characters themselves and more broadly in the fictive world they inhabit. Episodes 8–14 and 16–21 (with the intermission of the "recap" episode 15) are accompanied by "side episodes." The ones contained in the 8–14 set have a predominantly feel-good quality, while the ones attached to the 16–21 set overflow with riddles that by and large tie in with the main plot. These do not, however, provide unequivocal or transparent linkages, as they typically favor surreal sequences and montages over narrative drama, leaving it to the viewer to formulate hypotheses and thus contribute to the creative enterprise as an active party. Additionally, *Da Capo* abounds with self-reflective gestures. The performative dimension in particular is repeatedly foregrounded. A good example is the sequence in which Jun'ichi and Nemu pretend to be "lovers" for Yoriko's sake and their classmate Suginami directs the action as if it were a movie. Suginami's passion for filmmaking is again highlighted in an installment located just past the halfway point, where he offers a telescoped summary, replete with a bombastic commentary, of various moments from the series up to that juncture, focusing on its female characters' personalities. At the end of the episode, Suginami also warns the audience that *Da Capo*'s lighter moments are now over and that the second part will give way to "tears." The use of sepia-tinted and grayscale frames alongside standard polychromous ones lends the sequence an archival feel.

The visual-novel onscreen style is also evoked through frames consisting of a full-color "window" superimposed over a monochrome screen displaying the same shot, which acts as a reminder of the photoplay's eminently constructed status. The ludic dimension is also referred to by Jun'ichi in the finale, where he elliptically comments on the analogy between real life and play and draws attention to one of the visual novel's most distinctive attributes — namely, replayability as an incremental process sustained at each stage by lessons learned in previous phases of play: "People say that you can't reset life, like a game. But is that really true? If you stumble, you can always start over, like a *da capo*. ... that is not a start from zero." The discourse of cinema, for its part, is further invoked self-referentially in the sequence where Fushigi-san watches a film comprising a montage of frames from the side episodes in a derelict theater. The piece's climax is provided by flashes of his deliberately unexplained youthful relationship with Sakura (or maybe a Sakura double) and parting from the girl. The documentarist mode also comes into play in the episode recap with commentary by Utamaru, offering portrayals of the main personae from the cat's point of view.

Self-reflexivity is used by *Da Capo* to evoke a wide range of moods, including humor. A paradigmatic instance is the scene set in the haunted house mentioned earlier, where Mako chances upon an old manga and comments scornfully on its characters' huge eyes. The remark sounds ironic, if not downright ludicrous, when one considers the saucer-size proportions of the *Da Capo* heroines' own ocular attributes. Self-reflexivity also lends itself to sarcasm, as shown by the scene where Jun'ichi, having finally owned up to the nature of his feelings towards Nemu, derides the situation as akin to a "cheesy romance movie." As we watch *Da Capo*, we are asked to grasp the particular habitus underpinning its characters' goals and the strategies they utilize in order to achieve those goals, by turns identifying with their dominant desires and distancing ourselves from them, depending on the degree of self-referentiality (and hence defamiliarization), in which they are couched. As the ensuing analyses aim to illustrate, this remains true of both the second season and the distinct but related anime *Da Capo II*.

As intimated above, *Da Capo*'s first season posits the individual and the community as interdependent and mutually defining realities. This theme gains additional weight in *D. C. S. S. ~ Da Capo Second Season ~* (TV series; dir. Munenori Nawa, 2005). Set two years after the events proposed in the original anime's climax, the sequel initially focuses, on Jun'ichi's friends' efforts to assist the youth in Nemu's absence in the capacity of a self-appointed "Support Team." Feelings of nostalgia, regret and irretrievable loss are prominent in the early segments of the second season and are symbolically mirrored by the momentous transformation of the island's landscape, where the undying cherry trees appear to have given way to an ordinary stretch of arboreal life. The mood is also silently reinforced by shots of Nemu's school uniform hanging limply in her abandoned bedroom. The clothes operate as a metonym for the ubiquitous phantom of absence following Jun'ichi through each step of his solitary existence. There is something pointedly eerie about unoccupied clothing, since this draws attention to the life that could potentially fill it but is quite blatantly missing. (A similar point could be made about dolls and puppets.) The image of the discarded school uniform is analogously deployed in *Touka Gettan* following Momoka's disappearance.

On the generic plane, *D. C. S. S.* declares from its inceptive stages a penchant for nimble transitions from intense drama to humor and vice versa. Much of the comedy is provided by a new cast member, Aisia, a character in whom solemnity and infantilism come together in a seamless fusion of affects. Aisia is possessed by the dream of becoming a powerful magician in order to make everybody happy — an objective she has inherited from her illustrious grandmother — and her determination is conducive to a kaleidoscopic swirl of hilarious mishaps. Despite the exuberance exuded by Aisia's adventures, however, there can be little doubt as to the strength of her resolve, and this element increasingly imbues the action with a convincing sense of moral gravity. Aisia's project is grievously challenged, and the comedy accordingly superseded by serious drama, when she seeks to receive proper magical training from Sakura and is resolutely turned down. Magic, Sakura believes, does not unproblematically make people happy, but is in fact a hazardous tool that can lead to nefarious consequences even in the hands of practitioners not driven by evil intentions. This is a lesson Sakura has learned at her own cost, as borne out by the repercussions of her own magical exploits two years earlier.

The memory topos works as a diegetic pivot in the second season. It gradually accumulates dramatic weight through the introduction of Sakura as a key figure and through Aisia's revival of the giant cherry tree in an effort to ensure that everybody's wishes may be fulfilled, despite Sakura's terse advice against this move. Aisia's magic triggers the erasure of some memories and the resurgence of others, as the story's clock is rewound to the days preceding Nemu and Jun'ichi's romantic attachment. This preternatural intervention ultimately amounts to no less than a replacement of Hatsunejima's current reality by a parallel world. (Sakura at one point maintains the hypothetical viability of resetting the island's reality multiple times, which mirrors the parent game's inherent replayability.) One of the first symptoms of the magical *sakura*'s resurgence are allusions to Nemu and Jun'ichi by some of their friends suggesting that the two characters are still seen as siblings rather than lovers. Despite Sakura's assertion that people's genuine feelings are capable of withstanding the most portentous sorcery, and therefore the protagonists will preserve their love for each other, the path leading to the reestablishment of Hatsunejima's legitimate reality is destined to be very tortuous indeed.

When the reset engineered by Aisia is complete and the island is again covered with cherry trees in full blossom, Jun'ichi and Nemu themselves seem to harbor merely haphazard memories and live as though they had never been anything other than brother and sister except, that is, when symbols of their love such as letters and matching watches jolt them into a subliminal recognition of dormant emotions and related remembrances. The protagonists' disorientation is first conveyed by two parallel sequences connected through agile intercutting where Nemu and Jun'ichi glean mounting evidence for their friends' obliviousness to the true nature of their bond. The magical tree's power is ominously reinforced by the sheer physical pain its flowering inflicts on the protagonists: an aspect of the show which the artwork and animation communicate magisterially throughout the crowning episodes. It is not until Nemu collapses and Aisia realizes that the alternate reality she has forged can only lead to suffering that she finally grasps her friends' true feelings and — following in Sakura's footsteps at the close of the first season — resolves to bid them farewell as the *sakura* petals likewise disappear once more. The deserved culmination of Jun'ichi and Nemu's journey of self-discovery is at last on the horizon and, as the seasons swiftly roll by, it is indeed achieved by means of an aesthetically uplifting ending of palpable beauty. In this respect, the conclusion to *D. C. S. S.* evinces greater dramatic concreteness than the first season's resolution.

The second *Da Capo* visual novel, released in 2006 with the title *Da Capo II*, utilizes a playing system analogous to the one employed in the first game. Comprising six story arcs developing the narrative in ramifying directions, *Da Capo II* is divided into three main segments. The first pivots on the imminent Christmas party, the second unfolds in the course of the winter holiday and the skiing trip at its center, and the third follows the characters' school lives in the new year. The events presented in the 2006 game are articulated by *D. C. II S. S.* ∼ *Da Capo II Second Season* ∼ (TV series; dir. dir. Hideki Okamoto, 2008), whereas the first series, *D. C. II* ∼ *Da Capo II* ∼ (TV series; dir. Hideki Okamoto, 2007), focuses on events punctuating the preceding school months. In both the source game and its anime adaptation, the setting is again the magic-imbued island of Hatsunejima. However, the story takes place fifty-three years after the events presented in the original *Da Capo* and the only characters it retains from its predecessor are Sakura and Jun'ichi. Nemu is merely mentioned. Its protagonist is Yoshiyuki Sakurai, a boy brought into existence by Sakura with the assistance of an artificial wish-granting, ever-blooming cherry tree. (His name literally means "Yoshiyuki born within Sakura.") As a surrogate for the son Sakura and Jun'ichi never had, Yoshiyuki exhibits many of the most salient traits seen in *Da Capo*'s original lead, including the abilities to summon *wagashi* (Japanese candy) from nothing and to peep into others' dreams.

The most important new characters are Otome and Yume Asakura, Jun'ichi and Nemu's granddaughters. A skillful magician, Otome displays an engagingly composite personality. In the anime's first season, the story does not bring her preternatural abilities overtly into play but tends to underscore her profound sense of responsibility towards Yoshiyuki at the individual level and towards the school whose student council she presides at the collective level. The second season, conversely, foregrounds Otome's role as a self-proclaimed "magician of justice" determined to uphold the highest moral standards. Yet it also consolidates the impression of a multifaceted identity by intimating that Otome was once reserved to the point of defensiveness and that it was thanks to Yoshiyuki she learned how to open up to others and assume a more active role in her community. Her younger sister Yume appears to have inherited her grandfather's oneiric affiliations, but in the girl's case the magical skill is more clearly refined as an ability to foresee the future through her dreams. Though susceptible to loneliness, Yume is blessed with a magnanimous disposition and plays a particularly supportive role in relation to the robot girl Minatsu Amakase: a character loosely modeled on Miharu from the original *Da Capo*'s first season but endowed with a distinctive mentality and hence placed at the core of events radically different from those surrounding Miharu. Firstly, while Miharu seemed unproblematically drawn to humans, Minatsu at first claims to detest them. Secondly, the discovery within the school's population that she is a mechanical entity makes people deeply suspicious of her, which gives the anime scope for engaging in some intelligent reflections on the dread of alterity among well-adjusted and smugly self-righteous citizens. The character of Minatsu also supplies the first season with a perfect opportunity to deliver a striking instance of generic flexibility in its finale. This sets out with a positive moment of reconciliation between Self and Other as Minatsu, who has learned to accept humans, inspires erstwhile hostile fellow students to adopt a comparably commodious stance toward members of her own species. This celebratory mood gives way to somber drama as it transpires that a callous board of directors' decision to expel Minatsu from Kazami Academy — despite the students' en-masse boycott of their lessons — is irrevocable. The atmosphere alters again in the direction of sadness-tinged cheeriness, as an honorary graduation ceremony crowned by a stirring rock performance by Yoshiyuki and his friends is held solely for the robot's benefit.

Other personae worthy of note in this context are Nanaka Shirakawa, who follows in Kotori's steps by being cast as the school idol and a musically gifted mind-reader; Koko Tsukishima, a touchingly fragile and klutzy adolescent; Anzu Yukimura, a reclusive playwright endowed with a formidable yet peculiarly sapping memory; and Suginami, a lookalike of his predecessor displaying the very same proclivities and quirks. On the aesthetic plane, in embarking upon the first season of *Da Capo II* it is very intriguing to see characters who look just like the first *Da Capo*'s main personae holding quite different roles. This raises some challenging questions regarding the part played by character design in the fashioning of visual novels and their spawn as instrumental in the construction of compelling worlds, and hence in stoking the player's or viewer's creative urges: questions, as shown in this chapter's introductory part, that are axial to an adequate comprehension of the media under scrutiny here. In this particular case, we are enjoined to wonder what exactly makes *Da Capo II*'s characters special despite their somatic closeness to a previous cast. A good example of the anime's delicate variations even when it appears to imitate slavishly its predecessor's designs is provided by the character of Koko. While closely modeled on the persona of Miharu from the first show, Koko hosts quite distinct psychological attributes and accordingly exhibits individual attitudes. In the early part of *Da Capo II*, in particular, the girl comes across as inhibited and reticent whereas Miharu by and large shone forth as the epitome of frank exuberance. This departure from the model permeates Koko's physiognomy, resulting in a more subdued overall appearance and a penchant for blushing. Another subtle variation pertaining to the character of Koko and its connection with Miharu is that the robot presented in *Da Capo II*, the aforementioned Minatsu, does not look anything like the Miharu android, though she shares her family name, and that whereas Miharu had a fetishistic obsession with bananas, Minatsu loathes the item despite her metabolic dependence on regular doses of a substance indigenous to it termed "bananamin."

A Yoriko lookalike clad in the iconic maid costume makes recurrent cameo appearances as a mannequin displayed in a shop window. This is revealed to be one of legion mass-produced robots carefully drained of all emotions by their exploitative manufacturers to ensure their docility. Utamaru is no longer a visible cast member (though an ice-cream kiosk is named after him) but finds a worthy heir, visually speaking, in the comparably toylike puppy Harimao. Both Otome and Yume are faithfully based on Nemu, embodying the original character's maternally caring attitude and her impulsiveness respectively. Yoshiyuki, for his part, sharply resembles the first anime's male lead in physical terms, while also replicating Jun'ichi's refreshingly unsentimental stance, unflinching loyalty, altruism and — somewhat ironically given his other assets — blindness to some of his closest friends' deepest feelings. The youth's natural tendency to take full responsibility for his actions, accidental ones included, is clearly demonstrated by his attitude towards Minatsu. Although the robot is at first furious with him for inadvertently activating her when all she wanted was to sleep for a long time in her insulated subterranean pod, he generously assents to his teacher's request that he watch after the creature and keep her nature a secret. On the one hand, Yoshiyuki accepts responsibility for ushering Minatsu into the human world against her wishes. On the other, he is intrigued by the intimation that although robots are reputed to harbor no feelings, Minatsu is clearly endowed with a temper alluding to the possession of human emotions.

The bulk of *Da Capo II*'s actual drama unfolds in the course of the second season, gaining momentum as it builds up, methodically but ineluctably, to Sakura's revelation that the ever-blooming tree is a synthetic outcome of her research and that Yoshiyuki is the product of her wish, granted by the tree in response to her plea for companionship. The *sakura*'s survival and the youth's own existence are therefore inextricable from each other. Sakura's and

Hatsunejima's troubles begin when the tree starts malfunctioning and hence granting wishes indiscriminately regardless of their intentions. As an ever-swelling spate of malevolent desires comes to fruition, the island is beset by legion baleful incidents. Sakura is at first able to minimize the effects of these events by protecting the potential victims with her sorcerous powers. This external filter becomes ineffective, however, and the witch resolves to sacrifice her own being by operating as an internal firewall, which entails her merging with the artificial *sakura*. Alas, her noble action proves futile, as does the now elderly Jun'ichi's attempt to emulate her effort. At this point, it becomes unequivocally evident that to put an end to the calamities, the tree must be caused to wither — which will cause Yoshiyuki's disappearance — and that Otome is the only person endowed with the power to accomplish such a feat. While the girl is well aware that to protect the island she has no choice but to exterminate the undying blossom, her private feelings towards the male lead painfully militate against her obligation as a magician of justice. The inner rifts experienced by both Sakura and Otome in these poignant moments are sensitively portrayed, and eloquently attest to the second season's psychological richness. As the overall tone darkens through a carefully paced accumulation of sinister premonitions (which include Yoshiyuki's troubling dreams), the characters' actions and motives acquire unprecedented intensity.

The mounting sense of foreboding is fueled by several of the favorite tropes found in visual novels and their televisual progeny, and specifically by a seamless interweaving of oneiric visions, secrets, promises and mystical phenomena. These motifs, already prominent in the first *Da Capo* and in *D. C. II*'s first season, are complicated in *D. C. II S. S.*, especially in its pictorially exquisite symbolic openings accompanied by Sakura's alternately melancholy and sorrowful voiceovers. The abiding force of memory is the cohesive agent binding those tropes indissolubly together. Looking specifically at this topos, it is worth pointing out that *D. C. II S. S.* offers an inspired variation on the flashback technique by traveling back not only to earlier moments in its characters' pasts, but also intertextually to events seen in the original *Da Capo* anime. This is most evident in the sequence where Otome and Yoshiyuki, having read old tomes documenting Hatsunejima's legendary history and believing that the accounts are simply myths, ask old Jun'ichi about his opinion on the matter. To Jun'ichi, of course, those accounts are quite accurate as they reflect crucial occurrences from his own youth. Although Otome and Yoshiyuki initially respond to the old man's report as a joke and their condescending smiles suggest that they might consider him a victim of senile dementia, Jun'ichi's words come to sound disquietingly true. Any audience familiar with the diegetic backdrop behind *D. C. II S. S.* is bound to enjoy the dramatic tension between discordant generational perspectives.

In assessing *D. C. II S. S.* specifically in terms of its enhancement of psychological complexity as a major narrative stimulus, the development of Sakura's character is arguably its most outstanding manifestation. The seemingly immortal sorceress is no longer the admixture of mischievous playfulness and seriousness seen in the first *Da Capo* anime, and maintained by and large in *Da Capo II*'s first season. In fact, she appears preoccupied at all times and haunted by a dark knowledge she is not at liberty to share with anyone until the drama reaches its climax. Even when her engaging mien is wreathed in smiles, an undertone of sadness makes itself felt and this imparts her otherwise unaltered juvenile physiognomy with dolefully mature connotations. Sakura even rises to the stature of a tragic persona as she advances towards the fulfillment of her unpalatable destiny, dispassionately blaming herself for the evils that have befallen the island and for the pain in store for her loved ones once the magical tree has been appeased at last. The sequence in which she discloses the truth to Otome before resolving to be introjected by the *sakura* and the dream in which she finally unveils to Yoshiyuki the truth regarding his origins are some of the most pathos-laden moments in the whole franchise. Also unforgettable is the scene where she has Jun'ichi cut off her lush mane in preparation for the sacrifice, which exudes the mood of a cleansing ritual of old. The scene's solemnity is felicitously counterbalanced by the bittersweet tone of the exchange between Sakura and Jun'ichi, where she harks back to their youth in remarking on her friend's tendency to dismiss his own conduct as "annoying" whenever he feels embarrassed and Jun'ichi, in turn, calls her "Sakurambo," as he was wont to do in childhood.

The intense psychodrama staged by *D. C. II S. S.* in its crowning moments reaches its apotheosis as, in the aftermath of the magical tree's withering, the wishes it has fulfilled evaporate and Yoshiyuki, concomitantly, is erased from the memories of even his closest friends. These complications echo the climactic events seen in the original *Da Capo* but lead to a dénouement marked by a more overtly supernatural tenor as Sakura, realizing that Yoshiyuki has not been entirely removed from Hatsunejima's memory and that his friends sense (though only in an inchoate fashion) that someone important is missing from their lives, implores the tree to "let these feelings become miracles."

\* \* \*

In both the ludic and animated formats, *Clannad* eloquently endorses the proposition that well-defined personae operate as visual stimuli and arresting emotive agents, capable of fostering immersive experiences for players and viewers alike, in both its ludic and its animated incarnations. Thorough characterization helps us engage affectively with the drama's convolutions and comprehend the motivations and goals governing not only the protagonists but also members of the supporting cast or even purely peripheral presences. Accordingly, it prompts us to embrace those objectives as springboards for our own decoding and narrativizing enterprises. At the same time, character appeal is bolstered by a minutely detailed habitat in which aspects of Japanese design typified by both traditional customs and contemporary vogues blend with Western influences — e.g., in the depiction of household and scholastic interiors, vestimentary styles, culinary practices and artisanal products — while functional attributes elegantly coalesce with decorative motifs. While some facets of *Clannad*'s graphic world are so minimalistic as to bring to mind the values of simplicity and sparseness inspired by Zen Buddhism, others exude an appetite for flamboyantly cute ornamentation consonant with the aesthetic of *kawaii* on the basis of which all of the female characters are portrayed. The symbolic and occasionally surreal sequences highlighting some key moments in the protagonists' journeys of self-discovery illustrate the former modality, whereas the snippets of action revolving around domestic interactions or personal hobbies (and related fetishes) exemplify the latter. Taken in tandem, these contrasting aesthetic proclivities tend to yield an atmosphere of freshness and enthusiasm even when the focus is on painful experiences of disillusionment or loss, thereby providing an Aladdin's cave of ideas for both videogame and anime aficionados.

The visual novel and anime are complemented by an artbook distinguished by outstanding quality. This is demonstrated not only by its contents (including character profiles, illustration galleries, charts, music sheets) but also by its material constitution as an object of autonomous caliber attesting to the Japanese dedication to the arts of typography, papermaking, wrapping and packaging. Furthermore, while the title of the companion volume, *Clannad Visual Fan Book*, might bring to mind a collection of pictures intended merely to gratify devotees already familiar with the franchise and its cast, the book in fact offers a unique compendium of design styles capable of supplying estimable insights into myriad aspects of both traditional and contemporary Japanese aesthetics. An essential aspect of the book in its entirety is its emphasis on the aesthetic of *kawaii* (here examined in some depth in Chapter 1). Both the character designs and the artwork detailing various features of the distinctive *Clannad* world clearly indicate that the cultivation of cuteness in Japanese visual culture at large is a phenomenon that transcends status, age and gender, while concurrently blurring the boundary between fact and fantasy. The book's lavish plates also intimate, on numerous occasions, that the ethos of *kawaii* does not only inform the entertainment sector — even though it has undeniably governed it to memorable effect for decades, and most famously in the interrelated domains of anime, manga and videogaming.

In fact, it extends to the realm of graphic design, prolifically unleashing merchandise and services defined by logos and mascots that exhibit all of the classic *kawaii* traits: round and soft contours, gentle lineaments, pastelly hues, pie eyes and a disarming aura of innocence, vulnerability and childlike curiosity.

The original *Clannad* visual novel was released in 2004, spawning alternate versions of the game between 2006 and 2009, while the anime offshoots comprise the TV series *Clannad* (2007), the one-installment OVA *Another World: Tomoyo Chapter* (2008) and the TV series *Clannad After Story* (2008–2009), all three of which were directed by Tatsuya Ishihara and produced by Kyoto Animation, and the movie *Clannad* (2007), directed by Osamu Dezaki and produced by Toei Animation. The *Clannad* visual novel encompasses two arcs, "School Life" and "After Story." The latter only becomes available once the player has worked through the first segment's various scenarios and collected eight "orbs of light," — one of which disappears in "School Life" but features again in the second arc. "School Life" focuses on the final high-school year of the protagonist, Tomoya Okazaki, in the course of which he interacts with all of the key characters in the game, particularly its five main heroines: Nagisa Furukawa, Kyou Fujibayashi, Tomoyo Sakagami, Kotomi Ichinose and Fuko Ibuki. "After Story" covers the decade following the principal characters' graduation, concentrating on Tomoya and Nagisa's life as a couple and featuring characters from the first arc as ancillary actors. In order to experience the visual novel's authentic resolution, the player must collect a totality of thirteen orbs of light.

Tomoya, whose role the player is required to assume, is a third-year student who has gained an unsavory reputation as a delinquent due to his defiance of authority, poor attendance record and alternately circumspect and apathetic attitude towards life in general. So frank as to appear downright rude at times, Tomoya is primarily characterized by an unflinchingly loyal and selfless disposition — though he tends to dismiss his devotion to others on the grounds that he simply has nothing better to do. The character's disaffected stance is largely a corollary of the loss of his mother Atsuko in a car crash when he was just a child, in the wake of which his father Naoyuki descended into a sad spiral of gambling and alcoholism. Emotionally plagued by his father's proclivity to treat him as though he were a mere acquaintance, Tomoya has also been physically incapacitated (and hence disabled from taking part in the school's baseball club) by the older man's unintentional violence. Nagisa, *Clannad*'s main heroine, is a gentle and insecure girl who has been forced by a weak constitution to be absent from school for protracted periods and is hence repeating the third year when Tomoya first meets her on the way to school, amidst the blossoming cherry trees marking the start of the new academic year. Despite her lack of self-confidence, Nagisa is resolved to reform her school's disbanded drama club against all odds and enact a play she has long been rehearsing in private. (Amusingly, though the girl is passionate about theatre, she has never seen a play in her life.) Nagisa's characterization is originally enhanced by two charming idiosyncrasies: the tendency to mutter the names of her favorite food items as charms meant to give her strength and motivation, and an unconditional adoration of the fictional cartoon characters known as the "Dango Family."

Kyou is scurrilous and aggressive, yet secretly harbors a kindly and protective personality (especially towards her meek younger sister Ryou), while Tomoyo is a formidable fighter feared by even the most notorious street gangs, aspiring to become the president of the student council. Kotomi is a solitary genius girl, immediately distinguished by dismal communication skills counterbalanced by a disarmingly magnetic aura of childlike innocence. Fuko, one of *Clannad*'s most enigmatic personae, is a first-year student temporarily enabled by the desire to help her elder sister Kouko achieve happiness at any price to project her vision onto reality and interact with her fellow students, although she is in fact lying unconscious in a hospital following a traffic accident. While Nagisa echoes *Kanon*'s Ayu in her role as central heroine and Shiori in virtue of her checkered medical history, Fuko shares Ayu's oneiric/projective stature and Kotomi recalls Mai through her unsocial and withdrawn behavior. Alongside the characters who people *Clannad*'s real world are a girl and a robot-like doll inhabiting an imaginary realm dreamt by Tomoya: the former symbolizes Ushio, Tomoya and Nagisa's daughter, after her death, while the latter consists of a nameless creature manufactured by the girl out of scrap metal as a substitute for Tomoya. In this alternate domain, *Clannad*'s supernatural strand gradually unfolds, reaching a climax in the game's true ending.

The *Clannad* anime closely follows its ludic precursor in the adoption of a two-arc structure, each of the parent segments corresponding to one of the TV series helmed by Ishihara. (As we shall see, the movie offers a telescoped and altogether darker retelling of the whole story, with an emphasis on the more intense dramatic aspects of the second segment.) *Clannad* echoes *Kanon*, Ishihara's previous hit in the domain of anime adapted from visual novels, in capitalizing on the narrative principle of multiperspectivalism by orchestrating a thoroughly integrated ensemble of interrelated stories and respective journeys of self-discovery. *Clannad* is so devoted to the cultivation of plural points of view as to refrain from prioritizing incontrovertibly any one single actor at any one stage in the story. Even its primary heroine is repeatedly made to cede ground to other personae and their own emotional pilgrimages. This is borne out at an early juncture by Ishihara's use of what could be termed a deliberate false start. The plot might initially seem to revolve around Nagisa, her determination to revive the drama club and her incremental involvement with Tomoya, marked by his introduction to the girl's parents and unplanned recruitment as a reliable supporter of her quest. However, Nagisa does not dominate the set since Tomoya, in the course of this inceptive portion of the anime, also begins to interact with Fuko, Kyou, Ryou and Kotomi.

Fuko soon gains center stage while Nagisa temporarily moves of her own accord to the periphery of the action, recognizing that her thespian aspirations must be put on the back burner in order to advance the younger girl's more pressing goal. This is to organize a wedding ceremony for her sister Kouko to be attended by the staff and students of their school, where Kouko herself was formerly employed as an art teacher. To attract the intended guests, Fuko tirelessly carves starfish out of wood and distributes them throughout the school as invitations. The person performing these actions, it transpires, is actually a projection of her unconscious self emanating from her dream, which the strength of her love for Kouko renders provisionally visible to others. Nagisa and her parents are so eager to nourish Fuko's dream, which they know to be ephemeral, as to spend entire sleepless nights engaged in the manufacture of wooden starfish. As the real Fuko's condition deteriorates, leading the doctors to opine that she might never emerge from her coma, more and more students become oblivious to her existence, and the erstwhile perceptible projection rapidly acquires the uncanny status of an absent presence. Even Nagisa and Tomoya end up forgetting Fuko, and it is only because her feelings are so powerful as to ultimately reach all the people that ever received a starfish token that the doomed girl is able to witness the fulfillment of her dream before vanishing from the world of consciousness altogether. As she does so, Fuko magically leaves behind the vestigial rumor concerning a cute, innocent and earnest kid constantly running through the school. Fuko will make some cameo appearances as a seemingly real, flesh-and-blood presence in later installments, including the one in which Tomoya and his entire "harem" have fun in town together. Fuko also features in the sequence where the protagonist (temporarily suspended from school as a result of his assumption of responsibility for a fight actually triggered by Tomoyo's notoriety) is showered with all sorts of delicious dishes by Tomoyo herself, the Fujibayashi sisters and Kotomi, all of whom seem to be vying for Tomoya's romantic attention at this stage in the drama.

Once, the Fuko arc has reached its resolution, the anime's attention returns to Nagisa's efforts to pursue her theatrical aspirations. Yet insofar as Tomoya's determination to abet Nagisa's goal by recruiting more members for the club draws the youth into frequent interaction with various other characters, the camera is not, even at this juncture, undilutedly trained on the main female persona. First, the narrative concentrates on Kotomi's story, with frequent forays into the Fujibayashi sisters' parallel experiences. Subsequently it shifts to Tomoyo's turbulent past and her current juggling of both presidential ambitions and martial duties. The segment devoted to Kotomi revolves around the genius student's gradual acceptance of traumatic childhood experiences through a tortuous journey of self-discovery on which she embarks, unwittingly at first, at Tomoya's behest. A major turning point in the arc coincides with Tomoya's realization that he knew Kotomi as a kid and was for a while her sole friend. Around that time, Kotomi's parents perished in a plane crash and the orphan proceeded to burn what she believed to be her dad's groundbreaking research to prevent its illegitimate appropriation by unscrupulous parties. Kotomi's psychological ordeal is haunted by the figure of an enigmatic man whom the girl dreads insofar as she deems him hellbent on stealing her father's work. In fact, the man turns out to be her legal guardian who wishes to give her a birthday present purchased by Kotomi's parents just prior to their tragic demise: a teddy bear that miraculously survived the accident and was passed from hand to hand for years until he found it.

The sequence chronicling the toy's peregrination from country to country, as kindly strangers unquestioningly agree to look after it and convey it to the next person to help it eventually reach its intended destination, is one of the most remarkable portions of *Clannad* as a whole (and possibly of Ishihara's oeuvre generally). The distinctive atmosphere of each of the countries touched by the present in the course of its lengthy voyage is succinctly captured by recourse to instantly identifiable architectural, sartorial and climate-related symbols and offers an apt metaphor for Kotomi's own laborious journey of self-discovery. Having returned to Nagisa and her club-related quest for a few episodes, meanwhile taking the time to introduce new supporting characters that serve to enrich the narrative's community-oriented flavor, the anime turns to Tomoyo's story. Like Kotomi, Tomoyo carries a painful familial legacy. In her case, this is dominated by the daunting memory of her younger brother Takafumi, whose willingness to sacrifice his very life to prevent their parents' divorce enabled the Sakagamis to learn how to live like a proper family after years of indifference and tension. Tomoyo's chief objective, it gradually transpires, is to honor Takafumi's memory by protecting an avenue of cherry trees scheduled for felling in defiance of the authorities.

When Nagisa finally acquires virtually undisputed centrality in the anime, her characterization — already elaborate and subtly nuanced from the start — gains unprecedented levels of complexity. We thus discover that the girl is tormented by the intimation that she behaved reprehensibly towards her parents at some unspecified moment in the past but is powerless to recall the actual cause of this feeling. Although her parents dismissively claim that Nagisa must just be imagining the whole issue, Akio privately discloses to Tomoya the nugget of truth hiding behind the girl's disturbing sensation. Ten years earlier, we are informed, Nagisa was running a high fever and her parents left her on her own to go to work. Having found the girl in a critical condition upon their return, Akio and Sanae decided to relinquish their careers and dreams for their daughter's sake. Nagisa herself discovers the truth merely by chance when she bumps into some secreted boxes containing her parents' old diaries and photos. Unable to take her mind off Akio and Sanae's wrecked ambitions, she sinks into depression and when the longed-for opportunity to perform her play at the school festival finally arrives, Nagisa simply breaks down. However, conclusively enthroning the value of family ties as one of its principal preoccupations, *Clannad* chooses to rescue its heroine from her paralyzing impasse by bringing into play as central actors the hitherto secondary figures of Akio and Sanae. This dramatic reorientation reaches its climax in the scene where Akio proudly announces that he and his spouse's ultimate and most cherished goal has always been to see Nagisa make her own dream come true, which enables the performance to burgeon into a sensational success.

Revolving around a girl in "a world that has ended" who makes a doll by putting together "pieces of junk" in an effort to alleviate her abysmal loneliness, Nagisa's play directly mirrors Tomoya's dream — so much so that during its climactic performance at the close of the first anime, the sequences we are presented with actually consist of images from Tomoya's dream. The play deserves some attention at this point in the discussion, not only as a cardinal diegetic block but also as an artistic accomplishment in its own right. As a story-within-the-story, the piece encapsulates Japanese art's age-old devotion to simplicity as a means of communicating essential realities and universal themes unencumbered by mimetic obligations. As Natalie Avella has noted, "For Americans, simplicity means presenting information with clarity. To the Japanese, simplicity means a sparse aesthetic purity that eliminates superfluous detail, and even informational clarity, so the viewer has to seek out the message in the design" (Avella, p. 15). (This stance is reminiscent of the aesthetic ethos promulgated in the West by Renaissance courtly art, where the principles of clarity, illumination and radiance do not imply a lack of complexity or a promise of explicit revelations but are actually inseparable from a cultivation of richly allusive language requiring audiences to deploy their interpretative skills and actively engage with the text.) Artists have frequently resorted to the use of "lack of detail or void spaces around an object in order to leave the interpretation up to the audience." In so doing, they have implicitly conveyed the aesthetic significance of emptiness as a quality far exceeding plenitude and abundance in evocative power. The art of *ikebana*, Avella suggests, neatly exemplifies this idea: "In *ikebana*, only a few flowers and branches are used, arranged in a way that is not found in nature. The Japanese sensibility sees no beauty in a mass of flowers in a vase. The single flower loses its effect in the mass, and opulence alone is not considered a virtue in an arrangement. Economy in the use of material is at the same time an economy in the use of space. This balancing act of space and material is also the way many of Japan's most renowned designers seem to work" (p. 99). The *haiku*, one of the most popular forms of Japanese poetry, and garden design further demonstrate the penchant for simplicity.

The first anime series engages with all of the essential themes and motifs seen to operate recurrently in both visual novels and their anime offspring. Creative enterprises are accorded an integral part — most pointedly through Nagisa's theatrical exploits, but also through less conspicuous activities. For Tomoyo, the preservation of the *sakura* trees is itself a pursuit comparable to an artistic accomplishment. Kotomi, for her part, will not refrain from playing the violin even though the resulting performance is downright intolerable. As in other titles here studied, gastronomic practices are frequently invested with artistic status in *Clannad*: for Sanae, baking increasingly audacious types of bread and cake is a veritable raison d'être despite the frequent unpalatability of the outcome, while Kyou vaunts a reputation as a proficient chef and Nagisa, regards food as a magical tool. Even the habitually impractical Kotomi at one point gives vent to culinary enthusiasm by baking a stunningly professional apple pie for Tomoya. Fuko's relentless creation of starfish sculptures further reinforces the topos of artistic self-expression. Tomoya's own creativity is humorously illustrated by the scene where the protagonist deploys the "Faked-Rip-Van-Winkle" trope at Youhei Sunohara's expense, maintaining that while his friend slept through the day's lessons, one hundred years elapsed, and claiming to be first a hologram and then a cyborg. Tomoya also indulges in comical artistry in the sequence based on the popular "After-the-End" trope — i.e., the dramatic formula that envisions the future in accordance with all the conventional trappings of postapocalyptic anime. In the yarn improvised by Tomoya, Fuko is cast in the role of an imaginary hero's secret superweapon.

*Clannad*'s multifarious creative ventures are matched by inspired flourishes of self-referentiality. As Tomoya's best friend, the risibly inept Sunohara, engages in hopeless fights with Tomoyo in order either to expose her latent weakness or demonstrate that she is actually a bloke in disguise, the action is framed so as to mimic a filmed event and equipped with a combo counter of the kind found in fighting games, which adds up over time as the series progresses. Self-referentiality also comes into play in the scenes where the action switches to the RPG mode. When Tomoya manages to pull off a prank on Fuko, for instance, the screen sometimes displays a laudatory message (e.g., "you have mastered a new skill!") matched by an old-fashioned videogame-style tune. In one scene, Sunohara announces his intention to help Nagisa reestablish the defunct drama club at all costs, even if it entails fighting members of the student council who oppose the initiative. (The boy's actions do not reflect any particularly noble habitus at this stage, since he is guided solely by the desire to obtain unlimited supplies of bread from the Furukawa Bakery.) The animation suddenly switches to the visual-novel format, as Tomoya inwardly notes that if this were an RPG, the player would feasibly face multiple choices, all of which here amount to incongruously extreme options, 1. "slay"; 2. "smoke bomb"; 3. "magic." The screen accordingly displays the relevant lines of text and character sprites for Sunohara and Nagisa. The style adopted in this scene recalls Visual Art's/Key's 2007 visual novel *Little Busters*, where the dating-sim and fighting-game modalities felicitously coalesce.

Dreams and visions feature pervasively in *Clannad*, reaching their apotheosis in the recurrent symbolic sequences pivoting on the imaginary girl and her robotic garbage doll. Depicting a realm beyond time traversed by bewitching light spheres, these sequences abide in memory not only by virtue of their thought-provoking status in relation to the main action but also as a result of the unique animation techniques and cinematography employed in their execution. At such junctures, the anime exhibits what is typically described as an "art shift"—a sudden and intentional transition from the anime's regular style to a different visual tenor, effected to convey especially poignant emotions or to allude to cryptic layers of meaning that escape the ordinary process of semiosis and therefore require the viewer to shift to alternate interpretative modalities. Where the oneiric dimension is concerned, also notable is the surreal dream (worthy of Federico Fellini's cinema at its most adventurous) experienced by Tomoya when he meets Kotomi at the school library on a Sunday and consumes her wonderful apple pie. The conceit of a vision associated with the consumption of special food brings to mind the universe of *Alice in Wonderland*. In addition, memories and traumas punctuate the drama from start to finish. Tomoya sets the trend by declaring his longing to consign unwanted reminiscences to oblivion in the anime's opening moments. Fuko is motivated, throughout her transient visionary existence, by memories of her beloved Kouko while Kouko herself, in turn, is haunted by images of Fuko as a reclusive kid pathologically dependent on the sororal bond. Nagisa is increasingly troubled by inchoate recollections of her supposedly hurtful behavior towards her parents, whereas Tomoyo is driven by the desire to commemorate her little brother's sacrificial heroism, and Kotomi labors under the curse of baleful specters associated with her parents' tragic death and with her presumed persecution by a malevolent adult.

*Clannad* also alludes to the pervasiveness of mythical undertones in the apparently mundane here-and-now. The character of Fuko, as hinted, is enveloped in the codes and conventions of the classic ghost story, while Tomoyo is endowed with legendary stature by her martial prowess. The mythical dimension is allowed to reign supreme in Tomoya's dream, where the magical atmosphere exuded by the visuals and the animation techniques climactically colludes with the thematic deployment of miraculous occurrences. This blend of mythological and down-to-earth ingredients is complemented by the dialectical juxtaposition of symbolic settings (e.g., the *sakura*-flanked hill leading to the school where Nagisa and Tomoya first meet, the sunset-drenched roads witnessing some of the main characters' most significant exchanges) and pictorial naturalism. The latter is epitomized by the representation of the school itself. As noted with reference to *Kanon*, the visual-novel studio Visual Art's/Key often utilizes real-world locations in its games. In *Clannad*, the high school so central to the first anime's entire diegesis is overtly based on the junior-high and high school Komaba situated in Setagaya, Tokyo, affiliated to the University of Tsukuba. Concurrently, the axial role played throughout the narrative by the interplay of the individual and the community is attested to by the title itself: "*clannad*" indeed means "family" or "clan" in Irish. Parental figures feature prominently, in various guises, in Tomoya's, Nagisa's and Kotomi's personal journeys. Sisters play integral roles in Fuko's and Kyou's stories, and special significance is accorded to a brother in Tomoyo's. In Nagisa's case, the motif is reinforced by the recurrent appearance of the fictional Dango family. The ultimate "family" is the drama club itself: an assortment of disparate personalities brought together by the catalyst of Nagisa's infectious enthusiasm.

Finally, *Clannad* offers a magisterial exercise in multigeneric experimentation, oscillating even in the space of single installments between slice-of-life realism and densely symbolic action, between zany comedy and situations so somber as to occasionally verge on the tragic. Some of the most entertaining comic moments coincide with the sequences in which Tomoya encourages Sunohara to give up fighting with Tomoyo and mischievously advises him to ingratiate himself with the girl by addressing her ceremoniously while performing all manner of utterly inappropriate moves — such as "naturally stretching," "naturally doing a Hindu squat" and "pretending to bowl" — in the full knowledge that this will only serve to augment Tomoyo's exasperation. However, it is noteworthy, that even when the anime indulges most expansively in clownishness by recourse to familiar stereotypes, the characters associated with these situations are not portrayed as mere vehicles for comic relief. In fact, the actors exhibit subtly nuanced psychological facets that preclude univocal categorization. Sunohara, for example, reveals a sensitive disposition when he begins to forget Fuko, and his initial confusion turns into actual pain as he struggles to recapture the memories that tenaciously elude his grasp.

Nagisa's parents are downright farcical in their displays of either culinary pride or uxoriousness. Also ludicrous is the scene where they endeavor to invest Tomoya with a more memorable designation, and suggest as viable options words such as "Galaxy," "Cosmos" and "Eternal" — which inexplicably degenerates into "Ethanol" from one sentence to the next. Nevertheless, both characters evince outstanding emotional sophistication at various stages in the story: for example, in their treatment of Fuko and in the climax of the first anime. The second anime enhances *Clannad*'s appetite for generic limberness. Its early segments in particular abound with jocular complications, yet the comedy is subtly intersprinkled with allusions to serious emotional and psychological preoccupations. For example, in the episodes where Tomoya and Nagisa endeavor, with Mrs. Furukawa's generous support, to match Sunohara with a "fake girlfriend" so that his sister Mei will believe he has finally settled down and quit worrying about his immaturity, the situation provides plenty of opportunities for exhilarating humor, yet there is little doubt as to the extent of Mei's concern or the gravity of the state of affective inertia blighting Sunohara as a result of his deep-seated sense of failure.

As is commonly the case in visual novels, the gameplay requires the user to engage with lengthy and richly detailed textual passages and choose alternate routes from a number of options at designated decision points. There are five pivotal plot strands for the player to experience (one for each of the main female actors), each of which may be explored through multiple replays, and a total of thirteen mutable endings. The *Clannad* anime transposes the visual novel's characteristic penchant for variations on a set of core themes into a vital component of its narrative pattern and release history. Permutational options occur both within each of the two main series, as the focus shifts from one persona to another and one self-exploratory voyage to another, and across the franchise as a whole. A variation on the first show's resolution is supplied by the Tomoyo-centered OVA. The second TV series incorporates even more drastic tonal alternatives by incrementally morphing its prequel's school-based dimension first into an adult world and finally into an existence that transcends everyday reality altogether. With the movie, a further spectrum of variations is provided through the story's distillation into a pointedly symbolic experience. The OVA accomplishes a unique feat in the field by according a secondary heroine the pivotal role in the story's conclusion. Its alternate ending indeed casts Tomoyo as the male lead's companion in the journey towards adulthood instead of Nagisa.

Approximately one third of *After Story* chronicles occurrences unfolding during Tomoya's final semester as a senior high-schooler, evincing a gradual shift of mood as the action progressively moves from domestic, romantic and comical situations to serious drama haunted by separation and loss and punctuated by supernatural motifs. The graver atmosphere is predominant in the segments of the anime focusing on Tomoya and Nagisa's life as a couple, which culminates with their marriage, Nagisa's demise shortly after giving birth to their daughter Ushio, and Tomoya's descent into dejection and squalor. The turning point in the male lead's downhill ride is marked by his reunion with Ushio, initially entrusted to Akio and Sanae's care, and his life as a father. Having inherited her mother's weak physique, the little girl herself eventually falls prey to consumption, leaving Tomoya once again to face on his own the horror of irretrievable loss. As in *Kanon*, the anime's tragic finale is rectified by the intervention of a supernatural agency. At this stage in the drama, the full significance of Tomoya's recurrent dream finally transpires, as the true identities of the girl and her robot are disclosed and Tomoya is enabled to reverse history, thereby entering a life in which Nagisa miraculously survives Ushio's birth and the couple are able to raise their child together. The ethereal light orbs seen to course the oneiric world throughout the anime are appropriately shown floating through the city just as Nagisa and Tomoya give Ushio her first bath.

On the whole, the *Clannad* movie is, quite faithful to the original yarn but adopts a deliberately darker tone. (In this regard, it echoes the theatrical version of *Air*, also helmed by Dezaki.) The filmic version of Tomoya, in particular, is more somber than his TV incarnation. This aspect of the protagonist's personality is especially notable in the segment of the movie where he recounts his past life, from the moment of his first encounter with Nagisa through the establishment of the drama club and finally, to Nagisa's death. While all the other characters have managed to move on, however haphazardly or laboriously, Tomoya himself is stuck in the past and unable even to acknowledge his daughter's existence. Mirroring *After Story*'s narrative trajectory, the drama climaxes with Tomoya and Ushio's reunion. The film's most memorable contribution to the *Clannad* franchise lies with its distinctive visual style, epitomized by the use of watercolor effects in the scene cuts accompanying especially poignant moments, and its unique symbolic repertoire. The latter reaches its apotheosis in the depiction of the central characters inhabiting the "World of Nothingness" — shared by Tomoya and Nagisa since childhood — no longer as an imaginary girl and a junk doll but as masked puppets. This point is worth stressing not only because of its somewhat harrowing graphic lure but also because of its iconic significance in relation to Japanese tradition. Puppets, alongside dolls of various kinds, have played an important role in several aspects of Japan's entertainment history and customs for centuries, operating both as substitutes for humans and as emblematic reminders of human limitations. In terms of cinematography, the theatrical release capitalizes on techniques that bring to mind Japanese woodblock art, particularly the custom described by Avella as follows: "edges of pictures are cut in unexpected ways, often slicing through a subject, so that it appears to loom out of the frame in an energetic and dynamic way. Figures are seen from behind, in shadow, or partly obscured" and "the use of blank space, unusual angles and viewpoint" is pervasively notable (Avella, p. 10). (Interestingly, these are also some of the key techniques underpinning poster design — a practice that has gradually risen to the status of a legitimate art form since the late nineteenth century not only in Japan but also. In the West thanks to the influence exerted by Japanese graphic design on European and American culture.)

The anime's commitment to a design philosophy that maximizes the sensory appeal of characters and settings underscores the tactile properties of immersion. In the portrayal of its characters, *Clannad* concomitantly asks us to engage in a psychological process of immersion, encouraging speculation on those personae's hypothetical behavior in real-life circumstances, whereas in the depiction of its settings the anime promotes spatial immersion in a world that seems perceptually convincing despite its blatant fictitiousness. At the same time, the challenges posed by the story's more cryptic layers render immersion a cerebral task of strategic decoding. Tactile and cerebral aspects of the viewer's experience collude in what could be described as affective immersion — the sensation that one has entered a palpable world and is receiving stimulation from it. To support this experience, the anime brings into play various facets of temporality: order (the sequence in which certain events happen and/or are presented by the story); frequency (the reiteration of the same basic events with shifts of perspective and point of view); and speed (the compression or dilation of events as ways of prioritizing how they are experienced over their effective duration). These three facets of *Clannad*'s temporal dynamics are enriched by the anime's openness to revisiting: with each successive viewing, our sense of order, frequency and speed alters in accordance with the memories retained from previous viewings and attendant expectations. For example, we may formulate alternate interpretations of the anime's arrangement of events, of different actors' perceptions of those occurrences, and of the weight of the drama as a value independent from its actual extension. In other words, there is no obvious path forward except the one we come to choose, often unconsciously, as the narrative possibilities branch, twist and intersect.

It is through an unflinching dedication to character design that both the

*Clannad* game and the resulting anime succeed not only in absorbing us into convincing worlds but also in offering us vehicles for the exploration of our own reality. In several forms of videogaming, characters do not need to have a personality since their role is entirely functional: they are a means of getting the action to progress and there is no point in wondering what they think or feel about it. This is not the case with visual novels, where the emphasis on elaborate textual formations entails the ideation of personae that closely resemble literary characters and are capable of undergoing development and even behaving in unexpected ways. When such game-based actors are translated into animated presences, and thus inserted into a dynamic drama, the opportunities for development multiply — especially when, as in *Clannad*, the focus is essentially on ordinary human relationships, arguably the most convoluted facet of existence. It is also at this point that we are invited to reflect on the relevance of the characters' experiences to the actual world we inhabit, thereby questioning the ideological assumptions that underpin (often invisibly) our personal journeys of self-discovery. Fantasy elements imbued with mystical motifs do not impair the process but actually enhance it by contributing a challenging metaphorical dimension to the more realistic level of the story.

By encouraging us to step back and adopt a critical stance towards both the story's world and our own reality, *Clannad* deploys immersion not so much to induce a suspension of disbelief as to help us distance ourselves from the action and think about what we are watching as a construct, by tearing down the set's fourth wall. This move is perfectly consonant with traditional Japanese art's tendency to expose the work's artificiality in defiance of mimesis. A resplendent example of this trend is supplied by the opus of Utagawa Kuniyoshi (1797–1861), where stirring depictions of moments from Japan's ancient past coexist with mundane scenes focusing on beautiful courtesans or Kabuki actors, as well as poetic landscapes that have inspired many Impressionist and Post-Impressionist artists in the West. The passion for styles and imagery that frankly foreground the artwork's madeness pervades Kuniyoshi's output, flowing out of his color woodblocks and rough sketches alike as legendary warriors confront fantastic creatures from popular illustrated literature, powerful politicians become the butt of trenchant satire encoded in visual riddles, contemporary geishas are disguised as heroic ladies from history, familiar sceneries are viewed from eccentric angles replete with low horizons and ragged clouds, and grotesque erotic animals irreverently engage in human activities. In the context of the anime at hand, the exposure of artificiality makes the drama not so much a goal per se as a tool for stimulating thought. Hence, resolutions are not envisioned as primary objectives, as demonstrated by *Clannad*'s proclivity for alternate outcomes. What matters most is not "what happened" but "what could happen": the variable options stretching well beyond the spatial and temporal confines of the story as it is shown on the screen. In this respect, the construct yielded by the anime is not simply a drama but a meta-drama: a drama that allows for the conception of several possible dramas.

* * *

*Tsuyokiss* (TV series; dir. Shinichiro Kimura, 2006) overtly echoes one of *Clannad*'s principal diegetic motifs insofar as its protagonist, Sunao Konoe, is driven throughout by the resolve to form a drama club against all manner of seemingly intractable odds in the school to which she has recently transferred. *Tsuyokiss* also invokes the image of a girl fantasizing about being all alone in the world so central to Nagisa's play (as indeed it is to Chihiro's novel in *ef—a tale of memories*) through the character of the somber and reclusive Nagomi Yashi. A further intertextual homage to the work of Visual Art's/Key is the inclusion of the sword-wielding martial champion and "Director of Discipline" Otome Kurogane, who instantly brings to mind *Kanon*'s Mai. (The image of the champion of justice with which the girl comes to be associated also recalls Otome from *D. C. II.*) While *Clannad*'s mood is predominantly wistful despite the anime's inspired insertion of comic vignettes, *Tsuyokiss*'s overall tone is that of the typical "feel-good" program. Even the misunderstanding that threatens the development of the romantic liaison at the story's core is of an essentially playful character: the heroine's childhood friend and admirer Leo Tsushima inadvertently tarnishes the would-be actress's self-esteem by addressing her as a "*daikon*," which means a "ham performer," yet means to pay her a compliment since to him the *daikon* (i.e., Japanese white radish) symbolizes pure and elegant beauty.

Moreover, Sunao's "*daikon* complex" never succeeds in fully eradicating from her mind the memory of Leo as someone who has subliminally sustained her desire to act as a means of bringing happiness to others. On the whole, the protagonist's quest comes across as an authentic celebration of an essentially indigenous tenet: the upholding of "hard work and guts" famously encapsulated by the exhortation "*gambatte!*" (i.e., "do your best!" or "hang out there!"). In *Tsuyokiss*, this moral priority is not only seen to reach fruition at the private level: it is also posited as coterminous with the ability to share other people's feelings and thus regard any personal achievement as the outcome of a collective and collaborative effort. As in *To Heart*, the value of individual hard work is here posited as indissociable from the principles of solidarity and mutual support. This purview also extends to the audience, insofar as our recognition of those motivations and aims progressively influences the nature of the goals we wish to see fulfilled as the narrative advances.

*Tsuyokiss* repeatedly glories in self-reflexive flourishes of commendable tastefulness and invigorating liveliness. A particularly remarkable scene occurs in the opening installment, where the heroine tries to prove her thespian worth to the irritably arrogant president of the student council, known as "Princess Erika," and hence obtain permission to establish the sought-for club. In this segment, Sunao enacts the famous balcony scene from *Romeo and Juliet*, playing both parts by seamlessly switching places across the stage and thereby appearing to affect the scenery itself with each transition. An economically effective change of costume effected by merely donning a dark drape over Juliet's lacy garments contributes vitally to the overall mood. Moreover, the overt and intentional exposure of theatrical artificiality implicit in the sequence exudes a veritably Brechtian feel. The closing, post-credit sequence offered in the final installment stylistically mirrors the key sequence from the inaugural episode through its explicitly self-referential nature (thus also confirming the visual novel's penchant for self-reflexivity in its structural makeup). In this sequence, what would at first appear to be the resolution of Sunao's and Leo's fluctuating romance turns in to be a scene from a movie all of the key students and staff at the protagonist's school are shooting together — which indicates that Sunao has not merely managed to satisfy a personal aspiration but also to create an intersubjective network wherein everyone feels genuinely enthusiastic about the pleasures and challenges of performance.

Where self-reflexivity is concerned, it is also noteworthy that the anime's most assiduously recurrent visual trope is the "eyecatch." This term commonly designates a frame used to begin and end a commercial break in a Japanese TV program. In the show, the flow of the action is periodically halted by an eyecatch displaying one or more of the main characters, frequently in a fan-service mode, uttering the single word "Tsuyokiss" in a variety of tones and inflections. These frames recall character sprites from the visual-novel format. An additional expression of the self-referential urge is the couching of the twelve episodes' opening sequences as "mini-dramas" in a wide range of styles and genres (e.g., the thriller, romance, action adventure), generally framed within a dream or nightmare experienced by the heroine. (Sunao's journey of self-discovery is thus presented as indisseverable from her dream of embarking on a theatrical career in more ways than one.)

Of the recurring themes to be found in anime based on visual novels, the topos of the creative quest is therefore patently paramount in *Tsuyokiss*. At the same time, memories play an important part. Sunao's own evolution is punctuated by recollections of her childhood experiences as an aspiring performer beset by stage fright and rescued by the encouragement offered by a little boy who eventually turns out to be an infantile version of Leo himself. At the same time, memory is brought into play to individuate and flesh out some of the supporting characters. A primary instance is Nagomi, whose recollections of her now departed father evolve, as the narrative advances and she indirectly draws inspiration from the indomitable protagonist, from a disabling force that keeps her anchored to the past and its pain to a source of motivation and attendant desire to progress into the future. Whereas the *Tsuyokiss* anime prioritizes Sunao's quest as its principal diegetic thread from the start, the parent game of the same title (released for different platforms in 2005 and 2006) situates Leo as the protagonist and makes Erika and Otome central to his adventures and development.

* * *

The *Rumbling Hearts* anime (TV series; dir. Tetsuya Watanabe, 2003–2004) displays its origin in a visual novel primarily by virtue of its avoidance of sequential linearity in favor of a multiperspectival approach to the diegesis, which enables it to fare back and forth in time. The show sets out as a relatively straightforward teenage romance equipped with a fairly predictable cast: the sassy and athletic girl Mitsuki Hayase, her bashful friend Haruka Suzumiya, the impassive Takayuki Narumi and his spirited sidekick Shinji Taira. However, it rapidly morphs into something altogether darker as its protagonists' lives are radically disrupted by Haruka's involvement in a car crash that flings her into a three-year-long coma. The series' dramatic transition from an ostensibly familiar formula to a disquietingly original narrative drift is exhaustively documented by the artbook *Kimi ga Nozomu Eien Visual Complete*. The volume also helps us situate the anime's character portraits in their environmental, domestic and professional contexts, all of which evince the influence of indigenous graphic design. The accident shortly follows Haruka and Takayuki's first tentative date and occurs as the girl is waiting outside a station for her boyfriend in anticipation of an outing she has keenly been looking forward to.

Tormented by guilt, having obliquely contributed to the tragedy by showing up late, Takayuki precipitates into a paralyzing depression. Mitsuki, who also feels responsible for Haruka's mishap insofar as she has been the direct cause of Takayuki's tardy arrival at the rendezvous, tries to rescue the youth from his aboulic state and the two embark on a contorted affair. As they struggle to reconstruct their lives, having had to relinquish the dream of becoming a professional swimmer in Mitsuki's case and the resolve to take challenging college-entry exams in Takayuki's, the two characters oscillate almost addictively between a tendency to cling to the past and its oppressive ghosts and a search for fresh beginnings through which their shared guilt may be exorcized. When Haruka awakens, she has no idea that three years have elapsed since the accident and her physician enjoins the patient's friends and family to play along with the illusion that Haruka is still the girl she was at the time of her misfortune and accordingly that they have not altered either. This obligation generates a novel tide of emotional conflicts as Takayuki is pressured into choosing between his past — and Haruka — and his present — and Mitsuki. A sequel consisting of a four-part OVA titled *Rumbling Hearts — Next Season*, directed by Hideki Takayama and released in 2007–2008, provides an alternate story arc in which, following Haruka's recovery, she and Takayuki start dating again and revisit various places they fondly remember in an effort to retrieve the time they have both lost.

With the OVA sequel, *Rumbling Hearts* shows itself entirely allegiant to the parent visual novel's multibranching structure by foregrounding from the start a shift of emphasis in the articulation of the characters' convoluted psyches and attendant journeys of self-discovery. In the TV series, the male lead is unequivocally committed to Mitsuki even though he wishes to help Haruka recover to the best of his abilities, and is ultimately seen, to be no less responsible for the inception of his liaison with Mitsuki than Mitsuki herself. In the OVA, by contrast, it is intimated that Mitsuki has forced herself into the void left in Takayuki's heart by Haruka's loss of consciousness without much active involvement on the youth's part, even though it is also shown quite explicitly that Takayuki has developed genuine feelings towards Mitsuki over time. On the whole, the televisual version of the male lead comes across as rather self-absorbed and clueless (though these traits are by no means as pronounced as they are in Makoto from *School Days*), whereas the direct-to-video counterpart is portrayed as devoted and conscientious to self-denying extremes. This affective reorientation impacts on the sequel's overall mood. While the TV show's emotional import occasionally verges on the melodramatic, the tone adopted by the OVA is generally more sober and mature — except, perhaps, in the cliffhanging climax of the third installment, where shock again draws Haruka into sepulchral inertia. Relatedly, less emphasis is placed on romantic convolutions and emotional eruptions than on the characters' lucidly conceived — though not always palatable — reasons for electing certain courses of action in preference to others. The OVA's restrained tone affects its visuals, too, and this is principally evinced by character designs where a wider range of pensive and subtly modulated expressions is instantly noticeable, alongside toned-down and mellow palettes. Equally crucial to the sequel's atmosphere is a pervasive sense of wistfulness that makes itself plaintively audible even in the most auspicious moments. Haruka's haunting feeling that she is somehow to be blamed for the pain endured by others on her behalf, allied to the suspicion that Takayuki might be sacrificing his own career prospects for her sake, contributes substantially to this impression.

The *Rumbling Hearts* game, released in various phases between 2001 and

2008, is played from Takayuki's point of view and its dialogue attaches considerable weight to this character's introspective parable. The visual novel comprises two chapters. The first of these is set in 1997 and chronicles the events surrounding the inception of the romantic relationship between Takayuki and Haruka up to the latter's involvement in the fateful accident. Alternative narrative possibilities unfold depending on the kinds of relationships the male lead forms with the story's heroines: not only Haruka and Mitsuki but also Haruka's younger sister Akane and Manami, one of the nurses employed at the hospital where Haruka is cared for. The second chapter, set three years later, focuses on the liaison binding Takayuki and Mitsuki, the youth's working life as a part-time waiter and Haruka's eventual emergence from unconsciousness. The player is offered numerous options conducive to branching story arcs featuring different heroines as their centers of attention and hence to variable endings. In the Haruka-centered arc, Mitsuki leaves town to become a teacher while Takayuki and Haruka wind up together (this is the option elaborated by the OVA). In the arc focusing on Mitsuki, the latter becomes Takayuki's companion while Haruka devotes herself to the pursuit of a writing career. Although the TV series loosely adopts this ending, it leaves out the parent game's climactic introduction of Takayuki and Mitsuki's child, to whom Mitsuki is seen to read one of Haruka's books. There are also several variations revolving around secondary personae, such as Akane, the waitresses who work with Takayuki, Ayu and Mayu, and the nurses employed at the hospital. The TV series includes all of the game's principal personae, as well as a sprinkling of cameo appearances from some of its ancillary actors.

The mnemonic dimension plays a key role in the diegesis, with flashbacks increasingly punctuating the action as the story progresses. Retrospective visions are especially pivotal to the relatively late episode in which poignant moments from the story's main building blocks roll as a rapid montage through Takayuki's feverish brain. Additionally, flashbacks fill a substantial portion of the OVA's central installment, as Mitsuki recounts her vicissitudes to the former schoolmate and current host Tsujimura after her move to Tokyo in the wake of Haruka's return to reality. Notably, the timeline traced by Mitsuki in this account differs partially from the one presented in the original show. This results from the perspectival shift effected by the OVA at this juncture (fully consonant with the visual novel's formal predilections) that emplaces Mitsuki as the sole recorder of events, while in the TV series the polygonal approach is more persistently held. What deserves particular attention about the OVA's treatment of retrospection, both here and in subsequent segments, is its highly unusual incorporation of "quasi-flashbacks" or "pseudo-flashbacks"—i.e., snippets of past occurrences not actually chronicled in the original story but congruous with its visible developments.

Likewise notable is the theme of the creative quest, which operates throughout the anime as an unobtrusive yet potent leading thread. This is highlighted from an early stage in the action by the pre-accident scenes in which Haruka tells Takayuki about her desire to become an author of children's books and about an illustrated tale very popular at that particular time, a copy of which she longs to own. This is the very book Takayuki is carrying on his journey to the station where he is supposed to meet Haruka on the day of the crash. The narrative hosted within the cherished volume will hold great symbolic value in the TV show's finale, where Haruka shares with Takayuki the lesson she has learned from its protagonist, the fairy Mayal — that is, the importance of acquiring the "gift of parting words," which is effectively the ability to know when and how to properly say goodbye to a loved one. The book's significance within the overall diegesis is also corroborated by the scene where, following Haruka's awakening, Takayuki obtains a fresh copy of the book for her with the assistance of his co-worker Ayu and her *yakuza*-like contacts. This moment is worth dwelling upon as it succinctly conveys the show's penchant for depth of characterization. Indeed, Ayu — normally seen as the generator of rambunctious outbursts of comic relief— here rises to the stature of a fully rounded character endowed with sensitivity and an authentically generous disposition.

The story's devotion to psychological profundity is also borne out, in both the TV series and the OVA, by the development of Akane's persona from a relatively stereotypical "little sister" into a complex mentality with inner conflicts and anxieties of her own. What is thus thrown into relief, above all other attributes, is Akane's unflinching forthrightness: a quality that would in itself deserve unconditional commendation, yet has a regrettable knack for impacting deleteriously on her beloved sister's mental health. In the OVA, a further instance of sensitive characterization comes with the aforementioned Tsujimura: an obviously peripheral actor who would merely be noted as the pretext for Mitsuki to recount events from her past were it not for some inspired insights into her own twisted psyche. Most felicitous, in this regard, is the scene where Mitsuki's host candidly admits to deriving consolation from the knowledge that there are people out there on whom destiny has smiled no less profligately than it has on her own life.

It is not until the OVA's closing installment that we see Haruka herself acquire suitable psychological depth. Such an asset is logically to be expected of a character presented from the start as imaginative and sensitive well above average. However, Haruka has had no chance to evolve into a full-fledged personality as long as the overarching drama has required her to fulfill the Sleeping-Beauty role. With the OVA's final chapter, the young woman bravely asserts her determination to embrace adult responsibilities and duties from which her fate has thus far exempted her, discover what it is like to be treated as anything other than a kid or an invalid, and face up to the often unsavory repercussions of her ordeal on the lives of others. Her feelings towards Takayuki in particular are clouded by the recognition that it is because of her that the youth has relinquished his most treasured ambitions. Most importantly, Haruka is confronted with the unyielding reality of irreversible change, culminating with her sensation that in the world that has come into being during her coma and she now faces as though she were a newborn, "nobody" has "remained the person" she "once knew." Compounded with this crippling sense of confusion is guilt — a self-persecuting proclivity already glimpsed in Haruka in the TV series' early parts. This results from the awareness that although Takayuki has forsaken his goals for the sake of a hypothetical future with her, Haruka is still pursuing the aims entertained prior to the accident.

The vital lesson comes from a hitherto marginal character, Haruka's mother, who claims that if two people are to build a life together, they must first of all be able to appreciate and value their ineradicable difference from each other instead of struggling to efface their personal identities. This proposition brings to mind Luce Irigaray's idea that men and women involved in close relationships "have the duty" not only "of preserving the human species and of developing its culture" but also of "respecting their differences" (Irigaray 2000a, p. 129). The stereotypical assumption that reciprocal commitment should be conducive to symbiosis or possession is thus drastically challenged, to the point that Irigaray promulgates the transformation of "to love" into an intransitive verb: "Far from wanting to possess you in linking myself to you, I preserve a 'to'.... This 'to' safeguards a place of transcendence between us, a place of respect which is both obligated and desired, a place of possible alliance" (Irigaray 2000b, p. 19). The distance between the sexes and its open acknowledgement are the prerequisites of an honest relationship based on mutual recognition: "I am sensible to you, leaving you to be you" (Irigaray 2000b, p. 9). Difference, in other words, is what allows identity to be preserved and honored rather than suppressed in the name of some romantic myth of fusion. Radically challenging the conventional notion that the distance between two people diminishes according to the intensity of their love for each other, this model argues that "we need to love much to be capable of such a dialectic" — that is, to be able to love the life of another person "without giving him one's own" (Irigaray 2000b, p. 12). It is on the basis of this lesson that Haruka resolves to "move forward" with Takayuki and "start anew." This is the philosophical message with which the finale of the *Rumbling Hearts* OVA reverberates, investing the overall animated package with an affecting sense of both gravity and promise.

Thus, even though the anime as a whole deliberately abstains from delving into large-scale metaphysical issues, its understated exploration of the nature and limits of human relationships and of their role in the shaping of a number of interconnected journeys of self-discovery should not go unheeded. The main body of the soundtrack, consisting of low-key piano pieces and symphonic melodies with just a few chirpier themes for the moments of comic relief, felicitously sustains the show's tenor. Also notable is the anime's utilization of a time zone not usually seen in romantic drama wherein high-school dynamics are by and large prioritized: namely, young adulthood with its mature and contorted preoccupations. The tone is concurrently abetted by a gracefully methodical, at times even slow-paced entry into the narrative's crucial phases. This allows the characters, their interrelations and their circumstances to evolve prior to the emergence of the problems associated with the accident, and thus helps us understand intimately why those problems should arise and view them as realistic outcomes when they do.

*   *   *

What is arguably both most memorable and most daunting about *School Days* (TV series; dir. Keitaro Motonaga, 2007) is the pure sense of unease it incrementally generates as its characters' twisted and even crassly perverse motives come to the surface. This murky atmosphere intensifies as the action's pace increases and the characters' choices and moves become so misguided, rash and self-destructive as to degenerate into undiluted lunacy. Attitudes that initially carry the flavor of innocent delusions spawned by half-digested romantic expectations thus morph into paranoid obsessions. It is hardly surprising, given this context, that the narrative should build up to a blood-soaked climax that feels gruesome and grotesque in equal measures. The ending is indeed redolent of a traditional Japanese formula known as suicide pact or double suicide (*shinjuu*), immortalized by Monzaemon Chikamatsu (1721) and usually staged as a *bunraku* (or puppet show). What renders *School Days'* finale shocking is the show's disarmingly simple narrative premise. Two relatively timid characters the male lead Makoto Itou and the coheroine Kotonoha Katsura — are brought together by a mutual friend, Sekai Saionjii, who also happens to harbor feelings for Makoto and would therefore appear to be acting against her own best interest, yet pretends to both herself and others to be concerned with selflessly supporting her mates despite private preferences or goals. This masquerade is not to endure, however, and *School Days* soon reveals its true colors as an uncompromising anatomy of warped and fallacious convictions.

    Makoto's and Sekai's emotional deterioration plays an axial part, in this respect. The boy's originally gentle and naive disposition increasingly turns into monstrous selfishness as his sole drive becomes the determination to satisfy his carnal desires, bullheadedly blinding himself to all ethical considerations in the process. At the same time, Sekai's deviousness is little by little exposed, and her unscrupulous preparedness to sacrifice others to achieve her own contorted goals is concurrently unveiled. For both characters, what could have been a fruitful journey of self-discovery becomes instead a dark careening plunge into squalid rapaciousness. The two characters' degeneration is rendered especially painful to behold by the failure of the relationship on which they embark when they realize — or rather dupe themselves into believing — that their sincere feelings naturally draw them towards each other and that this may allow them to interact effortlessly without the spurious aid of namby-pamby set pieces. On the surface, Makoto's choice of Sekai over Kotonoha would seem to indicate that he prioritizes friendship and psychological intimacy over mere infatuation as the reliable base of a sentimental liaison. In this regard, the male lead's stance recalls Rin's attitude in *Shuffle!* and Hazumu's in the *Kashimashi — Girl Meets Girl* OVA. Beneath the laudable front, alas, courses a frantic yearning for instant self-gratification that makes the connection between Makoto and Sekai no less dishonest, self-seeking and ultimately downright malignant than any of the myriad casual affairs peppering the last portion of the series. Makoto's and Sekai's conduct has got the word "misrecognition" writ large all over its vapid veneer of spontaneity and reciprocal trust.

As an unsentimental portrait of the fragility of the human mind and heart and of the deleterious repercussions of the betrayal of friendship, *School Days* has few competitors of equal merit in the field of anime adapted from visual novels. From a generic point of view, this makes the series a poignant — and often disquieting psychological drama. Even the jocose moments centered on the stereotypical persona of the ineffectual would-be ladykiller (Sawanagi, in this instance) do not indulge in pure comedy, as is normally the case when a show brings this modality into play. No less importantly, *School Days* functions as an acerbic indictment of the stultifying vagaries of consumerism. Various forms of advertising gravitate insidiously around the characters' daily activities like noxious satellites eager to absorb their planet's life-sustaining atmosphere. The cinematographical orchestration of these images as a means of evoking not merely a convincing ambience but also a symbolic allusion to an underlying sense of cultural crisis attests precisely to the sorts of societal and economic pressures discussed in the preliminary segment of this chapter. However, it is above all else the hegemony of the cell phone that quotidianly immolates the characters to the chimeric desires and designs of commodification.

The ubiquitous gadget, instead of operating as a convenient supplement, rises to the status of an indispensable prosthesis, insistently subordinating face-to-face interaction to faceless telecommunication and thus sealing the characters into a destiny of atomized reification. So unquestioned is the cell phone's hold over not only the actors' practical arrangements but also their entire emotional circuits that they go on using it as a means of contacting the person they long for even when their text messages have been repeatedly and deliberately denied access to the intended inbox. These scenes highlight the anime's harrowing substratum in wrenchingly pathetic, unilateral attempts to restore something that is irretrievably lost. So-called communication thus descends to the level of audienceless monologues that never lead to dialogue but actually become empty ends in themselves. While the visual novel as a form celebrates textuality as a vehicle for bringing the player's imagination and creativity into focus, emplacing videogaming as an eminently active pursuit, *School Days* daringly denounces the opposite side of textuality as the ultimate denial of dynamic exchange and, by extension, of any authentic opportunity for a dialectic exercise in inventive interplay.

The parent game (launched in 2005) is characterized by a tight internal hierarchy whereby the player's choices are "tree-structured" and hence branch out as alternate narrative arcs. While the overall ensemble is rigorously conceived, the ludic experience itself is contrariwise on the contrary, emphatically multidirectional and open-ended. Indeed, the available arcs are conducive to no less than twenty-one potential endings, which entails that for players to truly appreciate the scope of the game, they must replay it several times. Various stylistic factors render the *School Days* visual novel quite original compared to other packages in a germane mold. For one thing, it relies quite substantially on animated footage rather than merely on stationary frames. Furthermore, sequences of animated scenes are organized into episodes, each of which comes equipped with its own opening and closing sequences. (The game's distinctively cinematic orientation echoes Aaron Smuts' observations about videogames and film discussed at the close of Chapter 4.) *School Days* also evinces a rich acoustic gamut, abetted by both an extensive musical soundtrack and legions of sound effects. The gaming experience is simultaneously enhanced by technical options altering the way the game is played, including a video playback option and the possibility of viewing successive scenes as a dynamic continuum without having to pause except when decision points arise.

The psychological curve traced by Makoto's infelicitous transformation over time is especially worthy of attention. His pathological inclination to indulge his polyerotic fantasies without developing the ability to commit himself to any one partner — and hence to face up to his interpersonal responsibilities — turns an amiable and convivial youth into an apathetically egotistical sociopath: the incurable victim of endlessly revamped and hence endlessly insatiable cravings. Sekai also exhibits a double personality as her enthusiastic approach to life, frankness and playfulness give way first to solipsistic emotionalism and ultimately to sheer bestiality. The third party in the doomed triangle, Kotonoha, proves no less prone to dissolve into self-persecutory paranoia and erosive malice. The ending provides a perfect culmination for this convoluted tale, not so much because of its unexpectedness as by virtue of the spine-chilling momentum through which it is reached. It is hard to imagine a journey of self-discovery more brutally yet awesomely flawed than the one chronicled in *School Days*.[1]

* * *

Whereas *School Days* charts a journey vitiated by its male protagonist's ethical degeneration as Makoto blindly cruises from one casual liaison to the next, *White Album* (TV series; dir. Akira Yoshimura, 2009) concentrates on the psychological fluctuations occurring within one pivotal relationship and the ancillary interactions orbiting around it. The visual novel was originally launched in 1998 — the year in which the epoch-making double album by The Beatles bearing the same title was re-released to commemorate its thirtieth anniversary. The game underwent subsequent releases in alternate formats in 2003 and 2009. The *White Album* visual novel adopts an established style of gameplay in requiring the user to engage with substantial portions of text and periodically operate choices that will determine the plot's progression in a particular direction. An original feature of the game is its request that players plan a schedule at the start of each week in the story, which allows them to take part in diverse activities involving disparate personae (or even to take the occasional day off). In the course of several of these events, players may also engage in conversations addressing topics of their own choice. To view all of the available plot strands, the user will need to replay the game several times, selecting alternate schedules at the given decision points.

The player takes on the role of *White Album*'s male protagonist, Touya Fujii, a twenty-year-old university student in his second year. Although *White Album* differs from *School Days* in its overall emphasis, it echoes Motonaga's anime in its portrayal of the male lead as a multifaceted and flawed personality wherein demureness and insensitivity often coalesce, and long-term good intentions tend to be perverted by the yearning for immediate satisfaction. The show's central relationship dramatizes Touya's romantic attachment to Yuki Morikawa, an aspiring idol singer endowed with a serene and unassuming disposition. Other key actors include the bright and classy Rina Ogata, a popular idol singer who feels drawn to Touya out of sheer loneliness; Misaki Sawakura, a gentle student enamored of books and cuisine alike; the quiet and athletic Haruka Kawashima, one of Touya's closest childhood friends since kindergarten; and Mana Mizuki, an aggressive and insolent high-school student whom Touya is supposed to tutor (often to her deep resentment). While Touya cannot be given credit for making faithfulness his top priority, his pursuit of self-gratification does not lead to the fevered extremes evinced by Makoto's behavior. In fact, he is ultimately capable of appreciating the honesty and extent of Yuki's commitment to their relationship and is genuinely crushed by the disclosure that it is largely for his sake that Yuki wishes to become more confident, independent and self-determining. However, the show's finale remains deliberately inconclusive to pave the way to a second season slated for domestic release in the fall of 2009.

Characterization is indubitably one of the anime's most striking attributes, and is abetted throughout not only by an imaginative approach to design but also by a deliberately methodical pace, which allows the action to focus on the characters' emotions with arresting subtlety. By means of self-reflexive gestures echoing the source's textual slant, the anime occasionally enhances its psychological dimension by offering glimpses of its characters' thoughts and feelings as lines written on the screen. The decision to display inner states as snippets of text rather than audible monologues conveys the idea that the characters are somewhat reluctant to express themselves openly (as a result of either their inherent timidity or their secretiveness), which invests the show with a pointedly introspective flavor. Another vehicle for the elliptical expression of thoughts and feelings is the book of Robert Browning's poetry with which several key characters come into contact. The volume, dexterously integrated into the action as a metaphorical catalyst for silent interaction, gradually becomes a supporting character of unique appeal.

The *White Album* anime closely mirrors its ludic antecedent in its proclivity to draw the audience into its world by recourse to both diegetic and intradiegetic forms of immersion. The former refers to our interactive contribution to meaning production as we watch the action unfold. The latter designates our involvement in the imaginary space of the story. Diegetic immersion is akin to the experience undergone by the reader of an engrossing novel, whereas intradiegetic immersion is fostered by the viewer's insertion into the anime as an experiential space. Thus, we are enjoined to act both on and within the anime's universe. We are allowed to influence the game's coming into being as a narrative through ongoing interpretation, and simultaneously express our creativity within the fictive domain as engaged actors. *White Album* establishes the sense of experiential space right from the start at both the macrocosmic and the microcosmic levels. On the one hand, it clearly situates the narrative in a specific societal and historical context, Japan in 1986. Concomitantly, it sets up its spatial coordinates with reference to a particular sector of the entertainment industry that found inception in the early 1970s and began to wane in the 1990s: the world of idol singers, their making, their promotion and their inexorable decline. On the other hand, the story focuses on a skein of private relationships, involving Touya and the five aforementioned heroines, as experiential spaces in their own right within which thoroughly individuated personalities juggle their emotions and varyingly strive to negotiate their singular developmental odysseys.

On the diegetic and the intradiegetic fronts alike, immersion does not amount to a state of passive absorption but rather to a process of evolving participation. This aspect of the phenomenon is beautifully captured by Janet Murray: "our brains are programmed to tune into stories with an intensity that can obliterate the world around us.... We seek the same feeling from a psychologically immersive experience that we do from a plunge in the ocean or swimming pool: the sensation of being surrounded by a completely other reality ... that takes over all of our attention, our whole perceptual apparatus." In the context of an explicitly "participatory medium," Murray adds, immersion entails, metaphorically speaking, "learning to swim, to do the things that the new environment makes possible" and hence savor it as "a participatory activity" (Murray, pp. 98–99). Moreover, the visual novel as a form demonstrates that technological tools able to achieve absolute photorealism are not indispensable to the evocation of a habitat potentially conducive to immersion. In fact, it succeeds in accomplishing that effect to enviable degrees by deploying a highly stylized graphic framework that never attempts to efface the work's inherent artificiality in the service of realist imperatives. *White Album* shows an inclination to lay bare the material foundations of its visuals by foregrounding the cumulative creative process unfolding from the initial designs and storyboards to the screen through frames executed in watercolors with only minimalistic animation (especially in the lovingly crafted previews). In their unsurpassed simplicity, these images underline the affective import of certain scenes more memorably than many of the overtly realistic and dynamic shots. At the same time, they contribute vitally to the consolidation of the anime's typically quiet mood, in conjunction with a nacreous finish and gently modulated lighting. When flashes of bright color enhanced by the use of a pastel crayon filter occasionally appear, they serve to reinforce the show's dominant atmosphere by ironic contrast.

* * *

Given the nature of the arguments pursued in the foregoing analyses, it will be quite evident from the discussion that follows what particular formal and thematic attributes make *Kashimashi—Girl Meets Girl* (TV series; dir. Nobuaki Nakanishi, 2006) an ideal candidate for translation into a visual novel. The game in question is *Kashimashi — Girl Meets Girl: The First Summer Story* (2006). Most relevant are the anime's deployment of a subtly depicted character gallery, its proficient treatment of the love-triangle structure in conjunction with the coming-of-age topos, the integration of poignant flashbacks and a pictorially tangible repertoire of both natural and architectural backgrounds. A stylistic blend combining romance with elements of comedy, science fiction and a sprinkling of farcical set pieces likewise matches the visual novel's preference for generic cocktails. In both the anime and its ludic offshoot, a sensitive approach to design, bolstered throughout by a meticulous integration of local and Western styles in the depiction of settings and objects, is instrumental in providing the viewer or player with emotive and pictorial stimuli capable of generative opportunities for both interaction and immersion.

Climbing Mount Kashima in search for peace, following his rejection by classmate Yasuna Kamiizumi, the meek and nature-loving high-school student Hazumu Osaragi is hit by an alien spaceship and terminally injured. However, the extraterrestrials engineer a way of reviving the hapless Earthling and reconstructing his body. In doing so, however, they also inadvertently manage to turn the boy into a charming adolescent girl. The aliens declare proudly that they have saved Hazumu "in accordance with the Law for the Protection of Planetary Beings," adding somewhat nonchalantly that a "complete regeneration has been performed, except his sex has been reversed." Although they proffer their "deepest apologies," they are clearly pleased to announce that Hazumu has become a "perfect, complete female." The extraterrestrials appear to honor high moral standards, as evinced by their address to humans: "Regarding this Earthling, we hope that you treat her with all human dignity and civility." Nevertheless, these principles are not accompanied by what humans might call emotions. As a result, the aliens do not seem in the least bothered by the fact that the "operation cannot be reversed." This clinically objective, detached and analytical stance to Hazumu's predicament is ironically juxtaposed with the highly emotive reactions (verging on slapstick in the case of the protagonist's parents) evinced by Hazumu's family and friends in response to the message, divulged by the aliens all over the world by means of tremendously sophisticated technology capable of translating its contents into all human languages. *Kashimashi*, incidentally, shows little orthodox respect for adults, who are often portrayed as selfish or immature. In the case of Hazumu's father, even a note of perversity enters the character, as he seems besotted with his offspring's female version in ways that exceed paternal affection. Yet, Hazumu's parents are also depicted as very warm and hospitable people who do not hesitate to welcome the aliens observing Hazumu and her/his friends into their household and to address them most ceremoniously as though this were the only obvious and considerate thing to do.

Hazumu's basic personality is unchanged by the accidental gender switch but s/he soon realizes that s/he must learn how to live as a female practically from scratch. Mastering the appropriate patterns of behavior, attitudes and mannerisms proves considerably demanding but the hero/ine is devotedly assisted by his childhood friend Tomari Kurusu: a vibrant and athletic girl who has harbored feelings for Hazumu from an early age but carefully disguised her longings by acting as Hazumu's guardian and protecting him from bullies contemptuous of timid boys. Initially, Tomari finds it arduous to accept Hazumu's metamorphosis even as she endeavors to turn her friend into a "proper girl" but gradually realizes that her feelings have not evaporated in the wake of the event. Yasuna's own feelings for Hazumu, in turn, grow exponentially as a result of the gender reversal and she declares her love at a relatively early stage in the series. Through these affective vicissitudes, what could have degenerated into mawkish soap opera had the director pandered to melodramatic eruptions in fact turns out to be a deeply rewarding experience, able to offer a dispassionate exploration of diverse gender roles and positions. Through a deft handling of multiperspectivalism and a sensitive depiction of the characters' tortured emotions, *Kashimashi* enables its actors to transcend the limitations of conventional anime stereotypes and to elicit assiduously the spectator's empathy. *Kashimashi* concurrently suggests that while an individual's memories amount to a continuum in which the past, the present and the future seamlessly coalesce, it is important to recognize the significance of juvenile recollections as mental contents that do not impact unquestionably on subsequent experiences. Hence, Tomari must ultimately accept that her memories of her early connection with Hazumu must be cherished in the context of their childhood and not be automatically assumed to determine the present, let alone the future. The ability — and perhaps more importantly the willingness — to acknowledge the status of the past *as* past is a vital aspect of self-maturation.

While Tomari must learn how to reconcile her relationship with Hazumu following the gender switch and her memories of the male Hazumu embedded in her psyche since infancy, Yasuna must find ways of owning up to the disabling condition that isolates her from adults and peers alike by confronting the bundle of submerged longings associated with its first manifestation. This consists of the girl's inability to see men as anything other than blurred grayscale masses, which has afflicted her since childhood, and subsequent loss of the ability also to see women distinctly in the aftermath of a shock. These interwoven experiences are enriched throughout by Nakanishi's emphasis on delicate emotional twists foregrounding the complexity of the characters' yearnings rather than on manipulative melodrama of the kind often regaled by the bucketful in the dramatization of love triangles in anime. An ancillary but by no means insignificant part is played by the aliens that infiltrate Hazumu's quotidian existence in the hope of learning more about human beings and human feelings, focusing on the lovelorn Yasuna as their principal case study.

With the introduction of the extraterrestrial observers, Nakanishi is not simply supplementing the main narrative with a subplot intended to supply comic relief. In fact, the aliens' experiences provide a metacommentary on Hazumu's own rite of passage. In trying to learn about humans, the aliens hope to find a solution to their predicament. Indeed, we discover that in order to eradicate the threats of war and discord, their race has suppressed all regular drives, including sexual desire, and is now therefore on the verge of extinction. Rediscovering the occluded instinct is axial to their survival. Hazumu, likewise, must find ways of negotiating between his old and new selves to understand what desire truly is (and whether or not it ultimately matters which gender s/he is drawn to) if s/he is to retain a sense of identity. Hazumu's initial interest in girls could have been displaced by the gender switch and translated into a fascination with boys. Yet it could just as feasibly have survived as an integral part of the character's personality, possibly inspired by Hazumu's attraction to both Tomari and Yasuna against all odds.[2]

The *Kashimashi — Girl Meets Girl* OVA (dir. Yukimaru Katsura, 2006) supplies an alternate ending, consonant with the visual novel's passion for diversified resolutions, where Yasuna concludes that her journey of self-discovery has finally led her to grasp the full value of autonomy thanks to Hazumu. Now able to stand on her own two feet, she wishes to confront life's challenges with a commodious and inquisitive disposition and to be single — which enables the protagonist and Tomari to come together at long last. In the TV series, crucial emphasis is laid on the importance of overcoming childhood expectations and ideals. The direct-to-video supplement, for its part, concentrates on the value of elective affinities built on mutual understanding and respect. The OVA exhibits all of the traits found in the TV show that render *Kashimashi* suitable for ludic adaptation. Moreover, it deploys the miracle trope so dear to many visual novels as pivotal to its intensely Christmassy climax. In both the TV show and the OVA, it is ultimately the characters' honesty about their feelings and about the simmering desires that fuel them that enables them to inspire empathy even when they would appear to conform to crystallized stereotypes: for instance, the sophisticated rich missy (Yasuna), the tempestuously boyish girl (Tomari), the wide-eyed ingénue (Hazumu). The show's subtlety is further corroborated by a multiperspectival approach based on the deft alternation of viewpoints. This is in turn bolstered by the association of each angle with gentle, even understated modulations of the characters' expressions, tones of voice and verbal registers, as well as unobtrusively atmospheric backgrounds that betray no trace of self-conscious toil despite their technical refinement. No less notable is the adoption of toned-down warm color schemes shunning the glossy artificiality of many anime centered on cute females.

Through sophisticated characterization and a clear definition of their protagonists' goals, the titles here discussed enlist their design strategies to the accomplishment of three interrelated objectives. They encourage us to explore the internal dimension of an actor's subjective experiences and memories; chart the evolution of these experiences and memories as a meaningful concatenation of moments in time; and, last but not least, enable us to interact immersively with palpably identifiable worlds through metaphorical inhabitation of characters whose goals we can embrace as our own, and on the basis of which we can establish a sense of personal identity within the anime's universe. Loyal to the ludic form whence they emanate, the shows use both interactivity and immersion to challenge the concept of storytelling as an activity predetermined by authorial priorities and encoded in a singular textual stream. In so doing, they present themselves to viewers as caskets overflowing with possibilities, with potential stories that might arise from the expression of our own agency within a credible screen world. Instead of unproblematically upholding the genius enshrined in somebody else's work, they propose that the most powerful stories, ultimately, are the ones we are creatively responsible for.

# Filmography

## Primary Titles: Anime Based on Visual Novels

*Air* (2004–2005). *Original Title*: Air. *Status*: TV Series (12 episodes + 1 recap episode). *Episode Length*: 24 minutes. *Director*: Tatsuya Ishihara. *Original Creator*: Visual Art's/Key. *Series Composition*: Fumihiko Shimo. *Music*: Jun Maeda, Magome Togoshi, Shinji Orito. *Original Character Designer*: Itaru Hinoue (Visual Art's). *Character Designer*: Tomoe Aratani. *Art Director*: Jouji Unoguchi. *Chief Animation Director*: Tomoe Aratani. *Background Art*: Emi Kesamaru, Miyuki Hiratoko, Miyuki Tsukazaki, Mutsuo Shinohara, Naoki Hosokawa. *Chief Editor*: Seiji Morita. *Sound Director*: Yota Tsuruoka. *Special Effects*: Rina Miura. *Color Key*: Akiyo Takeda. *Animation Production*: Kyoto Animation. *Production*: Kyoto Animation (Yokujin Denshou Kai), Mubik (Yokujin Denshou Kai), Pony Canyon (Yokujin Denshou Kai), TBS (Yokujin Denshou Kai). *Sound Effects Production*: Gakuonsha.

*Air in Summer* (2005). *Original Title*: Air in Summer. *Status*: TV Special (2 episodes). *Episode Length*: 24 minutes. *Director*: Tatsuya Ishihara. *Original Creator*: Visual Art's/Key. *Series Composition*: Fumihiko Shimo. *Screenplay*: Fumihiko Shimo. *Music*: Jun Maeda, Magome Togoshi, Shinji Orito. *Original Character Designer*: Itaru Hinoue (Visual Art's). *Character Designer*: Tomoe Aratani. *Art Director*: Jouji Unoguchi. *Chief Animation Director*: Tomoe Aratani. *Producers*: Shinichi Nakamura, Yoko Hatta, Yoshihisa Nakayama. *Background Art*: Chioi Hosokawa, Emi Kesamaru, Miyuki Hiratoko, Mutsuo Shinohara. *Sound Director*: Yota Tsuruoka. *Sound Effects*: Eiko Morikawa. *Color Designer*: Akiyo Takeda. *Animation Production*: Kyoto Animation. *Production*: Kyoto Animation, Pony Canyon, TBS.

*Air: the Motion Picture.* (2005). *Original Title*: Air: the Motion Picture. *Status*: movie. *Length*: 91 minutes. *Director*: Osamu Dezaki. *Original Creator*: Visual Art's/Key. *Screenplay*: Makoto Nakamura *Music*: Yoshikazu Suo. *Original Music*: Jun Maeda, Magome Togoshi, Shinji Orito. *Original Character Designer*: Itaru Hinoue (Visual Art's). *Character Designer*: Akemi Kobayashi. *Art Director*: Shinzo Yuki. *Producers*: Iriya Azuma, Mamoru Yokota. *Editor*: Masahiro Goto. *Sound Director*: Shoji Hata. *Sound Effects*: Yukiyoshi Itokawa. *Color Coordination*: Tsutomu Tsukata. *Animation Production*: Toei Animation. *Production*: Frontier Works, Toei Animation. *Supervision*: Visual Art's/Key.

***Clannad*** (2007). *Original Title*: *Clannad*. *Status*: TV Series (24 episodes). *Episode Length*: 25 minutes. *Director*: Tatsuya Ishihara. *Original Creator*: Visual Art's/Key. *Series Composition*: Fumihiko Shimo. *Screenplay*: Fumihiko Shimo. *Music*: Jun Maeda, Magome Togoshi, Shinji Orito. *Original Character Designer*: Itaru Hinoue. *Character Designer*: Kazumi Ikeda. *Art Director*: Mutsuo Shinohara. *Chief Animation Director*: Kazumi Ikeda. *Animation Directors*: Chiyoko Ueno, Fumio Tada, Futoshi Nishiya, Hiroyuki Takahashi, Kazumi Ikeda, Kazuya Sakamoto, Mariko Takahashi, Shoko Ikeda, Yukiko Horiguchi. *Producers*: Naohiro Futono, Shinichi Nakamura, Yoko Hatta, Yoshihisa Nakayama. *Background Art*: Anime Workshop Basara. *Editor*: Kengo Shigemura. *Sound Director*: Yota Tsuruoka *Color Designer*: Akiyo Takeda. *Animation Production*: Kyoto Animation, *Production*: TBS.

***Clannad*** (2007). *Original Title*: *Clannad*. *Status*: movie. *Length*: 90 minutes. *Director*: Osamu Dezaki. *Original Creator*: Visual Art's/Key. *Screenplay*: Makoto Nakamura. *Music*: Yoshichika Inomata. *Original Character Designer*: Itaru Hinoue (Visual Art's). *Character Designer*: Megumi Kadonosono. *Art Designer*: Jirou Kouno. *Animation Director*: Youichi Ohnishi. *Editor:* Makoto Nakamura. *Sound Director*: Tomoaki Yamada. *Sound Effects*: Aki Yokoyama, Masakazu Yokoyama. *Color Designer*: Kunio Tsujita. *Animation Production*: Toei Animation.

***Clannad After Story*** (2008–2009). *Original Title*: *Clannad After Story*. *Status*: TV Series (24 episodes). *Episode Length*: 30 minutes. *Director*: Tatsuya Ishihara. *Original Creator*: Visual Art's/Key. *Series Composition*: Fumihiko Shimo. *Screenplay*: Fumihiko Shimo. *Music*: Jun Maeda, Magome Togoshi, Shinji Orito. *Original Character Designer*: Itaru Hinoue. *Character Designer*: Kazumi Ikeda. *Art Director*: Mutsuo Shinohara. *Chief Animation Director*: Kazumi Ikeda. *Animation Directors*: Chiyoko Ueno, Futoshi Nishiya, Hiroyuki Takahashi, Kazumi Ikeda, Mariko Takahashi, Saiichi Akitake, Yukiko Horiguchi. *Sound Director*: Yota Tsuruoka. *Color Designer*: Akiyo Takeda. *Animation Production*: Kyoto Animation

***D.C. ~Da Capo~*** (2003). *Original Title*: *D.C. ~Da Capo~*. *Status*: TV Series (26 episodes). *Episode Length*: 24 minutes. *Director*: Nagisa Miyazaki. *Original Creator*: Circus. *Scenario*: Katsuki Hasegawa, Katsumi Teratou, Kenichiro Katsura, Mamiko Ikeda, Masaharu Amiya, Masashi Suzuki, Nagisa Miyazaki, Yuji Moriyama. *Music*: Hikaru Nanase, Yuugo Kanno. *Character Conceptual Designer*: Naru Nanao. *Character Designer*: Shinobu Tagashira. *Art Director*: Chikako Shibata. *Producers*: Katsuaki Kikuchi, Tomoko Kawasaki. *Editor*: Jun Tano. *Sound Director*: Hiromi Kikuta. *Color Coordination*: Kumi Akiyama. *Animation Production*: ZEXCS. *Production*: Da Capo Production Committee.

***D.C.S.S. ~Da Capo Second Season~*** (2005). *Original Title*: *D.C.S.S. ~Da Capo Second Season ~*. *Status*: TV Series (26 episodes). *Episode Length*: 30 minutes. *Director*: Munenori Nawa. *Original Creator*: Circus. *Series Composition*: Katsumi Hasegawa. *Music*: Hikaru Nanase. *Character Designer*: Yuka Takashina. *Art Director*: Naoko Kosakabe. *Producers*: Katsuaki Kikuchi, Takeshi Shukuri, Tomoko Kawasaki. *Editor*: Jun Takuma. *Sound Director*: Hiromi Kikuta. *Color Coordination*: Hiromi Iwaida. *Animation Production*: Feel. *Production*: Da Capo SS Production Committee.

***D.C.II ~Da Capo II~*** (2007). *Original Title*: *D.C.II ~Da Capo II~*. *Status*: TV Series (13 episodes). *Episode Length*: 24 minutes. *Director*: Hideki Okamoto. *Original Creator*: Circus. *Series Composition*: Chihare Ameno. *Music*: Kaoru Okubo, Tomoki Kikuya. *Character Designer*: Noriko Shimazawa. *Editor*: Jun Takuma. *Sound Director*: Hiromi Kikuta. *Animation Production*: Feel. *Production*: Starchild Records.

***D.C.IIS.S. ~Da Capo II Second Season~*** (2008). *Original Title*: *D.C.IIS.S. ~ Da*

*Capo II Second Season* ~. *Status*: TV Series (13 episodes). *Episode Length*: 24 minutes. *Director*: Hideki Okamoto. *Original Creator*: Circus. *Series Composition*: Chihare Ameno. *Scenario*: Katsumi Hasegawa. *Character Designer*: Noriko Shimazawa. *Sound Director*: Hiromi Kikuta. *Color Designer*: Yumi Yuya. *Animation Production*: Feel. *Production*: Starchild Records.

**ef— a tale of memories** (2007). *Original Title*: *ef— a tale of memories*. *Status*: TV Series (12 episodes). *Episode Length*: 24 minutes. *Director*: Shin Oonuma. *Original Creator*: Minori. *Series Composition*: Katsuhiko Takayama. *Screenplay*: Katsuhiko Takayama. *Music*: Eiichiro Yanagi, Tenmon. *Original Character Designers*: 2C=Galore, Naru Nanao. *Character Designer*: Nobuhiro Sugiyama. *Art Director*: Megumi Kato. *Animation Directors*: Nobuhiro Sugiyama, Shuuji Miyazaki, Yoshiaki Ito. *Editor*: Kazuhiko Seki. *Sound Director*: Yota Tsuruoka. *Color Designer*: Jin Hibino. *Animation Production*: Shaft. *Production*: Ef Production Committe, Rondo Robe.

**ef— a tale of melodies** (2008). *Original Title*: *ef— a tale of melodies*. *Status*: TV Series (12 episodes). *Episode Length*: 24 minutes. *Director*: Shin Oonuma. *Original Creator*: Minori. *Series Composition*: Katsuhiko Takayama. *Screenplay*: Katsuhiko Takayama. *Music*: Eiichiro Yanagi, Tenmon. *Original Character Designers*: 2C=Galore, Naru Nanao. *Character Designer*: Nobuhiro Sugiyama. *Art Director*: Kohji Azuma, Toshihiro Kohama. *Chief Animation Director*: Nobuhiro Sugiyama. *Animation Directors*: Akihisa Takano, Fumio Matsumoto, Hatsue Nakayama, Hideki Furukawa, Kazuhiro Ota, Kazumi Tahata, Kazuya Shiotsuki, Masato Numazu, Megumi Noda, Nobuhiro Sugiyama, Shuuji Miyazaki, Yoshiaki Ito. *Animation Production*: Shaft. *Production*: ef Production Committe.

**Fate/stay Night** (2006). *Original Title*: *Fate/stay Night*. *Status*: TV Series (24 episodes). *Episode Length*: 30 minutes. *Director*: Yuji Yamaguchi. *Original Creator*: Type-Moon. *Series Composition*: Takuya Sato. *Original Concept*: Kinoko Nasu (Type-Moon). *Music*: Kenji Kawai. *Original Character Designer*: Takashi Takeuchi. *Character Designer*: Megumi Ishihara. *Art Director*: Toshihisa Koyama. *Chief Animation Directors*: Megumi Ishihara, Toshimitsu Kobayashi. *Animation Directors*: Asako Nishida, Mariko Emori, Megumi Ishihara. *Chief Producer*: Jun Nishimura. *Producers*: Masaaki Saito, Mitsutoshi Ogura (Geneon), Takayuki Matsunaga (Frontier Works Inc.), Tetsuo Gensho, Tomotaka Takeuchi (Notes). *Background Art*: Chitose Asakura, Fumie Kawaai, Haruka Ozawa, Junko Nagazawa, Megumi Ogawa, Naoki Aoyama, Rie Matsuzawa, Riko Sudo, Shin Watanabe, Wakana Okamoto, Yukiko Nakayama, Yukiko Ogawa. *Editor*: Masahiro Matsumura. *Sound Director*: Kouji Tsujitani. *Color Designer*: Shinji Matsumoto. *Animation Production*: Studio Deen. *Production*: CREi , Fate Project, Frontier Works, Geneon Entertainment, Inc., Notes, Studio Deen, TBS.

**H2O Footprints in the Sand** (2007). *Original Title*: *H2O Footprints in the Sand*. *Status*: TV Series (12 episodes). *Episode Length*: 24 minutes. *Director*: Hideki Tachibana. *Original Creator*: Makura. *Series Composition*: Jukki Hanada. *Music*: Junpei Fujita (Elements Garden). *Character Designer*: Atsushi Okuda. *Art Director*: Kazuhiro Takahashi. *Editor*: Jun Takuma. *Sound Director*: Takeshi Takadera. *Color Designer*: Hideo Kamiya. *Animation Production*: ZEXCS.

**Kanon** (2002). *Original Title*: *Kanon*. *Status*: TV Series (13 episodes). *Episode Length*: 23 minutes. *Director*: Naoyuki Itou. *Original Creator*: Visual Art's/Key. *Music*: Hiroyuki Kouzu. *Character Conceptual Designer*: Itaru Hinoue. *Character Designer*: Youichi Ohnishi. *Art Designer*: Eiko Sawada. *Art Directors*: Eiko Sawada, Osamu Honda, Tadao Kubota, Yuko Tahara. *Chief Animation Director*: Youichi Ohnishi. *Animation Directors*: Haruo

Ogawara, Hisashi Ishii, Masahiro Okamura, Naomi Miyata, Nobuhiro Masuda. *Producers*: Daisuke Kawakami, Mamoru Yokota. *Animation Production*: Toei Animation. *Production*: Toei Animation, Visual Art's/Key.

**Kanon** (2006–2007). *Original Title*: *Kanon*. *Status*: TV Series (24 episodes). *Episode Length*: 24 minutes. *Director*: Tatsuya Ishihara. *Original Creator*: Visual Art's/Key. *Series Composition*: Fumihiko Shimo. *Screenplay*: Fumihiko Shimo. *Music*: Jun Maeda, OdiakeS, Shinji Orito. *Original Character Designer*: Itaru Hinoue (Visual Art's). *Character Designer*: Kazumi Ikeda. *Art Designer*: Mutsuo Shinohara. *Art Director*: Mutsuo Shinohara. *Chief Animation Director*: Kazumi Ikeda. *Animation Directors*: Chiyoko Ueno, Futoshi Nishiya, Hiroyuki Takahashi, Kazumi Ikeda, Mitsuyoshi Yoneda, Satoshi Kadowaki, Shoko Ikeda, Yukiko Horiguchi. *Producers*: Naohiro Futono, Shinichi Nakamura, Yoko Hatta, Yoshihisa Nakayama. *Sound Director*: Yota Tsuruoka. *Sound Effects*: Eiko Morikawa. *Color Designer*: Akiyo Takeda. *Special Effects*: Rina Miura. *Animation Production*: Kyoto Animation.

**Kanon Kazahana** (2003). *Original Title*: *Kanon Kazahana*. *Status*: OVA Special. *Director*: Naoyuki Itou. *Music*: Hiroyuki Kouzu. *Character Conceptual Designer*: Itaru Hinoue. *Art Designer*: Eiko Sawada. *Animation Production*: Toei Animation. *Production*: Toei Animation, Visual Art's/Key.

**Myself; Yourself** (2007). *Original Title*: *Myself; Yourself*. *Status*: TV Series (13 episodes). *Episode Length*: 23 minutes. *Director*: Tetsuaki Matsuda. *Original Creator*: Yeti. *Series Composition*: Go Zappa. *Screenplay*: Go Zappa. *Original Character Designer*: Mutsumi Sasaki. *Character Designer*: Tomoya Hiratsuka. *Art Director*: Shinji Takasuga. *Chief Animation Director*: Tomoya Hiratsuka. *Editors*: Masaki Sakamoto, Yuri Tamura. *Color Designer*: Kei Ishiguro. *Production*: Happinet Pictures, Marvelous Entertainment, Myself; Yourself Production Committee, Pony Canyon Enterprises, The 5pb.

**Rumbling Hearts** (2003–2004). *Original Title*: *Kimi ga Nozomu Eien*. *Status*: TV Series (14 episodes). *Episode Length*: 24 minutes. *Director*: Tetsuya Watanabe. *Original Creator*: Age. *Scenario*: Katsuhiko Takayama, Kenichi Kanemaki. *Music*: Abito Torai, Kenichi Sudo, Ryouju Minami. *Character Conceptual Designer*: Masanori Sugihara. *Character Designer*: Yoko Kikuchi. *Art Directors*: Minfang Zhang, Xifeng Chen. *Animation Directors*: Anzu Takano, Hideki Araki, Kumi Ishii, Makoto Koga, Mariko Fujita, Masaaki Sakurai, Naoki Yamauchi, Takashi Shiwasu, Takashi Uchida, Takuji Yoshimoto, Tetsuya Takeuchi, Toshiyuki Fujisawa, Yuichiro Miyake, Yukiko Akiyama. *Mechanical Designers*: Kanetake Ebikawa, Tomohiro Kawahara. *Art Designer*: Takeshi Miyamoto. *Editor*: Kengo Shigemura. *Sound Director*: Hiromi Kikuta. *Color Coordination*: Eiko Inoue. *Animation Production*: Studio Fantasia. *Production*: Kiminozo Production Committee, Media Factory, Studio Fantasia.

**Rumbling Hearts — Next Season** (2007–2008). *Original Title*: *Kimi ga Nozomu Eien -Next Season-*. *Status*: OVA series (4 episodes). *Episode Length*: 29 minutes. *Director*: Hideki Takayama. *Original Creator*: Age. *Scenario*: Takamitsu Kouno. *Character Designer*: Kazuhiko Tamura. *Animation Directors*: Miyako Nishida, Sadahiko Sakamaki. *Background Art*: Hirokuni Shinoda, Jong Song Kim. *Color Setting*: Yuuko Satou. *Special Effects*: Tomomi Ishihara. *Animation Production*: Brains Base, Maruga Factory. *Production*: Bandai Visual.

**School Days** (2007). *Original Title*: *School Days*. *Status*: TV series (12 episodes). *Episode Length*: 25 minutes. *Director*: Keitaro Motonaga. *Original Creator*: Overflow. *Series Composition*: Makoto Uezu. *Screenplay*: Makoto Uezu. *Music*: Kaoru Okubo. *Character Designer*:

Junji Goto. *Art Directors*: Jiro Kawano, Megumi Suzuki. *Chief Animation Director*: Junji Goto. *Producers*: Katsumi Koike, Makoto Ito, Masanori Goto. *Editor*: Takashi Sakurai. *Color Designer*: Rumiko Suzushiro. *Animation Production*: TNK. *Production*: avex entertainment, Lantis, Marvelous Entertainment, Pony Canyon Enterprises, School Days Production Committee.

**Shuffle!** (2005–2006). *Original Title*: Shuffle! *Status*: TV Series (24 episodes). *Episode Length*: 24 minutes. *Director*: Naoto Hosoda. *Original Concept*: Navel. *Series Composition*: Masashi Suzuki. *Script*: Katsuhiko Takayama, Katsumi Hasegawa, Masashi Suzuki. *Music*: Kazuhiko Sawaguchi, Minoru Maruo. *Character Conceptual Designers*: Aoi Nishimata, Hiro Suzuhira. *Character Designer*: Eiji Hirayama. *Art Director*: Hachidai Takayama. *Chief Animation Director*: Eiji Hirayama. *Animation Directors*: Eiji Hirayama, Kazuhisa Nakamura, Keiji Gotoh, Maiko Okada, Masahide Koyata, Masashi Wakayama, Naoto Hosoda, Seiki Tanaka, Yoshiko Nakajima. *Art Setting*: Yoshimi Umino. *Executive Producers*: Nobuhiko Sakawa, Shiroharu Kawasaki, Shouji Udagawa, Shunji Inoue, Takeshi Yasuda. *Producers*: Chiaki Terada, Michiko Suzuki, Tokuji Hasegawa, Tsuneo Takechi. *Editor*: Junichi Itou. *Sound Director*: Yota Tsuruoka. *Color Designer*: Naoki Fukutani. *Animation Production*: asread. *Production*: Shuffle! Media Partners.

**Soul Link** (2006). *Original Title*: Soul Link. *Status*: TV Series (13 episodes). *Episode Length*: 30 minutes. *Director*: Toshikatsu Tokoro. *Original Concept*: Navel. *Series Composition*: Toshikatsu Tokoro. *Scenario*: Isao Shizuya, Katsumi Hasegawa. *Music*: Hiroyuki Sawano. *Original Character Designer*: Hiro Suzuhira. *Character Designer*: Yoshihiro Watanabe. *Art Director*: Mitsuharu Miyamae. *Editor*: Akimitsu Okada. *Sound Director*: Satoki Iida. *Color Designer*: Haruko Nobori. *Animation Production*: Picture Magic. *Production*: Soul Link Media Project.

**To Heart** (1999). *Original Title*: To Heart. *Status*: TV series (13 episodes). *Episode Length*: 25 minutes. *Director*: Naohito Takahashi. *Original Manga*: Ukyou Takao. *Original Story*: Aquaplus. *Music*: Kaoru Wada. *Original Character Designer*: Toru Minazuki. *Character Designer*: Yuriko Chiba. *Art Directors*: Hisayoshi Takahashi, Shichiro Kobayashi. *Chief Animation Director*: Yuriko Chiba. *Animation Production*: Oriental Light and Magic. *Production*: KSS.

**Touka Gettan** (2007). *Original Title*: Touka Gettan. *Status*: TV series (26 episodes). *Episode Length*: 30 minutes. *Director*: Yuji Yamaguchi. *Original Creator*: Root. *Series Composition*: Tomomi Mochizuki. *Scenario*: Ai Shimizu, Mamiko Noto. *Music*: Akifumi Tada. *Original Character Designer*: Carnelian. *Character Designer*: Asako Nishida. *Art Director*: Toshihisa Koyama. *Chief Animation Director*: Asako Nishida. *3D Animation*: Akira Inaba, Naoyuki Ikeno. *Background Art*: Katsuhiro Yamada, Masami Oishi, Megumi Ogawa, Naoki Aoyama, Yukiko Nakayama, Yukiko Ogawa. *Sound Director*: Kouji Tsujitani. *Color Designer*: Eiko Kitazume. *Animation Production*: Studio Deen. *Sound Production*: Darks Production.

**true tears** (2008). *Original Title*: true tears. *Status*: TV series (13 episodes). *Episode Length*: 24 minutes. *Director*: Junji Nishimura. *Original Creator*: La'cryma. *Series Composition*: Mari Okada. *Script*: Junji Nishimura, Mari Okada, Mayumi Morita. *Music*: Hajime Kikuchi. *Original Character Designer*: Yumehito Ueda. *Character Designer*: Kanami Sekiguchi. *Art Directors*: Satoko Shinohara, Yusuke Takeda. *Chief Animation Director*: Kanami Sekiguchi. *Animation Directors*: Kanami Sekiguchi, Misaki Suzuki, Yuuko Yoshida. *Editor*: Junichi Uematsu. *Sound Director*: Kazuhiro Wakabayashi. *Color Designer*: Katsushi Inoue. *Special Effects*: Masahiro Murakami. *Animation Production*: P.A. Works. *Production*: Bandai Visual.

***Tsukihime, Lunar Legend*** (2003). *Original Title: Shingetsutan Tsukihime. Status:* TV series (12 episodes). *Episode Length:* 24 minutes. *Director:* Katsushi Sakurabi. *Original Creator:* Type-Moon. *Original Concept:* Kinoko Nasu. *Script:* Hiroko Tokita. *Music:* Toshiyuki Omori. *Original Character Designer:* Takashi Takeuchi. *Character Designer:* Kaoru Ozawa. *Animation Director:* Kaoru Ozawa. *Producers:* Takeshi Jinguji, Yuichi Sekido, Yuji Matsukura. *Editor:* Shigeru Nishiyama. *Sound Director:* Jin Aketagawa. *Sound Effects:* Kouji Konno. *Color Designer:* Tomomi Andou. *Animation Production:* J.C. Staff. *Production:* Geneon Entertainment, Inc., J.C. Staff, MOVIC, Rondo Robe, TBS, Tsukihime Production Committee.

***Tsuyokiss — CoolxSweet*** (2006). *Original Title: Tsuyokiss CoolxSweet. Status:* TV series (12 episodes). *Episode Length:* 30 minutes. *Director:* Shinichiro Kimura. *Original Creator:* PrincessSoft. *Series Composition:* Yasutomo Yamada. *Scenario:* Yasutomo Yamada. *Music:* I've, Little Non, Yuichi Nonaka. *Character Designer:* Yoshimi Agata. *Art Director:* Kuniaki Nemoto. *Producer:* Saburo Omiya. *Editor:* Masaki Sakamoto. *Color Designer:* Yukiko Tadano. *Animation Production:* Studio Hibari, Trinet Entertainment. *Production:* Candy Soft, Tsuyokisu Production Committee.

***Utawarerumono*** (2006). *Original Title: Utawarerumono. Status:* TV series (26 episodes). *Episode Length:* 23 minutes. *Director:* Tomoki Kobayashi. *Original Creator:* Aquaplus. *Series Composition:* Makoto Uezu. *Music:* Hijiri Anze, Miyu Nakamura. *Character Designer:* Masahiko Nakata. *Art Director:* Kenji Kato. *Animation Directors:* Hirokazu Shouji, Kazuhisa Nakamura, Masahiko Nakata, Motoki Tanaka, Naoto Hosoda, Shinichi Yoshino, Takuji Yoshimoto, Takuya Matsumoto, Tomohiro Koyama, Yasunori Yamaguchi, Yumenosuke Tokuda. *Producers:* Katsumi Koike, Toshio Hatanaka, Yasuo Ueda, Yutaro Mochizuki. *Sound Director:* Susumu Aketagawa. *Color Designer:* Tatsue Ohzeki. *Animation Production:* Oriental Light and Magic. *Production:* Utawarerumono Production Team.

***When Cicadas Cry*** (a.k.a. *When They Cry—Higurashi*) (2006). *Original Title: Higurashi no Naku Koro ni. Status:* TV series (26 episodes). *Episode Length:* 24 minutes. *Director:* Chiaki Kon. *Original Creator:* Seventh Expansion. *Series Composition:* Toshifumi Kawase. *Script:* Rika Nakase, Toshifumi Kawase. *Music:* Kenji Kawai. *Character Designer:* Kyuuta Sakai. *Art Director:* Chikako Shibata. *Background Art:* Ken Arai, Mahiro Akiba, Nobuhiro Yano, Tadashi Kudo, Yasuhiro Okumura, Yukiko Takahashi. *Editor:* Masahiro Matsumura. *Sound Effects:* Takuya Hasegawa. *Sound Production:* Natsuki Fukuda, Tetsu Hirata. *Color Designer:* Shinji Matsumoto. *Animation Production:* Studio Deen. *Production:* "When Cicadas Cry" Production Committee.

***When Cicadas Cry — Solutions*** (2007). *Original Title: Higurashi no Naku Koro ni Kai. Status:* TV series (24 episodes). *Episode Length:* 24 minutes. *Director:* Chiaki Kon. *Original Creator:* Seventh Expansion. *Series Composition:* Toshifumi Kawase. *Script:* Fumihiko Shimo, Masashi Suzuki, Toshifumi Kawase. *Music:* Kenji Kawai. *Character Designer:* Kyuuta Sakai. *Art Director:* Chikako Shibata. *Chief Animation Director:* Kyuuta Sakai. *Producers:* Hiroyuki Oomori, Mika Nomura, Takeshi Okamura. *Design Work:* Chihomi Ohsawa. *3D Animation:* Hiroki Tanji, Naruhiro Baba. *Editor:* Masahiro Matsumura. *Sound Director:* Hozumi Gouda. *Sound Effects:* Shizuo Kurahashi, Takuya Hasegawa. *Color Designer:* Shinji Matsumoto. *Animation Production:* Studio Deen. *Production:* "When Cicadas Cry" Production Committee.

***When Cicadas Cry — Gratitude*** (2009). *Original Title: Higurashi no Naku Koro ni Rei. Status:* OVA series (5 episodes). *Episode Length:* 30 minutes. *Director:* Toshifumi Kawase. *Original Creator:* Seventh Expansion. *Series Composition:* Toshifumi Kawase. *Music:* Kenji Kawai. *Character Designer:* Kazuya Kuroda. *Animation Production:* Studio Deen.

*White Album* (2009). *Original Title*: *White Album*. *Status*: TV Series (13 episodes). *Episode Length*: 25 minutes. *Director*: Akira Yoshimura. *Original Creator*: Aquaplus. *Script*: Hiroaki Sato. *Original Character Designer*: Hisashi Kawata. *Character Designer*: Kou Yoshinari. *Art Director*: Shinji Katahira. *Animation Director*: Osamu Sakata. *Sound Director*: Yoku Shioya. *Animation Production*: Seven Arcs.

*Yami to Boushi to Hon no Tabibito* (2003). *Original Title*: *Yami to Boushi to Hon no Tabibito* (a.k.a. *Darkness, Hat and Book Traveler* or *Yami, the Hat and the Travelers of Books*. *Status*: TV Series (13 episodes). *Episode Length*: 30 minutes. *Director*: Yuji Yamaguchi. *Original Creator*: Orbit Co., Ltd. *Series Organization*: Tomomi Mochizuki. *Script*: Hideki Shirane, Rika Nakase, Tomomi Mochizuki, Toshifumi Kawase. *Music*: Akifumi Tada. *Original Character Designer*: Carnelian (Root). *Character Designer*: Asako Nishida. *Art Directors*: Shin Watanabe, Toshihisa Koyama. *Chief Animation Director*: Asako Nishida. *Animation Director*: Kyuuta Sakai. *Editor*: Masahiro Matsumura. *Sound Director*: Kouji Tsujitani. *Color Coordination*: Shinji Matsumoto. *General Producer*: Takayuki Nagasawa. *Production*: Studio Deen.

# Ancillary Titles: Anime Adapted into Visual Novels (Illustrative Samples)

*Aria the Animation* (2005). *Original Title*: *Aria*. *Status*: TV Series (13 episodes). *Episode Length*: 25 minutes. *Director*: Junichi Sato. *Original Creator*: Kozue Amano. *Series Composition*: Junichi Sato. *Scenario*: Ayuna Fujisaki, Reiko Yoshida. *Music*: Choro Club, Takeshi Senoo. *Character Designer*: Makoto Koga. *Art Director*: Junichiro Nishikawa. *Chief Animation Director*: Makoto Koga. *Animation Directors*: Etsuko Sumimoto, Hiroshi Kazui, Hiroyuki Yanase, Makoto Koga, Masatsugu Arakawa, Masayuki Onchi, Mikio Fujiwara, Tadahito Matsubayashi, Takayuki Hanyuu, Takeshi Kusaka, Takuji Yoshimoto, Tomohisa Shimoyama, Toshiyuki Fujisawa, Yukiko Miyamoto, Yuuji Kondou. *Producers*: Shigeru Tateishi, Tetsuo Uchida, Yasutaka Hyuuga. *Editor*: Shigeru Nishiyama. *Color Designer*: Yoshimi Kawakami. *Animation Production*: Hal Film Maker.

*Aria the Natural* (2006). *Original Title*: *Aria 2*. *Status*: TV Series (26 episodes). *Episode Length*: 24 minutes. *Director*: Junichi Sato. *Original Creator*: Kozue Amano. *Series Composition*: Junichi Sato. *Screenplay*: Ayuna Fujisaki, Kazunobu Fusegi, Kenichi Takeshita, Mari Okada, Reiko Yoshida, Tatsuhiko Urahata, Yoshimasa Hiraike. *Music*: Choro Club, Takeshi Senoo. *Character Designer*: Makoto Koga. *Art Director*: Hiroshi Yoshikawa. *Chief Animation Director*: Tetsuya Kumagai. *Art Setting*: Junichiro Nishikawa. *Design Work*: Hiroyuki Kasugai, Thomas Romain. *Editor*: Shigeru Nishiyama. *Color Setting*: Miyuki Kibata. *Animation Production*: Hal Film Maker. *Production*: ARIA Company.

*Aria the OVA ~Arietta~* (2007). *Original Title*: *Aria OVA*. *Status*: OVA (1 episode). *Length*: 30 minutes. *Director*: Junichi Sato. *Original Creator*: Kozue Amano. *Screenplay*: Junichi Sato. *Music*: Choro Club, Takeshi Senoo. *Character Designer*: Makoto Koga. *Art Director*: Hiroshi Yoshikawa. *Animation Director*: Hiroyuki Kaidou. *Design Work*: Hiroyuki Kasugai. *Editor*: Kentarou Tsubone. *Color Designer*: Yoshimi Kawakami. *Animation Production*: Hal Film Maker.

*Aria the Origination* (2008). *Original Title*: *Aria 3*. *Status*: TV Series (13 episodes). *Episode Length*: 25 minutes. *Director*: Junichi Sato. *Original Creator*: Kozue Amano. *Series*

*Composition*: Junichi Sato. *Script*: Ayuna Fujisaki, Kenichi Takeshita, Tatsuhiko Urahata. *Screenplay*: Ayuna Fujisaki, Reiko Yoshida, Tatsuhiko Urahata. *Music*: Choro Club, Takeshi Senoo. *Character Designer*: Makoto Koga. *Art Director*: Kenichi Tajiri. *Chief Animation Director*: Masayuki Onchi. *Editor*: Kentarou Tsubone. *Color Designer*: Yoshimi Kawakami. *Animation Production*: Hal Film Maker.

**The Familiar of Zero** (2006). *Original Title*: Zero no Tsukaima. *Status*: TV Series (13 episodes). *Episode Length*: 24 minutes. *Director*: Yoshiaki Iwasaki. *Original Creator*: Noboru Yamaguchi. *Series Composition*: Takao Yoshioka. *Script*: Takao Yoshioka. *Music*: Shinkichi Mitsumune. *Original Character Designer*: Eiji Usatsuka. *Character Designer*: Masahiro Fujii. *Art Director*: Yoshinori Hirose. *Chief Animation Director*: Masahiro Fujii. *Editor*: Masahiro Goto. *Sound Director*: Tsuyoshi Takahashi. *Color Designer*: Kyousuke Ishikawa. *Animation Production*: J.C. Staff. *Production*: GENCO, Zero no Tsukaima Production Committee.

**Kanokon** (2008). *Original Title*: Kanokon. *Status*: TV Series (12 episodes). *Episode Length*: 30 minutes. *Director*: Atsushi Ohtsuki. *Original Creator*: Katsumi Nishino. *Series Composition*: Masashi Suzuki. *Music*: Tsuyoshi Ito. *Original Character Designer*: Koin. *Character Designer*: Akio Takami. *Art Director*: Toshihiro Kohama. *Art Designer*: Yoshinori Shiozawa. *Sound Director*: Toshihiko Nakajima. *Color Designer*: Mitsuko Sekimoto. *Animation Production*: Xebe. *Production*: AT-X, Media Factory, MOVIC. The 5pb.

**Kashimashi — Girl Meets Girl** (2006). *Original Title*: Kashimashi — Girl Meets Girl. *Status*: TV Series (12 episodes). *Episode Length*: 30 minutes. *Director*: Nobuaki Nakanishi. *Original Text (manga)*: Satoru Akahori. *Original Illustrations (manga)*: Yukimaru Katsura. *Series Composition*: Jukki Hanada. *Script*: Jukki Hanada. *Music*: Hitoshi Fujima, Soushi Hosoi, Toshimichi Isoe. *Original Character Designer*: Sukune Inugami. *Character Designer*: Tomoko Iwasa. *Animation Director*: Tomoko Iwasa. *Background Art*: Eri Satou, Noriko Ikebata. *Sound Director*: Jin Aketagawa. *Animation Production*: Studio Hibari. *Production*: Bandai Visual, Kashimashi Production Team, Lantis, MediaWorks, Studio Hibari.

**Kashimashi — Girl Meets Girl** (2006). *Original Title*: Kashimashi — Girl Meets Girl. *Status*: OVA (1 episode). *Length*: 27 minutes. *Director*: Yukimaru Katsura. *Original Creator (manga)*: Yukimaru Katsura. *Original Character Designer*: Sukune Inugami.

# Chapter Notes

## Chapter 2

1. Dolls play an important part in Japanese culture. Known as "*ningyou*," i.e., "human figure," they have been traditionally shaped in a wide range of forms: children and warriors, fairytale characters and gods, heroes and demons, and still feature as central to popular festivities such as *Hina Matsuri* ("Doll Festival" or "Girls' Day") and *Kodomo no Hi* ("Boys' Day" or "Children's Day"). In the Heian Period (794–1185), dolls served principally ceremonial purposes and were held capable of absorbing a person's sins. In the Edo Period (1603–1867), dolls of astonishing artistic quality at the levels of materials, costumes and mechanical properties became pivotal to a vibrant market of collectible goods and greatly cherished by the growing ranks of affluent individuals. Dolls are still manufactured today in many regions of Japan as a local craft and purchased enthusiastically by shrine pilgrims and international tourists. The specimens created by Kikyou in *Touka Gettan* are redolent of classic *hina* types in virtue of their pyramidal bodies and use of colours.

2. *Aria*'s visuals obliquely evoke a variety of artistic sources — most memorably, depictions of Venice's unique natural environment and architecture yielded by masters such as Jacopo Tintoretto (1518–1594),

Canaletto (1697–1768), Bernardo Bellotto (1720–1780) and J. M. W. Turner (1775–1851).

## Chapter 3

1. *Kanon*'s setting — and even its cast, to some extent — vividly echo the following description of the proverbially snowy region of Hokkaido, Japan's northernmost island: "The natural landscapes of Hokkaido are rich in variety, with magnificent mountains, flowers in bloom, wetlands surrounded by primeval forests, and lovely alpine plants…. Hokkaido is a paradise of wild animals. Even in urban parks, you may encounter red foxes and squirrels" (*Nature Experiences*).

2. Hirito Kawasumi maintains that the importance of music in Ishihara's show is borne out precisely by its symbolic employment of Pachelbel's *Canon* (also more formally known, incidentally, as *Canon and Gigue in D major for three Violins and Basso Continuo* [*Kanon und Gigue in D-Dur für drei Violinen und Basso Continuo*]), adding the following comments: "One thing I derived from the usage of *Canon*, could be that in order for a perfect harmony between different people, there must be a certain level of synchronization between them," enabling them "to understand each other" and "lend a helping

hand when needed, which brings to the point of '*One can never walk alone*' or basically, Unity through Friendship" (Kawasumi).

## Chapter 4

1. *Fate/stay Night*'s seemingly unorthodox take on Arthurian lore should not come as a surprise when one considers that within that narrative realm, there is no such thing as a universally shared and recognized body of stories to which all scholars and enthusiasts unproblematically subscribe. In fact, as Chris Thornborrow pithily maintains, "To many questions in the Arthurian Lore, there are no definitive answers, only theories and a few, a very few, undisputed facts. History, legend, religion and myth all combine to make this subject both fascinating and mysterious. Differing authors provide differing answers to the same question" (Thornborrow).

## Chapter 5

1. The anime's release history was regrettably marred by a censorship-related issue: "The day before the final episode was scheduled to air, a sixteen-year-old girl killed her father with an axe in Kyoto. In response, TV Kanagawa replaced the episode, which was known to contain similarly violent

material, with half an hour of scenery and classical music to avoid association with the murder. Other stations airing the anime followed suit, except for AT-X, who remained indecisive at the time. In the following week, Overflow announced that a screening of the episode would take place in the Tokyo area as part of the release of the series' first DVD volume, and would require a copy of either the PC game or Summer Days PC game for admission. However, AT-X announced that they would air the last episode on September 27, 2007, with minor alterations in airing times. The screening of the episode that Overflow announced showed the uncut version of episode twelve, including the blood color change black to red, more sound effects, and fewer flashbacks. The uncut scene was included in the DVD release on February 27, 2008" (*Wikipedia, the Free Encyclopaedia — School Days*).

2. In anime and manga, the branch of romance dealing with homoerotic relationships pivoting specifically on female personae, precisely of the type dramatized through Hazumu, Tomari and Asuna in *Kashimashi*, is commonly known as "*yuri*." Another example offered by a title examined in this book is the relationship (in this case, pointedly understated) involving Mai Kawasumi and Sayuri Kurata from *Kanon* (please see Chapter 3).

# Bibliography

Aarseth, E. J. 1997. *Cybertext— Perspectives on Ergodic Literature*. Baltimore: Johns Hopkins UniversityPress.

*Air on TV*. 2005. MAG Garden Premium Art Collection.

*Air The Motion Picture*. 2005. MAG Garden Premium Art Collection.

Ando, T. "Tadao Ando Quotes." *Brainy-Quote*. <http://www.brainyquote.com/quotes/authors/t/tadao_ando.html>

Arnheim, R. 1974. *Art and Visual Perception: a Psychology of the Creative Eye*. Berkeley, CA: University of California Press.

Avella, N. 2004. *Graphic Japan: From Woodblock and Zen to Manga and Kawaii*. Hove, East Sussex: RotoVision.

Barthes, R. 1990. *The Pleasure of the Text*. Trans. R. Miller. Oxford: Basil Blackwell Ltd.

Bartle R. A. 1996. "Hearts, Clubs, Diamonds and Spades: Players Who Suit MUDs." <http://www.mud.co.uk/richard/hcds.htm>

Besen, E. 2003a. "Analogy and Animation: A Special Relationship: Part 1— Show and Tell." *Animation World Magazine*. <http://mag.awn.com/index.php?ltype=Columns&column=AnalogyAni&article_no=1895>

Besen, E. 2003b. "Analogy and Animation: A Special Relationship: Part 2 — Think Like an Animator, Walk Like a Duck." *Animation World Magazine*. <http://mag.awn.com/index.php?ltype=Columns&column=AnalogyAni&article_no=1918>

Besen, E. 2003c. "Analogy and Animation: A Special Relationship: Part 3 — Good Studios, Bad Films, v. 1." *Animation World Magazine*. <http://mag.awn.com/index.php?ltype=Columns&column=AnalogyAni&article_no=1954>

Borges, J. L. 1970. *Labyrinths*. Harmondsworth: Penguin Books Ltd.

Bourdieu, P. 1991. *Outline of a Theory of Practice*. Cambridge: Cambridge University Press.

Brooks, P. 1984. *Reading for the Plot*. New York: Knopf.

Caillois, R. 1961. *Man, Play, and Games*. New York: Schocken Books, 1961.

Carson, D. 2000. "Environmental Storytelling: Creating Immersive 3D Worlds Using Lessons Learned From the Theme Park Industry." *Gamasutra.com*. <http://www.gamasutra.com/features/20000301/carson_pfv.htm>

Chesterton, G. K. "Play." *Thinkexist.com*. <http://thinkexist.com/quotes/with/keyword/play/>

*Clannad Visual Fan Book*. 2004. Visual Art's/Key & EnterBrain Inc.

"A Close Look at an Anime Production House Part 1." 2008. *Kanon* DVD, vol. 1. ADV Films.

"A Close Look at an Anime Production House Part 2." 2008. *Kanon* DVD, vol. 2. ADV Films.

"A Close Look at an Anime Production House Part 3." 2008. *Kanon* DVD, vol. 2. ADV Films.

"A Close Look at an Anime Production House Part 4." 2008. *Kanon* DVD, vol. 3. ADV Films.

"A Close Look at an Anime Production House Part 8." 2008. *Kanon* DVD, vol. 6. Funimation.

Collingwood, R. G. 1938. *The Principles of Art*. New York: Oxford University Press.

Crawford, C. 1982. "The Art of Computer Game Design." <http://www.stanford. edu/class/sts145/Library/Crawford%20 on%20Game%20Design.pdf>

Derrida, J. 1978. *Writing and Difference*. Trans. A. Bass. London and Henley-on-Thames: Routledge & Kegan Paul.

Drazen, P. 2003. *Anime Explosion: The What? Why? & Wow! of Japanese Animation*. Berkeley, CA: Stone Bridge Press.

Eco, U. 1986. [1973.] "Dreaming the Middle Ages." In *Travels in Hyperreality*. Trans. W. Weaver. New York: Harcourt Brace.

Eco, U. 1984. *The Name of the Rose*. Trans. W. Weaver. London: Picador.

Eco, U. 1979. *The Role of the Reader*. London: Hutchinson.

Ekuan, K. 2000. *The Aesthetics of the Japanese Lunchbox*. Trans. D. Kenny. Cambridge, MA: MIT Press.

"Elements of a Traditional Japanese Interior." *The Yoshino Newsletter*. <http:// www.yoshinoantiques.com/Interior-article.html>

Ellory, R. J. 2007. *A Quiet Belief in Angels*. London: Orion.

Frasca, G. 2003. "Ludologists love stories, too: notes from a debate that never took place." <http://www.ludology.org/ articles/Frasca_LevelUp2003.pdf>

Frasca, G. 1999. "Ludology Meets Narratology." <http://www.ludology.org>

Gould, S. J. 1980. "A biological homage to Mickey Mouse." In *The Panda's Thumb: More Reflections in Natural History*. New York: W. W. Norton & Co. Ltd.

Heidegger, M. 1991. [1955–1956.] *The Principle of Reason*. Trans. R. Lilly. Bloomington: Indiana University Press.

Heliö, S. 2004. "Role-Playing: A Narrative Experience and a Mindset." <http:// www.ropecon.fi/brap/ch6.pdf>

Hetherington, J. 2006. "The Art of Gaming." *Animation World Magazine*. <http:// mag.awn.com/?article_no=2866>

Hume, N. G. 1995. *Japanese Aesthetics and Culture: A Reader*. Albany: State University of New York Press.

Irigaray, L. 2000a. *Democracy Begins Between Two*. Trans. K. Anderson. London: Continuum.

Irigaray, L. 2000b. *To Be Two*. Trans. M. M. Rhodes and M. F. Cocito-Monoc. London: Continuum.

"Japan smitten by love of cute." 2006. *The Age Company Ltd*. <http://www.theage. com.au/news/people/cool-or-infantile/ 2006/06/18/1150569208424.html>

Jenkins, H. 2004. "Game Design as Narrative Architecture." <http://newmediastudies.stockton.edu/pdf_library/jenkins %20game%20design.pdf>

Joyce, J. 1957. *Letters*. New York: Viking Press.

Jung, C. "Carl Jung Quotations." <http:// www.spaceandmotion.com/Philosophy-Carl-Jung.htm#Jung.Quotes>

Juul, J. 2001. "A Clash between Game and Narrative." <http://www.jesperjuul.net/ thesis/AClashBetweenGameAndNarrative. pdf>

Kandinsky, W. 1994. *Complete Writings on Art*, edited by K. C. Lindsay and P. Vergo. New York: Da Capo Press.

*Kanon Visual Memories*. 2007. Visual Arts's/Key Publications.

Kawai, H. 1995. *Dreams, Myths and Fairy Tales in Japan*. Einsiedeln, Switzerland: Daimon.

Kawai, H. 1988. *The Japanese Psyche: Major Motifs in the Fairytales of Japan*. Dallas, TX: Spring Publications, Inc.

Kawasumi, H. 2008. "Anime Review: *Kanon*." <http://hirito.blogspot.com/2008 /03/anime-review-kanon.html>

Kawin, B. 1978. *Mindscreen: Bergman, Godard and First-Person Film*. Princeton, IL: Princeton University Press.

Kim J. 1998. "The Threefold Model FAQ." <http://www.darkshire.net/~jhkim/rpg/ theory/threefold/faq_v1.html>

*Kimi ga Nozomu Eien Visual Complete.* 2004. Media Factory.

Kücklich, J. 2003. "Perspectives of Computer Game Philology." *Game Studies*, volume 3, issue 1, May. <http://gamestudies.org/0301/kucklich/>

Landow, G. P. 1997. *Hypertext: The Convergence of Contemporary Critical Theory and Technology.* Baltimore: Johns Hopkins University Press.

Lankoski, P. 2003. "Character Design Fundamentals for Role-Playing Games." <http://www.ropecon.fi/brap/ch12.pdf>

Lankoski, P., and Heliö, S. 2002. "Approaches to Computer Game Design — Characters and Conflict." <http://www.digra.org:8080/Plone/dl/db/05097.01201.pdf>

Lao Tzu. 1955. *Tao Te Ching: The Way of Lao Tzu.* Trans. R. B. Blakney. New York: The New American Library.

Larsen, J. L. 2001. "The Inspiration of Japanese Design." *Traditional Japanese Design: Five Tastes.* New York: Japan Society.

Lee, D. 2005. "Inside Look at Japanese Cute Culture." *Uniorb.* <http://uniorb.com/ATREND/Japanwatch/cute.htm>

Lindley, C. A. 2002. "The Gameplay Gestalt, Narrative, and Interactive Storytelling." <http://www.tii.se/zerogame/pdfs/CGDClindley.pdf>

Lonsdale, S. 2008. *Japanese Style.* London: Carlton Books Ltd.

Lorenz, K. 1961. [1949.] *King Solomon's Ring.* Trans. M. Kerr Wilson. London: Methuen.

Lynch, K. A. 1960. *The Image of the City.* Cambridge: MIT Press.

Mackay, D. 2001. *The Fantasy Role-Playing Game: A New Performing Art.* Jefferson, NC: McFarland.

McLane, D. 2008. *Japan Style*, edited by A. Taschen. Hong Kong, Köln, London, Los Angeles, Madrid, Paris, Tokyo: Taschen.

Matthews, J. 1993. "Foreword." In *The Illustrated Encyclopaedia of Arthurian Legend*, edited by R. Coghlan. Rockport, MA: Element Books.

Merleau-Ponty, M. 1962. *Phenomenology of Perception.* Trans. C. Smith. London: Routledge & Kegan Paul.

Murakami, H. "Haruki Murakami Quotes."

*Brainy Quote.* <http://www.brainyquote.com/quotes/authors/h/haruki_murakami.html>

Murray, J. 1997. *Hamlet on the Holodeck: The Future of Narrative in Cyberspace.* Cambridge, MA: MIT Press.

Nagatomo, S. 2006. "Japanese Zen Buddhist Philosophy." *Stanford Encyclopedia of Philosophy.* <http://plato.stanford.edu/entries/japanese-zen/>

*Nature Experiences.* "Charm of Hokkaido." <http://kanko.pref.hokkaido.jp/kankodb/foreign/e/trv_f003.htm>

Omni. 2007. "Random Musings — The Calm Before The Storm." *Random Curiority.* <http://randomc.animeblogger.net/2007/03/31/random-musings-the-calm-before-the-storm/>

Pohjola, M. 2004. "Autonomous Identities: Immersion as a Tool for Exploring, Empowering and Emancipating Identities." In *Beyond Role and Play: tools, toys and theory for harnessing the imagination*, edited by M. Montola and J. Stenros. Ropecon, Helsinki.

Poremba, C. 2003. "Player as Author: Digital Games and Agency," Thesis submitted in Partial Fulfilment of the Requirements for the Degree of Master of Applied Science, Department of Computing Arts and Design Sciences, Simon Fraser University. <http://www.shinyspinning.com/THESIS_PlayerAsAuthor.pdf>

Rapoport, A. 1966. *Two-Person Game Theory: The Essential Ideas.* Ann Arbor: University of Michigan Press.

Reeve, J. 2006. *Japanese Art in Detail.* London: The British Museum Press.

Ryan, M-L. 2001. "Beyond Myth and Metaphor — The Case of Narrative in Digital Media." *Game Studies*, volume 1, issue 1, July. <http://itp.nyu.edu/isco/pdfs/Ryan_BeyondMyth_and_Metaphor.pdf>

Saito, Y. 2007. "The Moral Dimension of Japanese Aesthetics." *Journal of Aesthetics and Art Criticism* 65 (1), 85–97. Blackwell Publishing: The American Society for Aesthetics.

Schklovsky, V. 1988. [1917.] "Art as technique." In *Modern Criticism and*

*Theory — A Reader*, edited by D. Lodge. London and New York: Longman.

Shirane, H. 2005. "Performance, Visuality, and Textuality: The Case of Japanese Poetry." *Oral Tradition*, 20/2.

Smuts, A. 2005. "Are Video Games Art?" *Contemporary Aesthetics*. <http://www.contempaesthetics.org/newvolume/pages/article.php?articleID=299>

Sontag, S. 2007. "Pay attention to the word." *The Guardian*. 17 March. <http://books.guardian.co.uk/print/0,,32974814 9-99930,00.html>

Stanley-Baker, J. 2000. *Japanese Art*. London and New York: Thames & Hudson.

Stern, E. 2002. "A Touch of Medieval: Narrative, Magic and Computer Technology in Massively Multiplayer Computer Role-Playing Games." <http://www.digra.org/dl/db/05164.03193.pdf>

Szilas, N. 1999. "Interactive drama on computer: beyond linear narrative." <http://www.lcc.gatech.edu/~mateas/nidocs/Szilas.pdf>

Tanizaki, J. 2001. [1933.] *In Praise of Shadows*. Trans. T. J. Harper and E. G. Seidensticker. London: Vintage.

Todorov, T. 1988. [1966.] "The typology of detective fiction." In *Modern Criticism and Theory — A Reader*, edited by D. Lodge. London and New York: Longman.

Ueda, M. 1967. *Literary and Art Theories in Japan*. Cleveland, OH: Case Western Reserve University Press.

von Glasersfeld, E. 1985. "Konstruktion der Wirklichkeit und des Begriffs der Objektivität." In *Einführung in den Konstruktivismus*, edited by H. Gumin and A. Mohler. Munich: Oldenburg.

*When They Cry/Higurashi Character and Analysis Book*. 2006. Jive Ltd.

*Wikipedia, the Free Encyclopaedia — School Days*. <http://en.wikipedia.org/wiki/School_Days_(visual_novel)#Delay_of_finale>

Wittgenstein, L. 1991. [1951.] *Philosophical Investigations*. Trans. G. E. M. Anscombe and E. Anscombe. Oxford: Wiley-Blackwell.

Yee, N. 2002. "Facets: 5 Motivation Factors for Why People Play MMORPGs." <http://www.nickyee.com/facets/home.html>

# Index